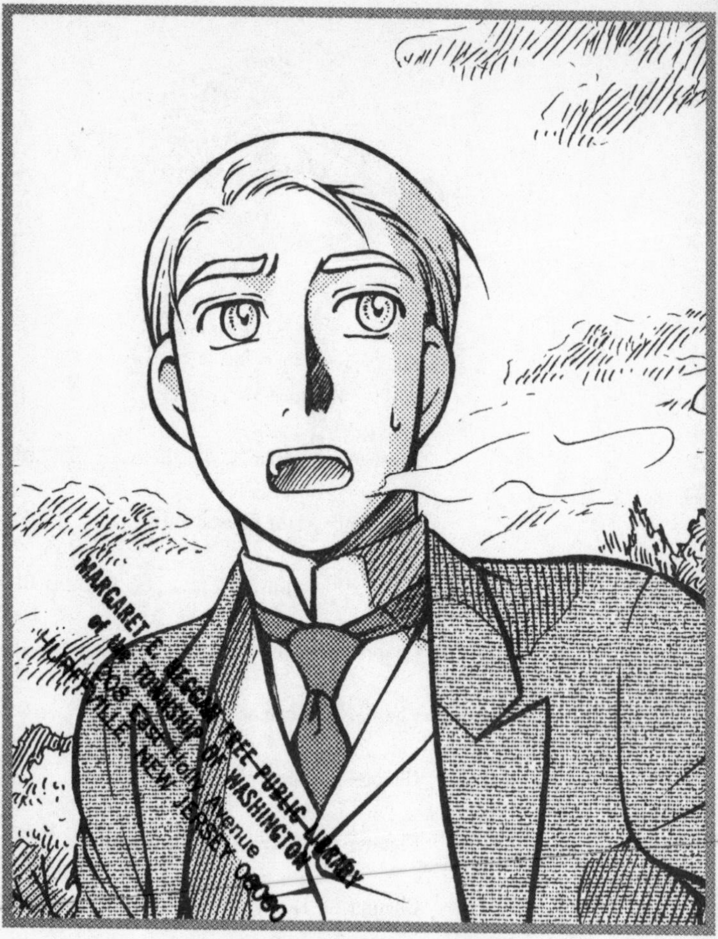

EMMA

Volume 2

By Kaoru Mori

-Contents-

☙ Dramatis personae ☙

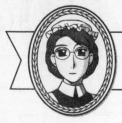

Emma
Maid employed by Mrs. Stownar.
Wears glasses, uncommon for someone
of her social class.

Mrs. Kelly Stownar
Married at 18 and widowed at 20.
Became a governess after that, working for
respectable families for over 30 years. Now
retired and living with Emma.

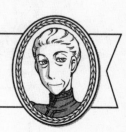

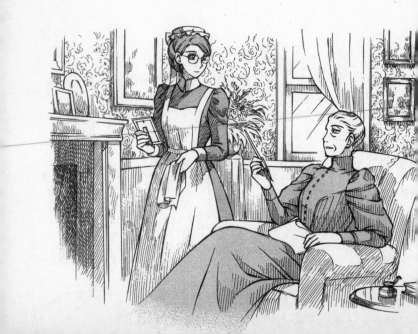

William Jones

Eldest son of the gentry-class Jones family. Taught by the stern Mrs. Stownar as a child and still unable to look her in the eye. Fell in love at first sight with Emma upon paying an overdue visit to his former governess.

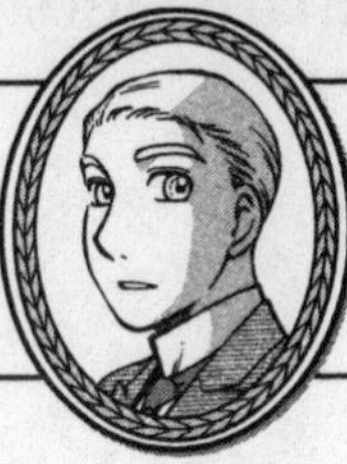

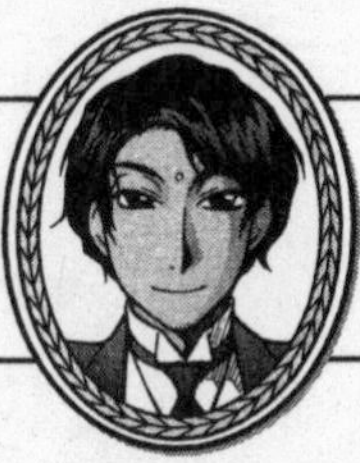

Hakim Atawari

A friend of William's who came riding in on an elephant from India to visit. The second son of the Maharajah Jayapool. Has 18 siblings (some with different mothers).

Hakim's Girls

Dancing girls who follow Hakim wherever he may go. Four, but they act as one.

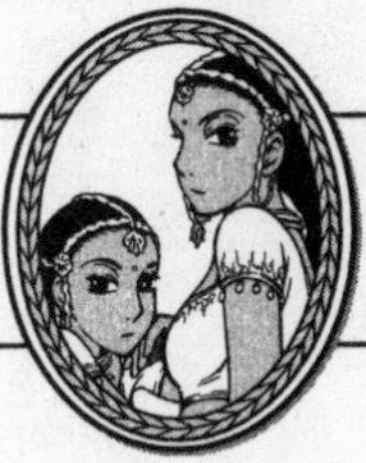

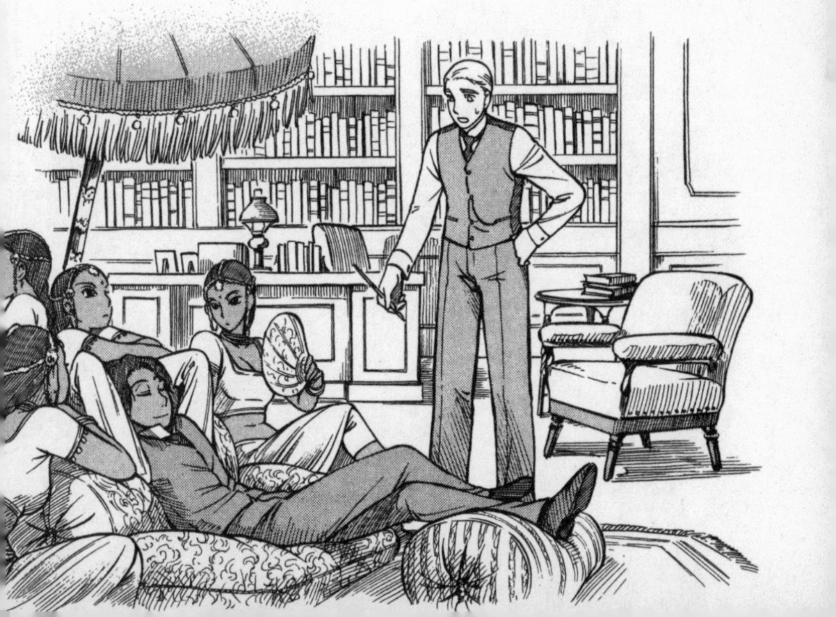

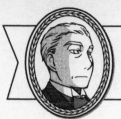

Richard Jones

William's father and the head of the Jones family. A sensible person who places great weight on order and tradition. Adamantly opposed to a relationship between William and Emma.

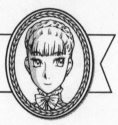

Eleanor Campbell

The third daughter of the viscount family Campbell.

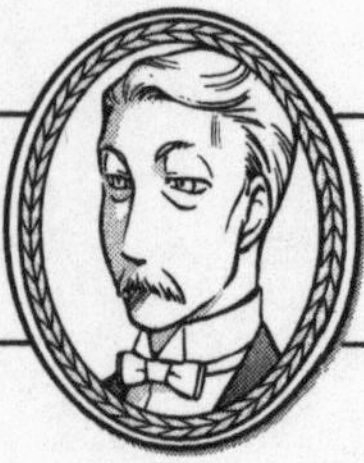

Stevens

Faithful butler to the Jones family. His father and grandfather were also butlers.

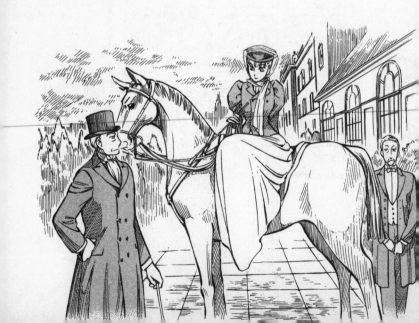

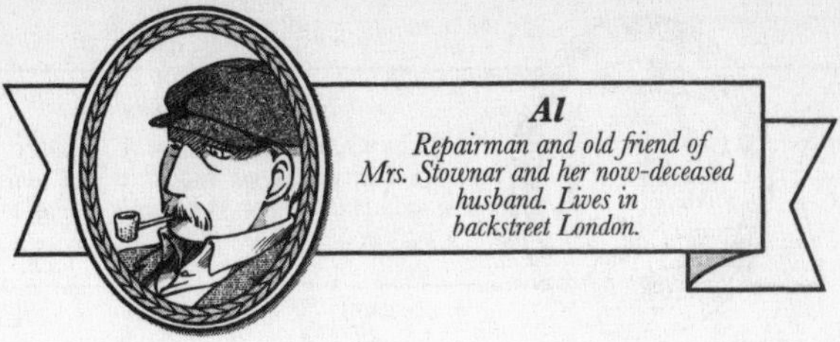
Al
Repairman and old friend of Mrs. Stownar and her now-deceased husband. Lives in backstreet London.

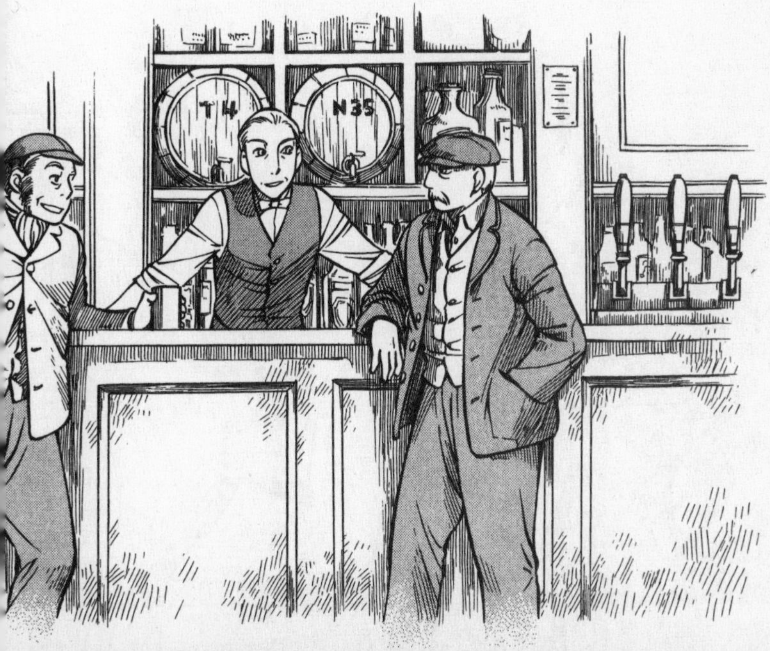
T4
N35

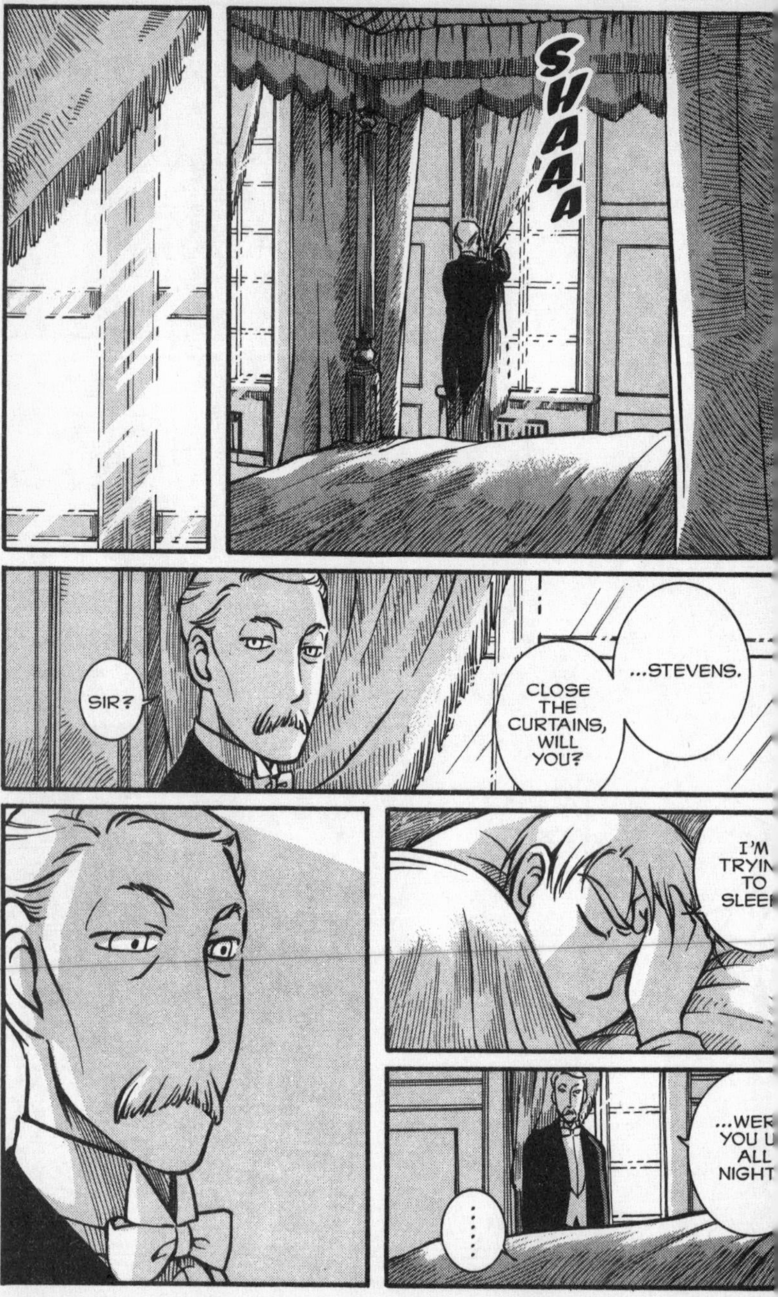
SHAAA
...STEVENS.
CLOSE THE CURTAINS, WILL YOU?
SIR?
I'M TRYIN TO SLEE
...WER YOU U ALL NIGHT
......

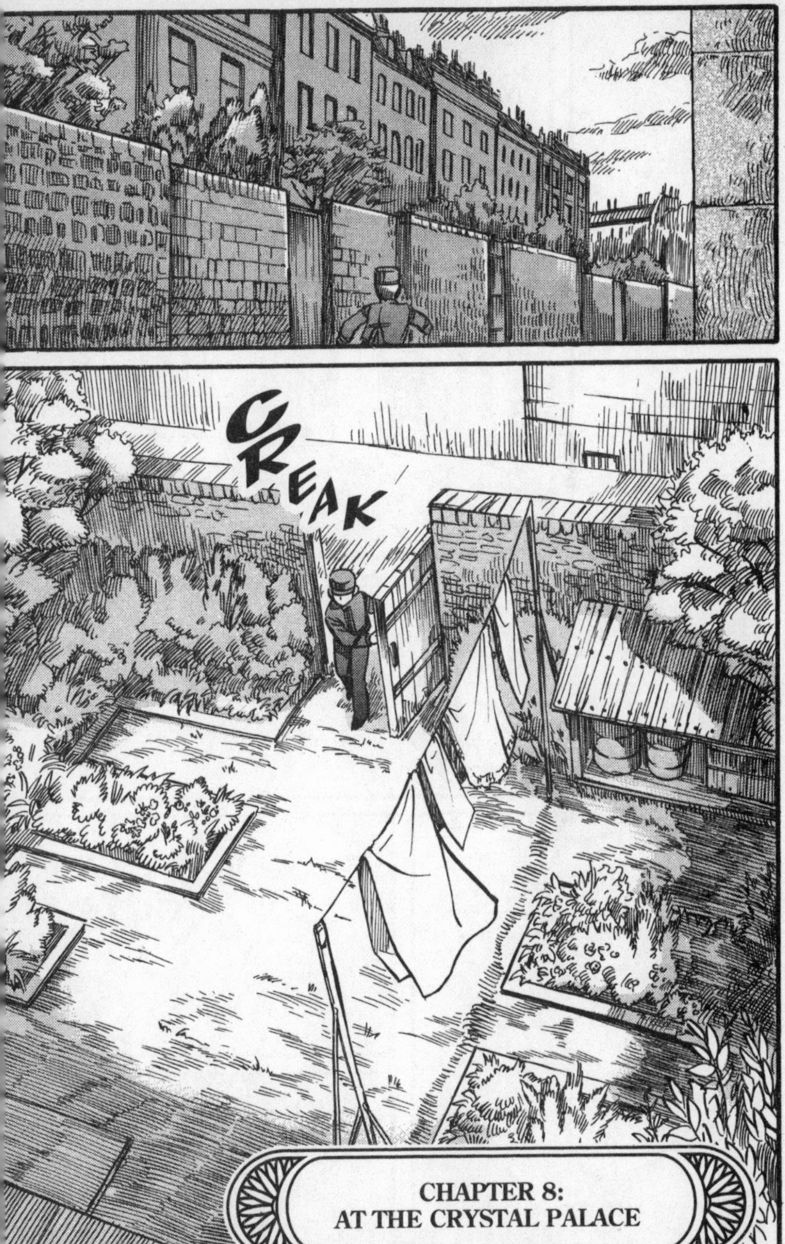
CREAK
CHAPTER 8:
AT THE CRYSTAL PALACE

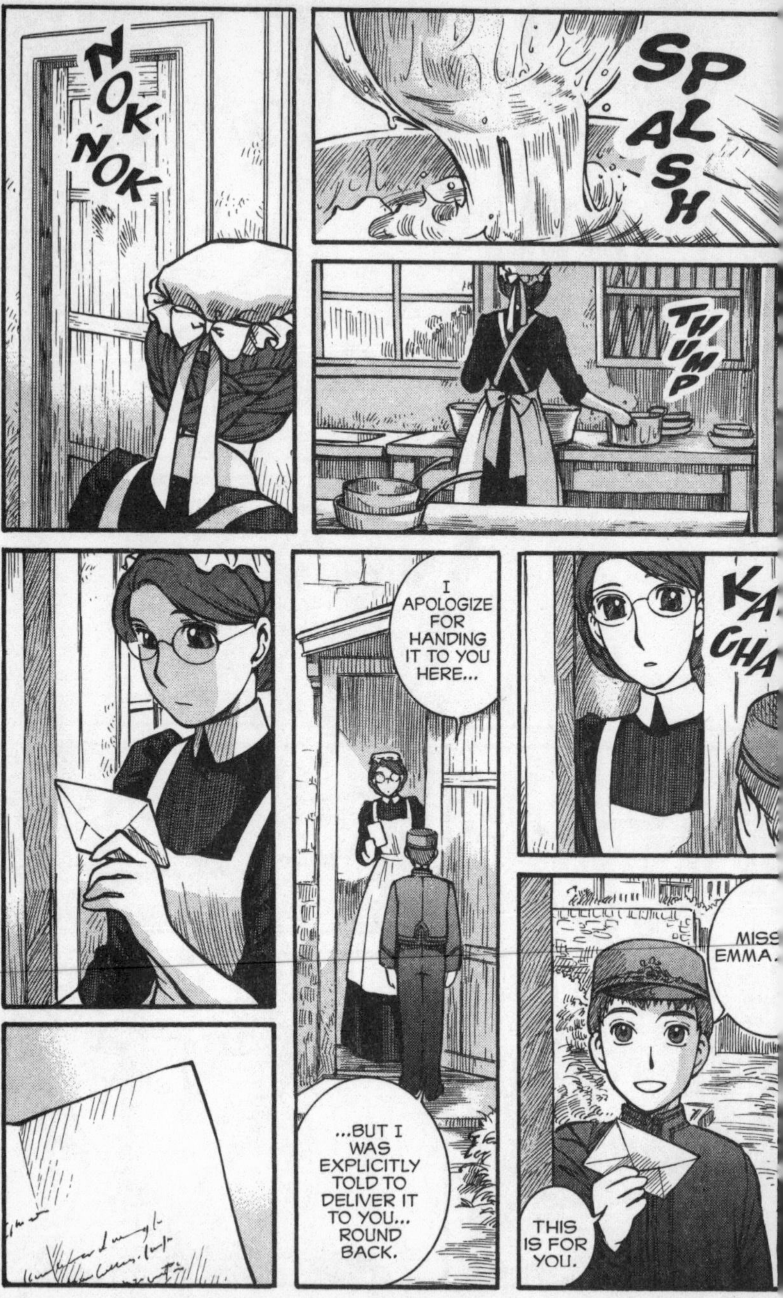
SPLASH
THUMP
NOK NOK
KA-CHA
MISS EMMA...
THIS IS FOR YOU.
I APOLOGIZE FOR HANDING IT TO YOU HERE...
...BUT I WAS EXPLICITLY TOLD TO DELIVER IT TO YOU... ROUND BACK.

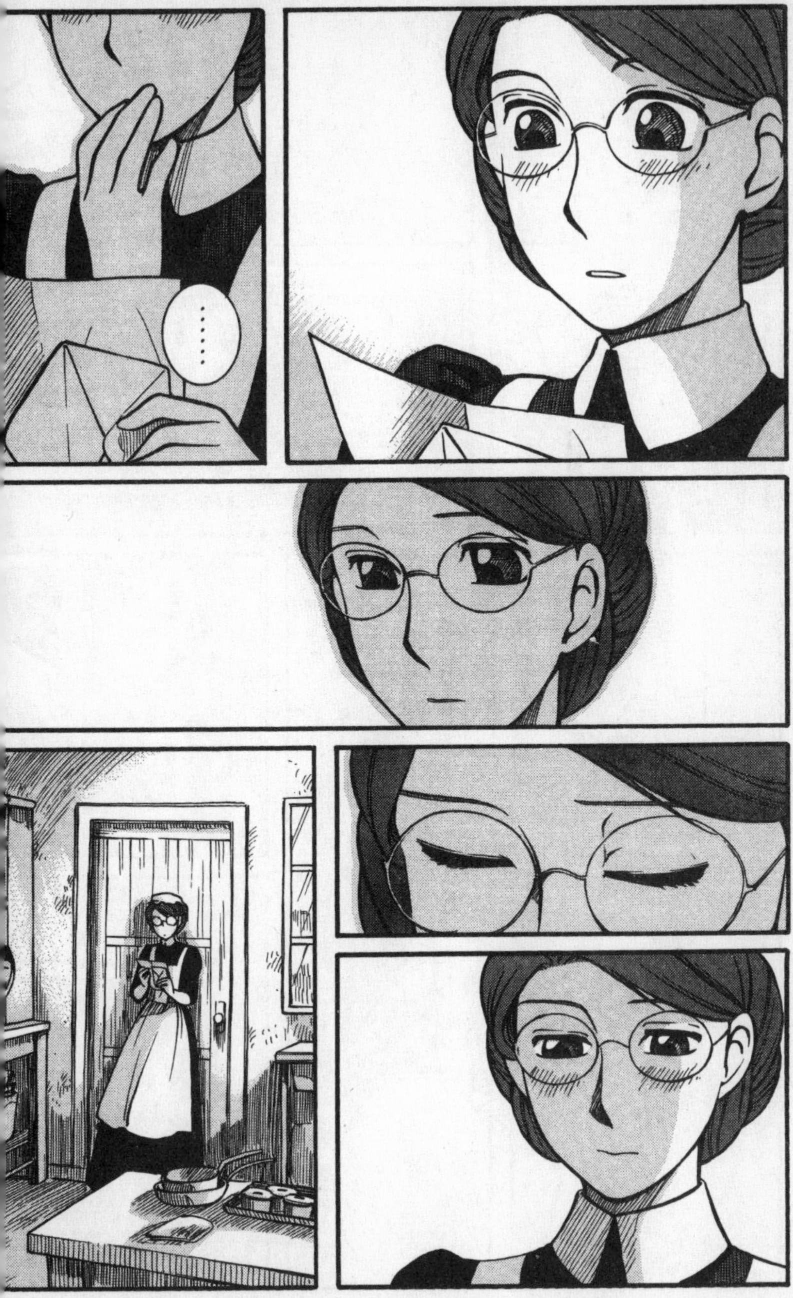
……

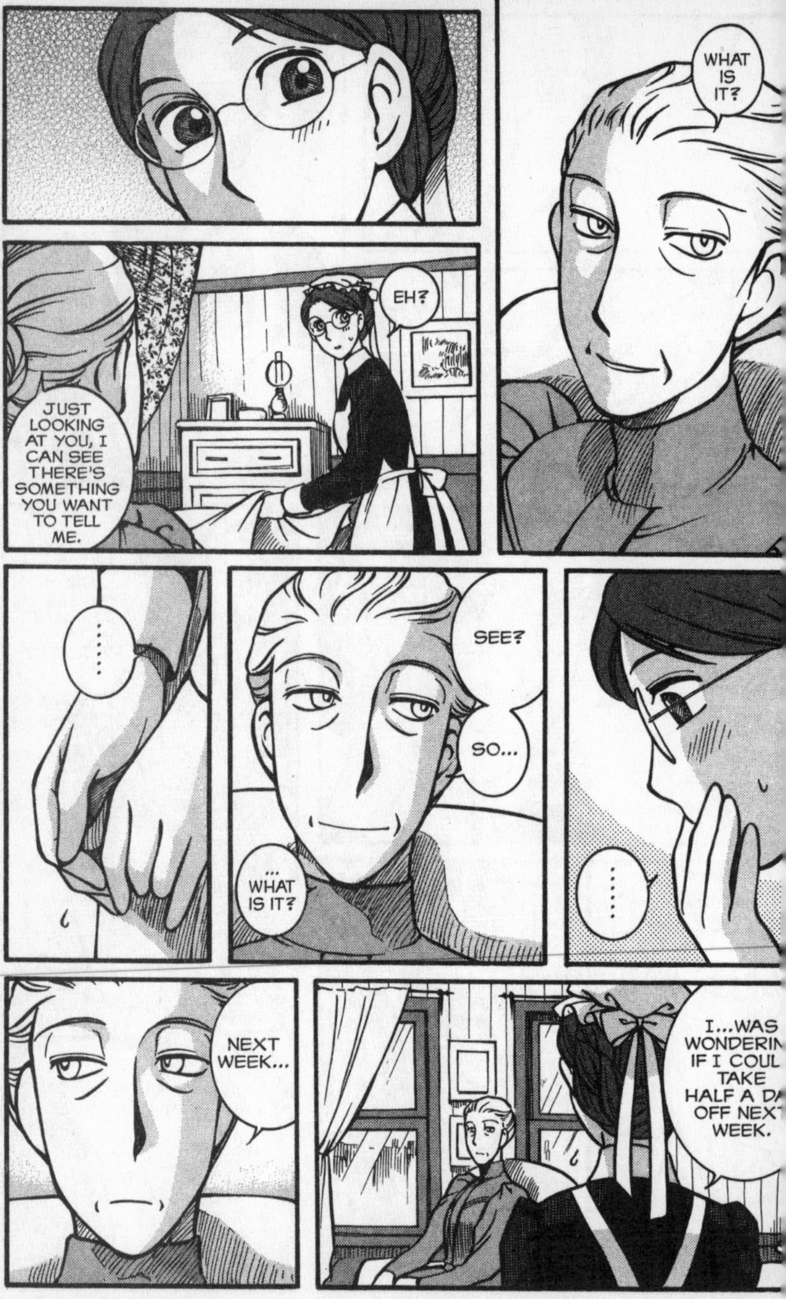
WHAT IS IT?
EH?
JUST LOOKING AT YOU, I CAN SEE THERE'S SOMETHING YOU WANT TO TELL ME.
......
SEE?
SO...
... WHAT IS IT?
......
I...WAS WONDERIN IF I COUL TAKE HALF A DA OFF NEXT WEEK.
NEXT WEEK...

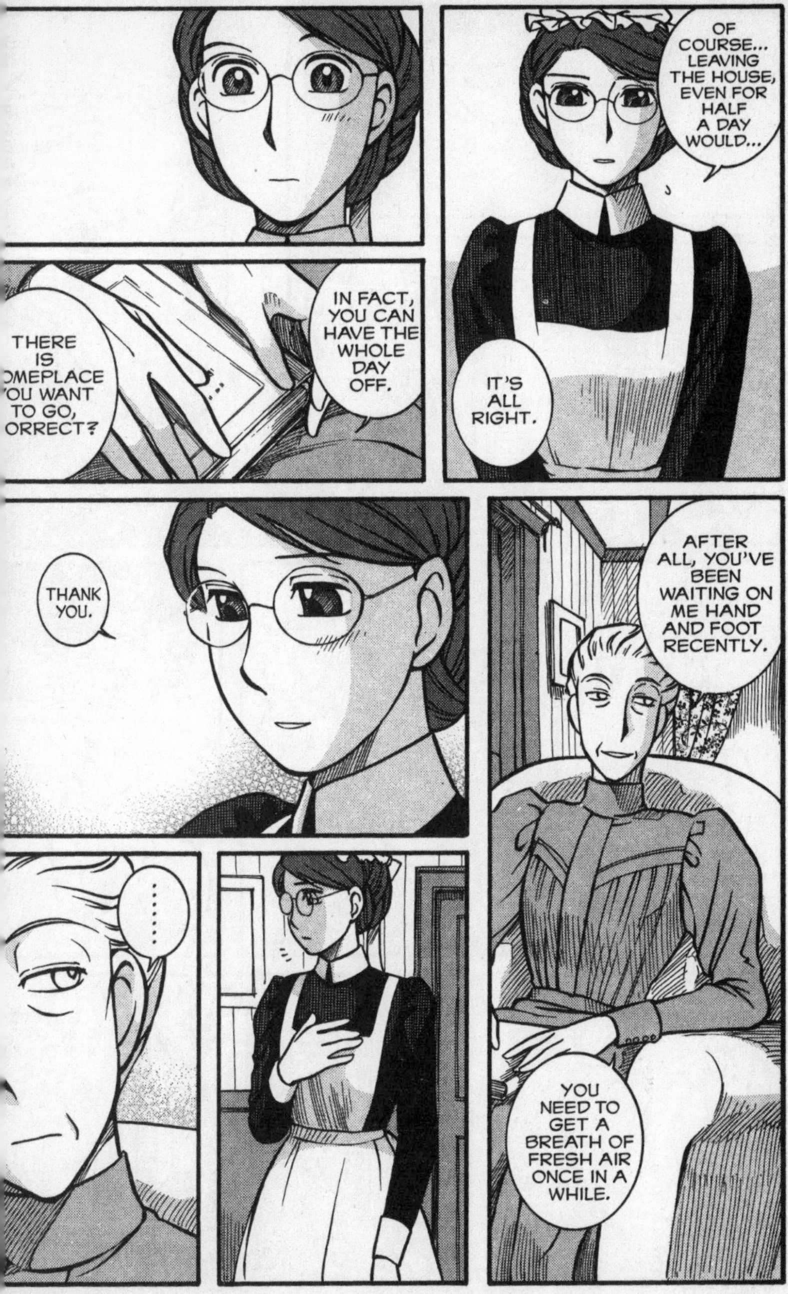
OF COURSE... LEAVING THE HOUSE, EVEN FOR HALF A DAY WOULD...
IT'S ALL RIGHT.
IN FACT, YOU CAN HAVE THE WHOLE DAY OFF.
THERE IS OMEPLACE OU WANT TO GO, ORRECT?
AFTER ALL, YOU'VE BEEN WAITING ON ME HAND AND FOOT RECENTLY.
YOU NEED TO GET A BREATH OF FRESH AIR ONCE IN A WHILE.
THANK YOU.
......

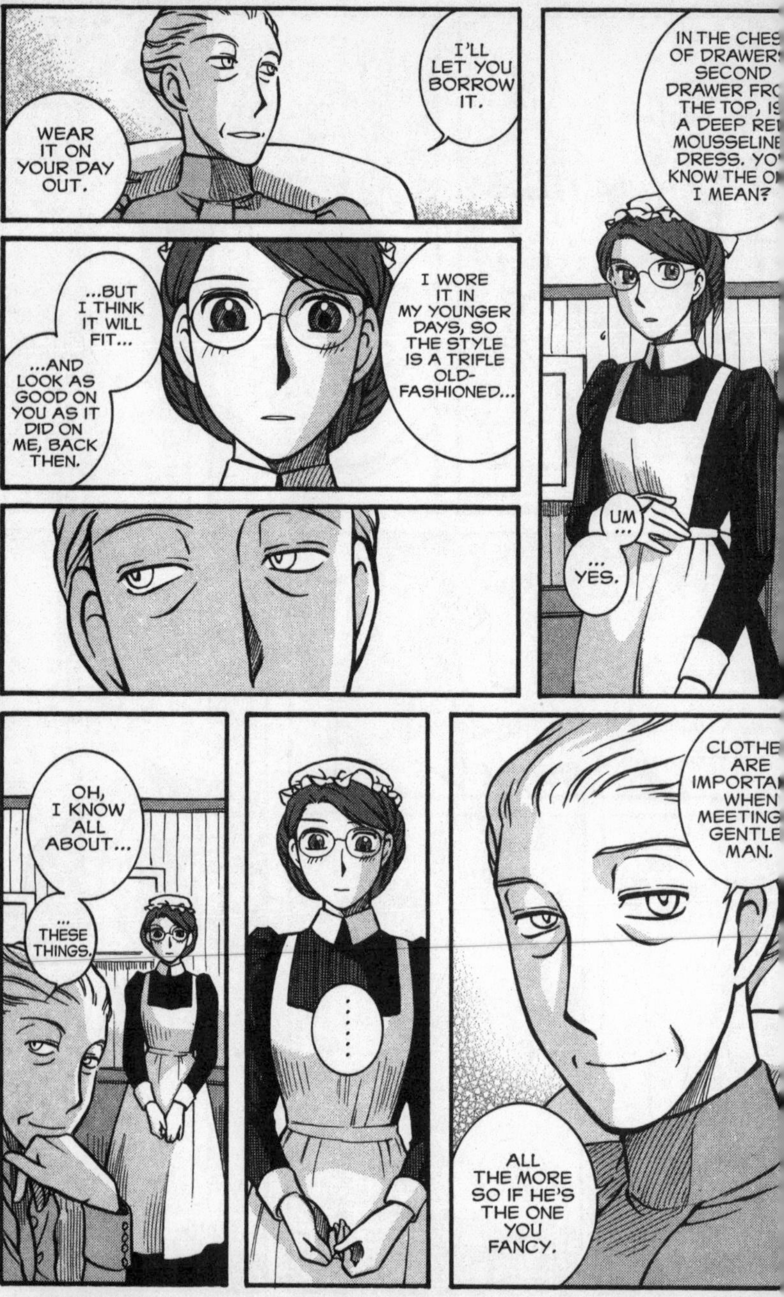
IN THE CHES OF DRAWER SECOND DRAWER FRO THE TOP, IS A DEEP RE MOUSSELINE DRESS. YO KNOW THE O I MEAN?
UM...
...YES.
I'LL LET YOU BORROW IT.
WEAR IT ON YOUR DAY OUT.
I WORE IT IN MY YOUNGER DAYS, SO THE STYLE IS A TRIFLE OLD-FASHIONED...
...BUT I THINK IT WILL FIT...
...AND LOOK AS GOOD ON YOU AS IT DID ON ME, BACK THEN.
CLOTHE ARE IMPORTA WHEN MEETING GENTLE MAN.
ALL THE MORE SO IF HE'S THE ONE YOU FANCY.
......
OH, I KNOW ALL ABOUT...
...THESE THINGS.

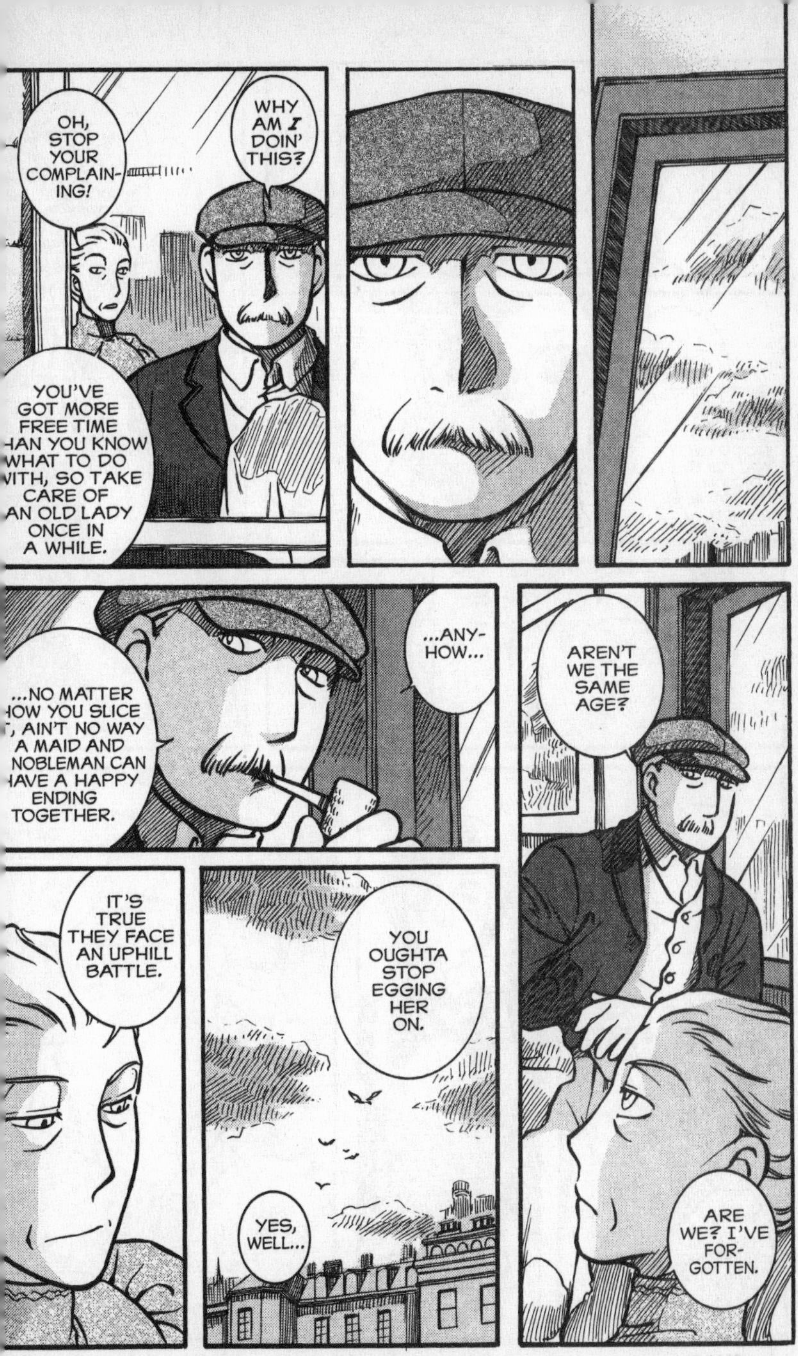
WHY AM I DOIN' THIS?
OH, STOP YOUR COMPLAINING!
YOU'VE GOT MORE FREE TIME HAN YOU KNOW WHAT TO DO VITH, SO TAKE CARE OF AN OLD LADY ONCE IN A WHILE.
AREN'T WE THE SAME AGE?
ARE WE? I'VE FOR-GOTTEN.
...ANY-HOW...
...NO MATTER HOW YOU SLICE T, AIN'T NO WAY A MAID AND NOBLEMAN CAN HAVE A HAPPY ENDING TOGETHER.
YOU OUGHTA STOP EGGING HER ON.
YES, WELL...
IT'S TRUE THEY FACE AN UPHILL BATTLE.

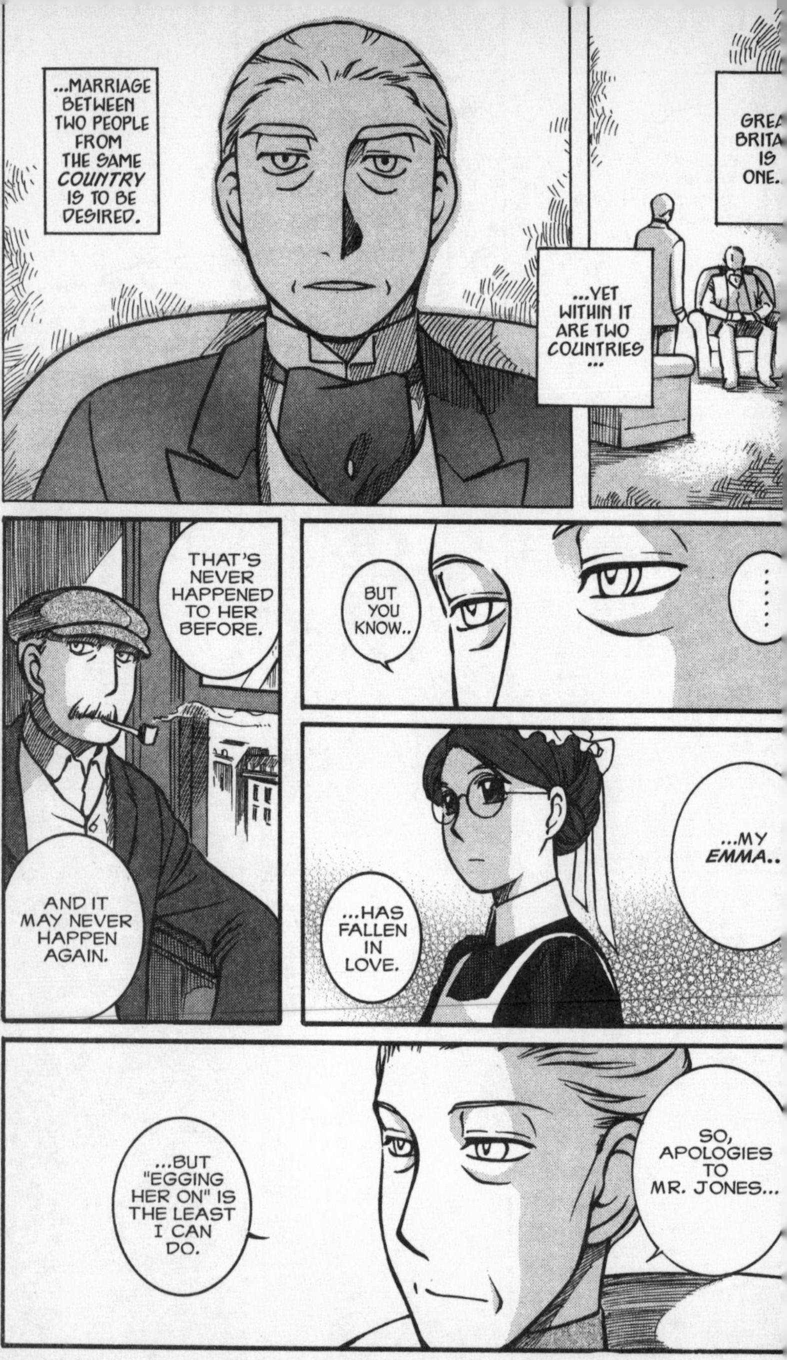
GREA BRITA IS ONE..
...YET WITHIN IT ARE TWO COUNTRIES ...
...MARRIAGE BETWEEN TWO PEOPLE FROM THE SAME *COUNTRY* IS TO BE DESIRED.
......
BUT YOU KNOW..
...MY *EMMA*..
...HAS FALLEN IN LOVE.
THAT'S NEVER HAPPENED TO HER BEFORE.
AND IT MAY NEVER HAPPEN AGAIN.
SO, APOLOGIES TO MR. JONES...
...BUT "EGGING HER ON" IS THE LEAST I CAN DO.

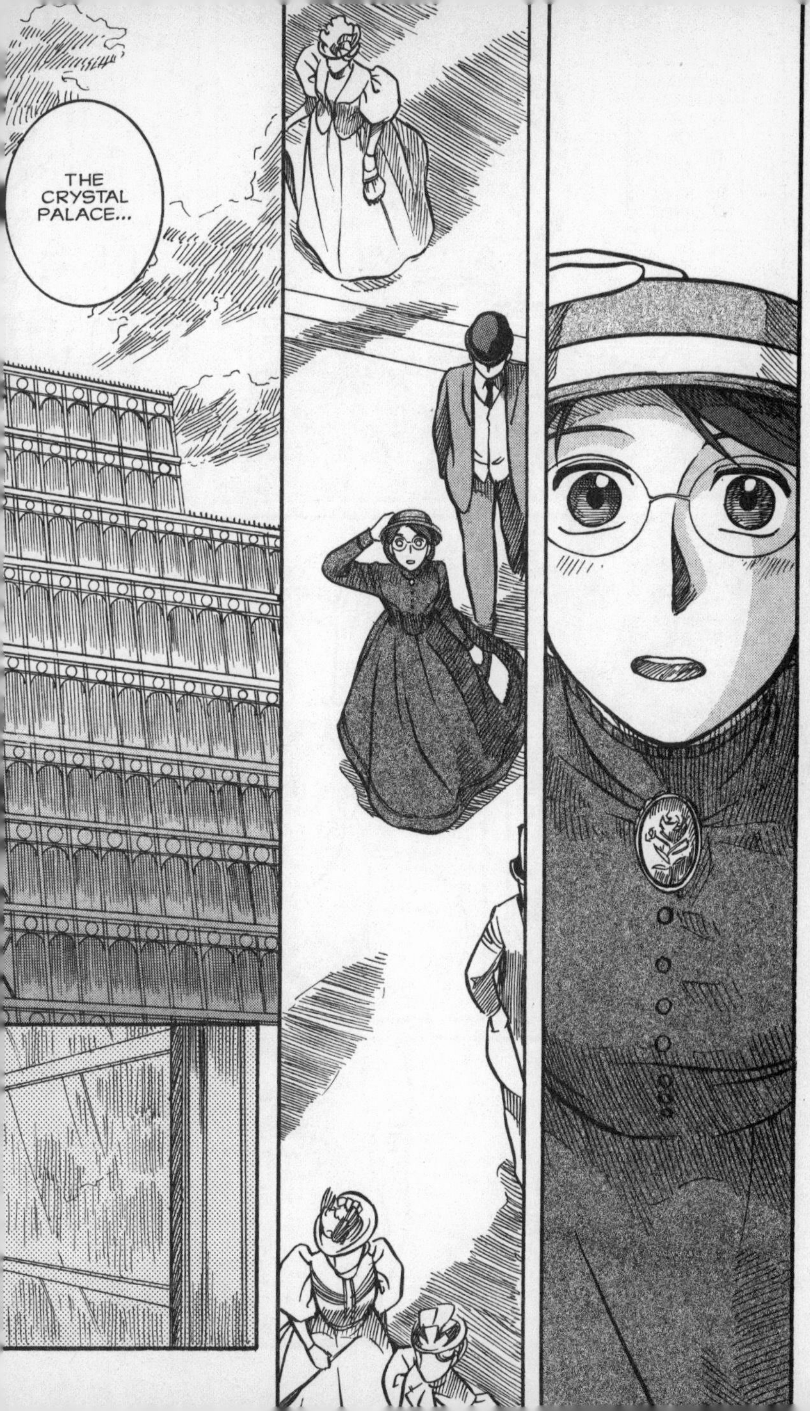
THE CRYSTAL PALACE...

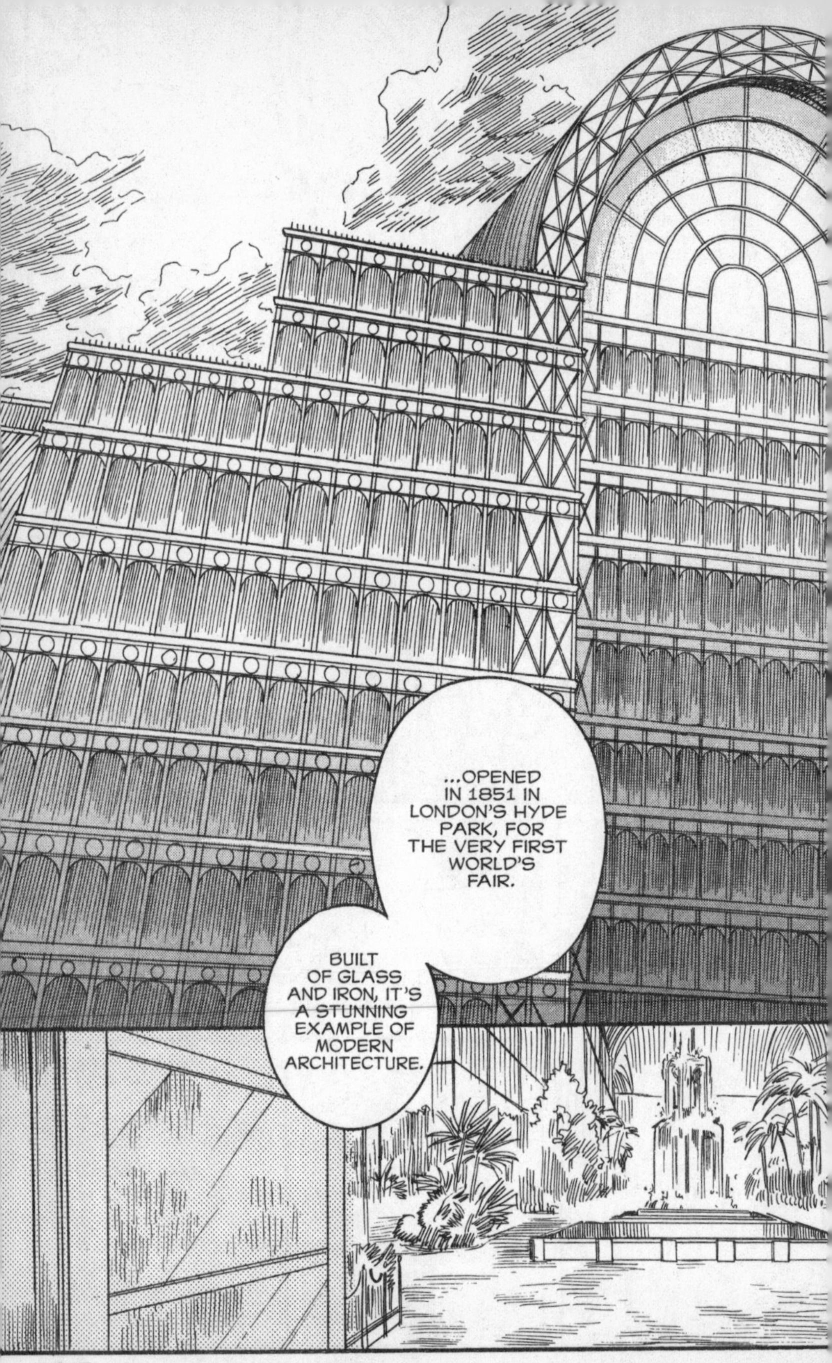
...OPENED IN 1851 IN LONDON'S HYDE PARK, FOR THE VERY FIRST WORLD'S FAIR.
BUILT OF GLASS AND IRON, IT'S A STUNNING EXAMPLE OF MODERN ARCHITECTURE.

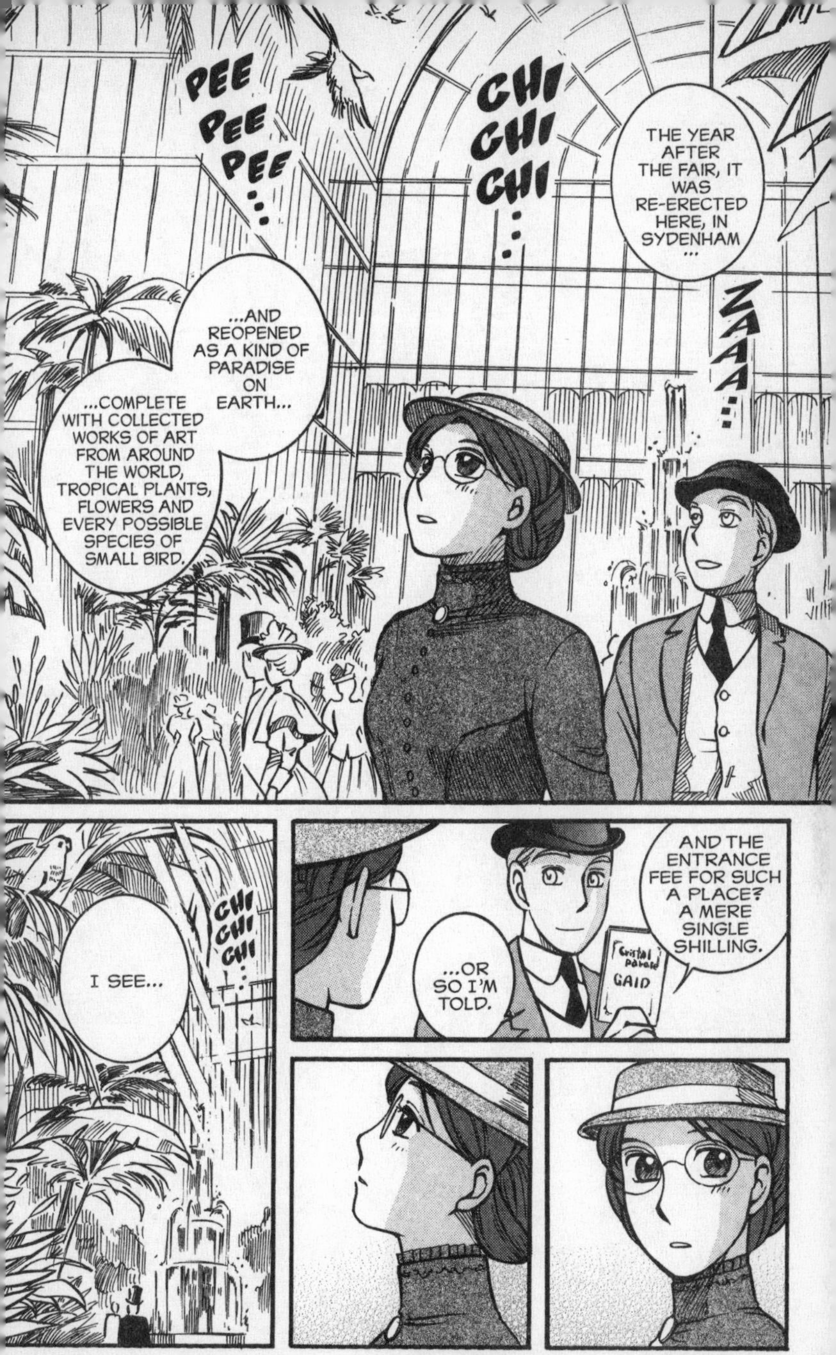
THE YEAR AFTER THE FAIR, IT WAS RE-ERECTED HERE, IN SYDENHAM ...
CHI CHI CHI...
PEE PEE PEE...
ZAAA...
...AND REOPENED AS A KIND OF PARADISE ON EARTH...
...COMPLETE WITH COLLECTED WORKS OF ART FROM AROUND THE WORLD, TROPICAL PLANTS, FLOWERS AND EVERY POSSIBLE SPECIES OF SMALL BIRD.
AND THE ENTRANCE FEE FOR SUCH A PLACE? A MERE SINGLE SHILLING.
...OR SO I'M TOLD.
I SEE...
CHI CHI CHI...

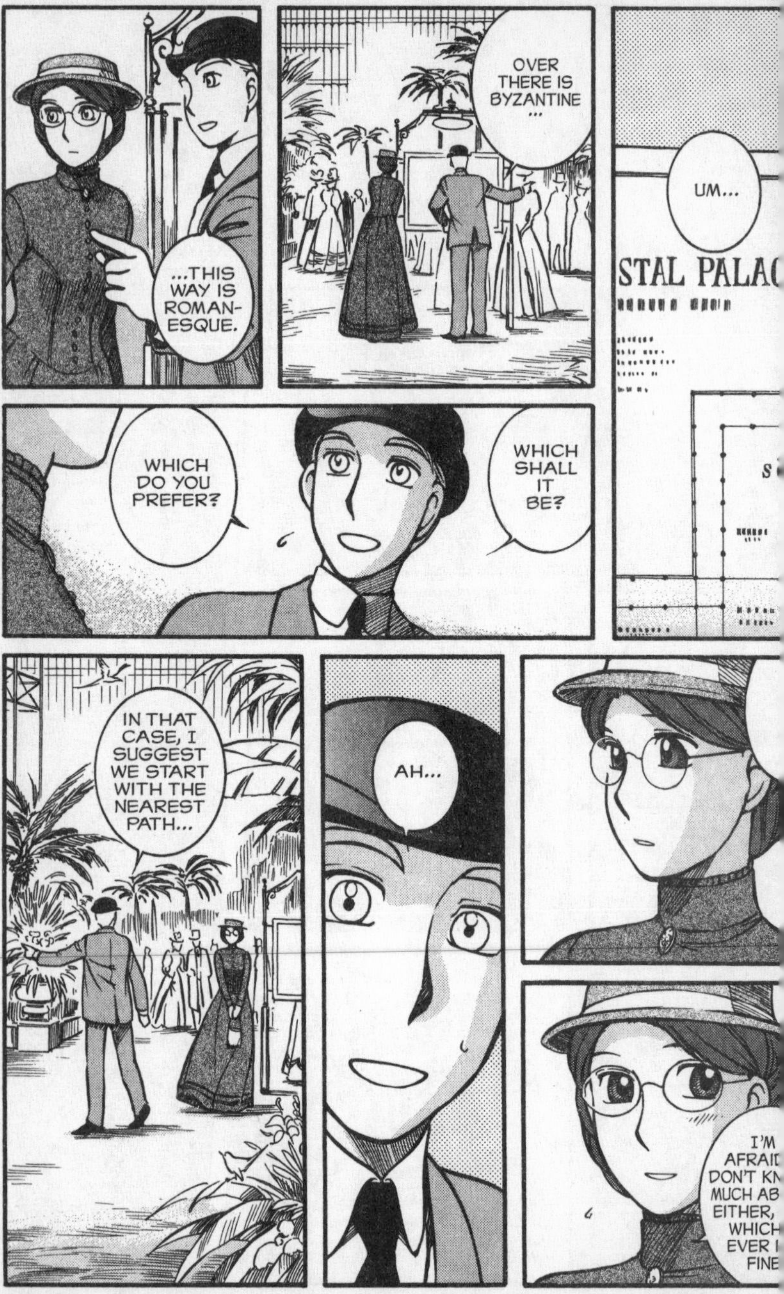
UM...
STAL PALAC
OVER THERE IS BYZANTINE ...
...THIS WAY IS ROMAN-ESQUE.
WHICH SHALL IT BE?
WHICH DO YOU PREFER?
I'M AFRAID DON'T KN MUCH AB EITHER, WHICH- EVER I FINE
AH...
IN THAT CASE, I SUGGEST WE START WITH THE NEAREST PATH...

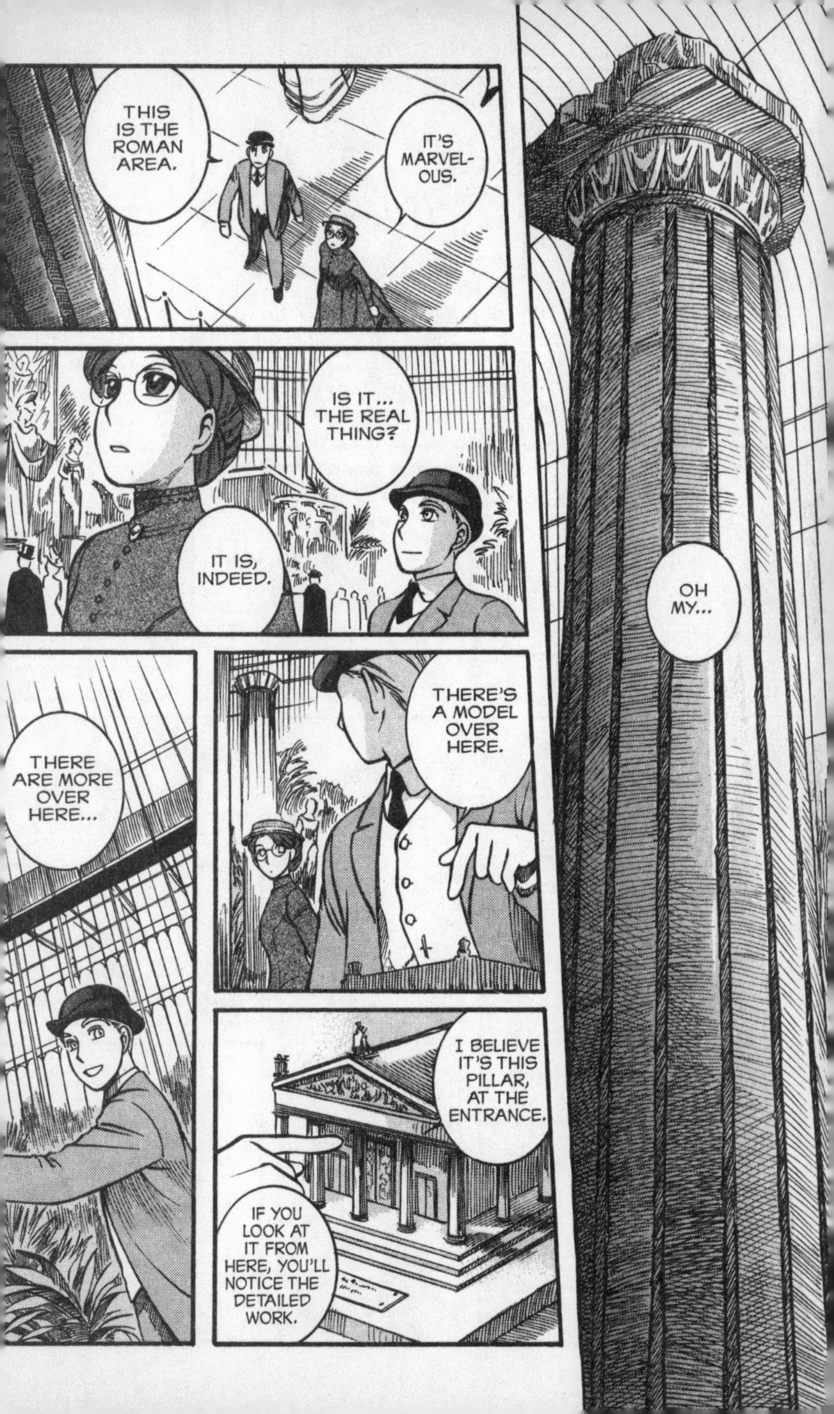
OH MY...
THIS IS THE ROMAN AREA.
IT'S MARVEL-OUS.
IS IT... THE REAL THING?
IT IS, INDEED.
THERE'S A MODEL OVER HERE.
THERE ARE MORE OVER HERE...
I BELIEVE IT'S THIS PILLAR, AT THE ENTRANCE.
IF YOU LOOK AT IT FROM HERE, YOU'LL NOTICE THE DETAILED WORK.

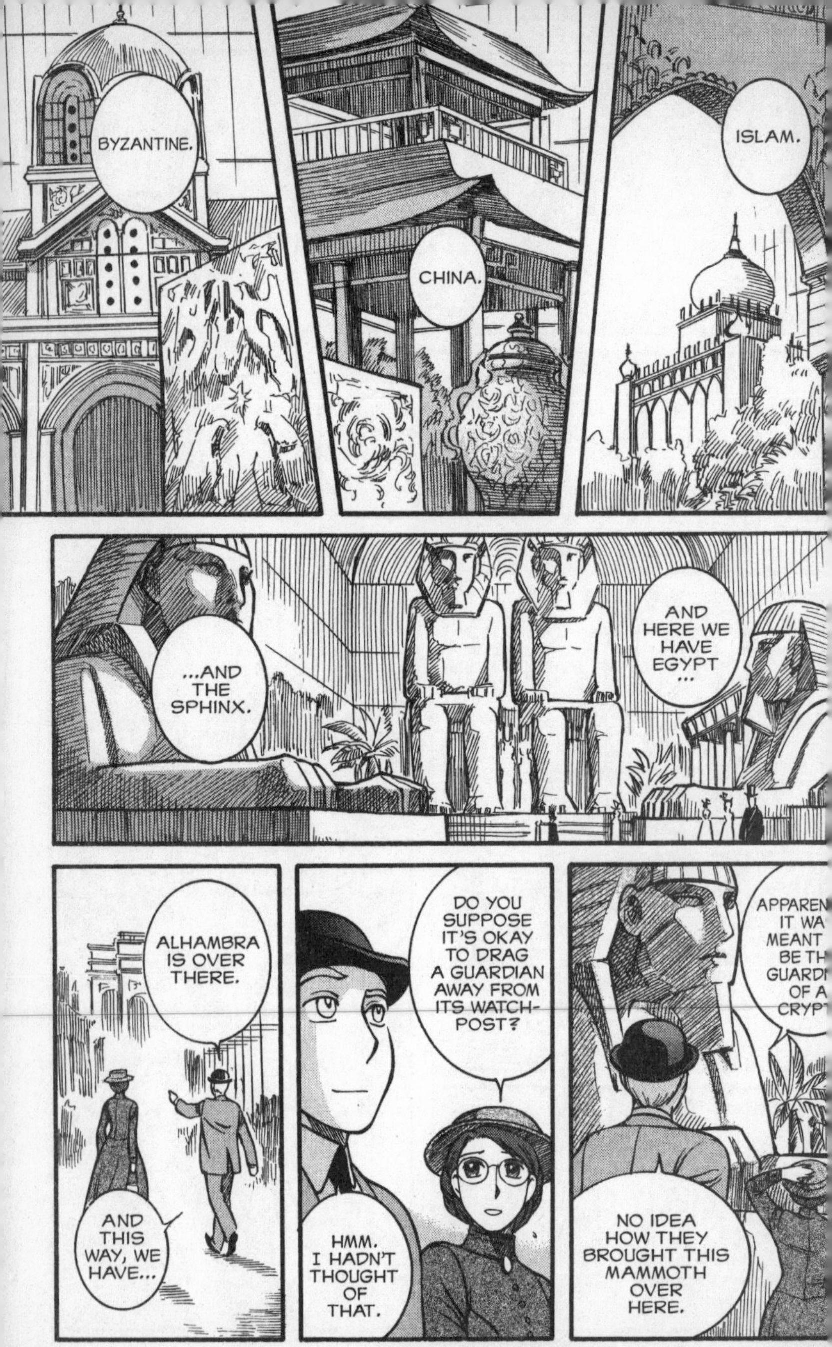
ISLAM.
CHINA.
BYZANTINE.
AND HERE WE HAVE EGYPT ...
...AND THE SPHINX.
APPAREN IT WA MEANT BE TH GUARDI OF A CRYPT
NO IDEA HOW THEY BROUGHT THIS MAMMOTH OVER HERE.
DO YOU SUPPOSE IT'S OKAY TO DRAG A GUARDIAN AWAY FROM ITS WATCH-POST?
HMM. I HADN'T THOUGHT OF THAT.
ALHAMBRA IS OVER THERE.
AND THIS WAY, WE HAVE...

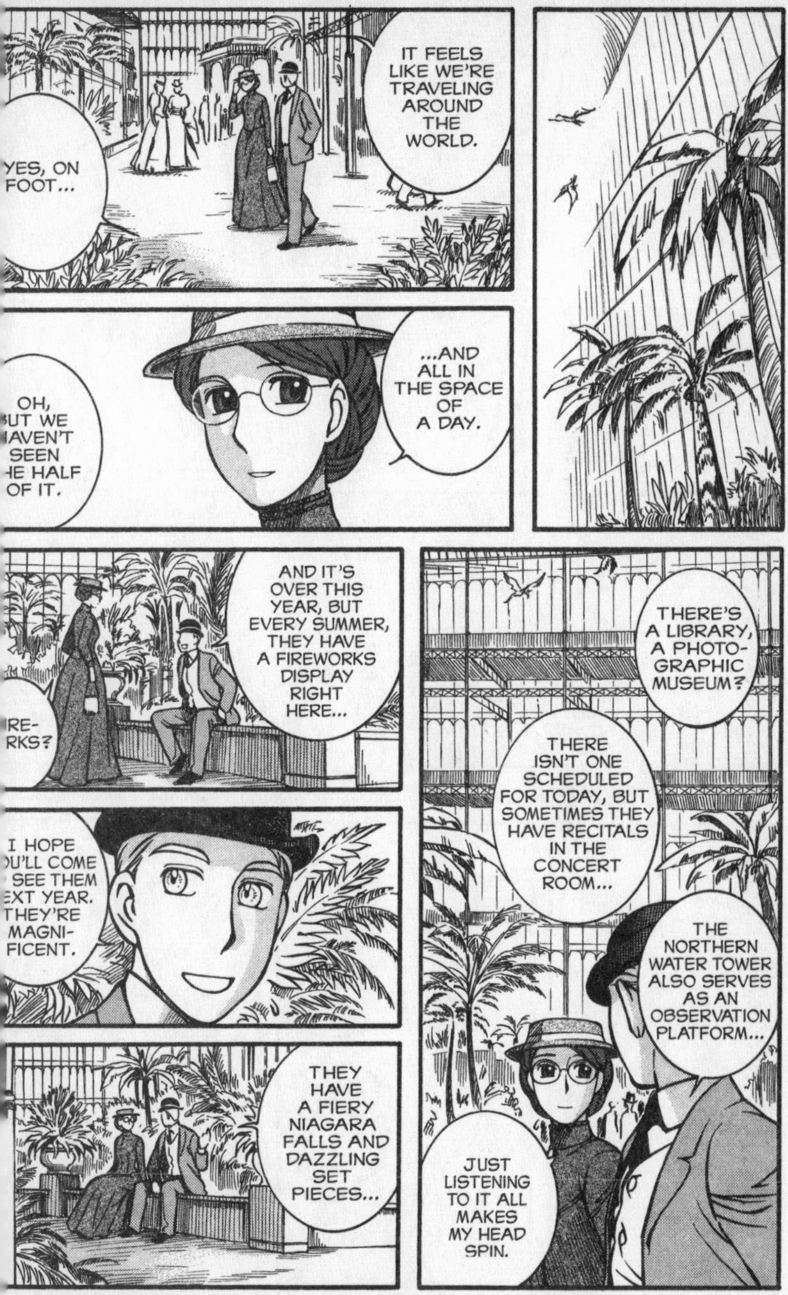
IT FEELS LIKE WE'RE TRAVELING AROUND THE WORLD.
YES, ON FOOT...
...AND ALL IN THE SPACE OF A DAY.
OH, UT WE AVEN'T SEEN HE HALF OF IT.
THERE'S A LIBRARY, A PHOTO-GRAPHIC MUSEUM?
THERE ISN'T ONE SCHEDULED FOR TODAY, BUT SOMETIMES THEY HAVE RECITALS IN THE CONCERT ROOM...
THE NORTHERN WATER TOWER ALSO SERVES AS AN OBSERVATION PLATFORM...
JUST LISTENING TO IT ALL MAKES MY HEAD SPIN.
AND IT'S OVER THIS YEAR, BUT EVERY SUMMER, THEY HAVE A FIREWORKS DISPLAY RIGHT HERE...
RE-RKS?
I HOPE OU'LL COME SEE THEM EXT YEAR. THEY'RE MAGNI-FICENT.
THEY HAVE A FIERY NIAGARA FALLS AND DAZZLING SET PIECES...

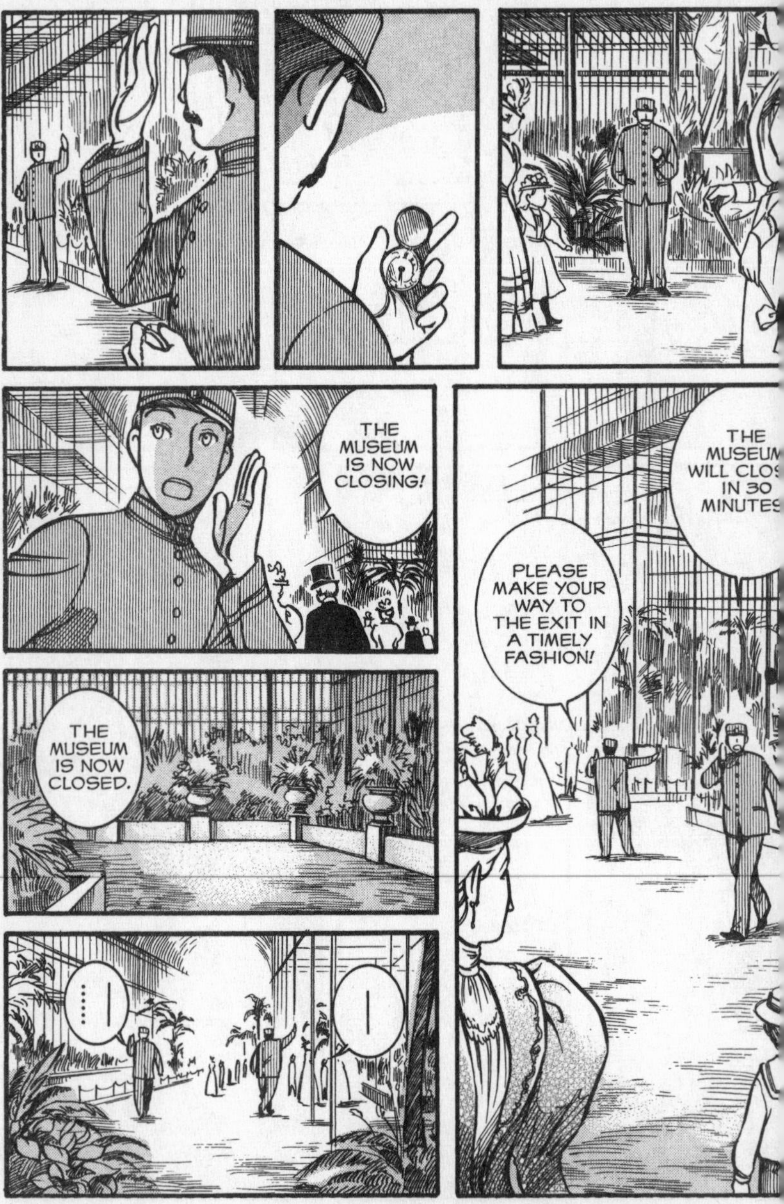
THE MUSEUM WILL CLOS IN 30 MINUTES
PLEASE MAKE YOUR WAY TO THE EXIT IN A TIMELY FASHION!
THE MUSEUM IS NOW CLOSING!
THE MUSEUM IS NOW CLOSED.
—
……—

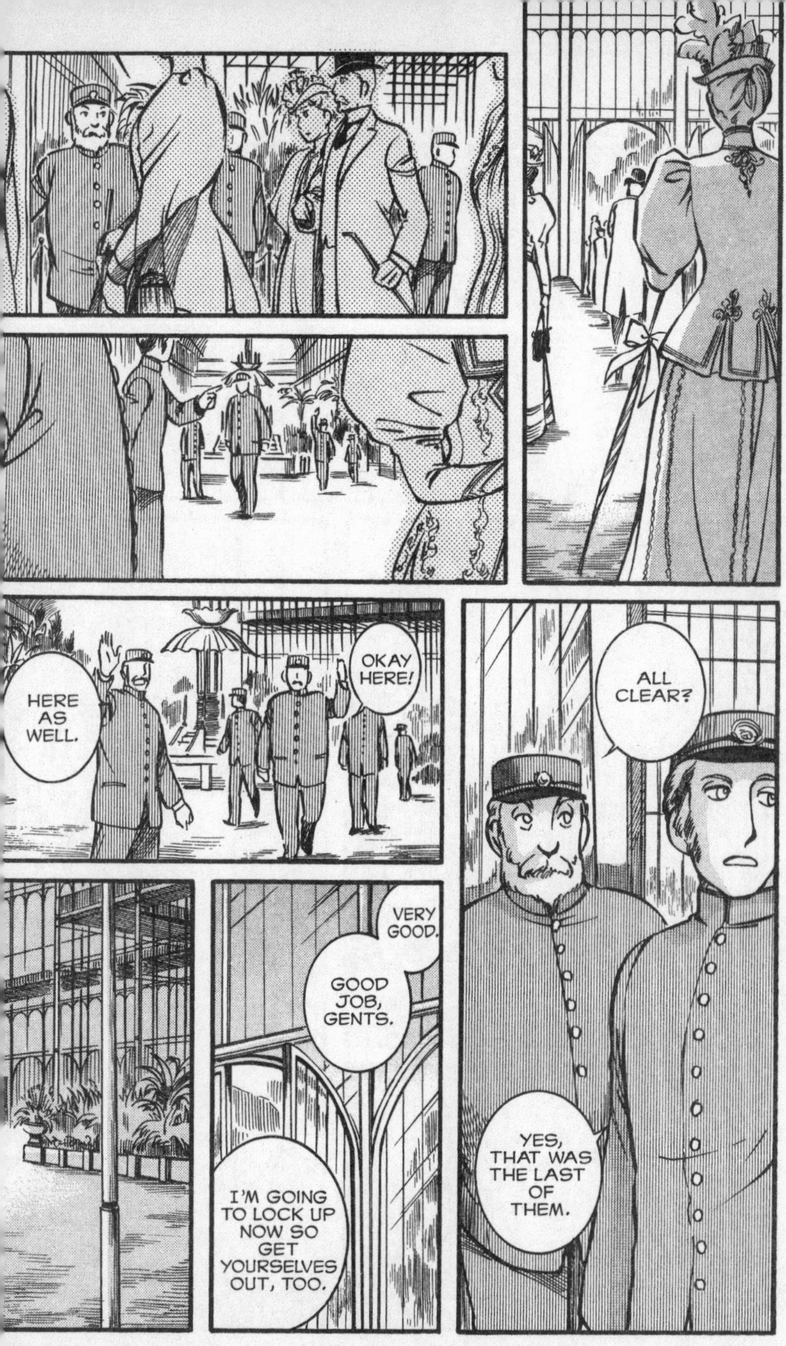
ALL CLEAR?
YES, THAT WAS THE LAST OF THEM.
OKAY HERE!
HERE AS WELL.
VERY GOOD.
GOOD JOB, GENTS.
I'M GOING TO LOCK UP NOW SO GET YOURSELVES OUT, TOO.

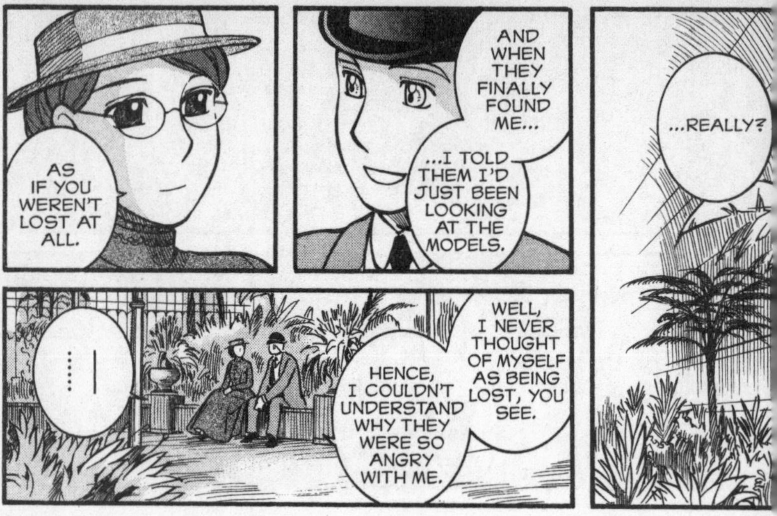
...REALLY?
AND WHEN THEY FINALLY FOUND ME...
...I TOLD THEM I'D JUST BEEN LOOKING AT THE MODELS.
AS IF YOU WEREN'T LOST AT ALL.
WELL, I NEVER THOUGHT OF MYSELF AS BEING LOST, YOU SEE.
HENCE, I COULDN'T UNDERSTAND WHY THEY WERE SO ANGRY WITH ME.
......

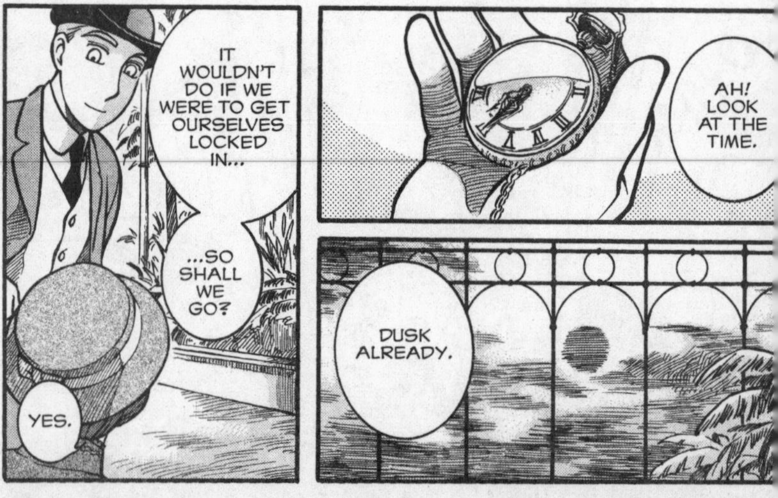
AH! LOOK AT THE TIME.
DUSK ALREADY.
IT WOULDN'T DO IF WE WERE TO GET OURSELVES LOCKED IN...
...SO SHALL WE GO?
YES.

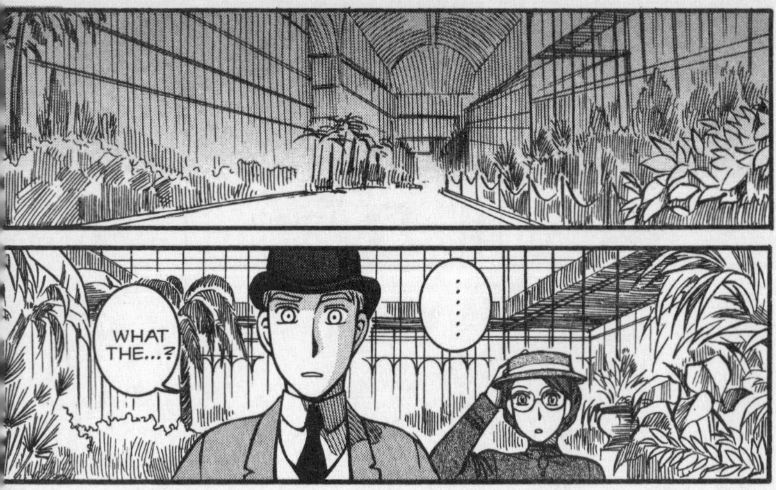
......
WHAT THE...?

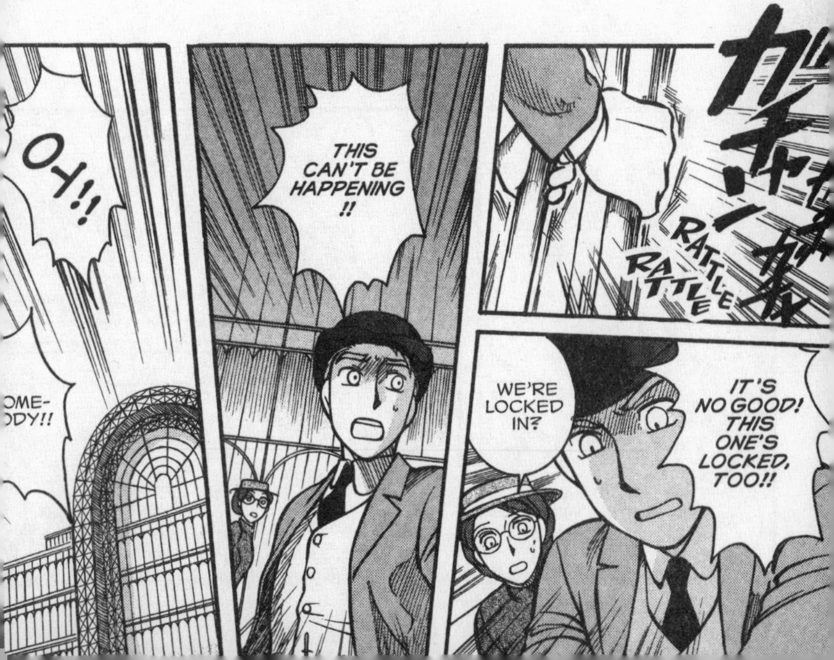
RATTLE RATTLE
IT'S NO GOOD! THIS ONE'S LOCKED, TOO!!
WE'RE LOCKED IN?
THIS CAN'T BE HAPPENING!!

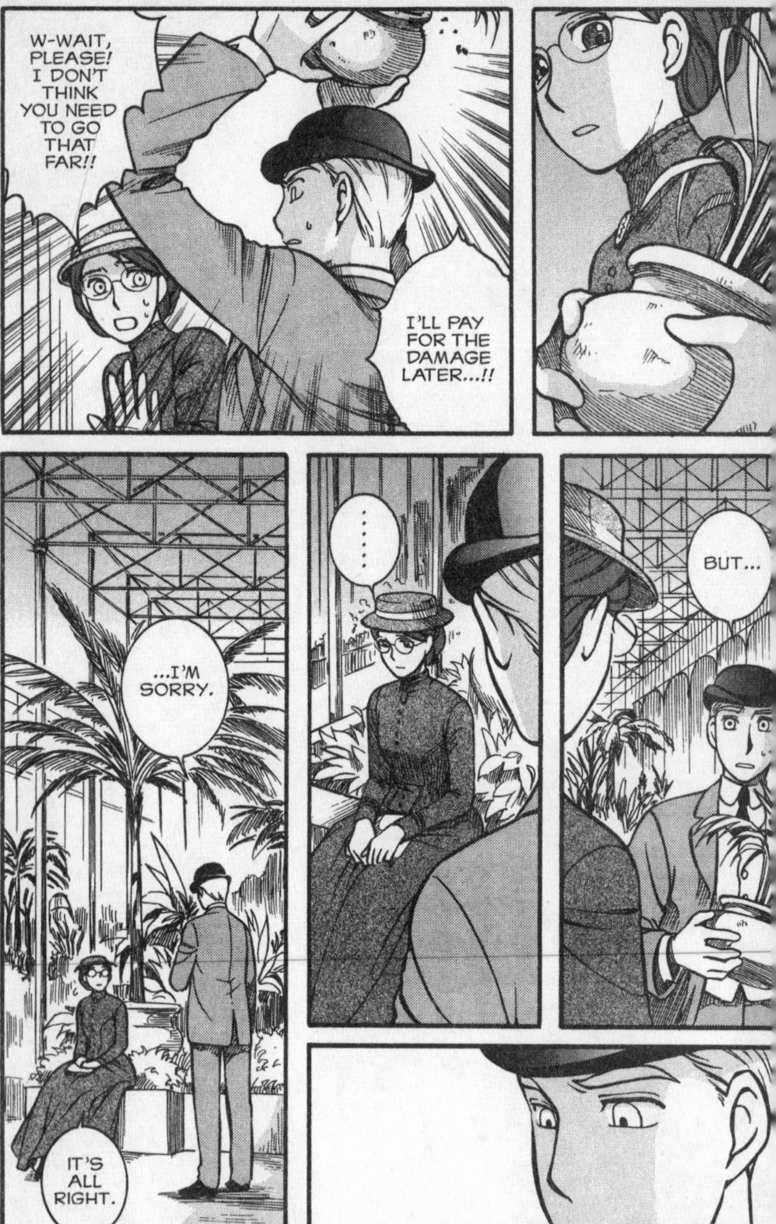
I'LL PAY FOR THE DAMAGE LATER...!!
W-WAIT, PLEASE! I DON'T THINK YOU NEED TO GO THAT FAR!!
BUT...
......
...I'M SORRY.
IT'S ALL RIGHT.

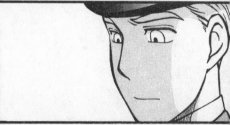

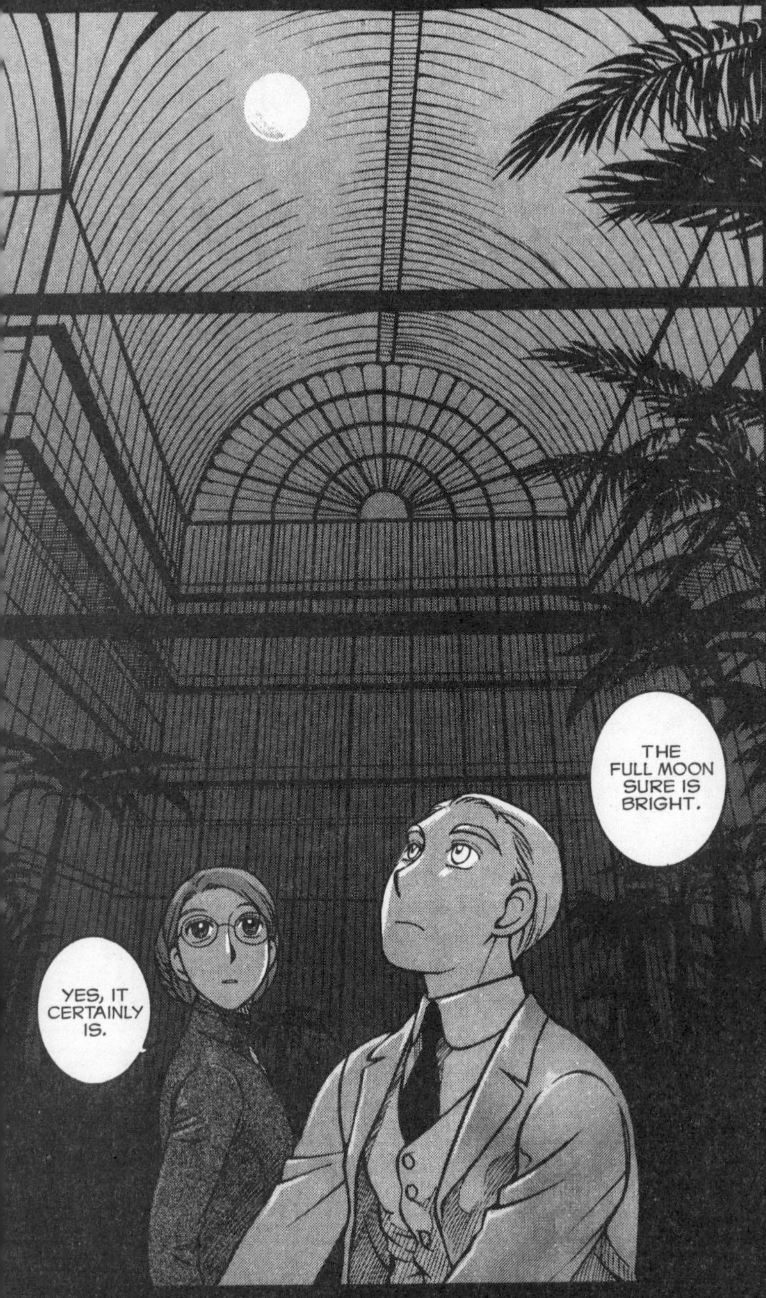
THE FULL MOON SURE IS BRIGHT.
YES, IT CERTAINLY IS.

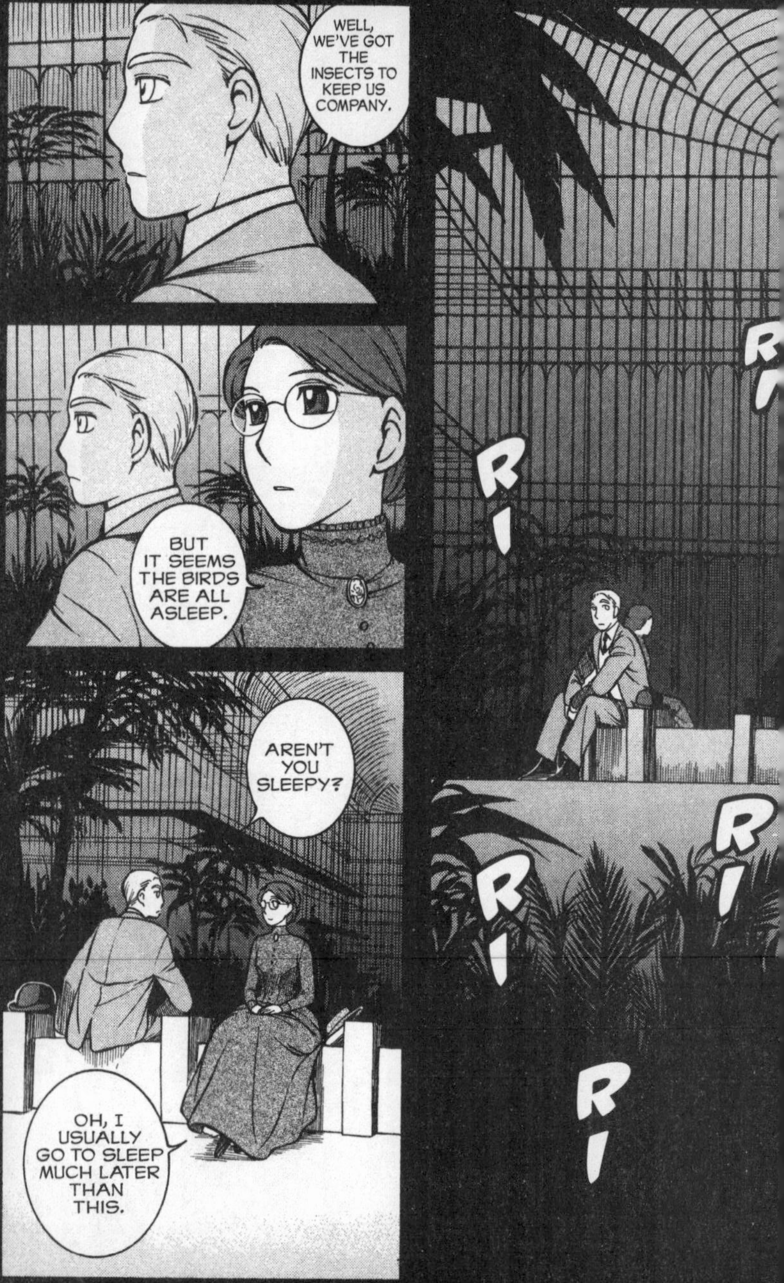
RI
RI
RI
RI
RI
WELL, WE'VE GOT THE INSECTS TO KEEP US COMPANY.
BUT IT SEEMS THE BIRDS ARE ALL ASLEEP.
AREN'T YOU SLEEPY?
OH, I USUALLY GO TO SLEEP MUCH LATER THAN THIS.

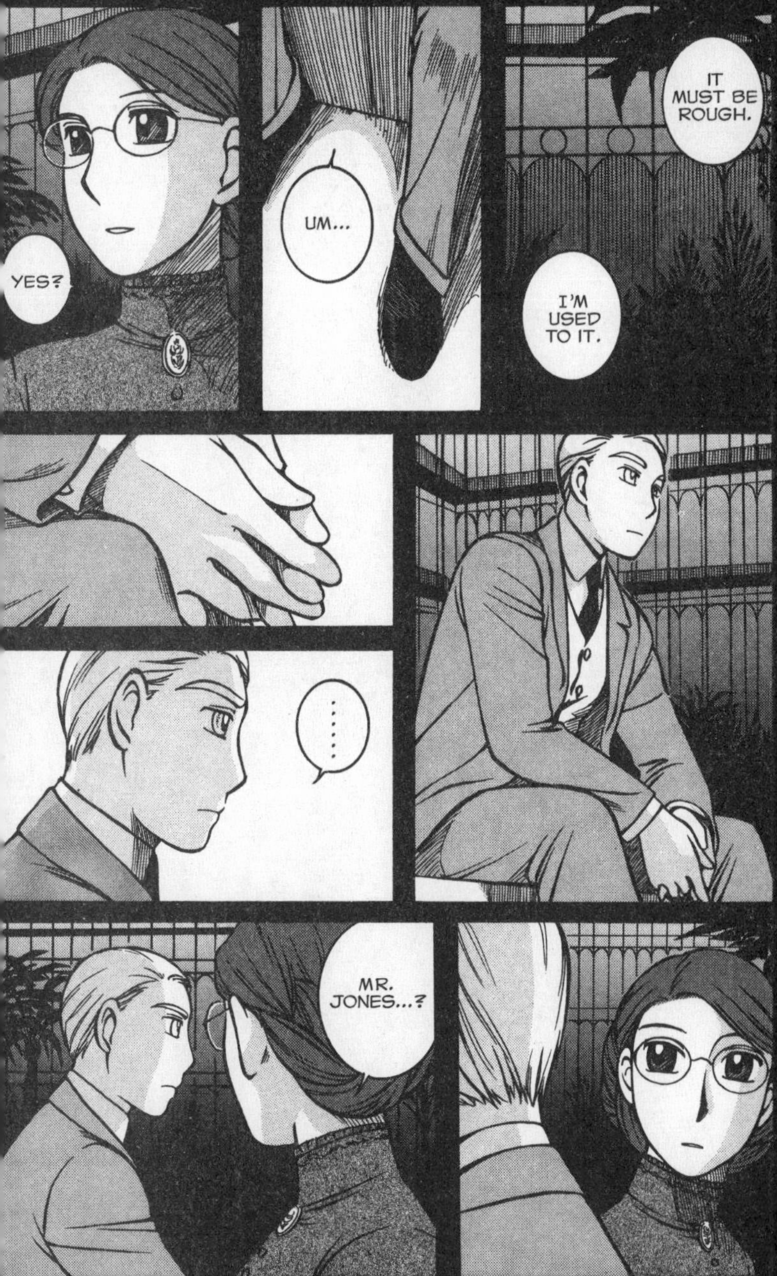
IT MUST BE ROUGH.
I'M USED TO IT.
UM...
YES?
......
MR. JONES...?

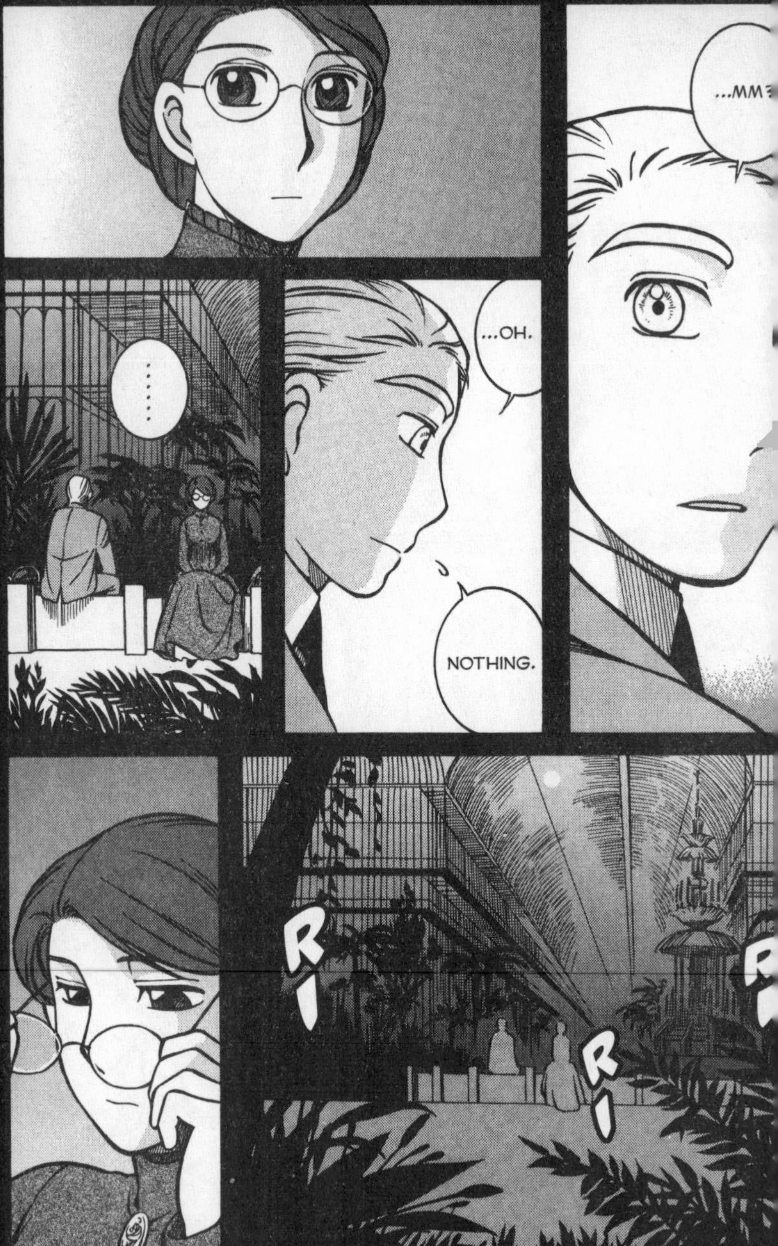
...MM
...OH.
NOTHING.
......
R
RI
RI

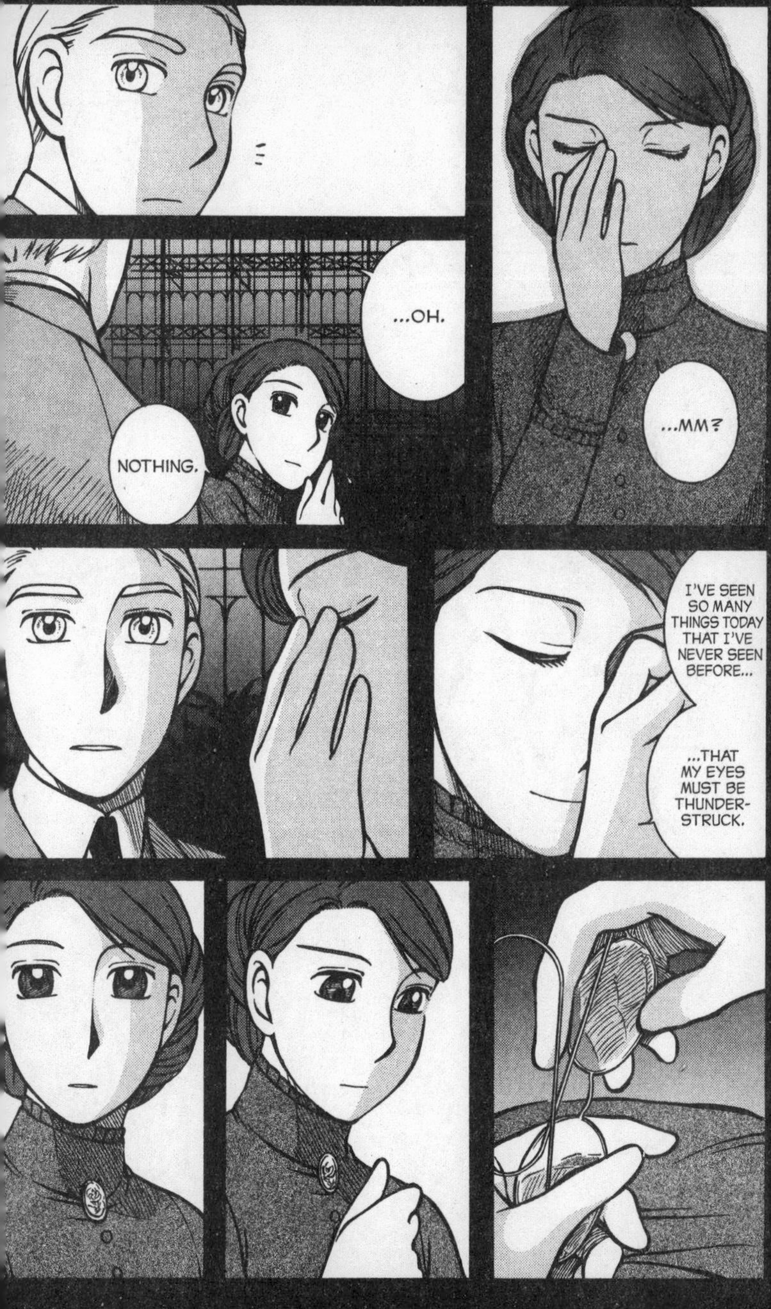
...MM?
...OH.
NOTHING.
I'VE SEEN SO MANY THINGS TODAY THAT I'VE NEVER SEEN BEFORE...
...THAT MY EYES MUST BE THUNDER-STRUCK.

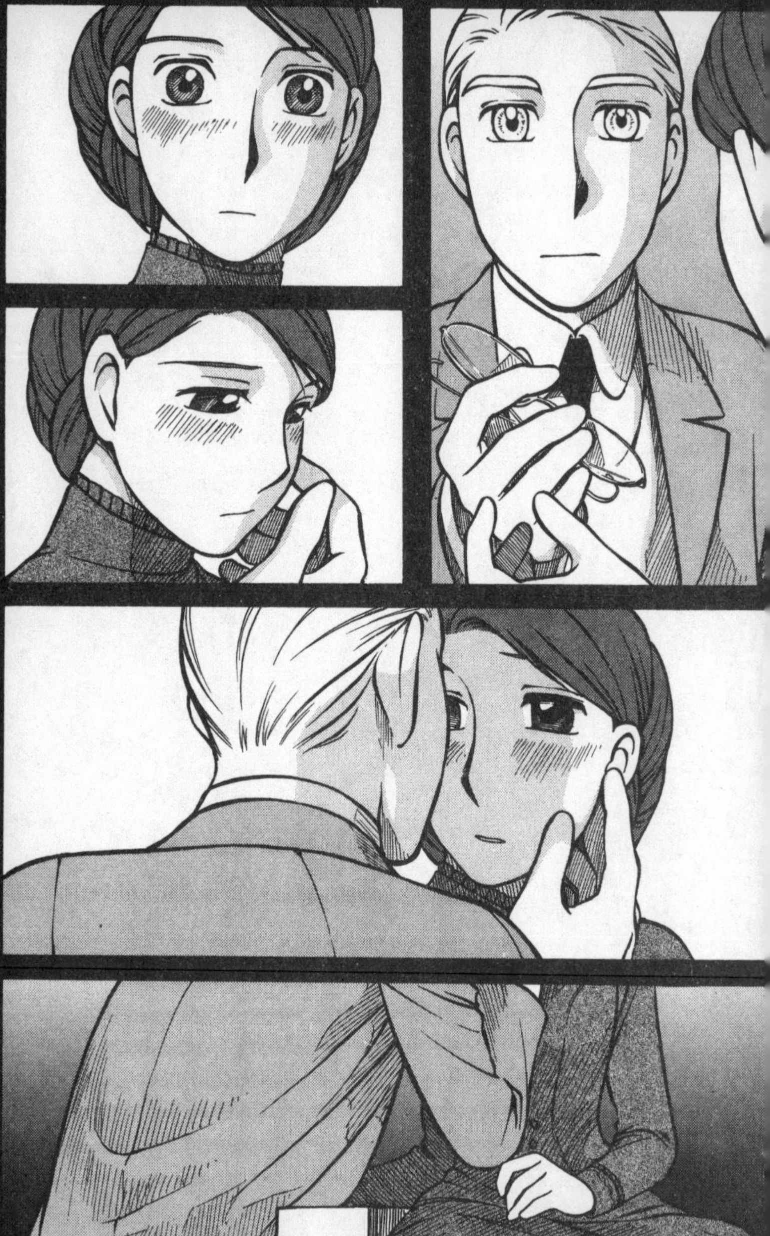

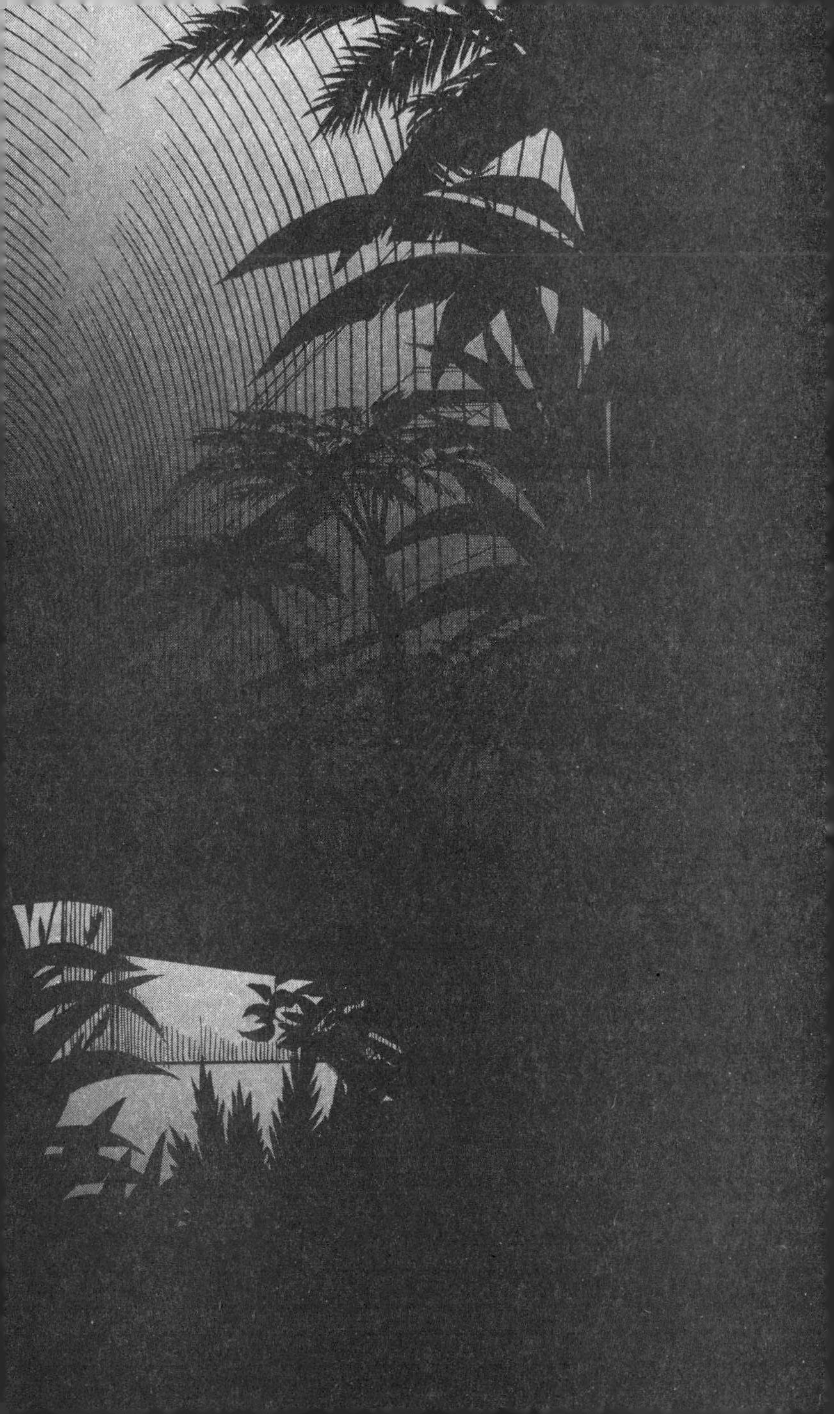

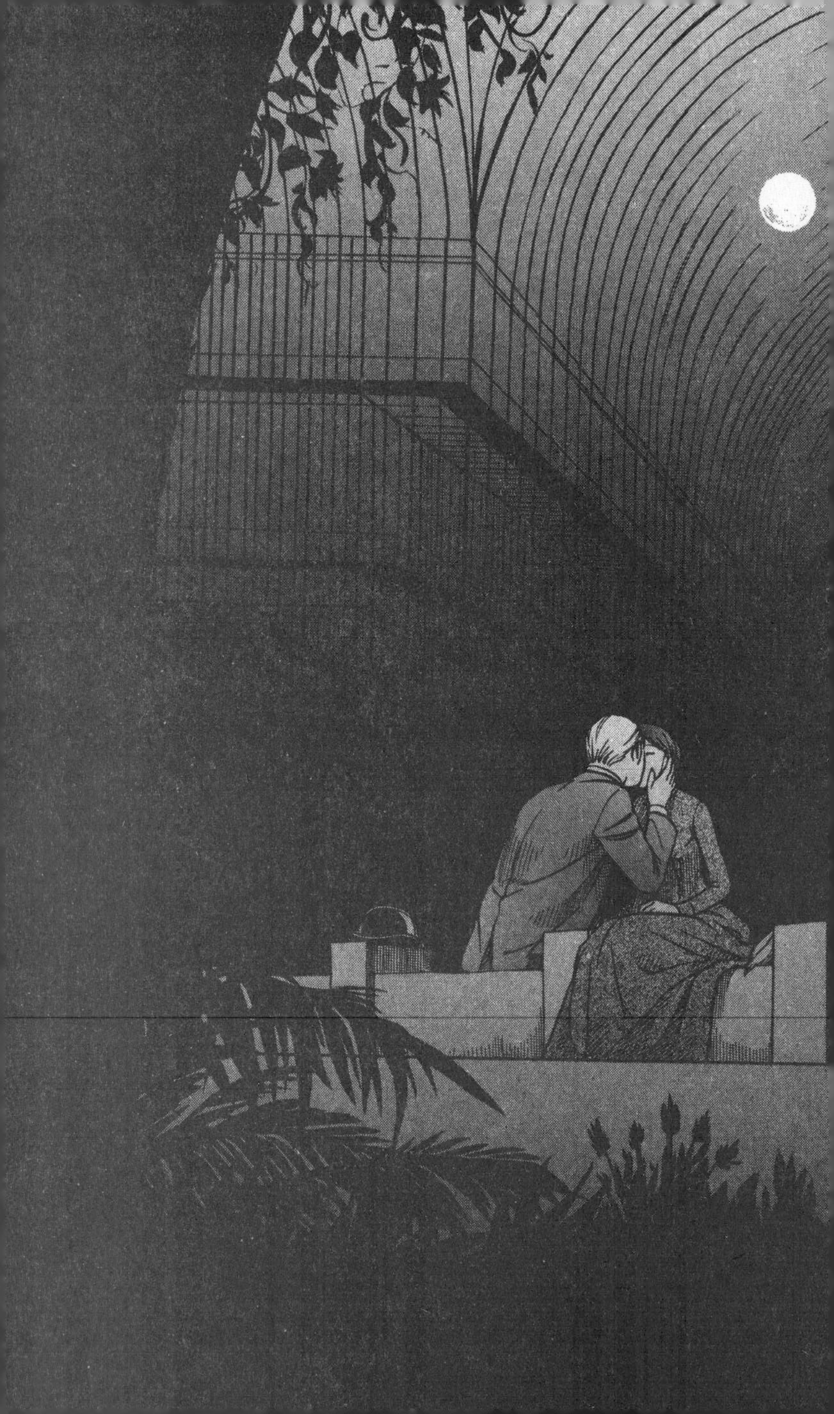

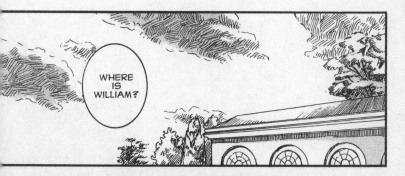

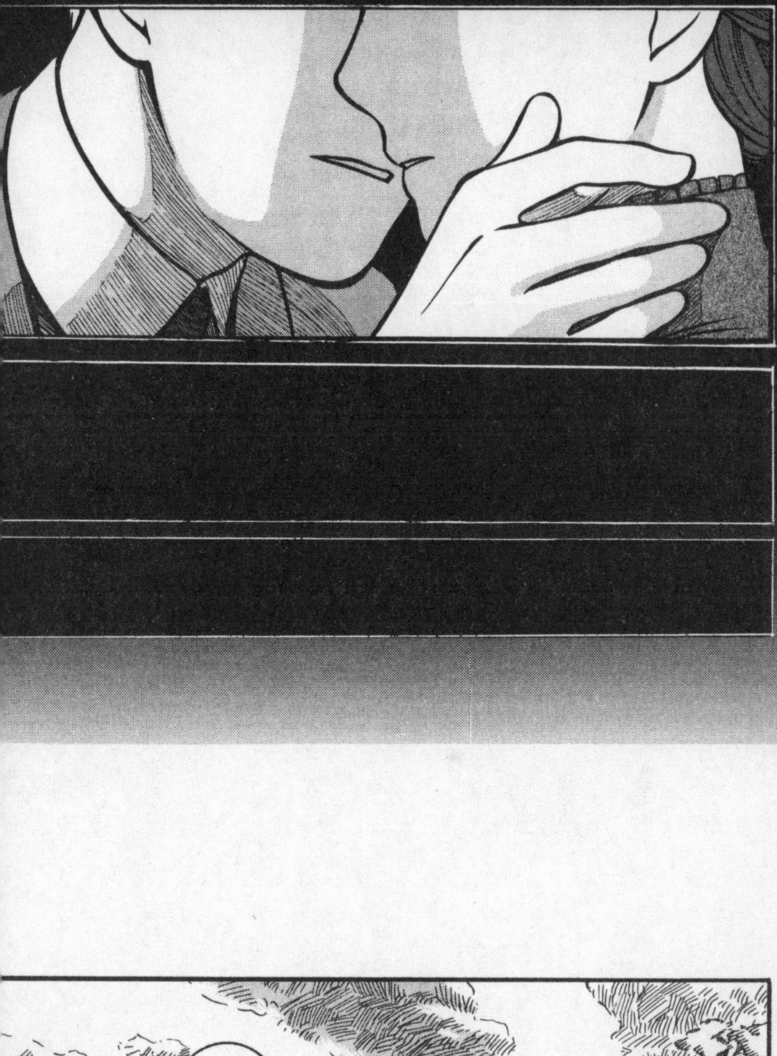
WHERE IS WILLIAM?

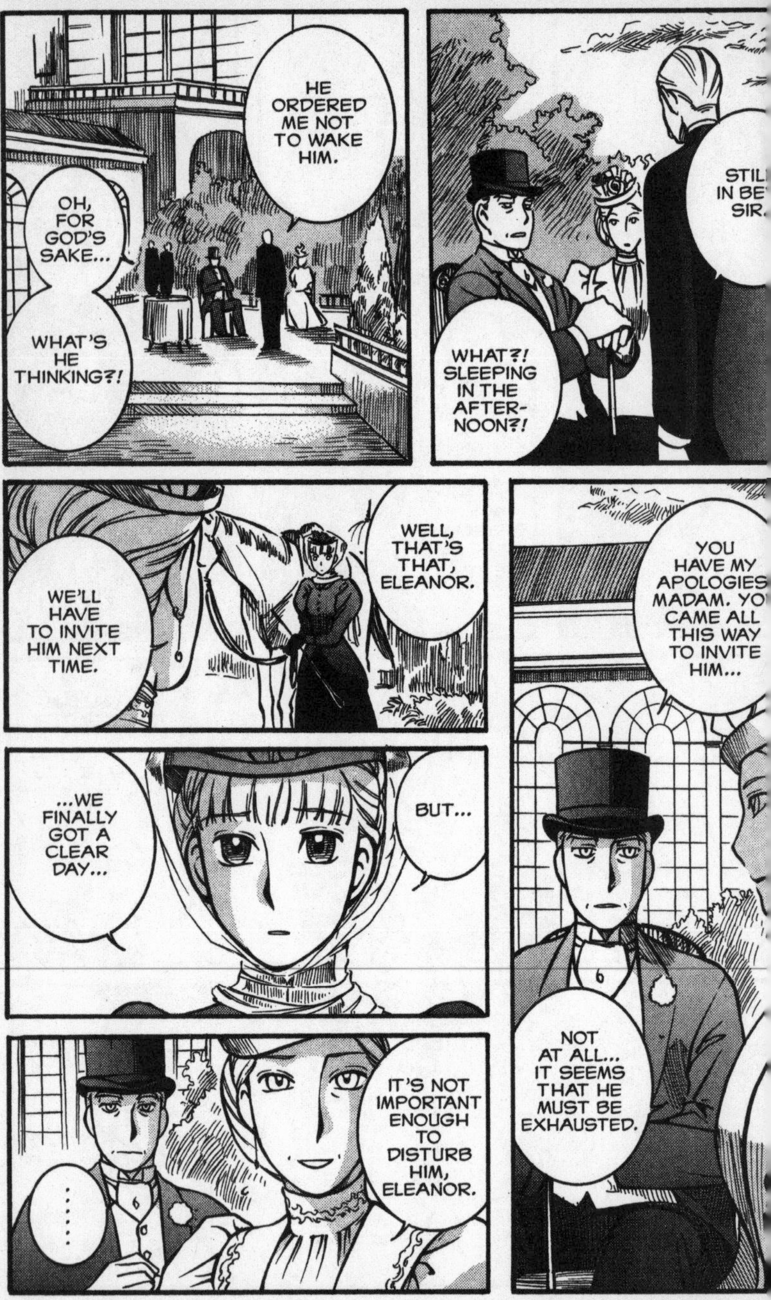
STIL IN BE SIR.
WHAT?! SLEEPING IN THE AFTER-NOON?!
HE ORDERED ME NOT TO WAKE HIM.
OH, FOR GOD'S SAKE...
WHAT'S HE THINKING?!
YOU HAVE MY APOLOGIES MADAM. YO CAME ALL THIS WAY TO INVITE HIM...
NOT AT ALL... IT SEEMS THAT HE MUST BE EXHAUSTED.
WELL, THAT'S THAT, ELEANOR.
WE'LL HAVE TO INVITE HIM NEXT TIME.
BUT...
...WE FINALLY GOT A CLEAR DAY...
IT'S NOT IMPORTANT ENOUGH TO DISTURB HIM, ELEANOR.
......

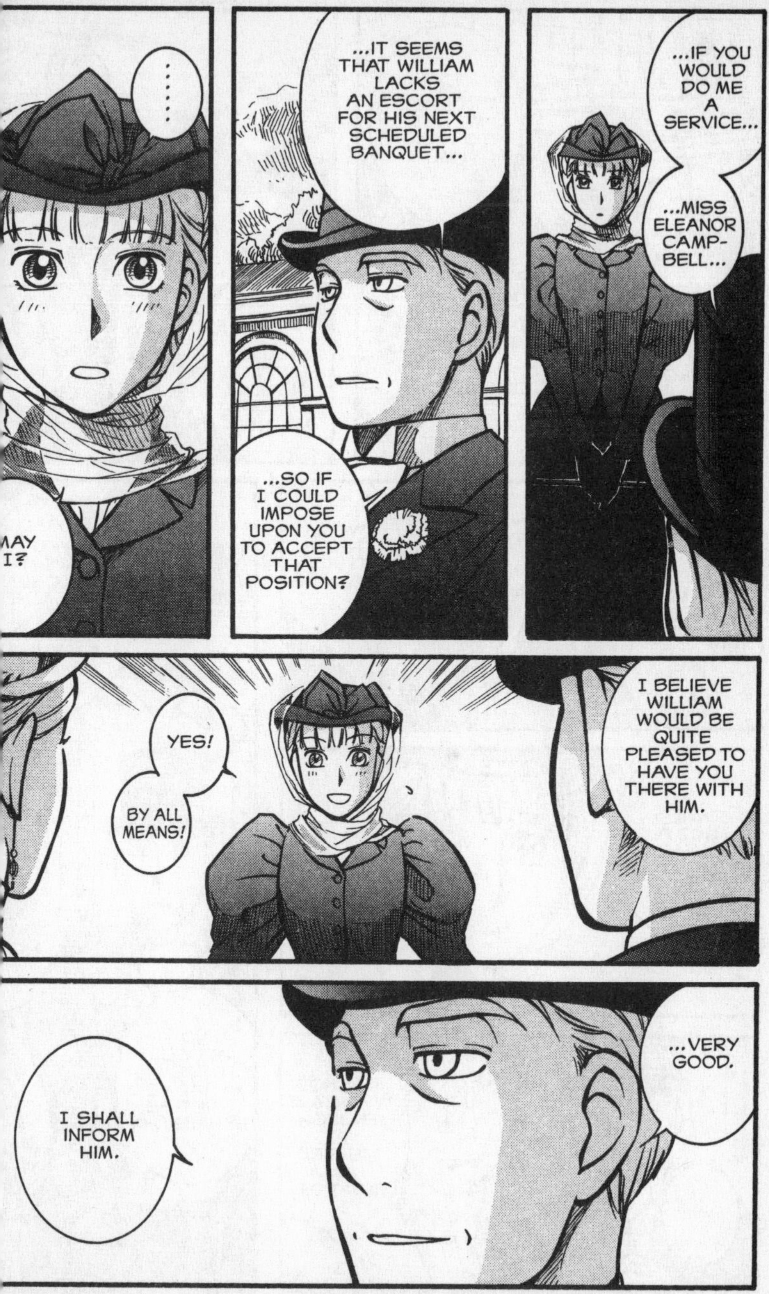
...IF YOU WOULD DO ME A SERVICE...
...MISS ELEANOR CAMP-BELL...
...IT SEEMS THAT WILLIAM LACKS AN ESCORT FOR HIS NEXT SCHEDULED BANQUET...
...SO IF I COULD IMPOSE UPON YOU TO ACCEPT THAT POSITION?
......
MAY I?
I BELIEVE WILLIAM WOULD BE QUITE PLEASED TO HAVE YOU THERE WITH HIM.
YES!
BY ALL MEANS!
...VERY GOOD.
I SHALL INFORM HIM.

EPILOGUE

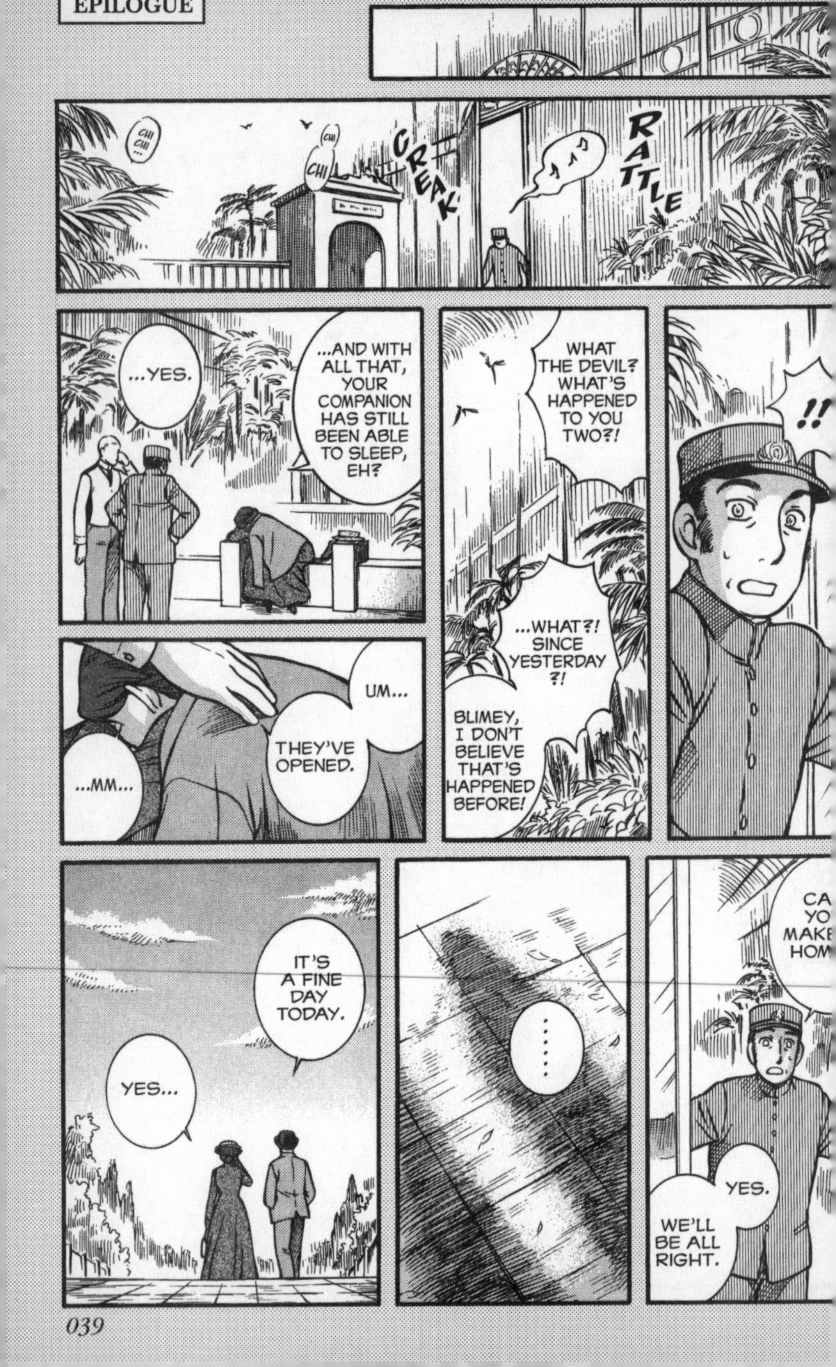

RATTLE
♪ ♪ ♪
CREAK
(CHI)
CHI
CHI CHI ...
!!
WHAT THE DEVIL? WHAT'S HAPPENED TO YOU TWO?!
...WHAT?! SINCE YESTERDAY ?!
BLIMEY, I DON'T BELIEVE THAT'S HAPPENED BEFORE!
...AND WITH ALL THAT, YOUR COMPANION HAS STILL BEEN ABLE TO SLEEP, EH?
...YES.
UM...
THEY'VE OPENED.
...MM...
CA YO MAKE HOM
YES.
WE'LL BE ALL RIGHT.
......
IT'S A FINE DAY TODAY.
YES...

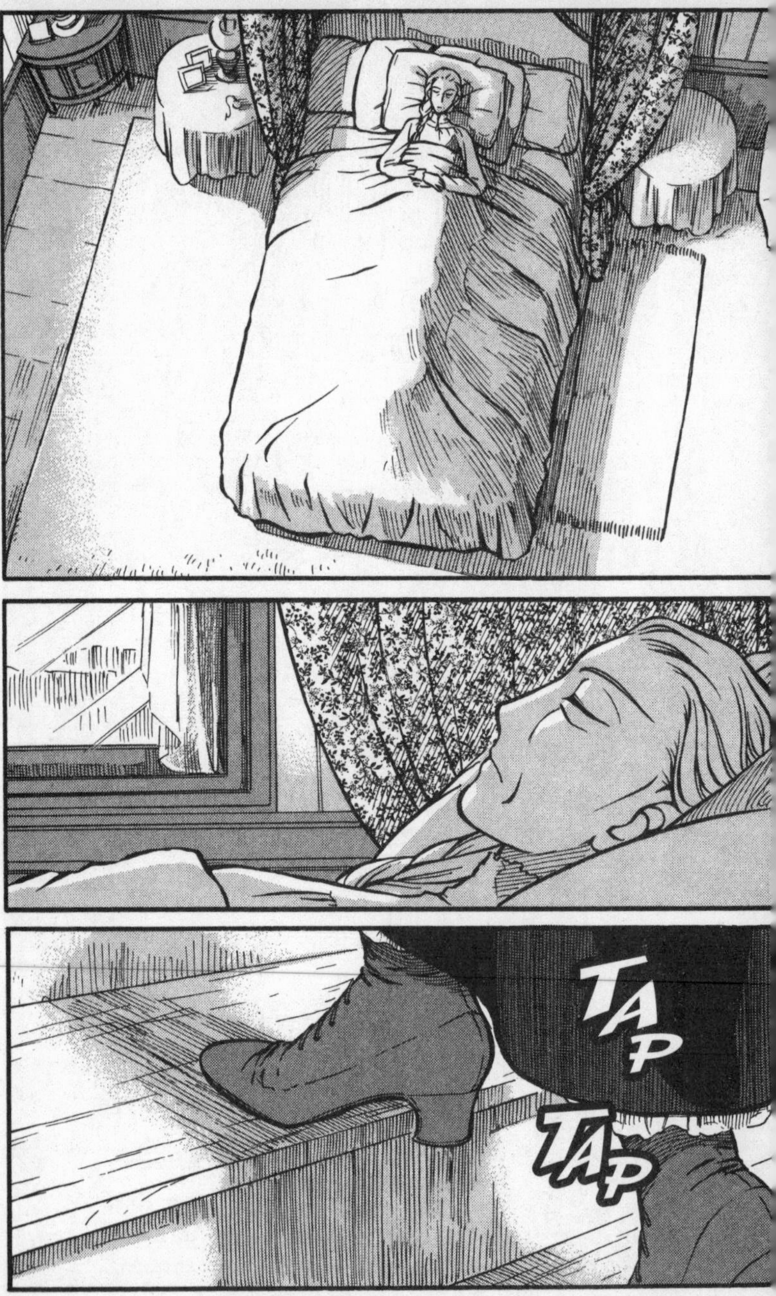
TAP
TAP

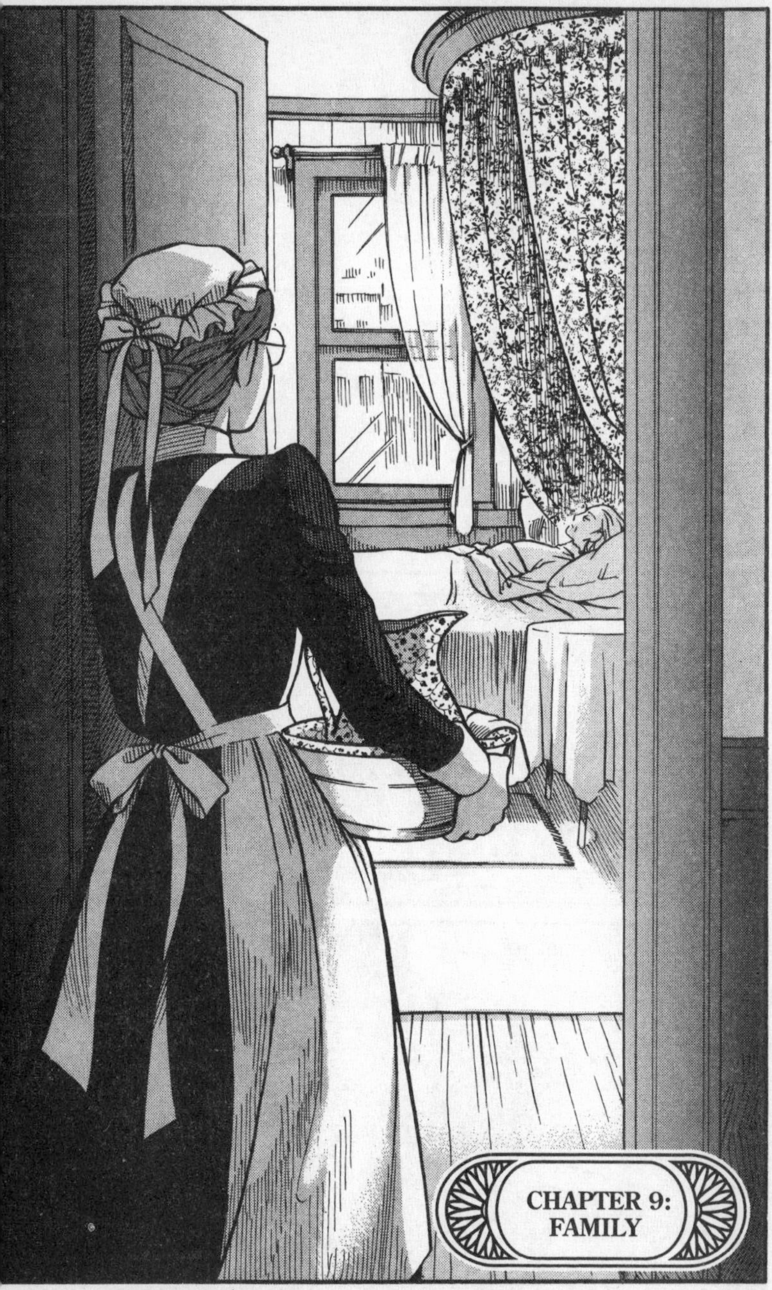
CHAPTER 9:
FAMILY

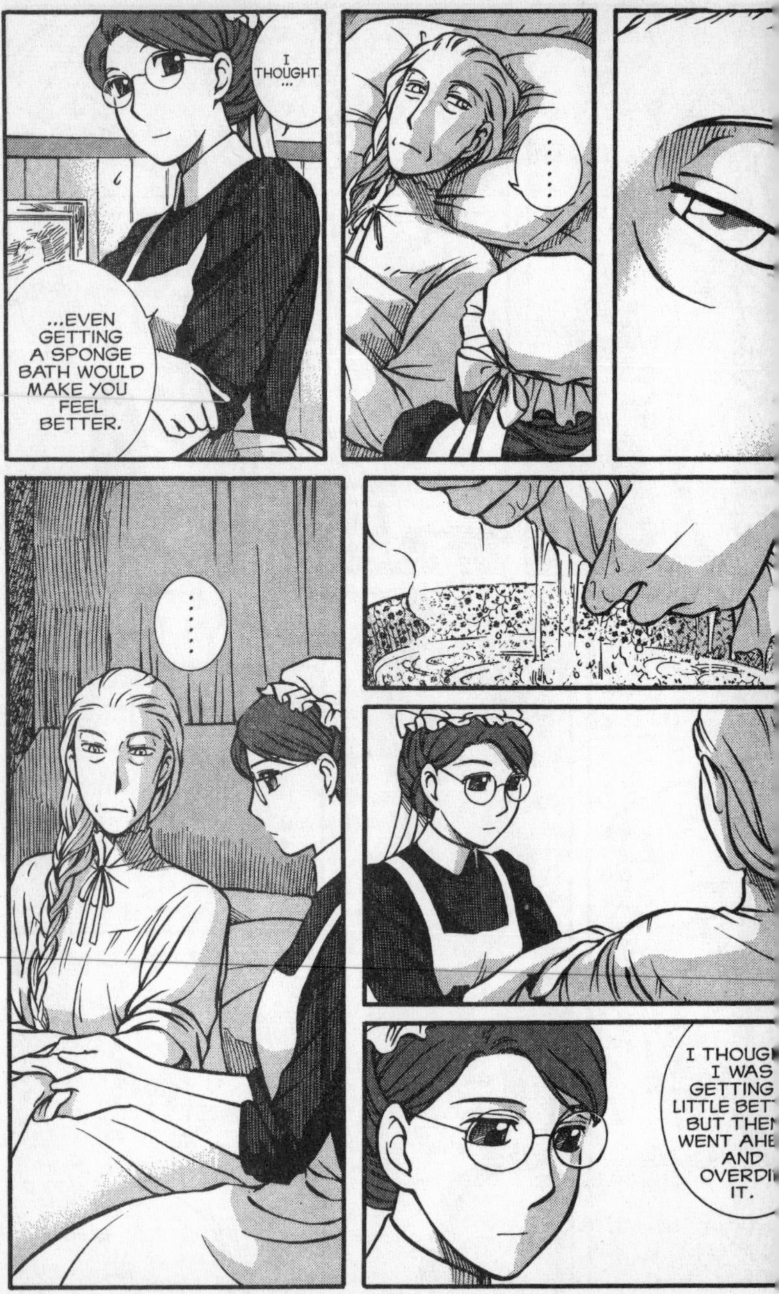
......
I THOUGHT ...
...EVEN GETTING A SPONGE BATH WOULD MAKE YOU FEEL BETTER.
I THOUG I WAS GETTING LITTLE BETT BUT THEN WENT AHE AND OVERDI IT.
......

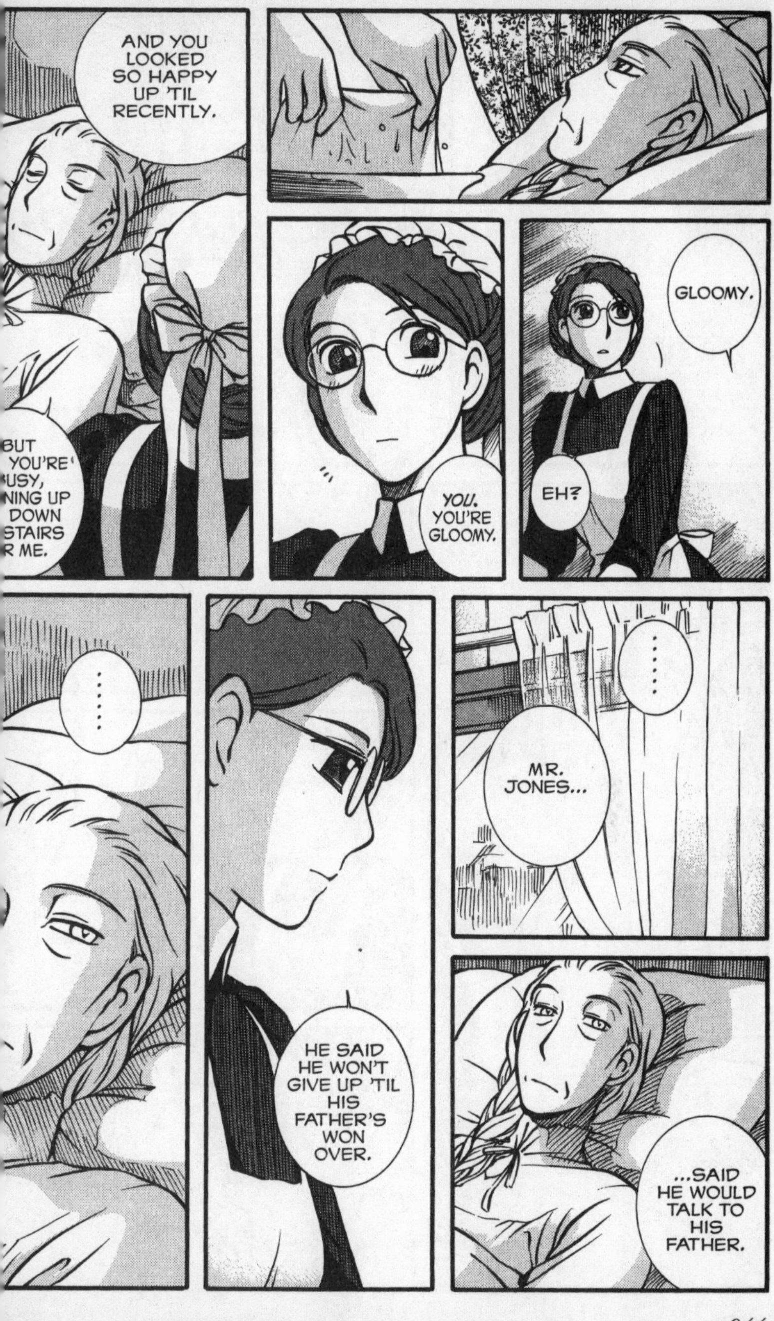
GLOOMY.
EH?
YOU. YOU'RE GLOOMY.
AND YOU LOOKED SO HAPPY UP 'TIL RECENTLY.
BUT YOU'RE USY, NING UP DOWN STAIRS R ME.
......
MR. JONES...
...SAID HE WOULD TALK TO HIS FATHER.
HE SAID HE WON'T GIVE UP 'TIL HIS FATHER'S WON OVER.
......

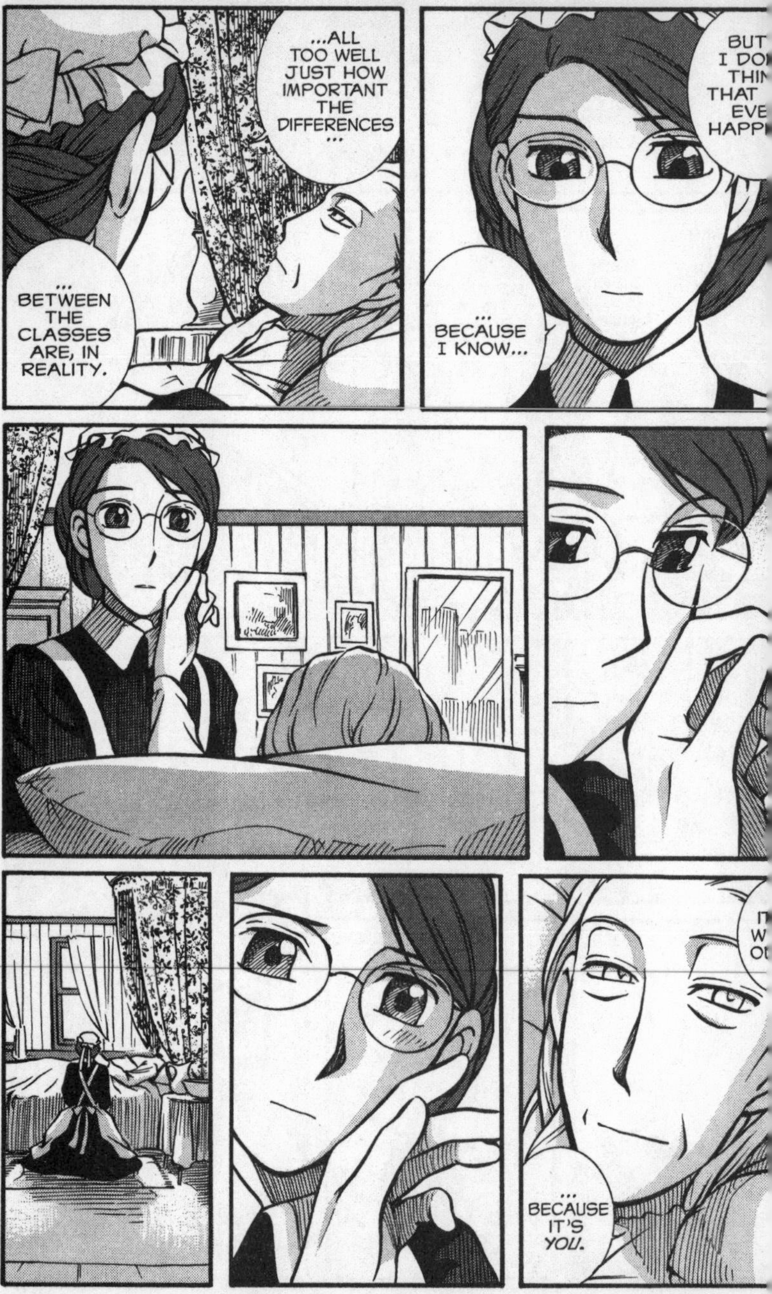
BUT I DO THIN THAT EVE HAPP
...BECAUSE I KNOW...
...ALL TOO WELL JUST HOW IMPORTANT THE DIFFERENCES...
...BETWEEN THE CLASSES ARE, IN REALITY.
IT W O
...BECAUSE IT'S *YOU.*

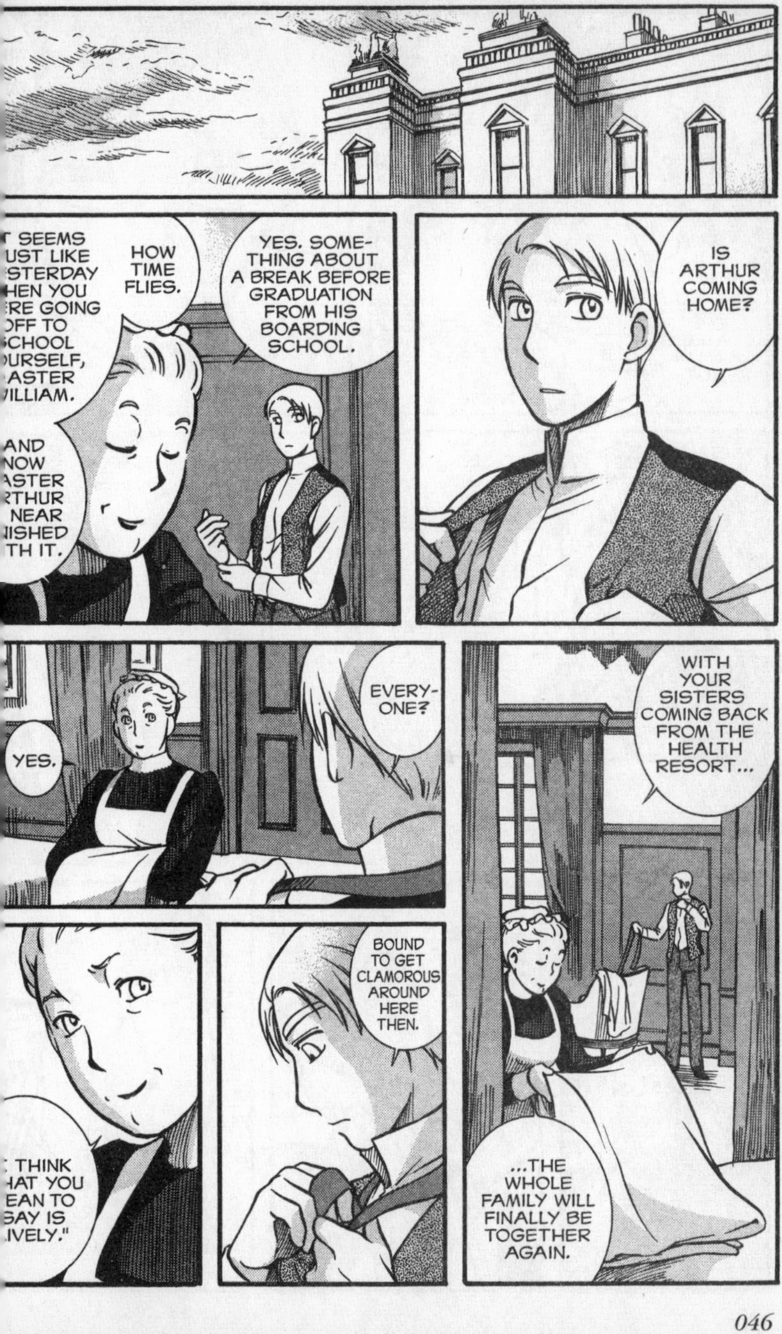

IS ARTHUR COMING HOME?
YES. SOME-THING ABOUT A BREAK BEFORE GRADUATION FROM HIS BOARDING SCHOOL.
HOW TIME FLIES.
T SEEMS UST LIKE STERDAY HEN YOU ERE GOING OFF TO SCHOOL OURSELF, ASTER VILLIAM.
AND NOW ASTER RTHUR NEAR NISHED TH IT.
WITH YOUR SISTERS COMING BACK FROM THE HEALTH RESORT...
...THE WHOLE FAMILY WILL FINALLY BE TOGETHER AGAIN.
EVERY-ONE?
YES.
BOUND TO GET CLAMOROUS AROUND HERE THEN.
THINK HAT YOU EAN TO SAY IS IVELY."

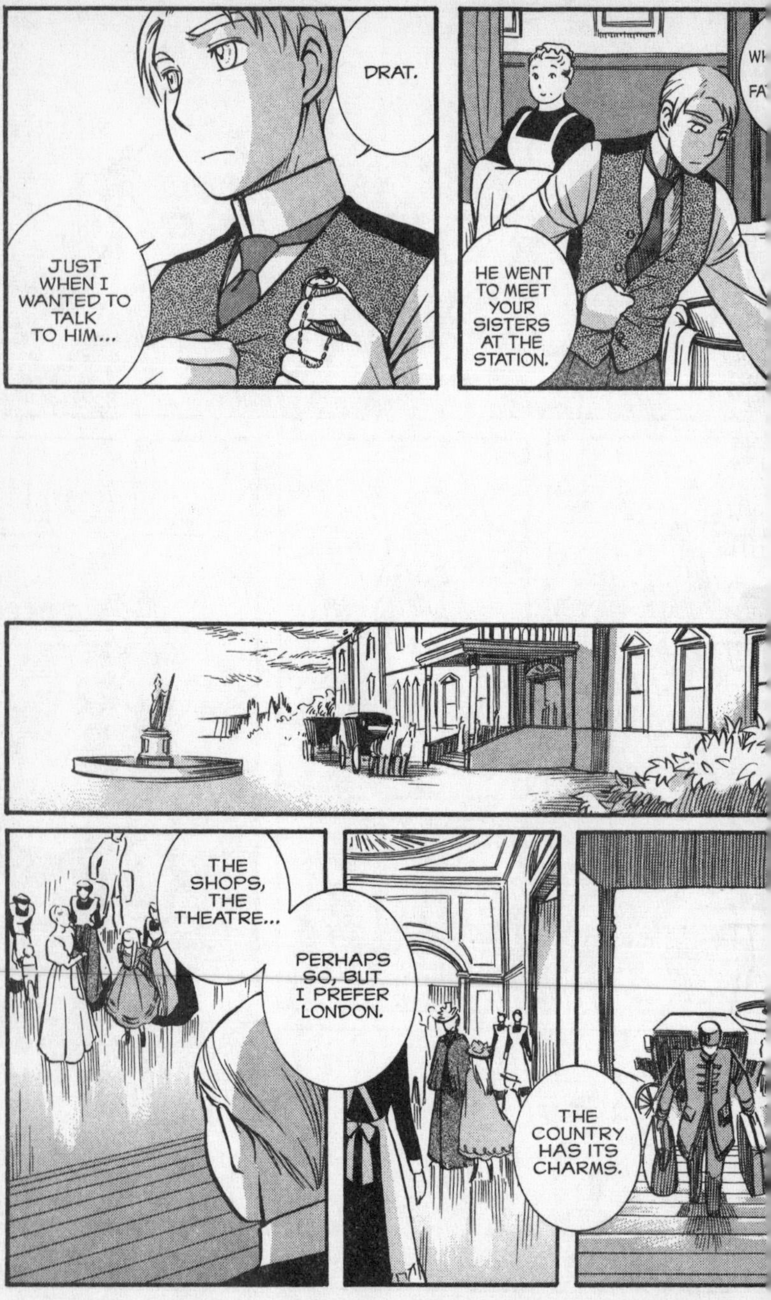
HE WENT TO MEET YOUR SISTERS AT THE STATION.
DRAT.
JUST WHEN I WANTED TO TALK TO HIM...
THE COUNTRY HAS ITS CHARMS.
PERHAPS SO, BUT I PREFER LONDON.
THE SHOPS, THE THEATRE...

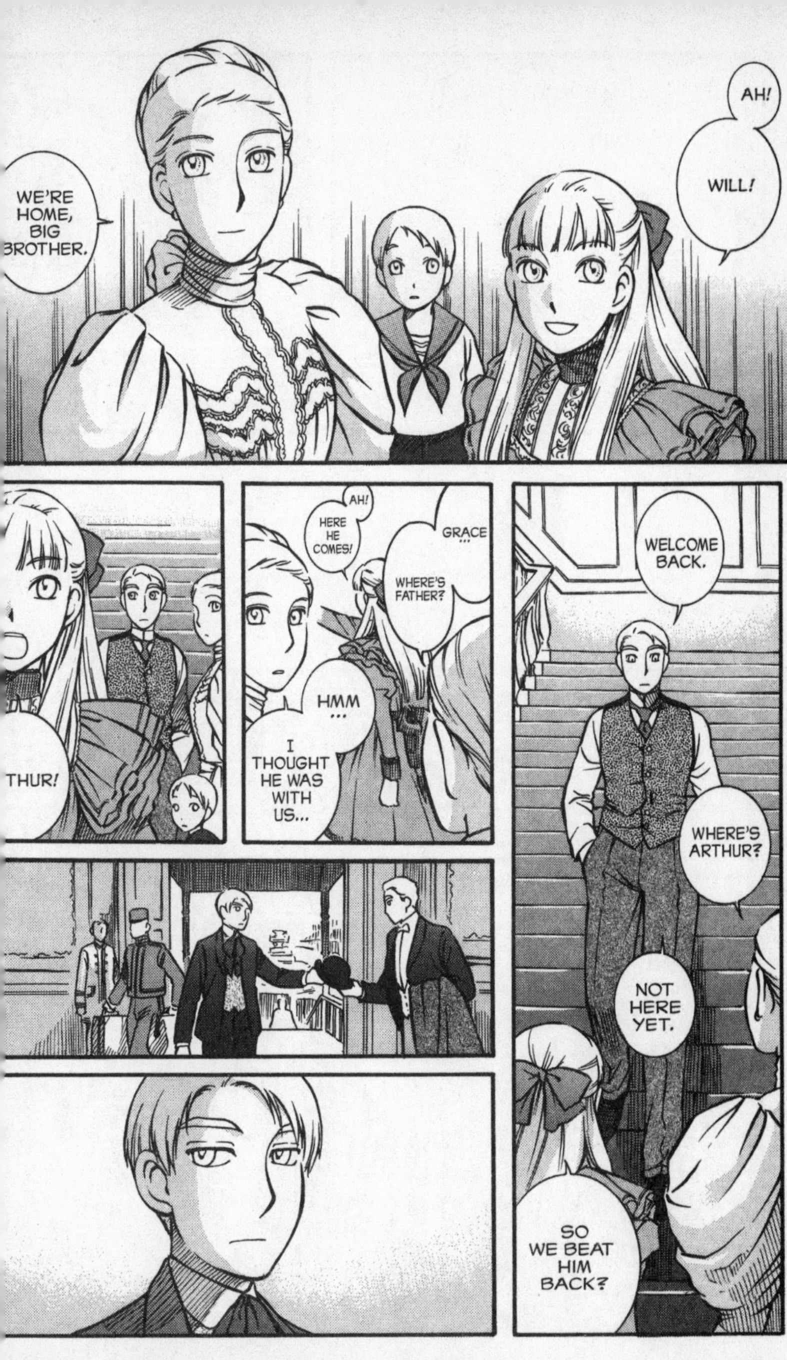
AH!
WILL!
WE'RE HOME, BIG BROTHER.
WELCOME BACK.
WHERE'S ARTHUR?
NOT HERE YET.
SO WE BEAT HIM BACK?
GRACE... WHERE'S FATHER?
HMM... I THOUGHT HE WAS WITH US...
AH! HERE HE COMES!
THUR!

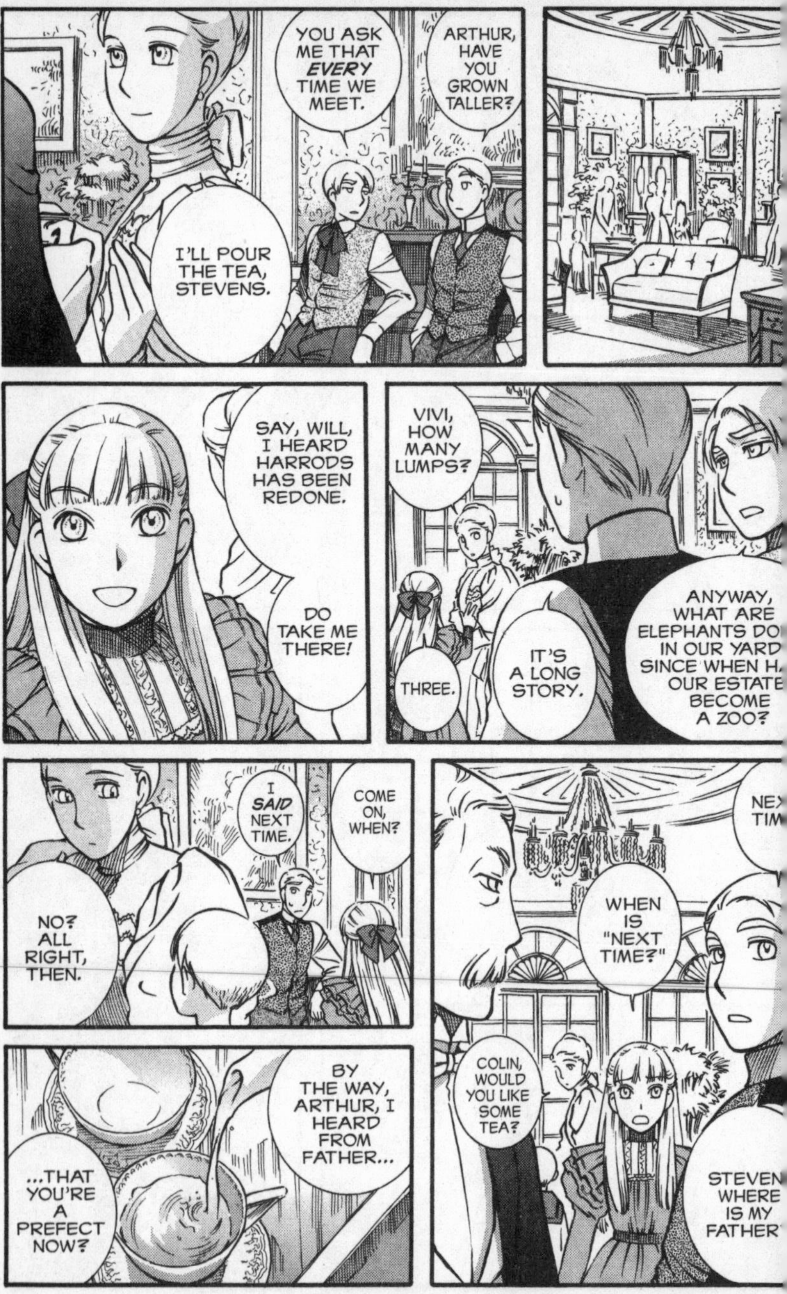
ARTHUR, HAVE YOU GROWN TALLER?
YOU ASK ME THAT *EVERY* TIME WE MEET.
I'LL POUR THE TEA, STEVENS.
VIVI, HOW MANY LUMPS?
ANYWAY, WHAT ARE ELEPHANTS DO IN OUR YARD SINCE WHEN H OUR ESTATE BECOME A ZOO?
IT'S A LONG STORY.
THREE.
SAY, WILL, I HEARD HARRODS HAS BEEN REDONE.
DO TAKE ME THERE!
NEX TIM
WHEN IS "NEXT TIME?"
COLIN, WOULD YOU LIKE SOME TEA?
STEVEN WHERE IS MY FATHER
COME ON, WHEN?
I *SAID* NEXT TIME.
NO? ALL RIGHT, THEN.
BY THE WAY, ARTHUR, I HEARD FROM FATHER...
...THAT YOU'RE A PREFECT NOW?

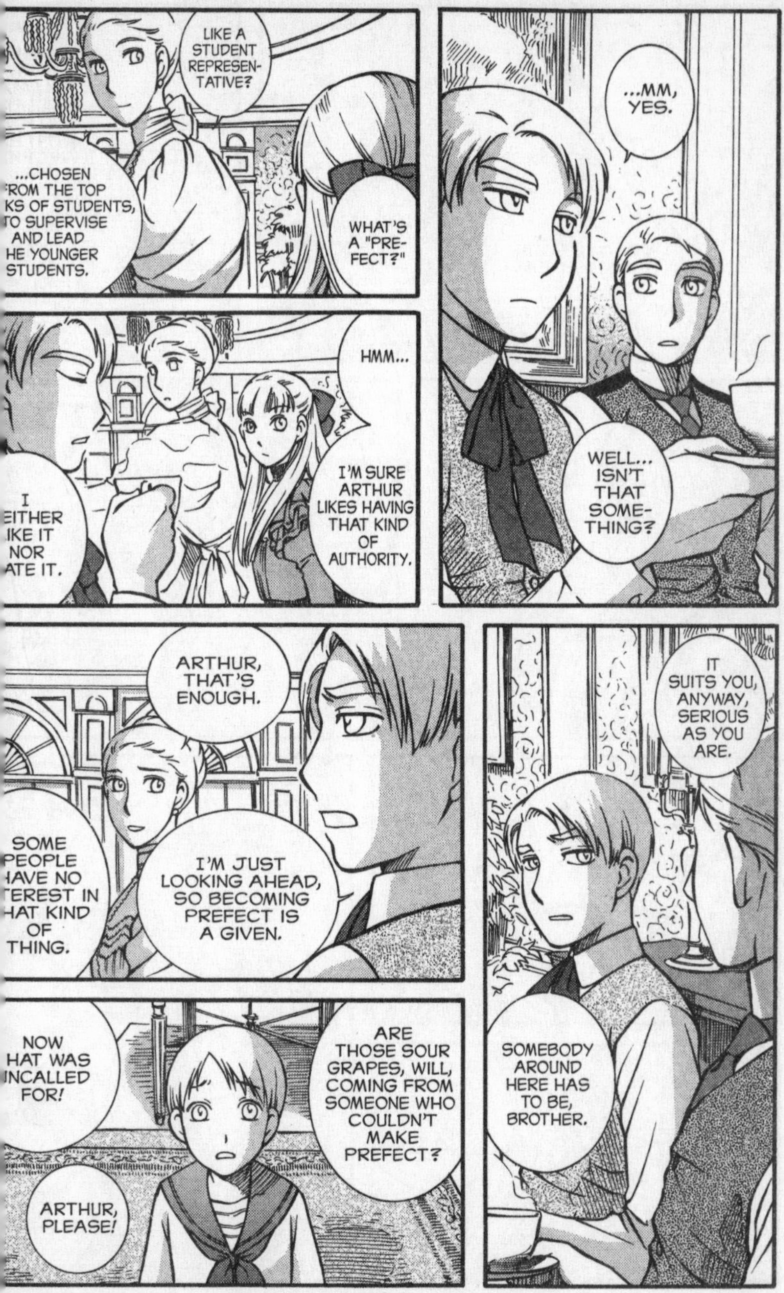
...MM, YES.
WELL... ISN'T THAT SOME-THING?
WHAT'S A "PRE-FECT?"
...CHOSEN FROM THE TOP KS OF STUDENTS, TO SUPERVISE AND LEAD HE YOUNGER STUDENTS.
LIKE A STUDENT REPRESEN-TATIVE?
HMM...
I'M SURE ARTHUR LIKES HAVING THAT KIND OF AUTHORITY.
I EITHER LIKE IT NOR ATE IT.
IT SUITS YOU, ANYWAY, SERIOUS AS YOU ARE.
SOMEBODY AROUND HERE HAS TO BE, BROTHER.
ARTHUR, THAT'S ENOUGH.
I'M JUST LOOKING AHEAD, SO BECOMING PREFECT IS A GIVEN.
SOME PEOPLE HAVE NO TEREST IN HAT KIND OF THING.
ARE THOSE SOUR GRAPES, WILL, COMING FROM SOMEONE WHO COULDN'T MAKE PREFECT?
NOW HAT WAS NCALLED FOR!
ARTHUR, PLEASE!

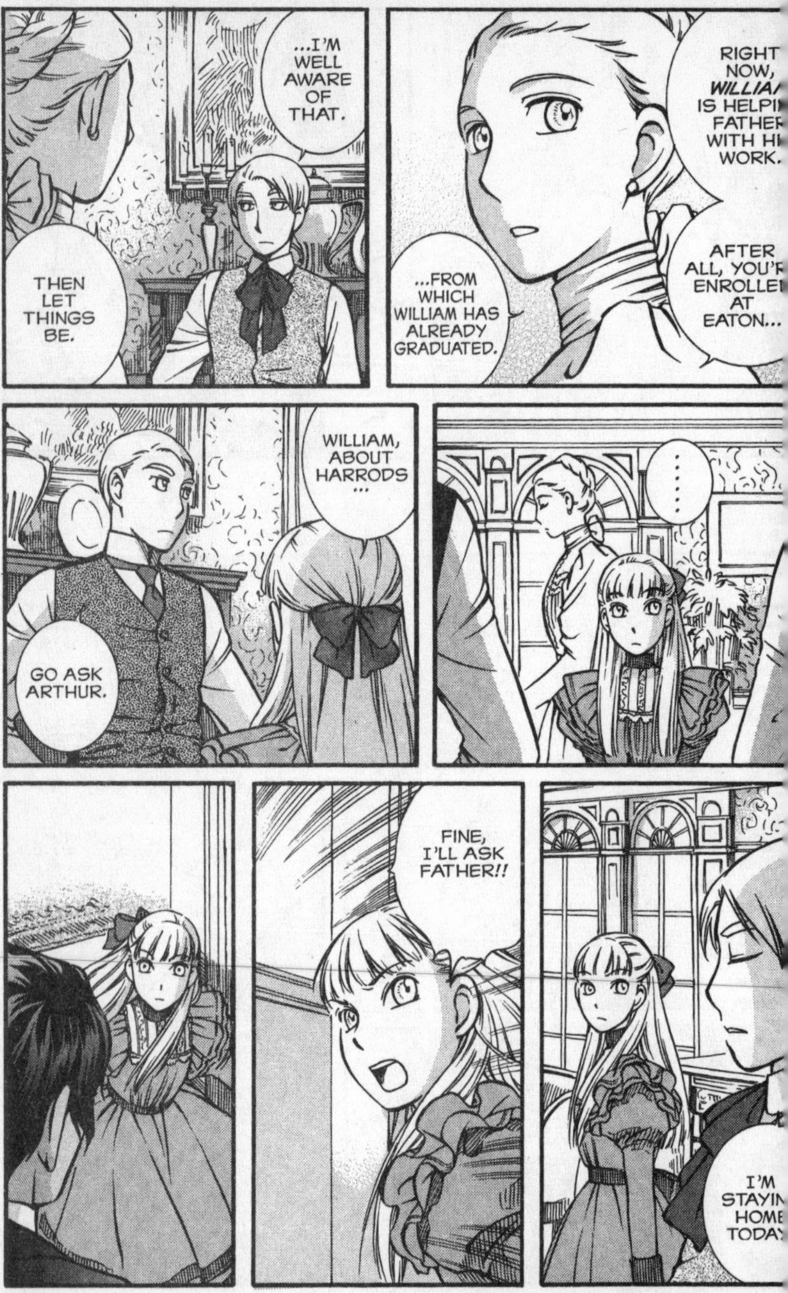
RIGHT NOW, WILLIA IS HELPI FATHER WITH HI WORK.
AFTER ALL, YOU'R ENROLLE AT EATON...
...FROM WHICH WILLIAM HAS ALREADY GRADUATED.
...I'M WELL AWARE OF THAT.
THEN LET THINGS BE.
......
WILLIAM, ABOUT HARRODS ...
GO ASK ARTHUR.
I'M STAYIN HOME TODA
FINE, I'LL ASK FATHER!!

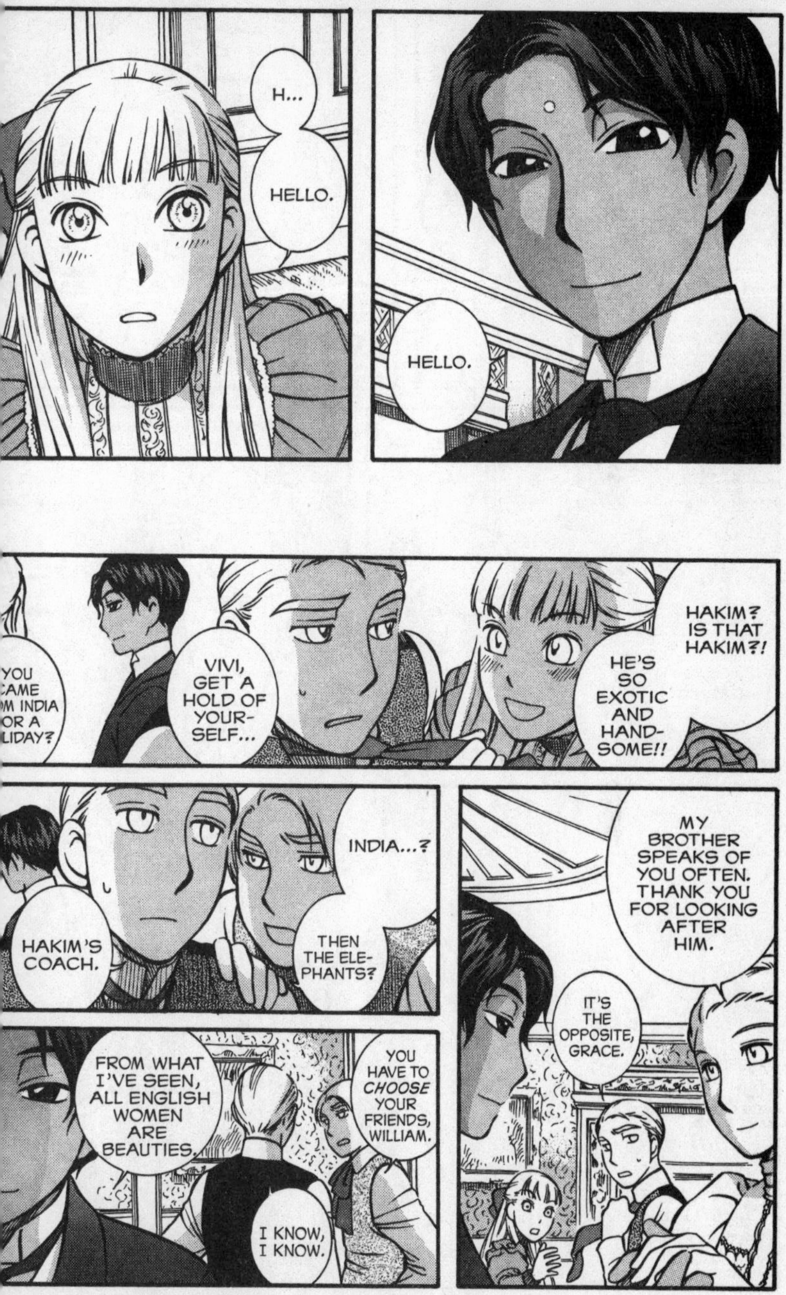
HELLO.
H...
HELLO.
HAKIM? IS THAT HAKIM?!
HE'S SO EXOTIC AND HAND-SOME!!
VIVI, GET A HOLD OF YOUR-SELF...
YOU CAME M INDIA OR A LIDAY?
MY BROTHER SPEAKS OF YOU OFTEN. THANK YOU FOR LOOKING AFTER HIM.
IT'S THE OPPOSITE, GRACE.
INDIA...?
THEN THE ELE-PHANTS?
HAKIM'S COACH.
YOU HAVE TO *CHOOSE* YOUR FRIENDS, WILLIAM.
FROM WHAT I'VE SEEN, ALL ENGLISH WOMEN ARE BEAUTIES.
I KNOW, I KNOW.

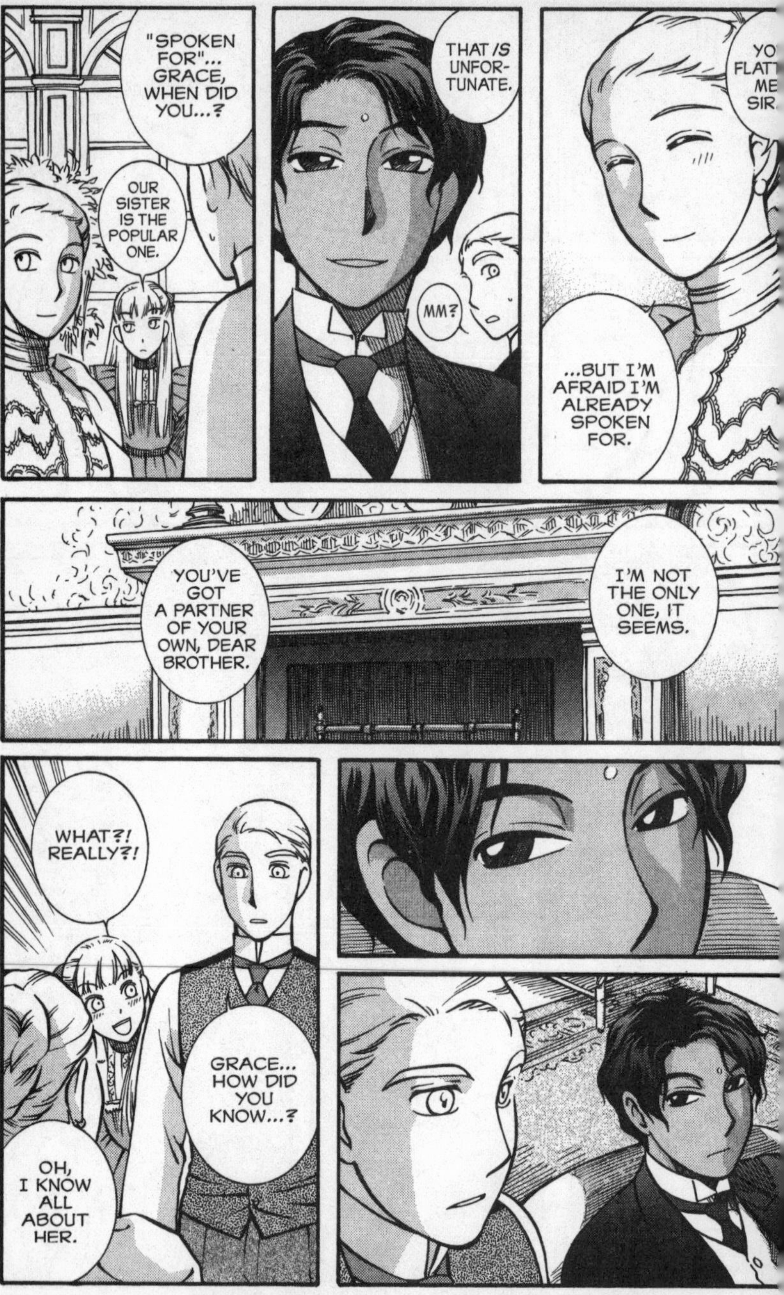
YO FLATT ME SIR.
...BUT I'M AFRAID I'M ALREADY SPOKEN FOR.
THAT *IS* UNFORTUNATE.
MM?
"SPOKEN FOR"... GRACE, WHEN DID YOU...?
OUR SISTER IS THE POPULAR ONE.
I'M NOT THE ONLY ONE, IT SEEMS.
YOU'VE GOT A PARTNER OF YOUR OWN, DEAR BROTHER.
WHAT?! REALLY?!
GRACE... HOW DID YOU KNOW...?
OH, I KNOW ALL ABOUT HER.

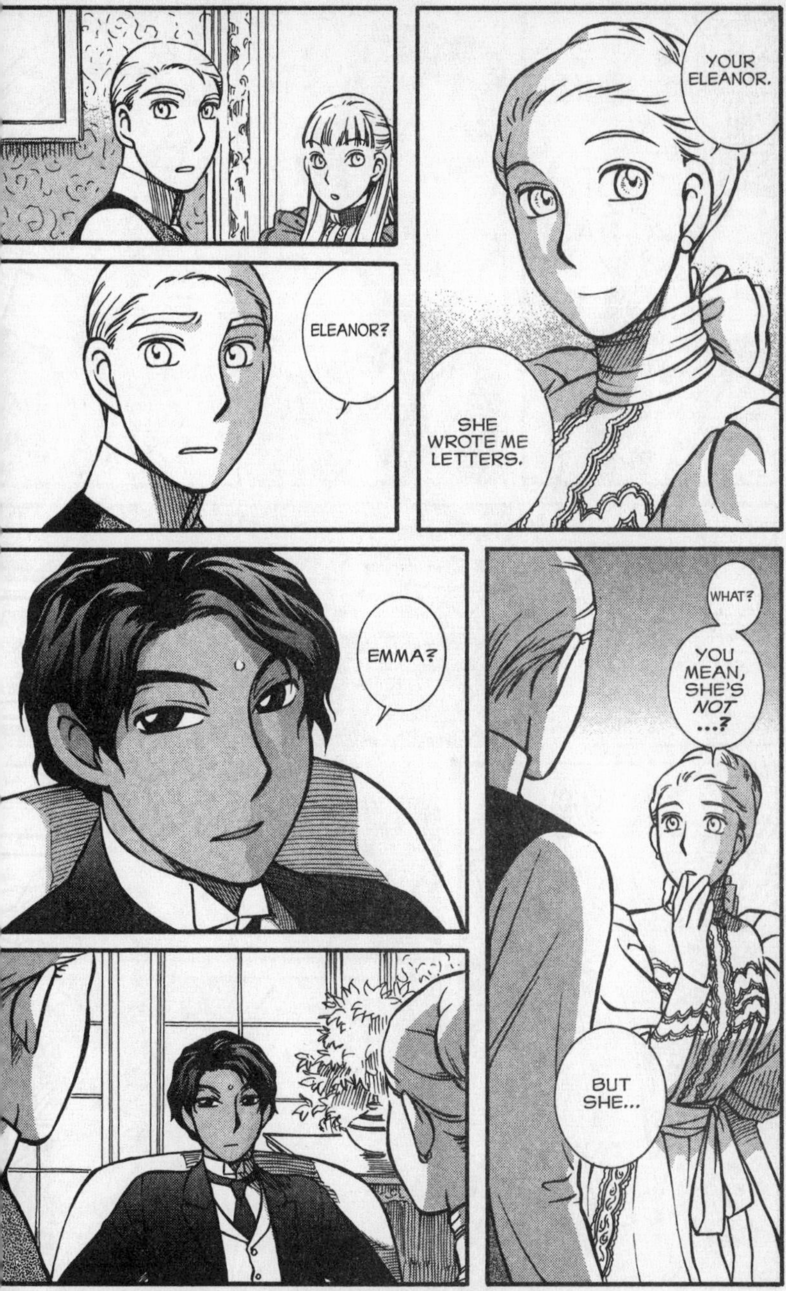
YOUR ELEANOR.
SHE WROTE ME LETTERS.
ELEANOR?
WHAT?
YOU MEAN, SHE'S *NOT* ...?
BUT SHE...
EMMA?

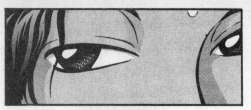

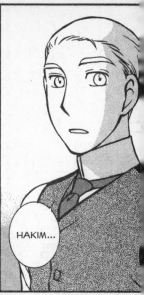

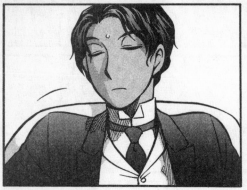

HAKIM...

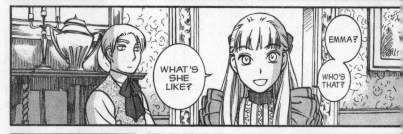

WHAT'S SHE LIKE?

EMMA?

WHO'S THAT?

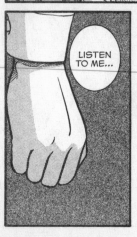

LISTEN TO ME...

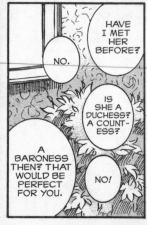

HAVE I MET HER BEFORE?

NO.

IS SHE A DUCHESS? A COUNTESS?

A BARONESS THEN? THAT WOULD BE PERFECT FOR YOU.

NO!

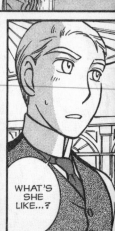

WHAT'S SHE LIKE...?

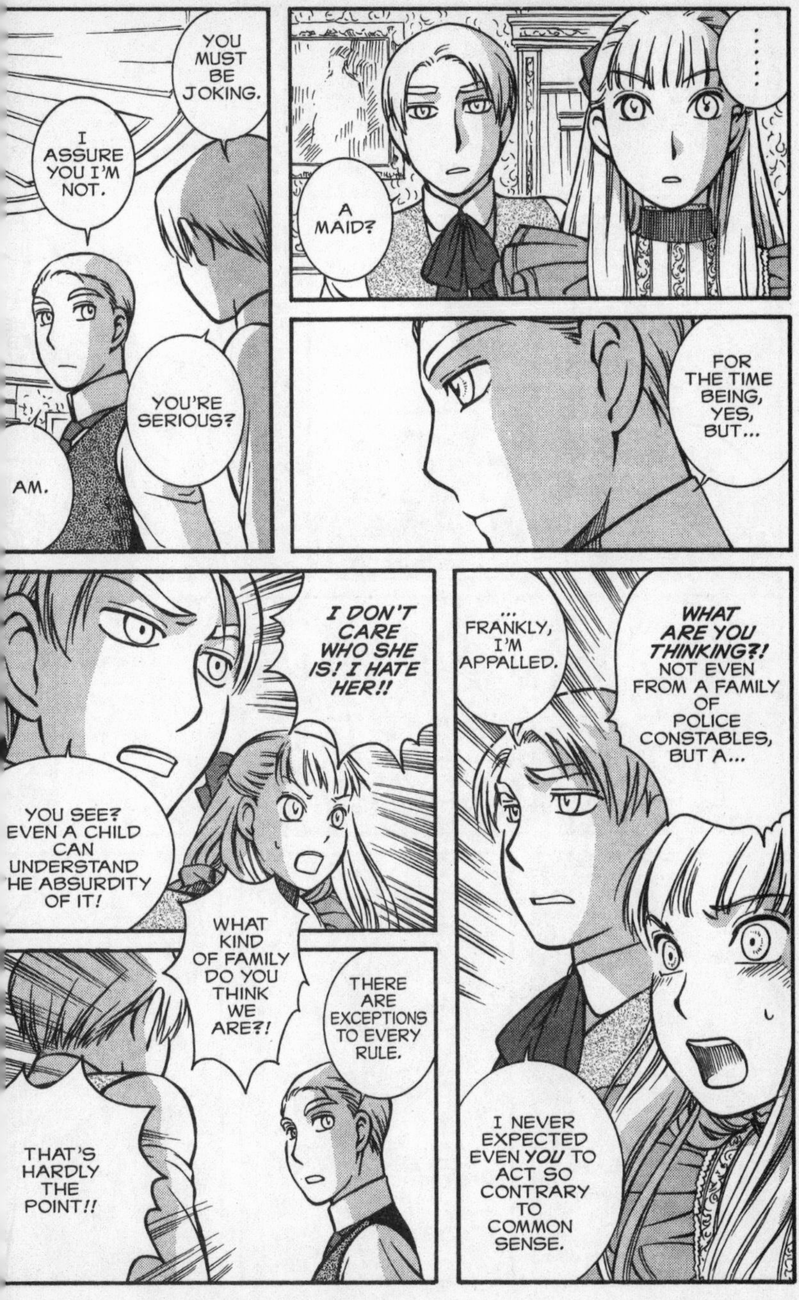
......
A MAID?
FOR THE TIME BEING, YES, BUT...
YOU MUST BE JOKING.
I ASSURE YOU I'M NOT.
YOU'RE SERIOUS?
AM.
WHAT ARE YOU THINKING?! NOT EVEN FROM A FAMILY OF POLICE CONSTABLES, BUT A...
... FRANKLY, I'M APPALLED.
I NEVER EXPECTED EVEN *YOU* TO ACT SO CONTRARY TO COMMON SENSE.
I DON'T CARE WHO SHE IS! I HATE HER!!
YOU SEE? EVEN A CHILD CAN UNDERSTAND HE ABSURDITY OF IT!
WHAT KIND OF FAMILY DO YOU THINK WE ARE?!
THERE ARE EXCEPTIONS TO EVERY RULE.
THAT'S HARDLY THE POINT!!

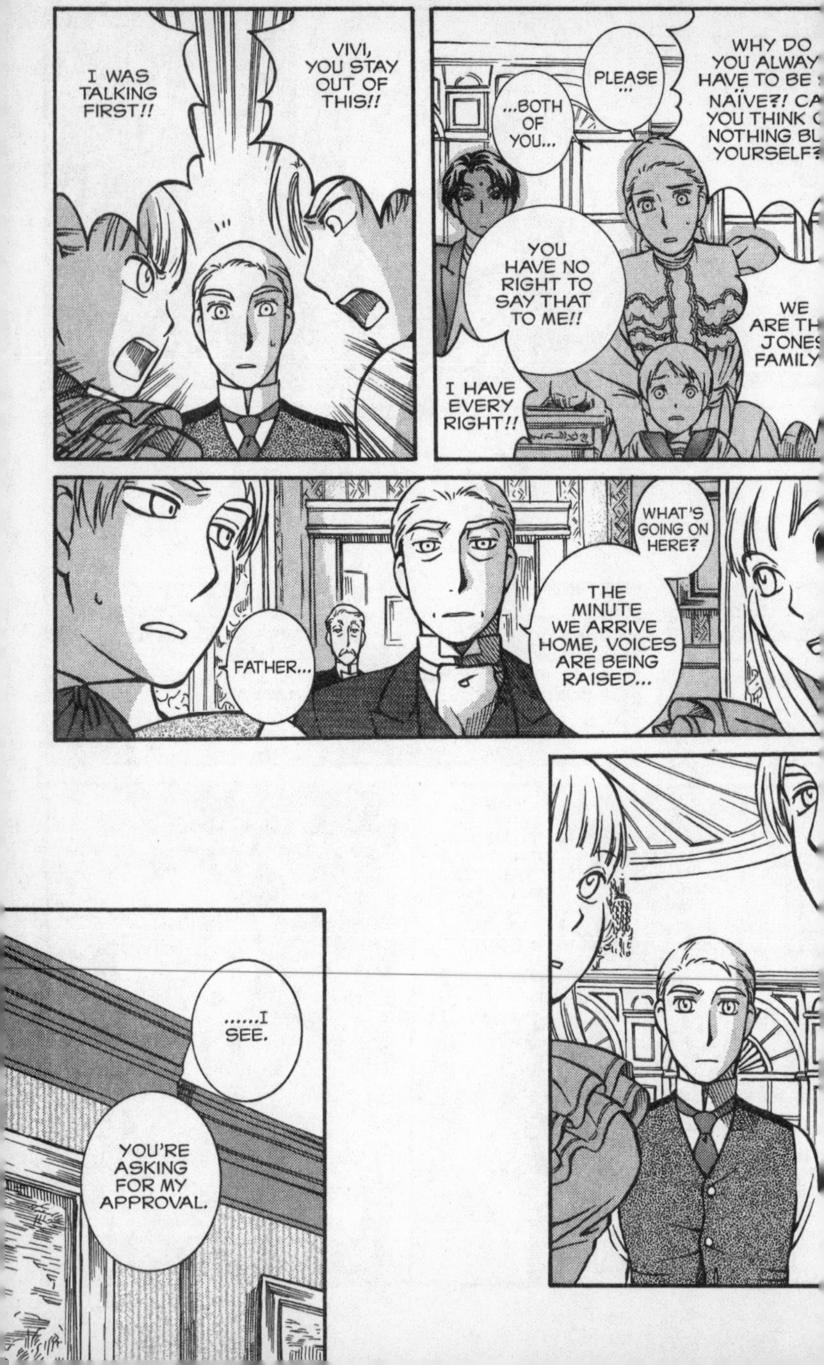
WHY DO YOU ALWAY HAVE TO BE NAÏVE?! CA YOU THINK NOTHING BU YOURSELF?
PLEASE...
...BOTH OF YOU...
WE ARE TH JONES FAMILY
YOU HAVE NO RIGHT TO SAY THAT TO ME!!
I HAVE EVERY RIGHT!!
VIVI, YOU STAY OUT OF THIS!!
I WAS TALKING FIRST!!
WHAT'S GOING ON HERE?
THE MINUTE WE ARRIVE HOME, VOICES ARE BEING RAISED...
FATHER...
......I SEE.
YOU'RE ASKING FOR MY APPROVAL.

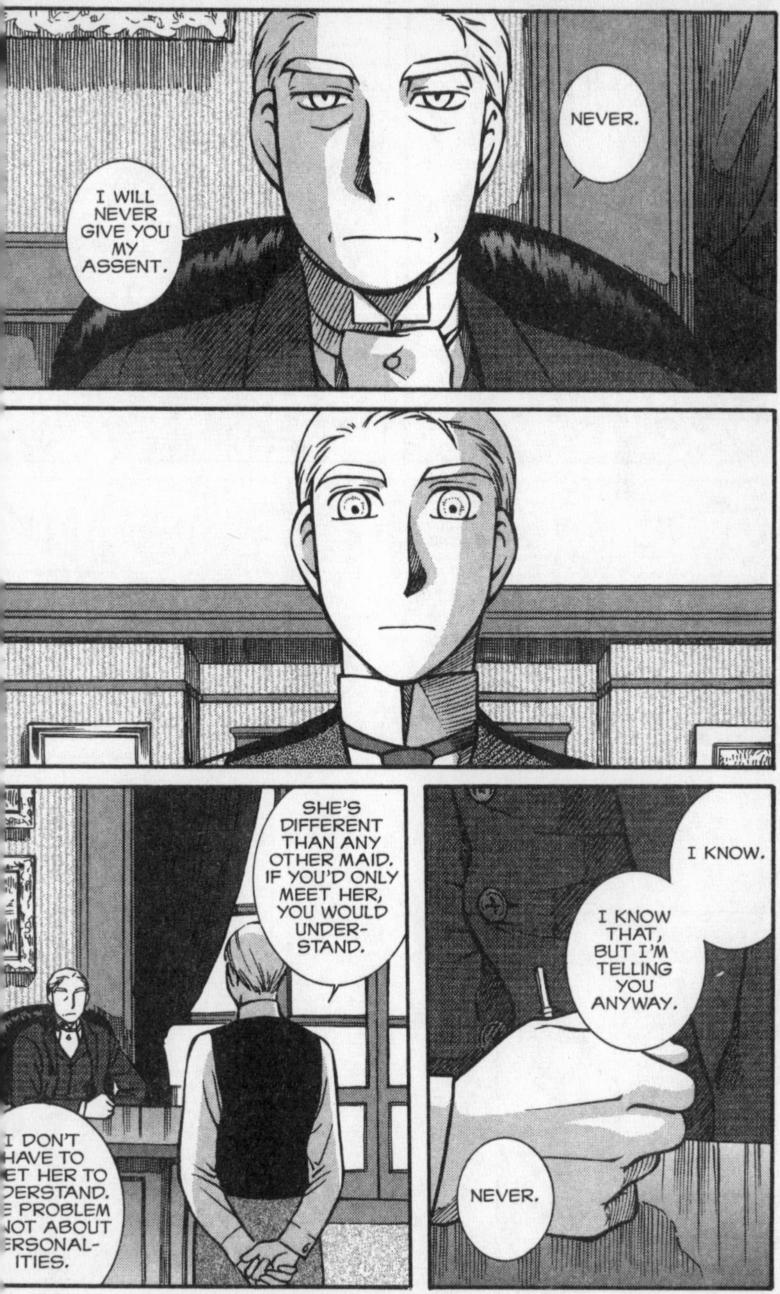
NEVER.
I WILL NEVER GIVE YOU MY ASSENT.
I KNOW.
I KNOW THAT, BUT I'M TELLING YOU ANYWAY.
NEVER.
SHE'S DIFFERENT THAN ANY OTHER MAID. IF YOU'D ONLY MEET HER, YOU WOULD UNDER-STAND.
I DON'T HAVE TO ET HER TO DERSTAND. E PROBLEM NOT ABOUT ERSONAL-ITIES.

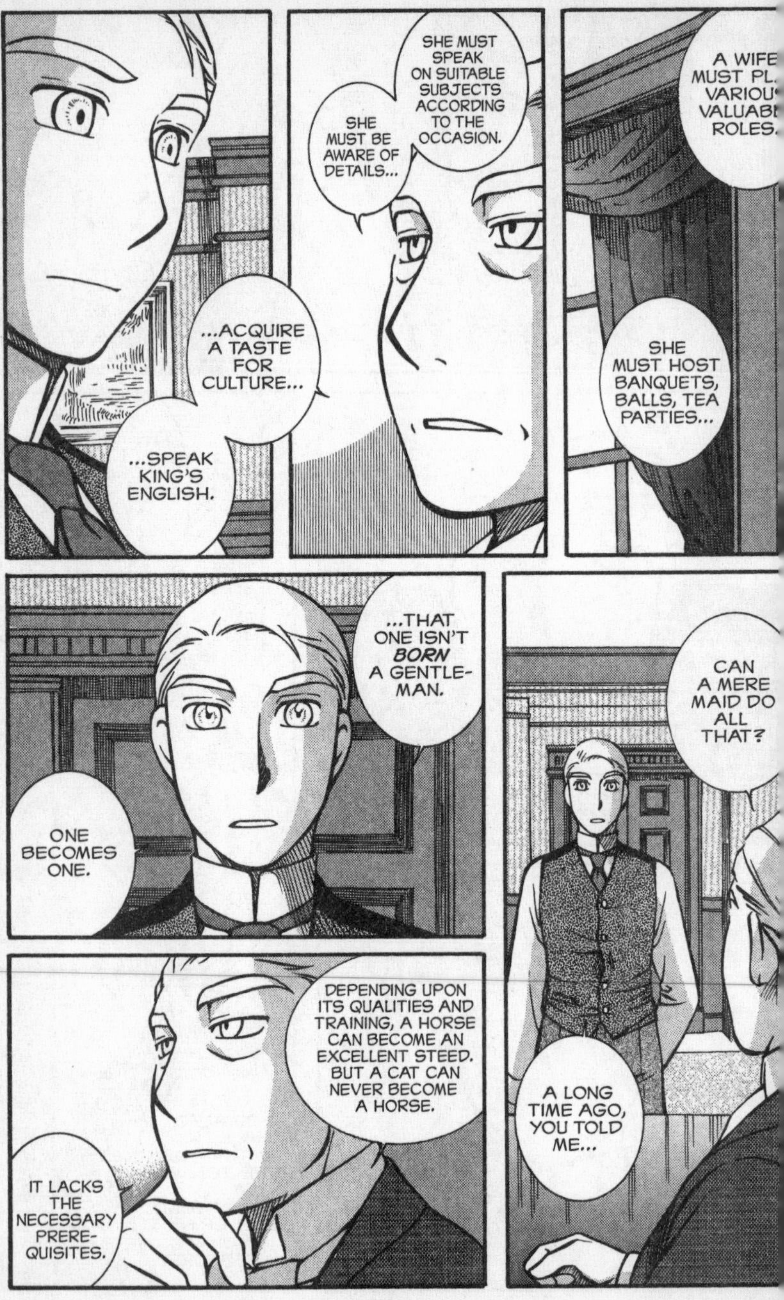
A WIFE MUST PL. VARIOU VALUAB ROLES.
SHE MUST HOST BANQUETS, BALLS, TEA PARTIES...
SHE MUST SPEAK ON SUITABLE SUBJECTS ACCORDING TO THE OCCASION.
SHE MUST BE AWARE OF DETAILS...
...ACQUIRE A TASTE FOR CULTURE...
...SPEAK KING'S ENGLISH.
CAN A MERE MAID DO ALL THAT?
A LONG TIME AGO, YOU TOLD ME...
...THAT ONE ISN'T *BORN* A GENTLE-MAN.
ONE BECOMES ONE.
DEPENDING UPON ITS QUALITIES AND TRAINING, A HORSE CAN BECOME AN EXCELLENT STEED. BUT A CAT CAN NEVER BECOME A HORSE.
IT LACKS THE NECESSARY PRERE-QUISITES.

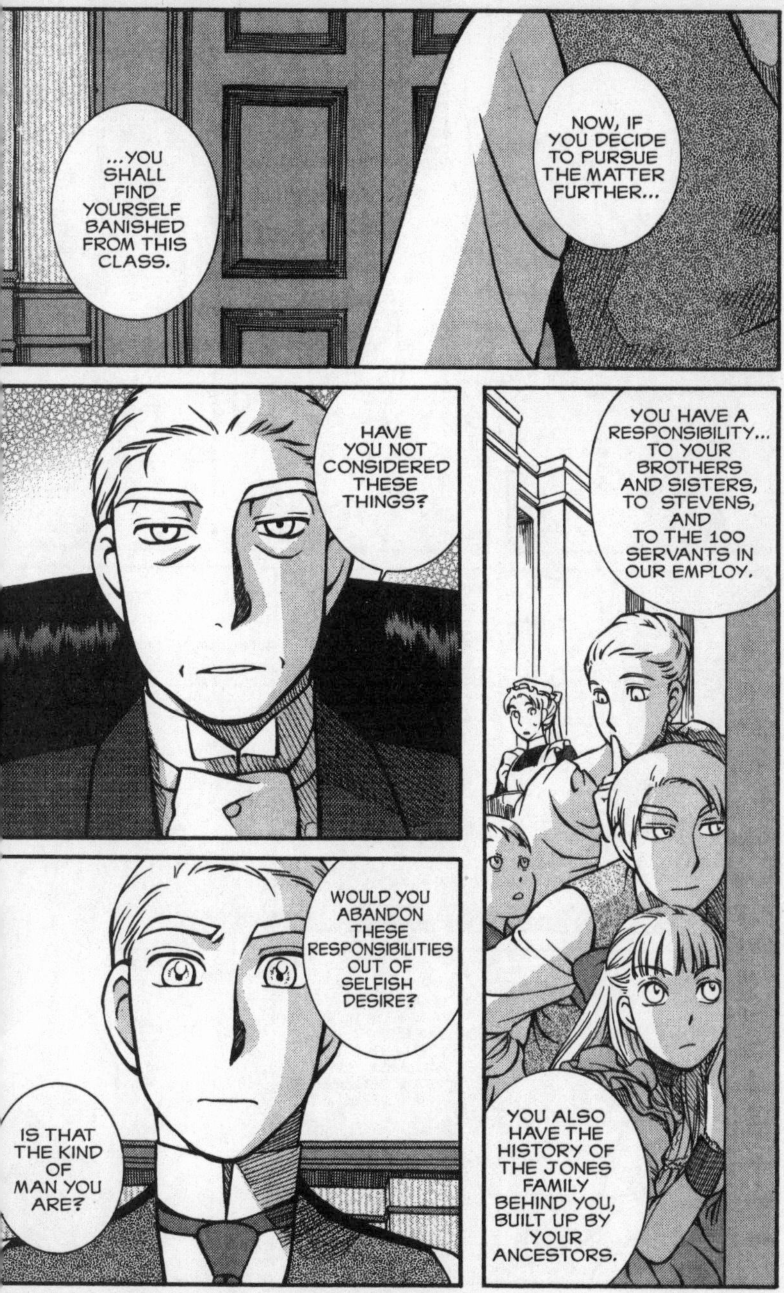
NOW, IF YOU DECIDE TO PURSUE THE MATTER FURTHER...
...YOU SHALL FIND YOURSELF BANISHED FROM THIS CLASS.
YOU HAVE A RESPONSIBILITY... TO YOUR BROTHERS AND SISTERS, TO STEVENS, AND TO THE 100 SERVANTS IN OUR EMPLOY.
YOU ALSO HAVE THE HISTORY OF THE JONES FAMILY BEHIND YOU, BUILT UP BY YOUR ANCESTORS.
HAVE YOU NOT CONSIDERED THESE THINGS?
WOULD YOU ABANDON THESE RESPONSIBILITIES OUT OF SELFISH DESIRE?
IS THAT THE KIND OF MAN YOU ARE?

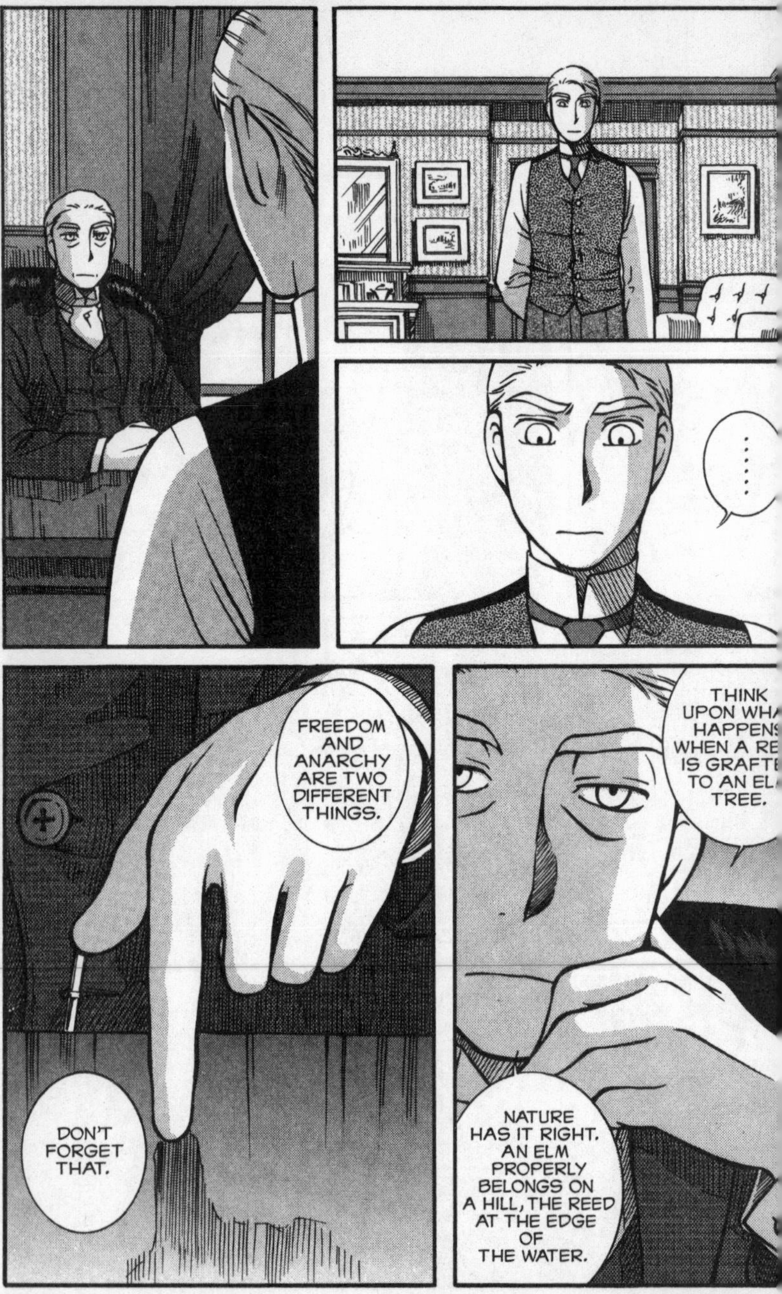
......
THINK UPON WHA HAPPENS WHEN A RE IS GRAFTE TO AN EL TREE.
NATURE HAS IT RIGHT. AN ELM PROPERLY BELONGS ON A HILL, THE REED AT THE EDGE OF THE WATER.
FREEDOM AND ANARCHY ARE TWO DIFFERENT THINGS.
DON'T FORGET THAT.

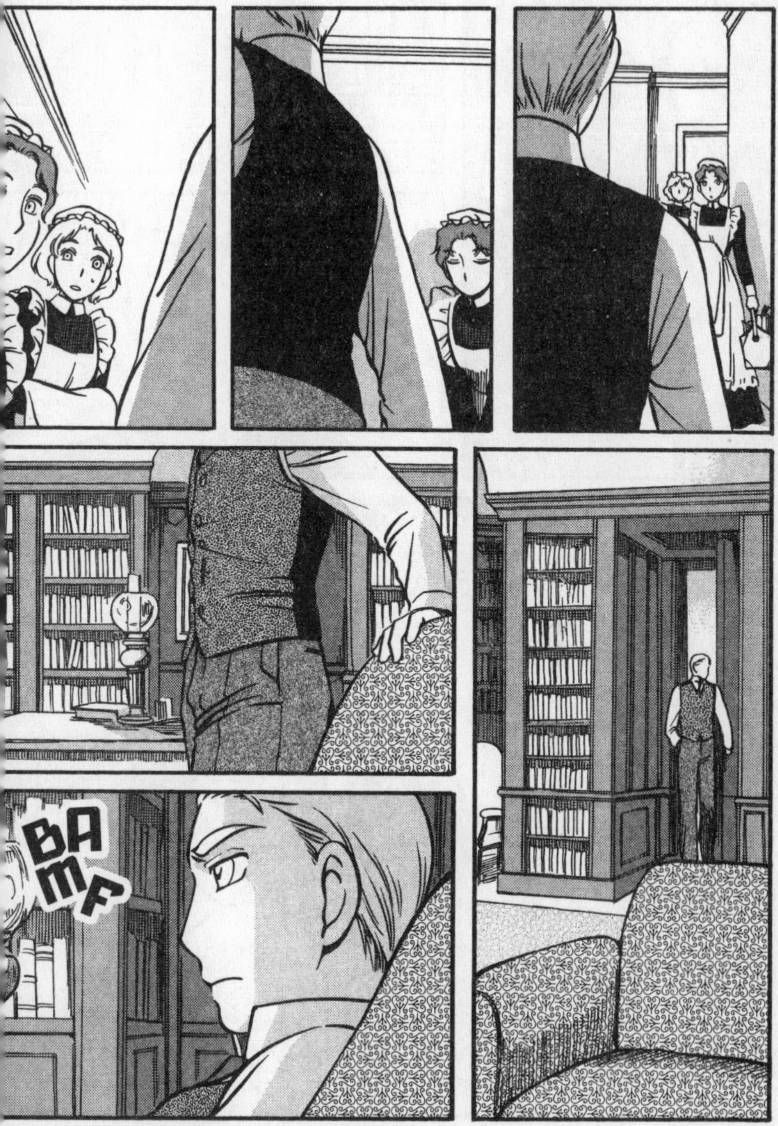
BAMF

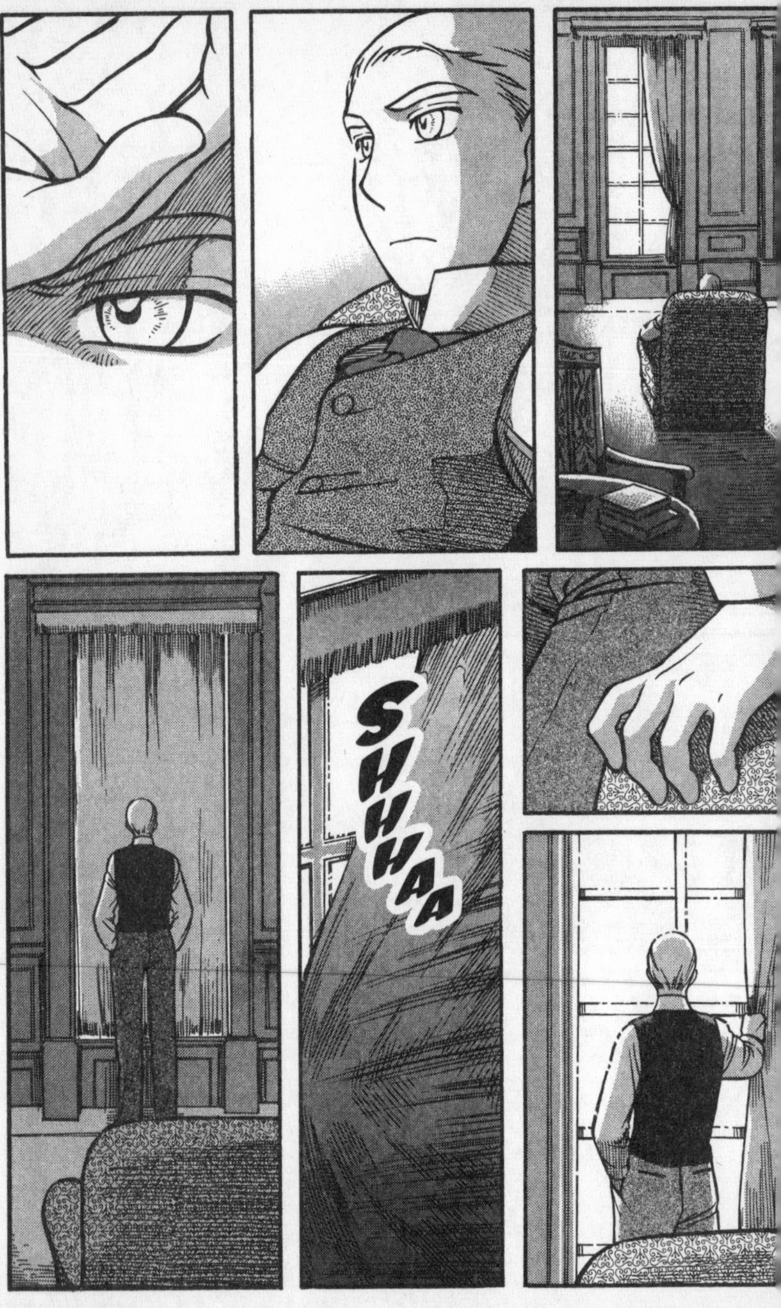
SHHHAA

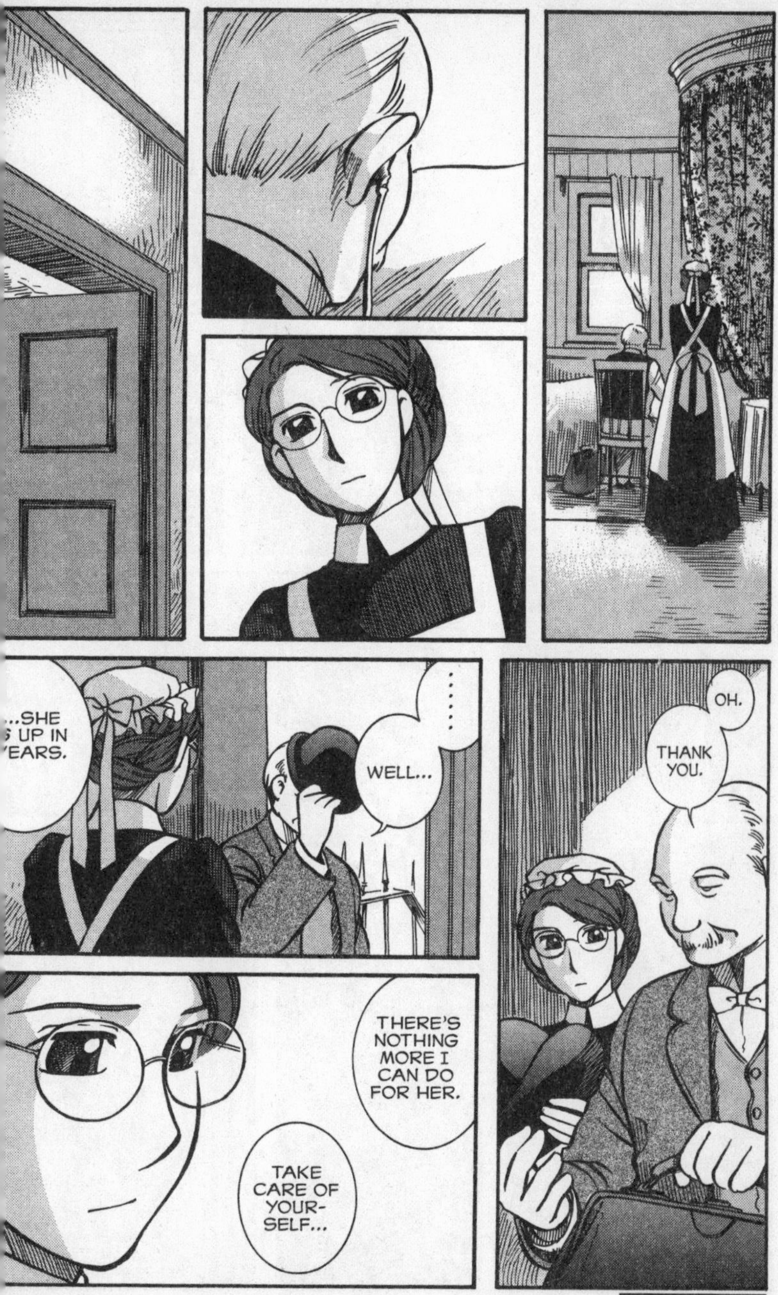
OH.
THANK YOU.
......
WELL...
...SHE S UP IN EARS.
THERE'S NOTHING MORE I CAN DO FOR HER.
TAKE CARE OF YOURSELF...

Chapter Nine: The End

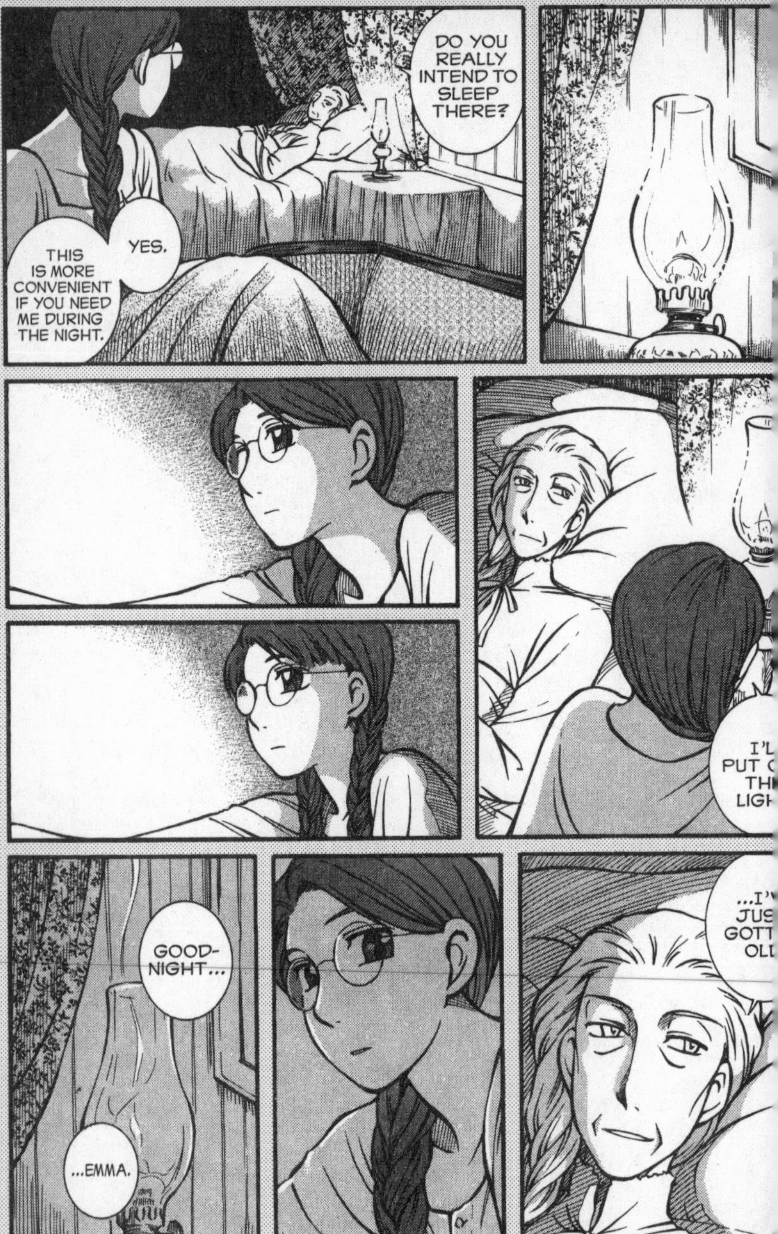
DO YOU REALLY INTEND TO SLEEP THERE?
YES.
THIS IS MORE CONVENIENT IF YOU NEED ME DURING THE NIGHT.
GOOD-NIGHT...
...EMMA.

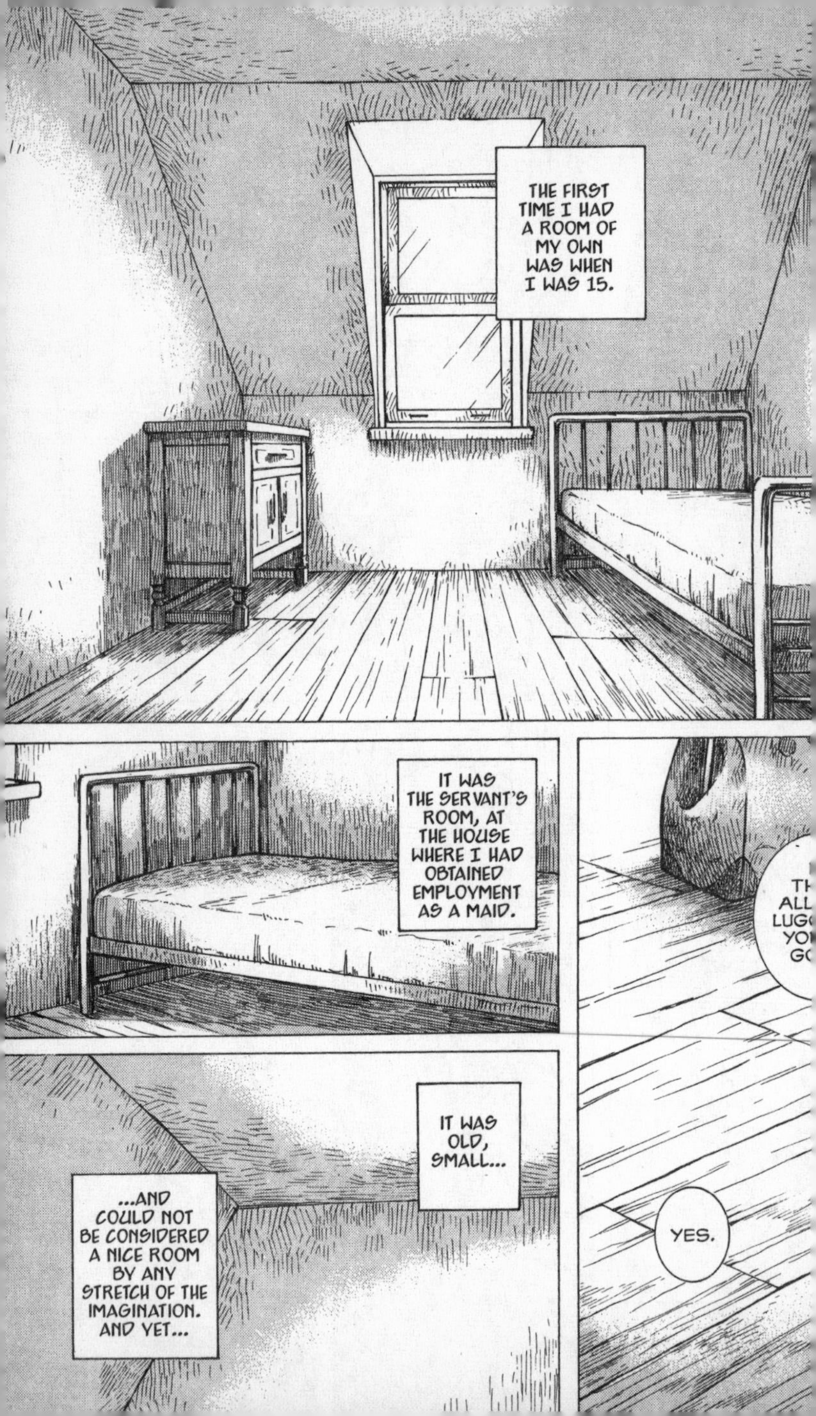
THE FIRST TIME I HAD A ROOM OF MY OWN WAS WHEN I WAS 15.
YES.
IT WAS THE SERVANT'S ROOM, AT THE HOUSE WHERE I HAD OBTAINED EMPLOYMENT AS A MAID.
IT WAS OLD, SMALL...
...AND COULD NOT BE CONSIDERED A NICE ROOM BY ANY STRETCH OF THE IMAGINATION. AND YET...

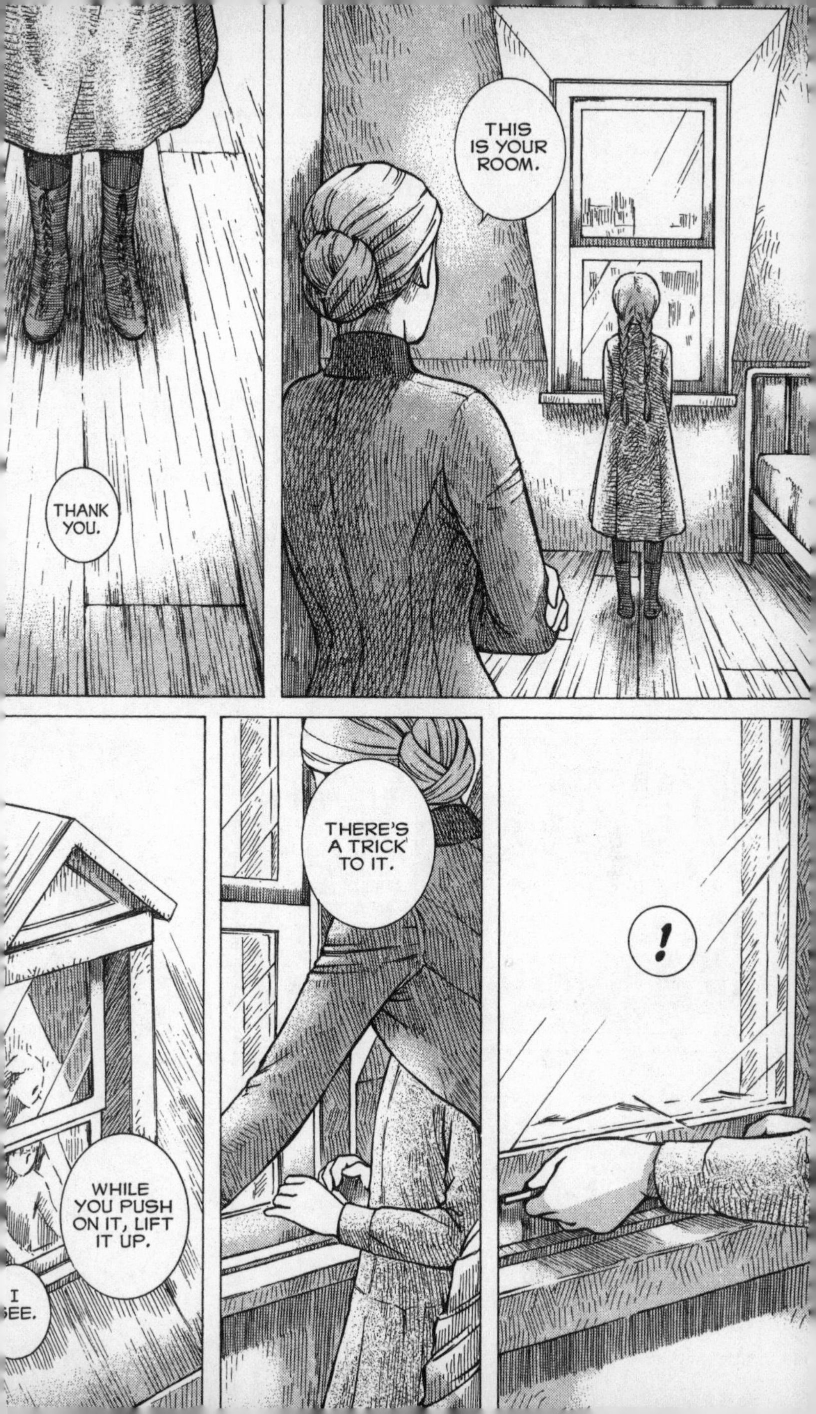
THIS IS YOUR ROOM.
THANK YOU.
!
THERE'S A TRICK TO IT.
WHILE YOU PUSH ON IT, LIFT IT UP.
I SEE.

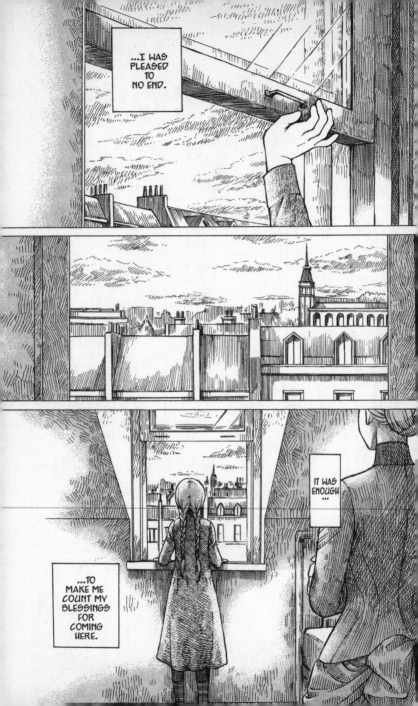

...I WAS PLEASED TO NO END.

IT WAS ENOUGH...

...TO MAKE ME COUNT MY BLESSINGS FOR COMING HERE.

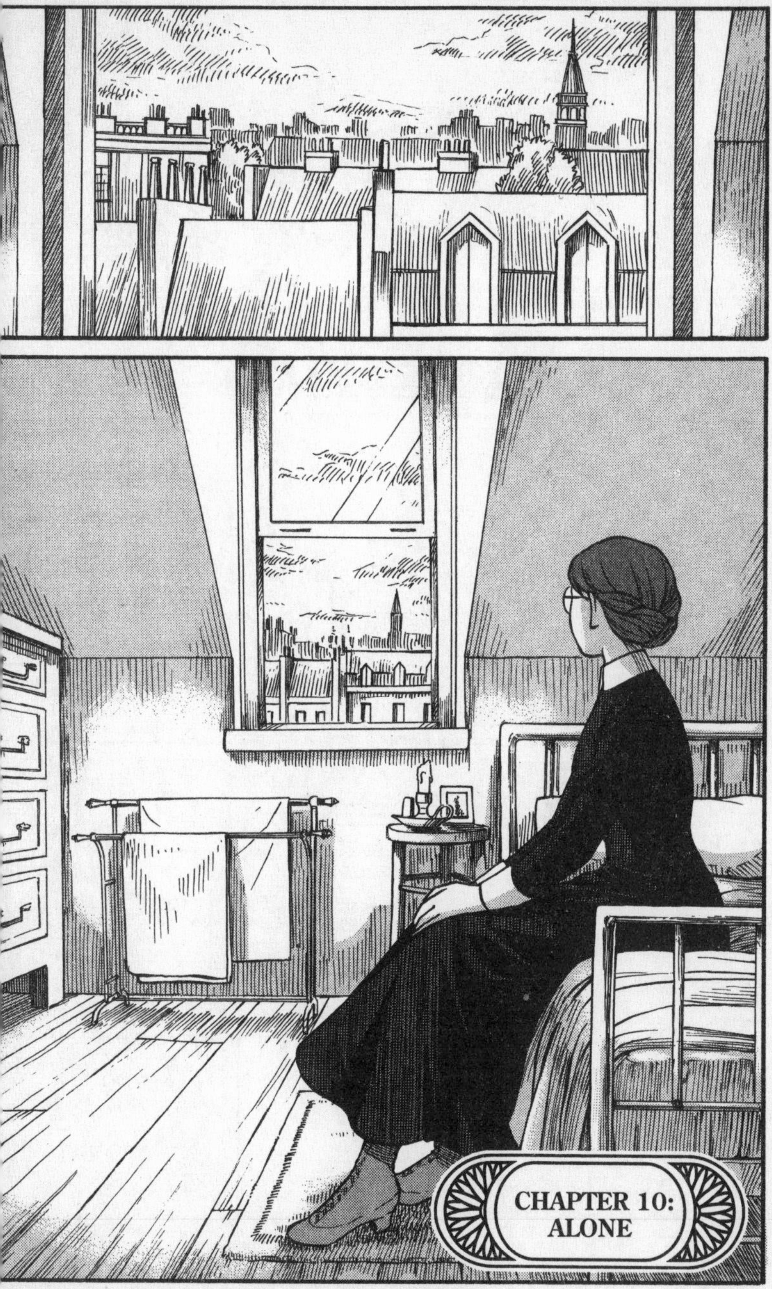
CHAPTER 10:
ALONE

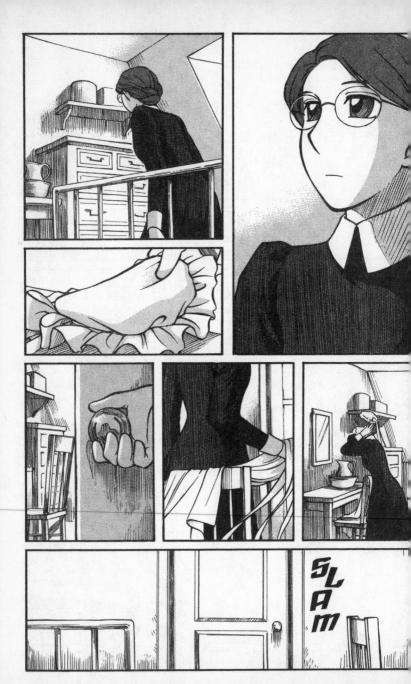

SLAM

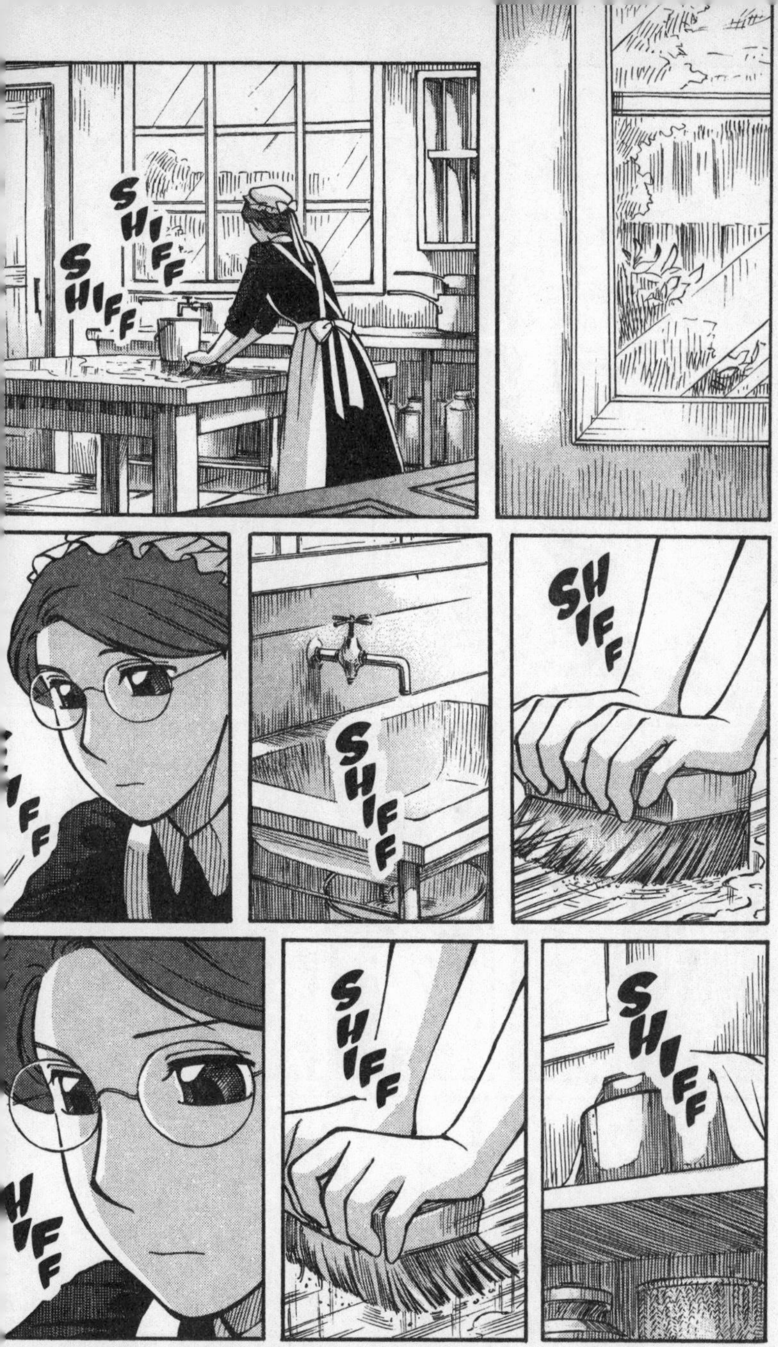
SHIFF
SHIFF
SHIFF
SHIFF
IFF
SHIFF
SHIFF
HIFF

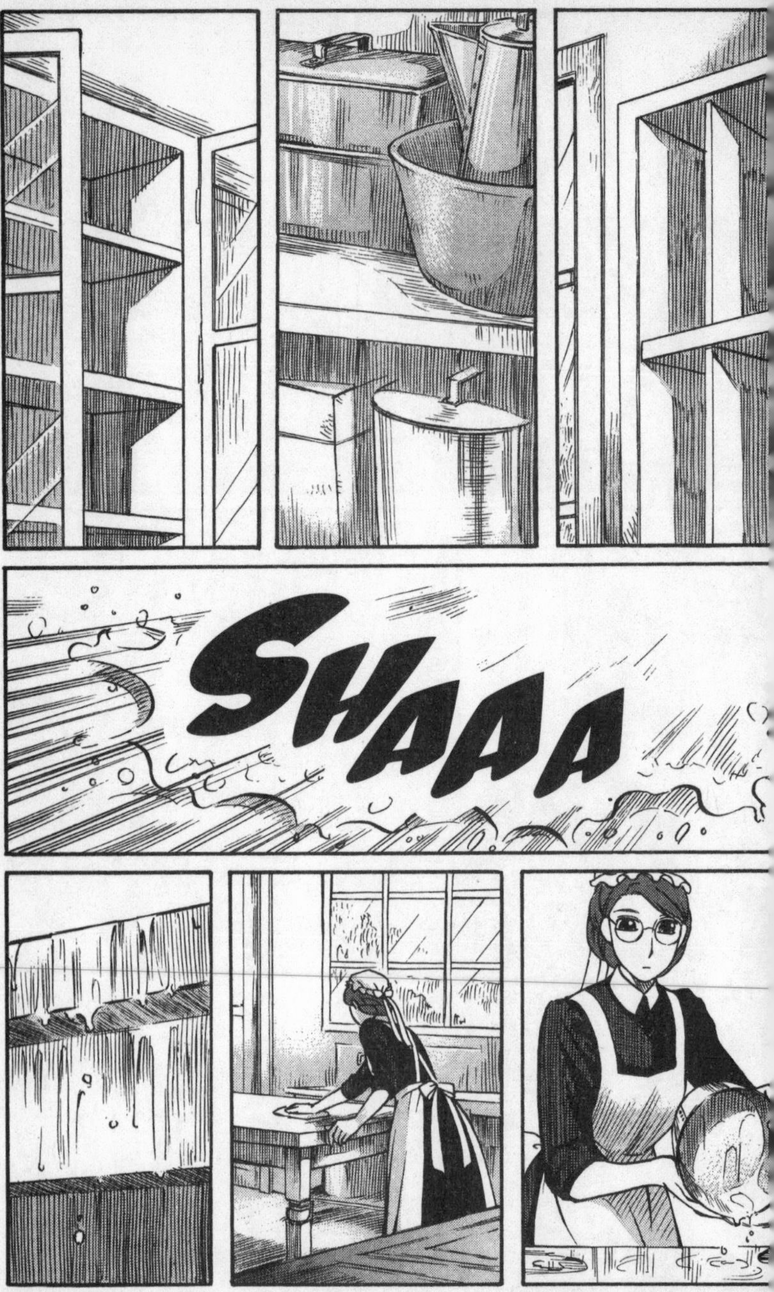
SHAAA

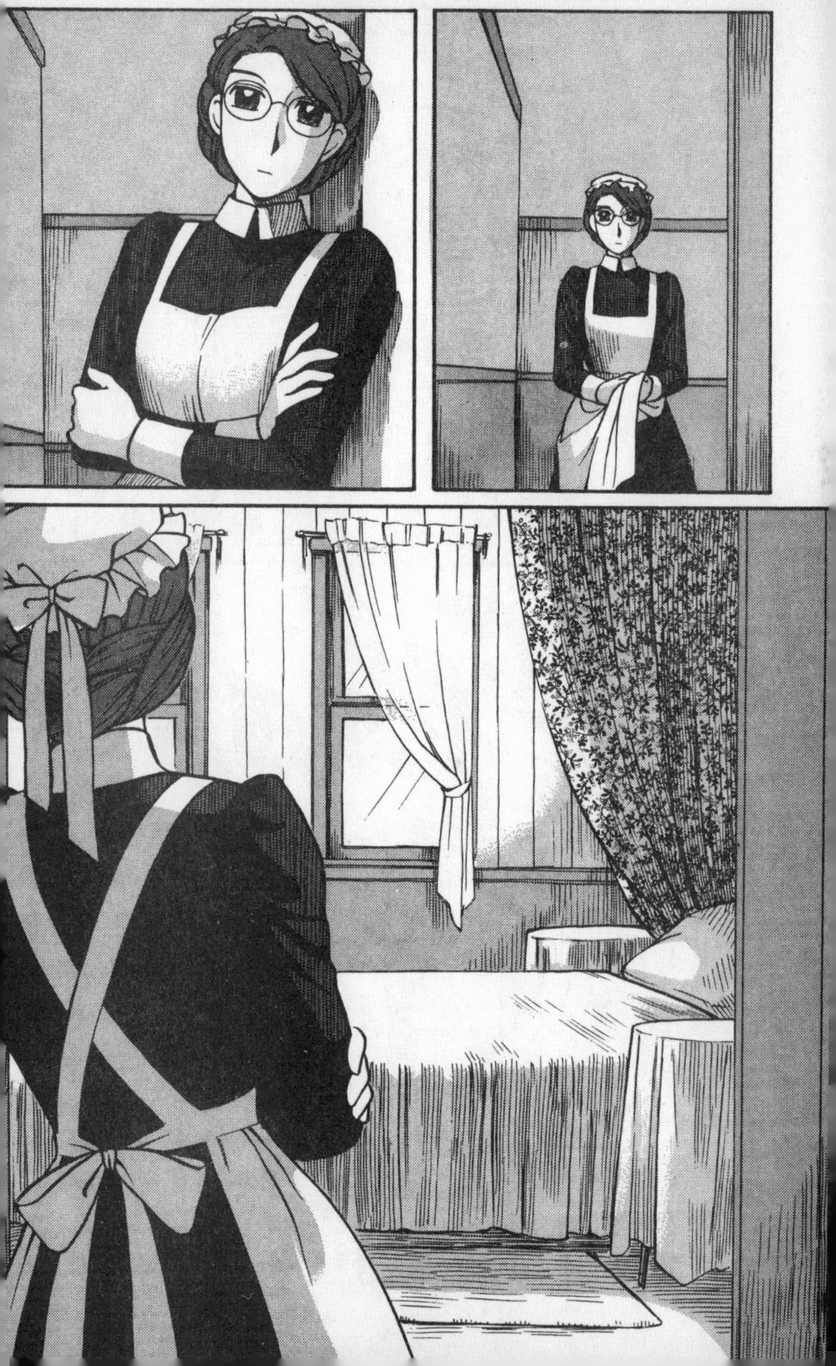

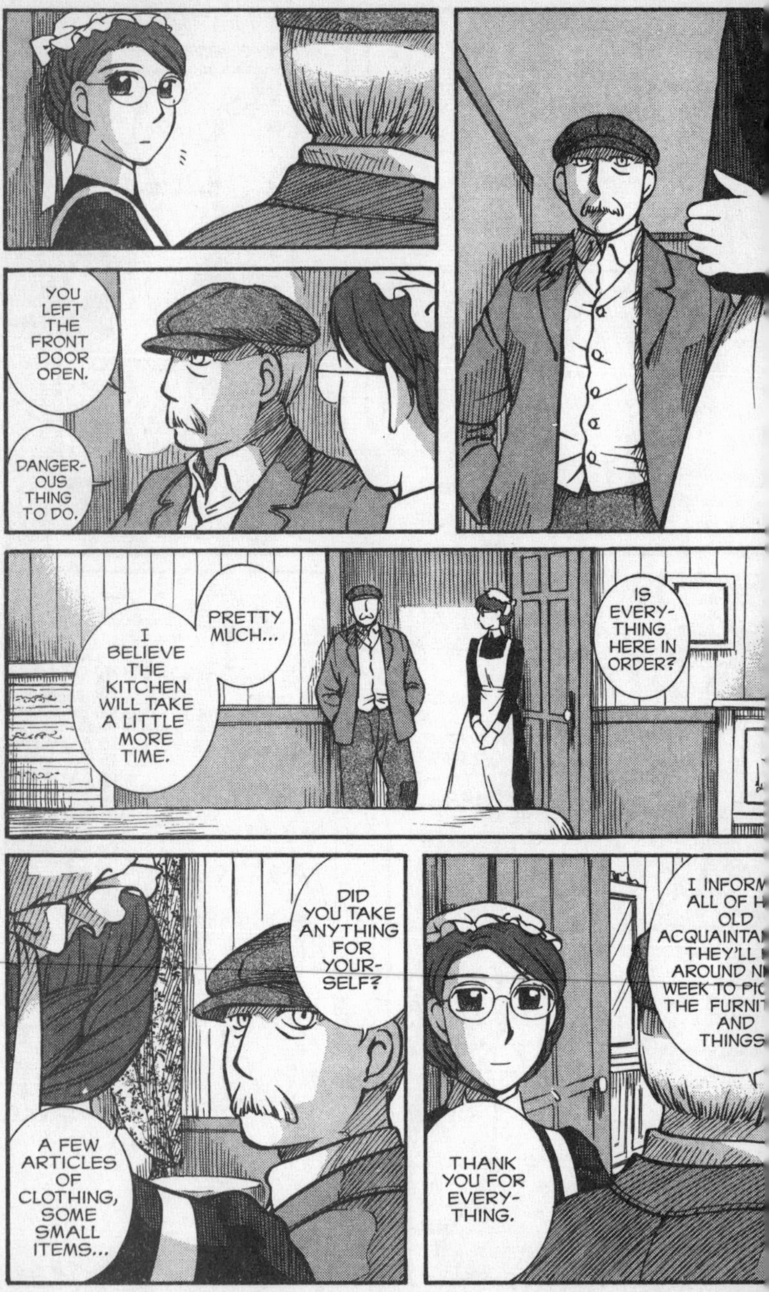
YOU LEFT THE FRONT DOOR OPEN.
DANGEROUS THING TO DO.
IS EVERYTHING HERE IN ORDER?
PRETTY MUCH...
I BELIEVE THE KITCHEN WILL TAKE A LITTLE MORE TIME.
I INFORM ALL OF H OLD ACQUAINTA THEY'LL AROUND N WEEK TO PI THE FURNIT AND THINGS
THANK YOU FOR EVERYTHING.
DID YOU TAKE ANYTHING FOR YOURSELF?
A FEW ARTICLES OF CLOTHING, SOME SMALL ITEMS...

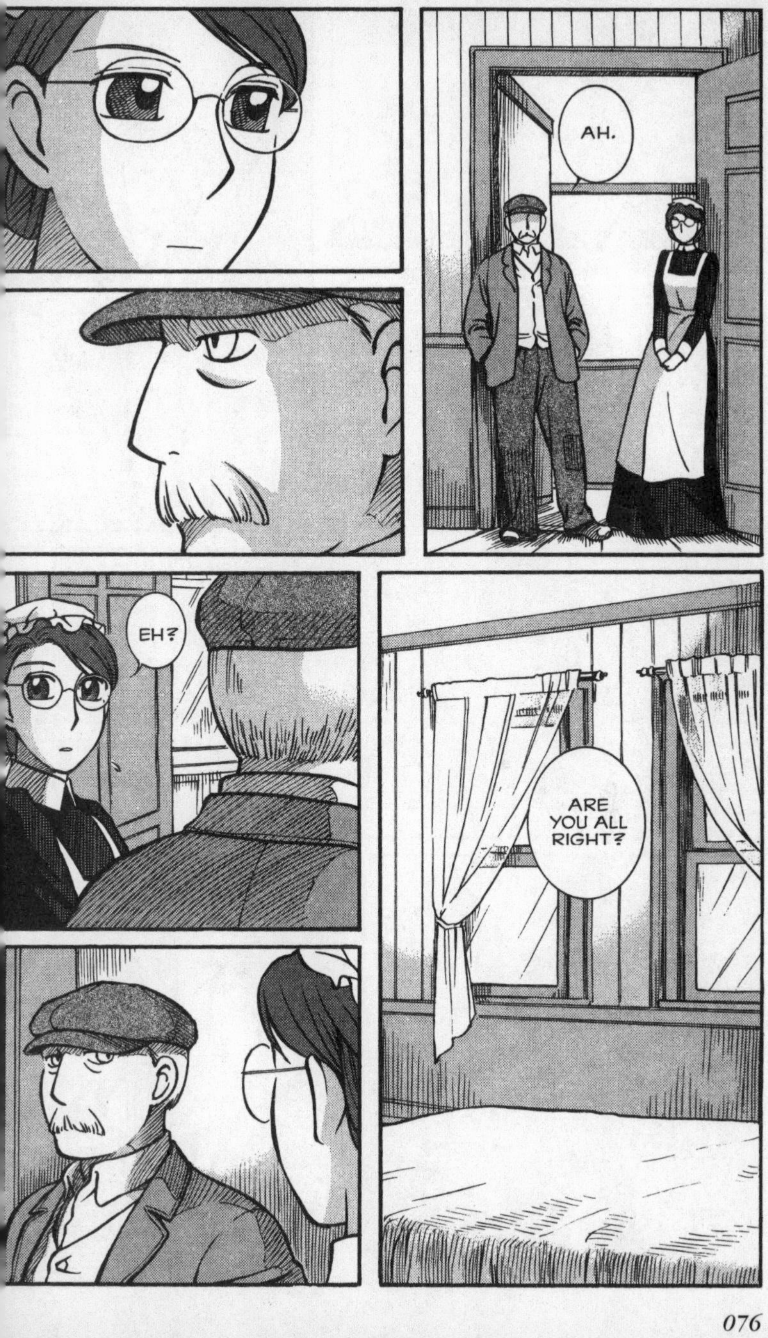
AH.
ARE YOU ALL RIGHT?
EH?

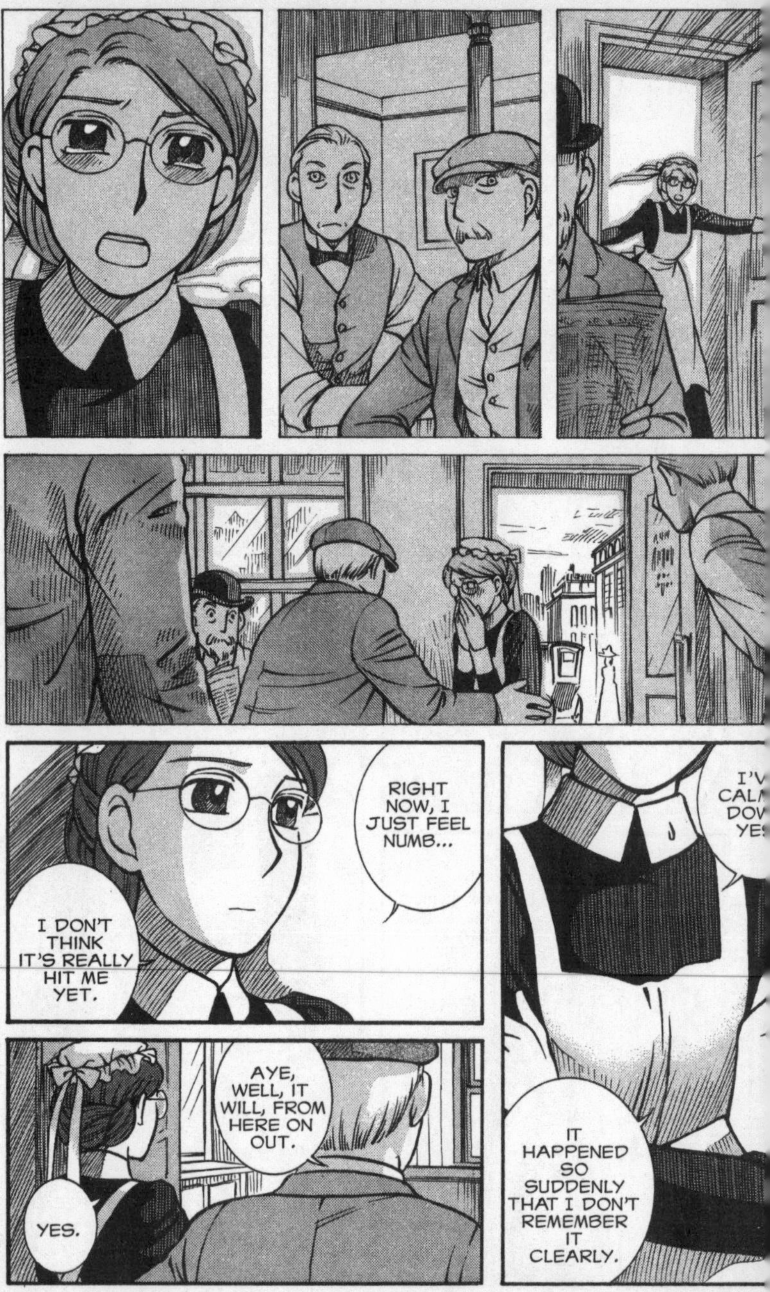
IT HAPPENED SO SUDDENLY THAT I DON'T REMEMBER IT CLEARLY.
RIGHT NOW, I JUST FEEL NUMB...
I DON'T THINK IT'S REALLY HIT ME YET.
AYE, WELL, IT WILL, FROM HERE ON OUT.
YES.

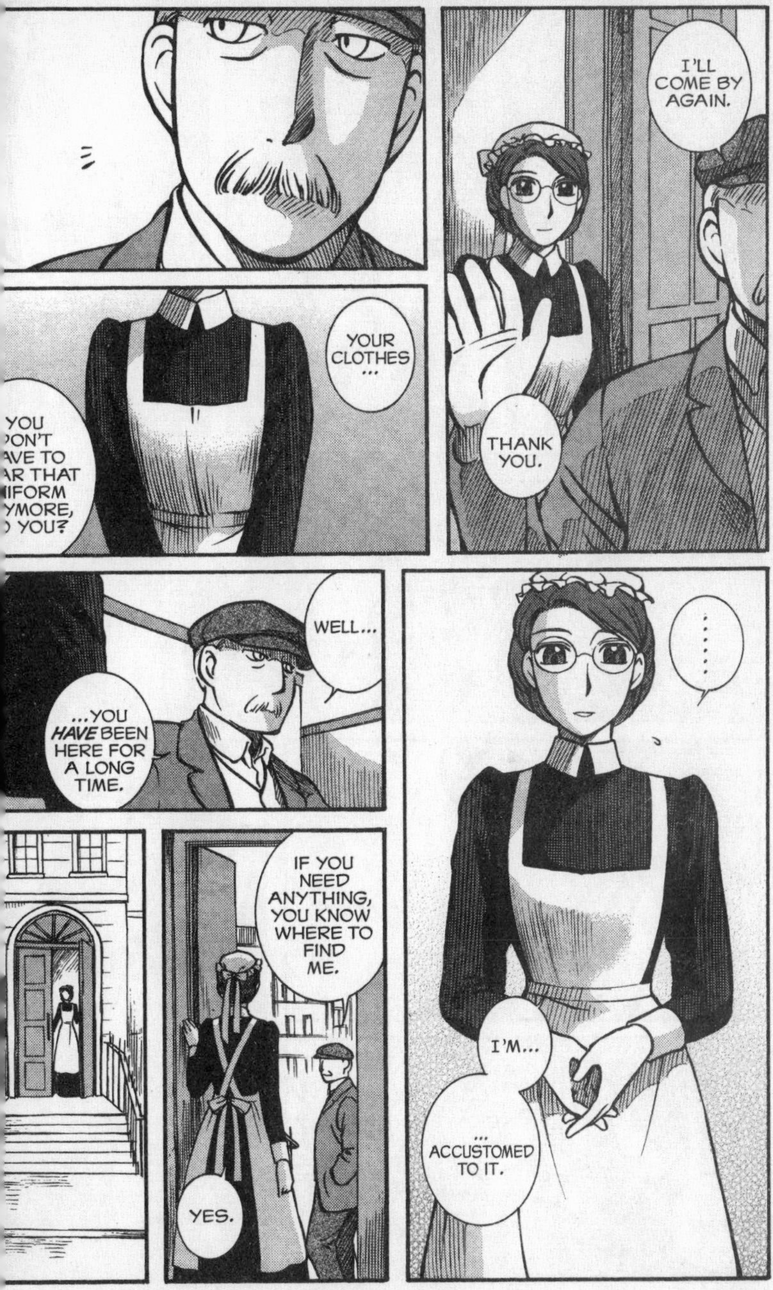
I'LL COME BY AGAIN.
THANK YOU.
YOUR CLOTHES ...
YOU ON'T AVE TO AR THAT IFORM YMORE, YOU?
......
I'M...
... ACCUSTOMED TO IT.
WELL...
...YOU *HAVE* BEEN HERE FOR A LONG TIME.
IF YOU NEED ANYTHING, YOU KNOW WHERE TO FIND ME.
YES.

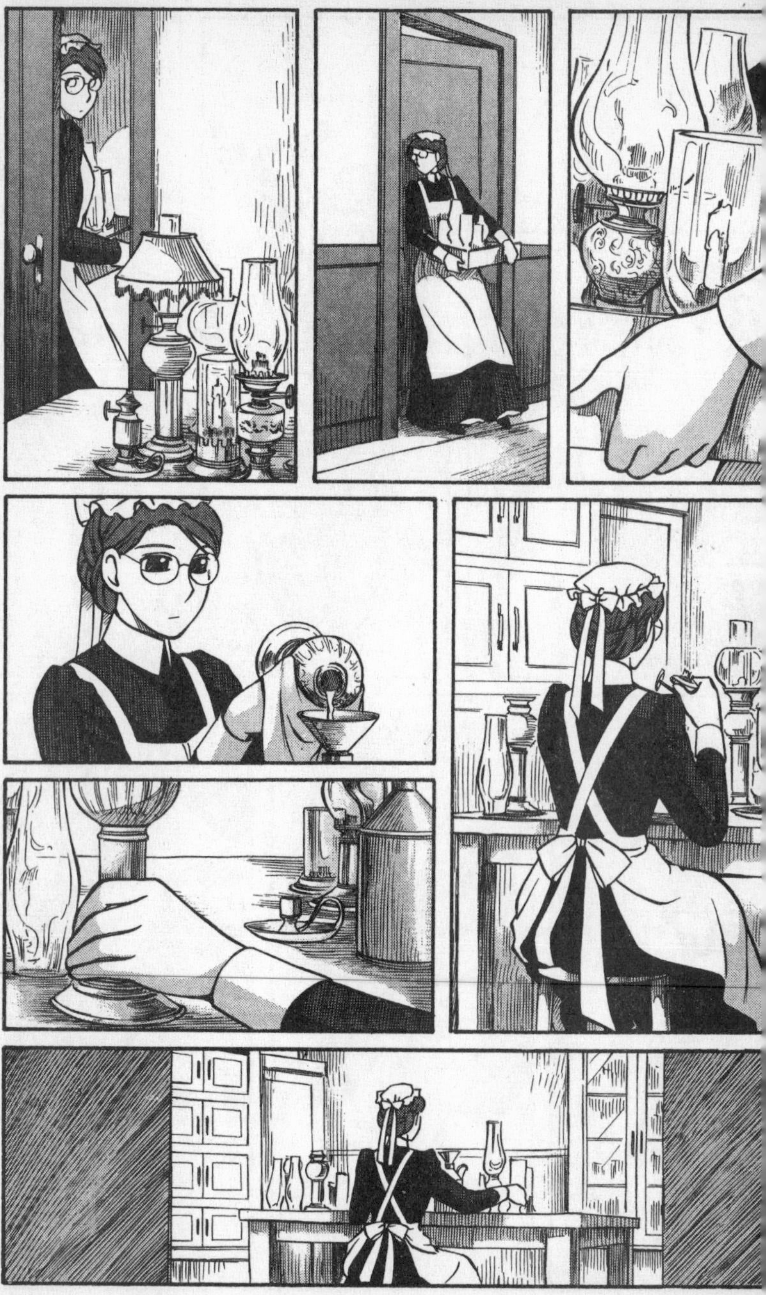

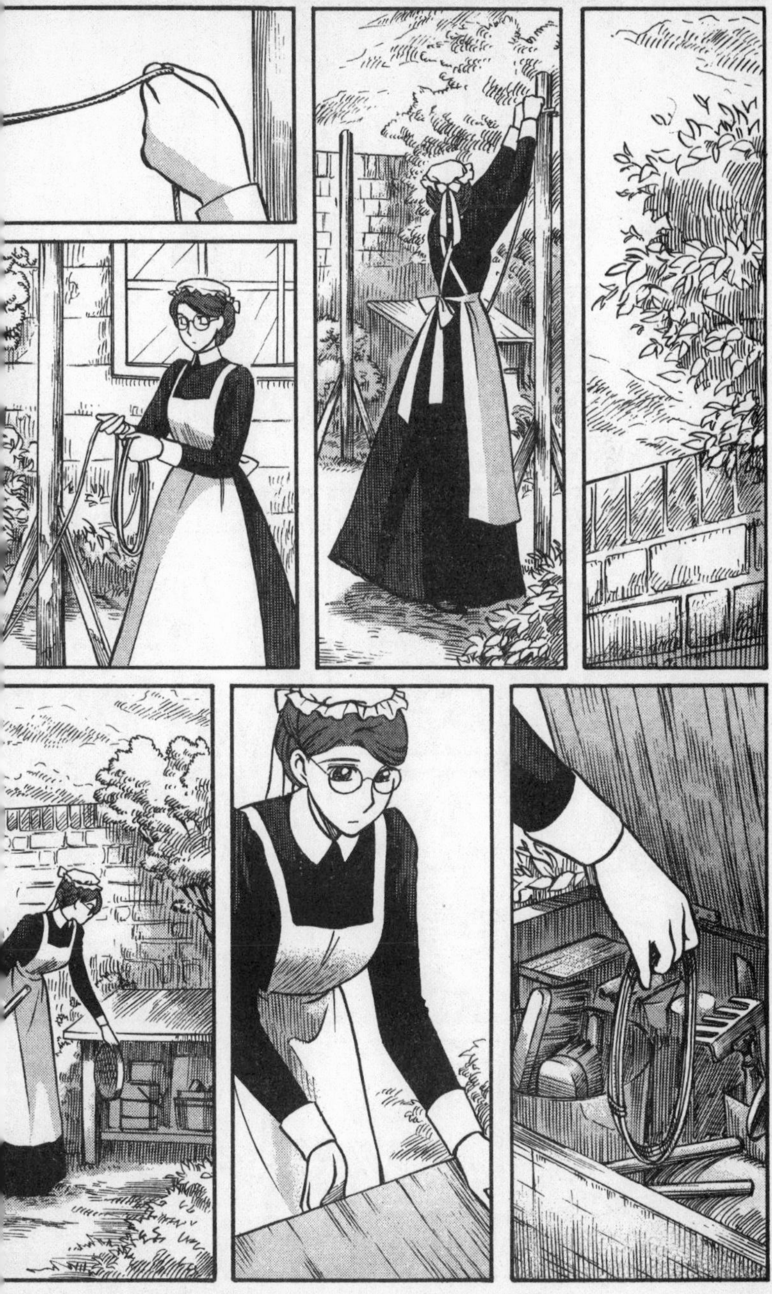

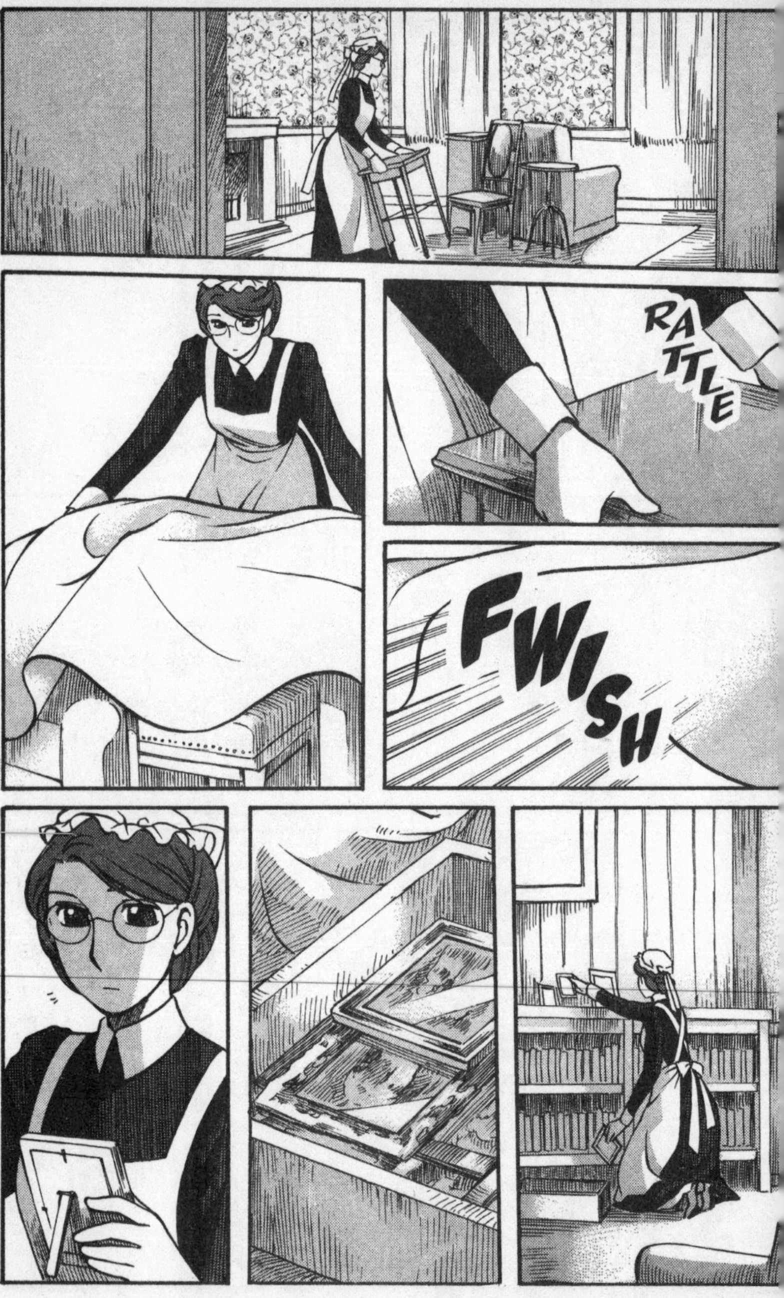
RATTLE
FWISH

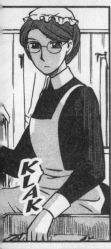

KLAK

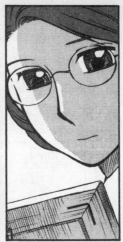

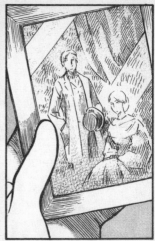

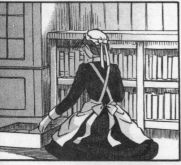

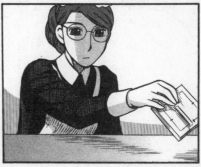

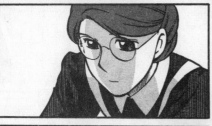

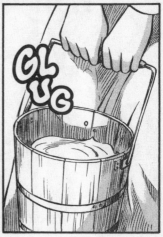

GLUG

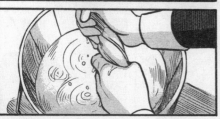

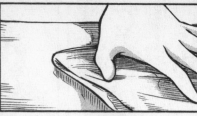

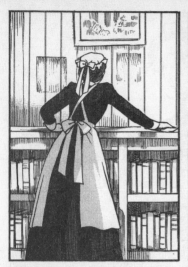

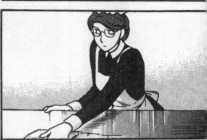

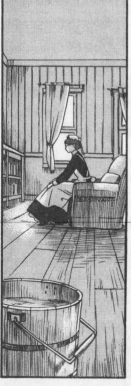

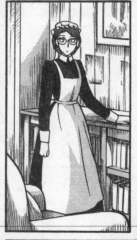

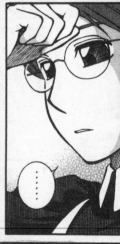

．．．．．

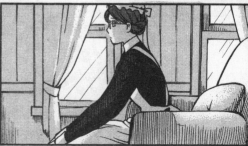

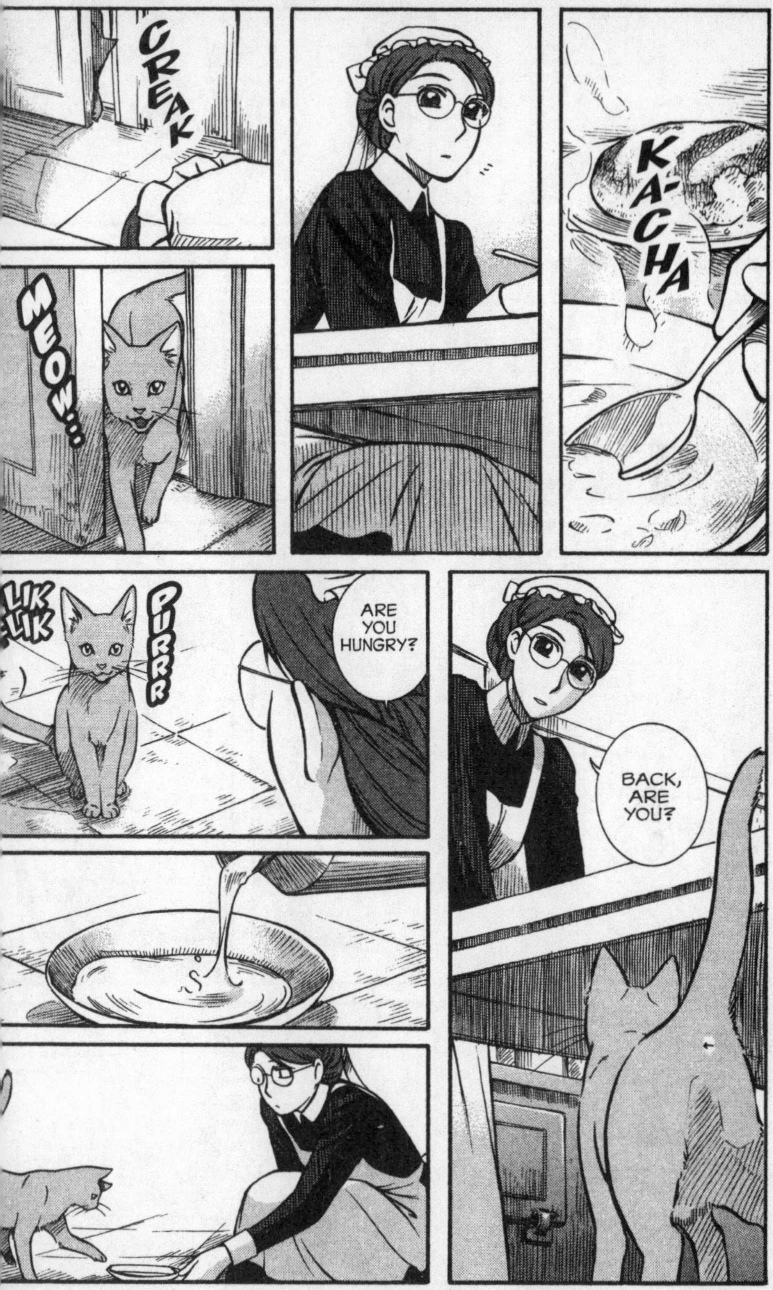
KA-CHA
CREAK
MEOW...
BACK, ARE YOU?
ARE YOU HUNGRY?
PURRR
LIK LIK

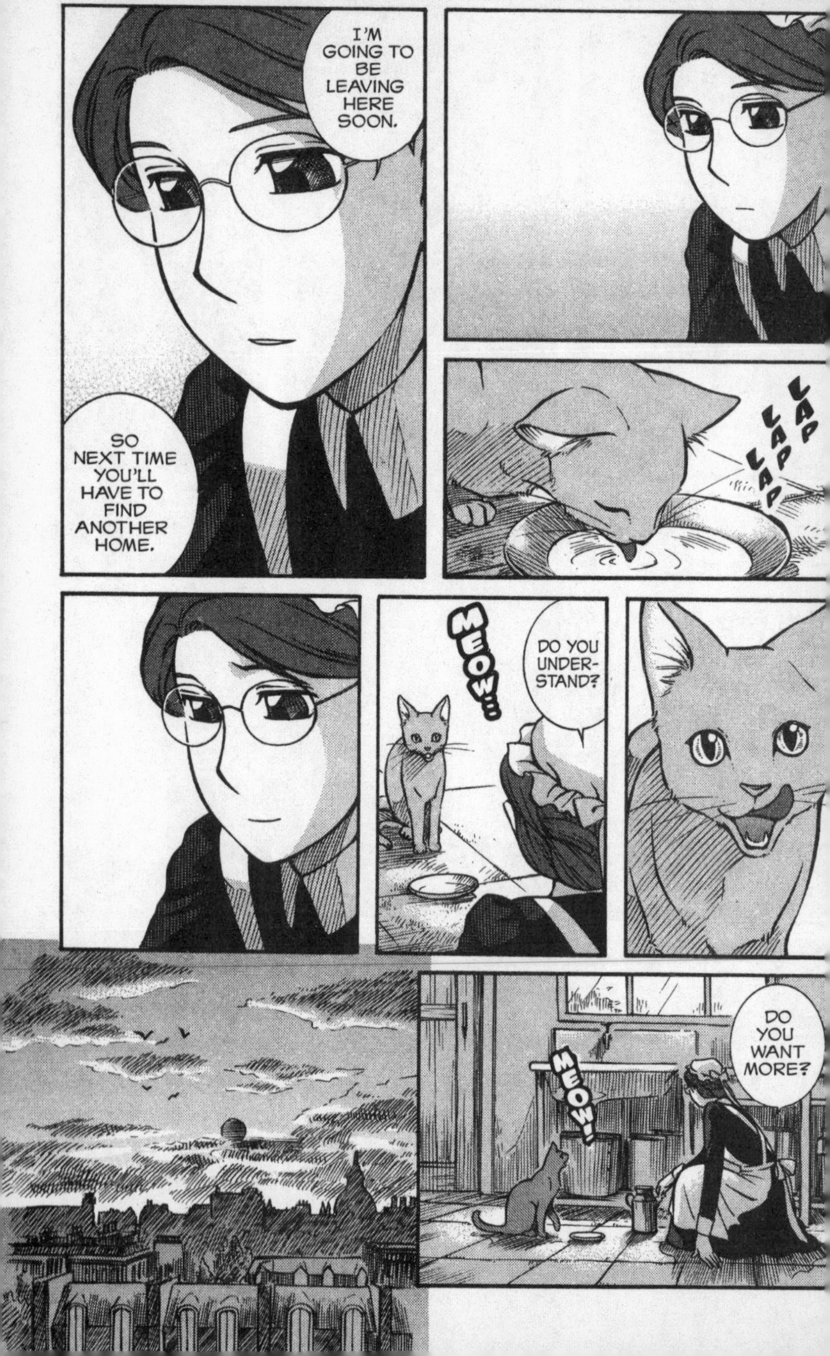
LAP LAP LAP
I'M GOING TO BE LEAVING HERE SOON.
SO NEXT TIME YOU'LL HAVE TO FIND ANOTHER HOME.
DO YOU UNDER-STAND?
MEOW!
DO YOU WANT MORE?
MEOW!

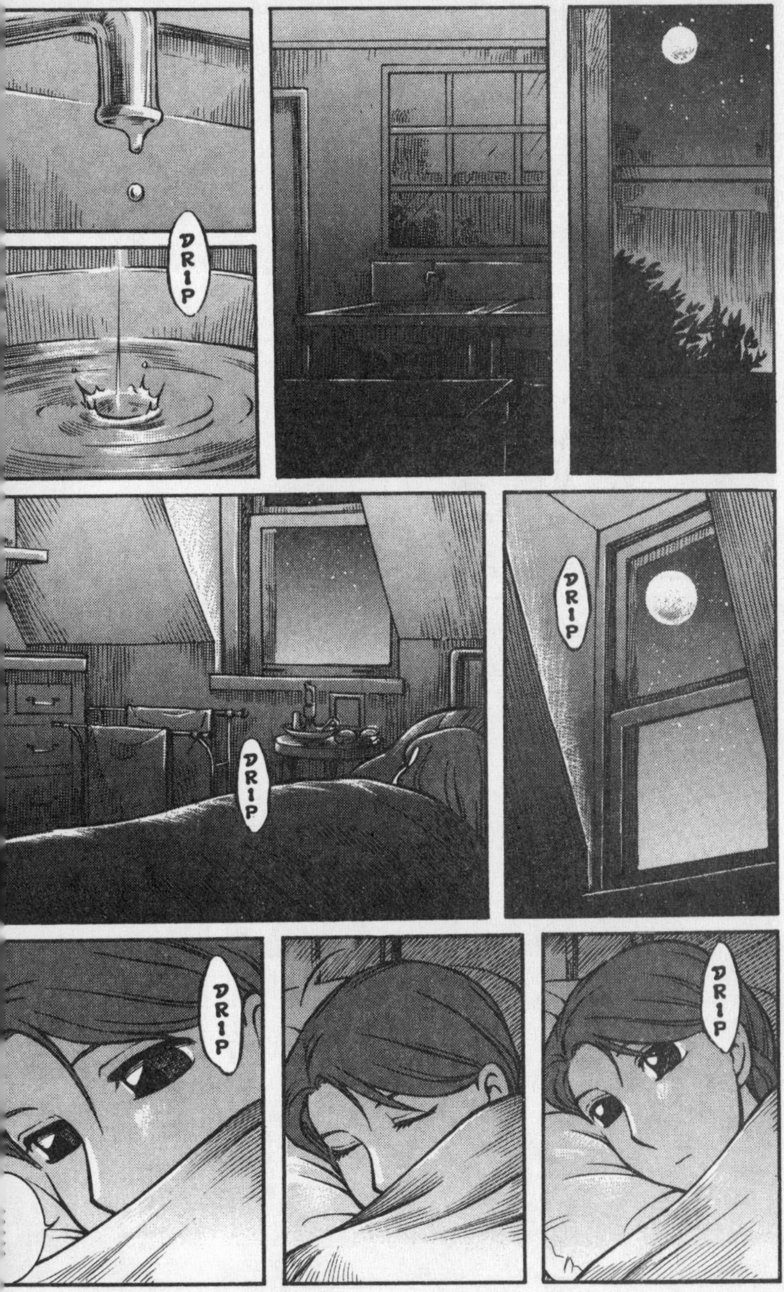
DRIP
DRIP
DRIP
DRIP
DRIP

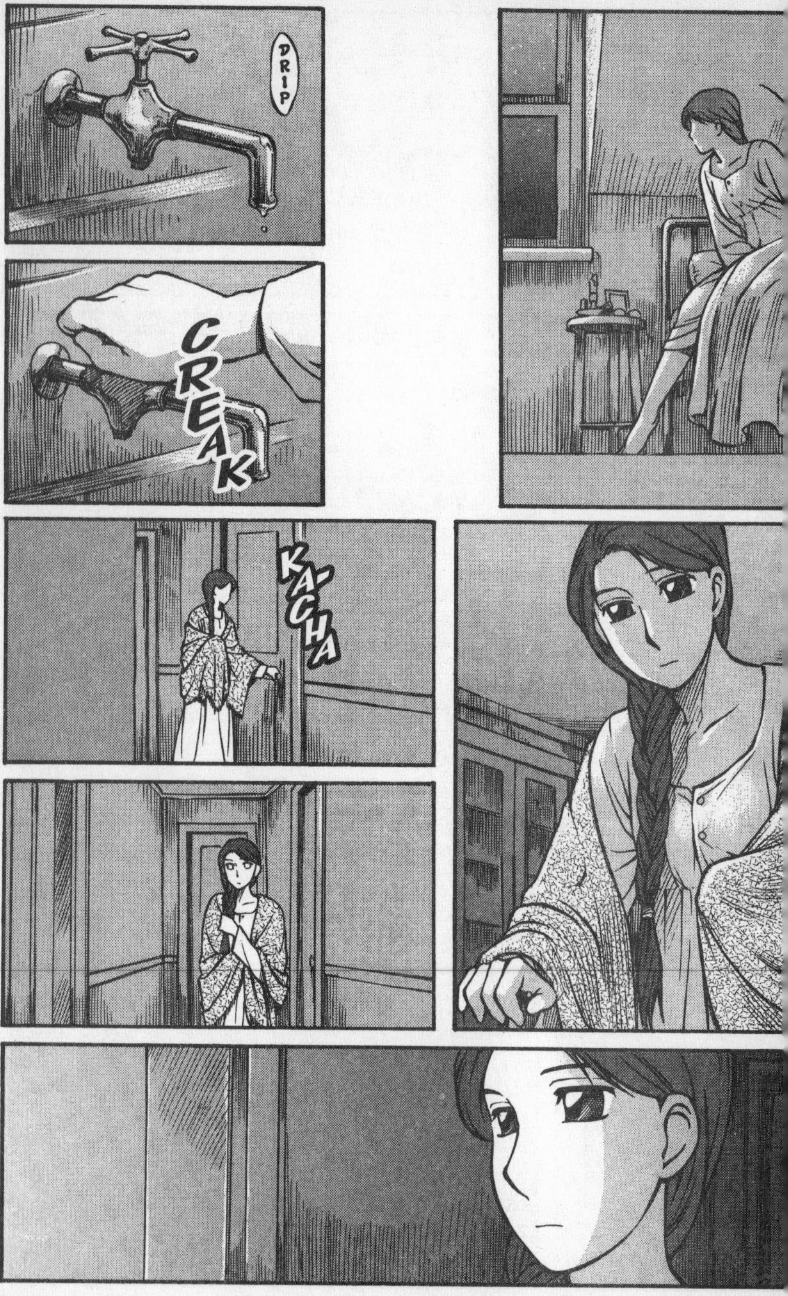
DRIP
CREAK
KA-CHA

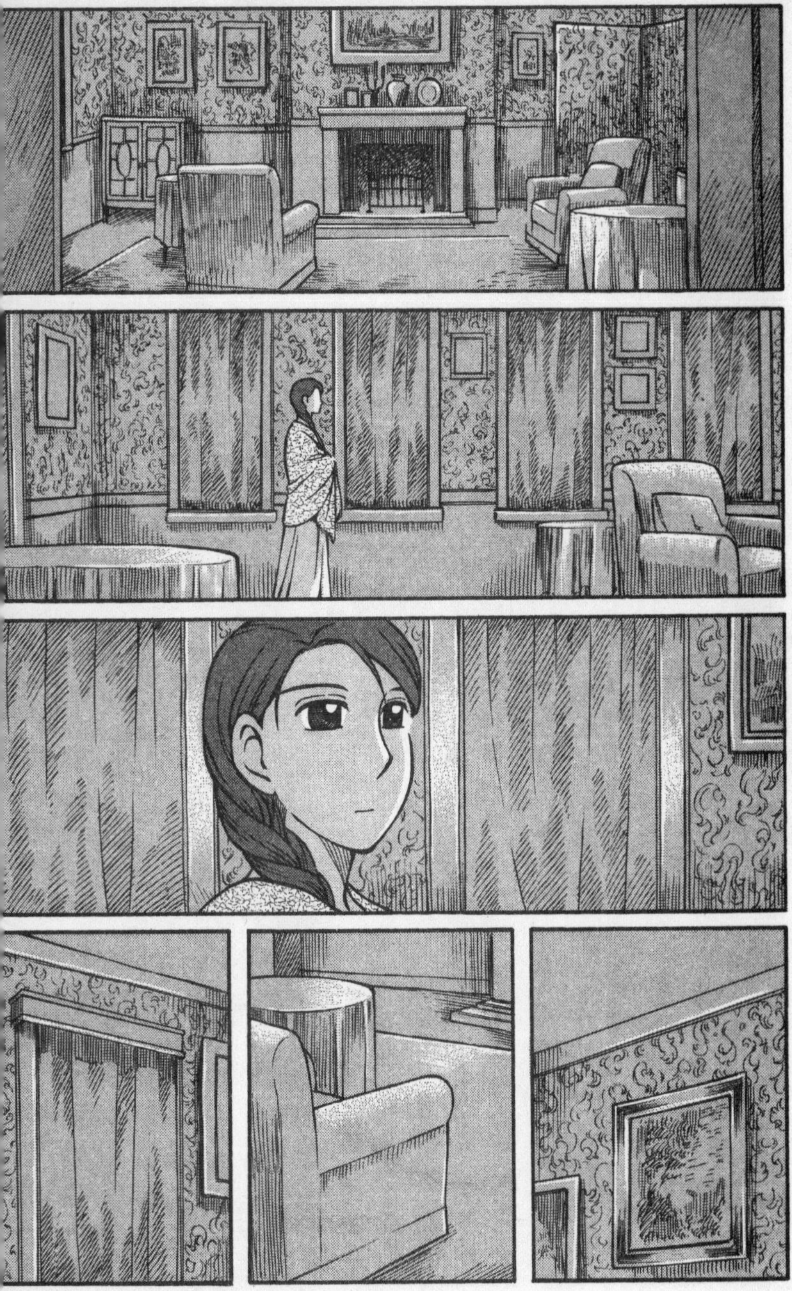

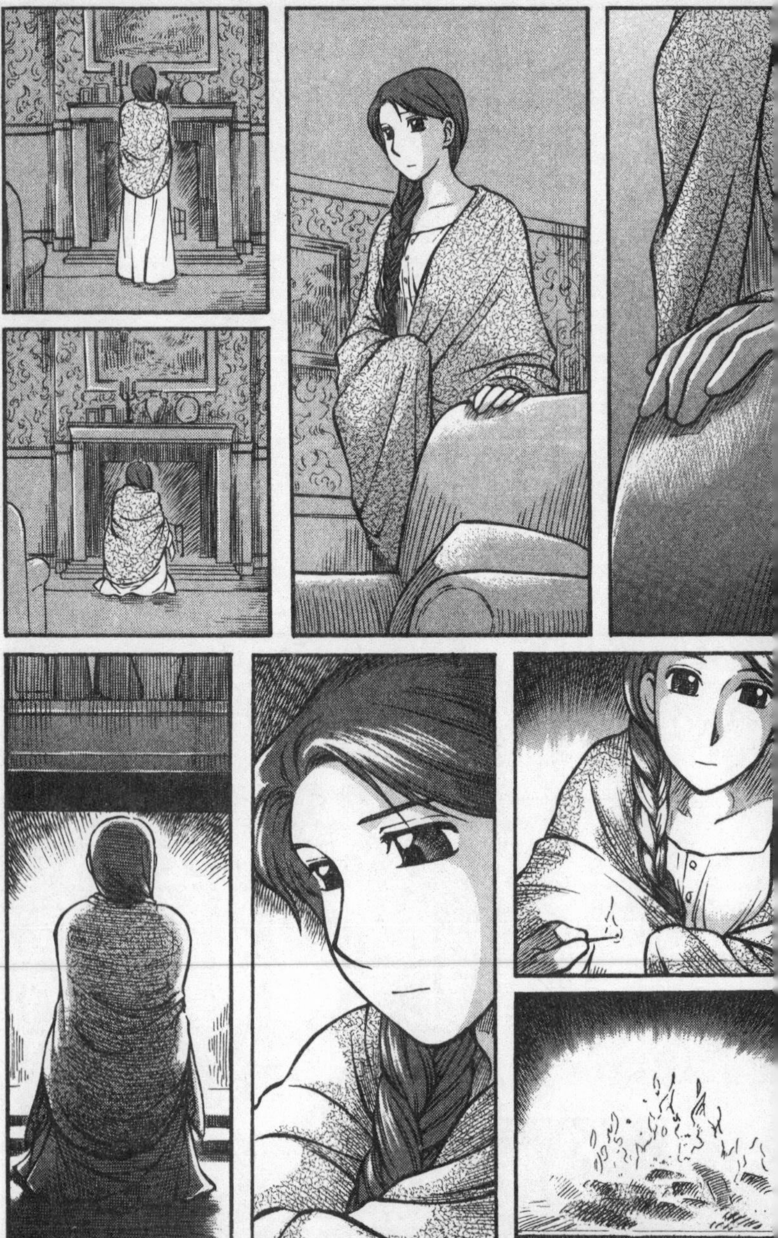

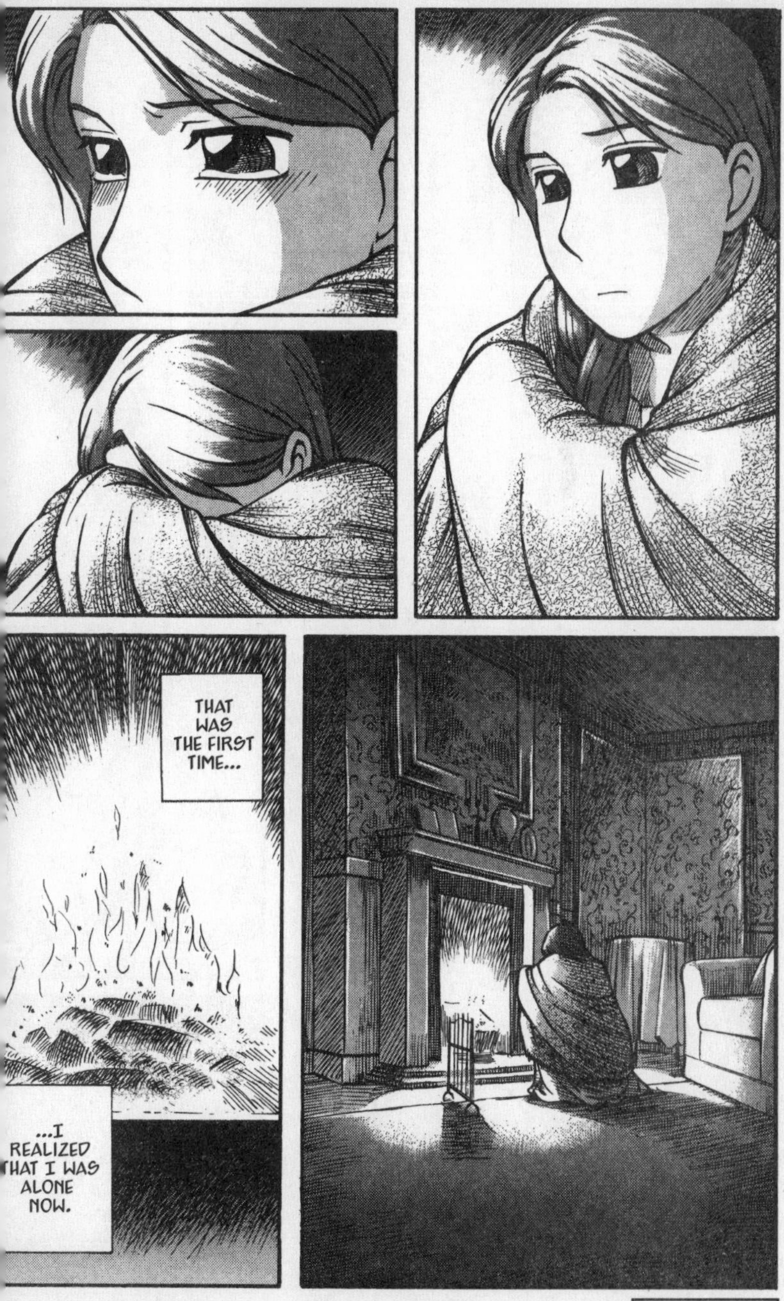
THAT WAS THE FIRST TIME...
...I REALIZED THAT I WAS ALONE NOW.

Chapter Ten:
The End

EPILOGUE

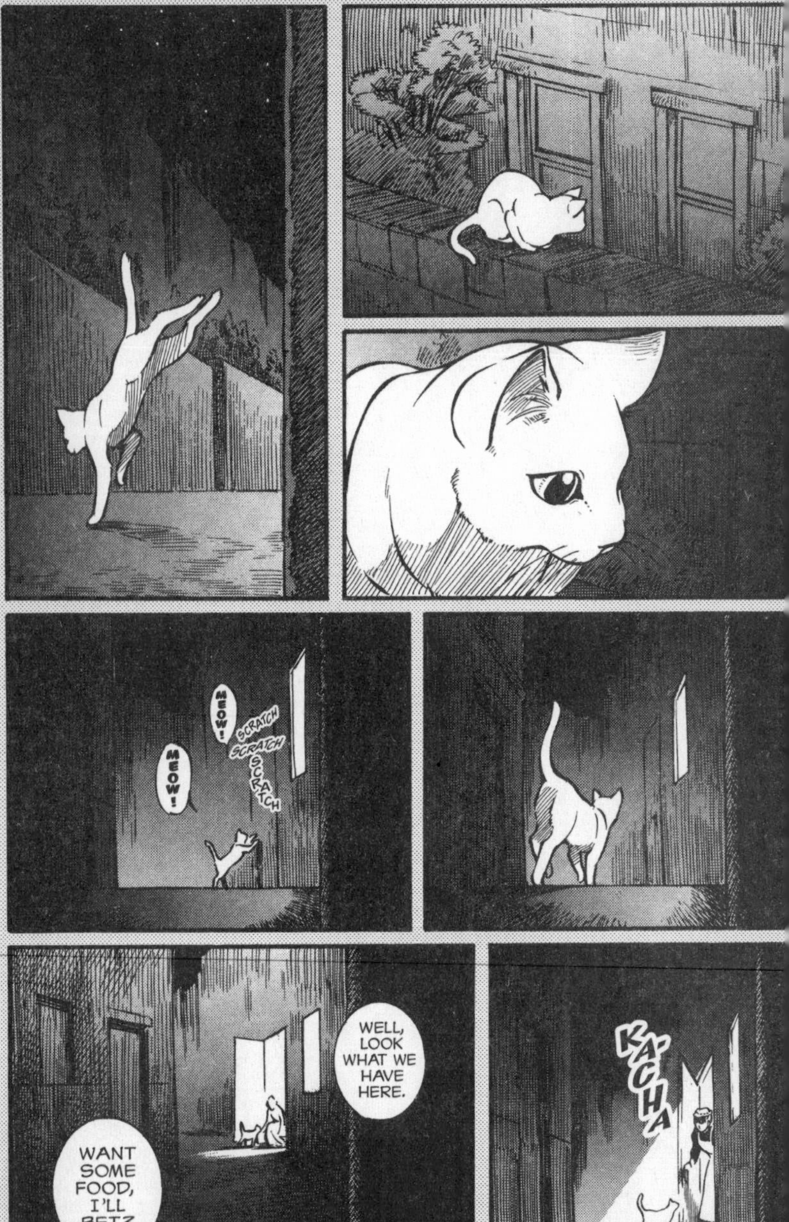
MEOW!
SCRATCH SCRATCH SCRATCH
MEOW!
KA-CHA
WELL, LOOK WHAT WE HAVE HERE.
WANT SOME FOOD, I'LL BET?

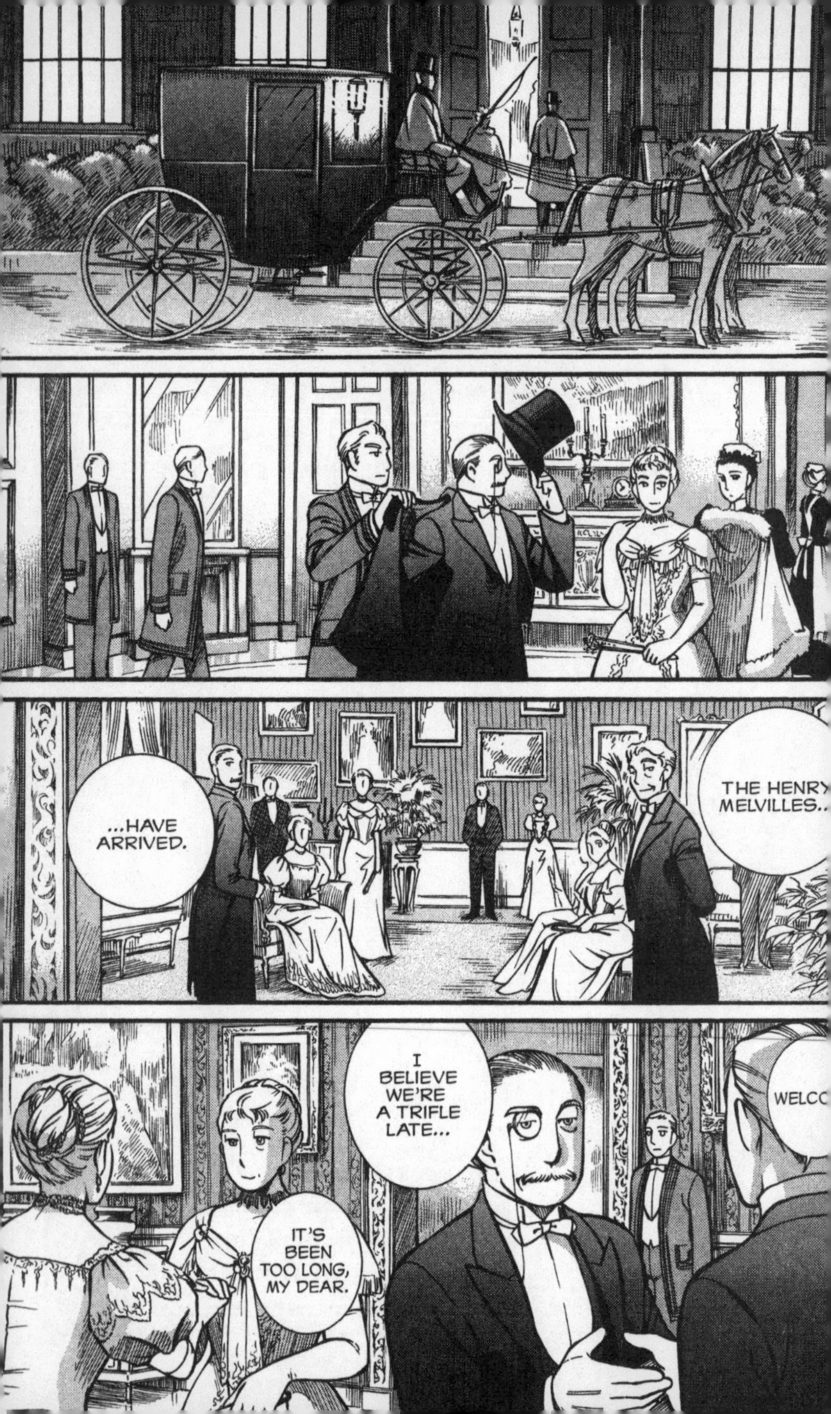
THE HENRY MELVILLES..
...HAVE ARRIVED.
WELCO
I BELIEVE WE'RE A TRIFLE LATE...
IT'S BEEN TOO LONG, MY DEAR.

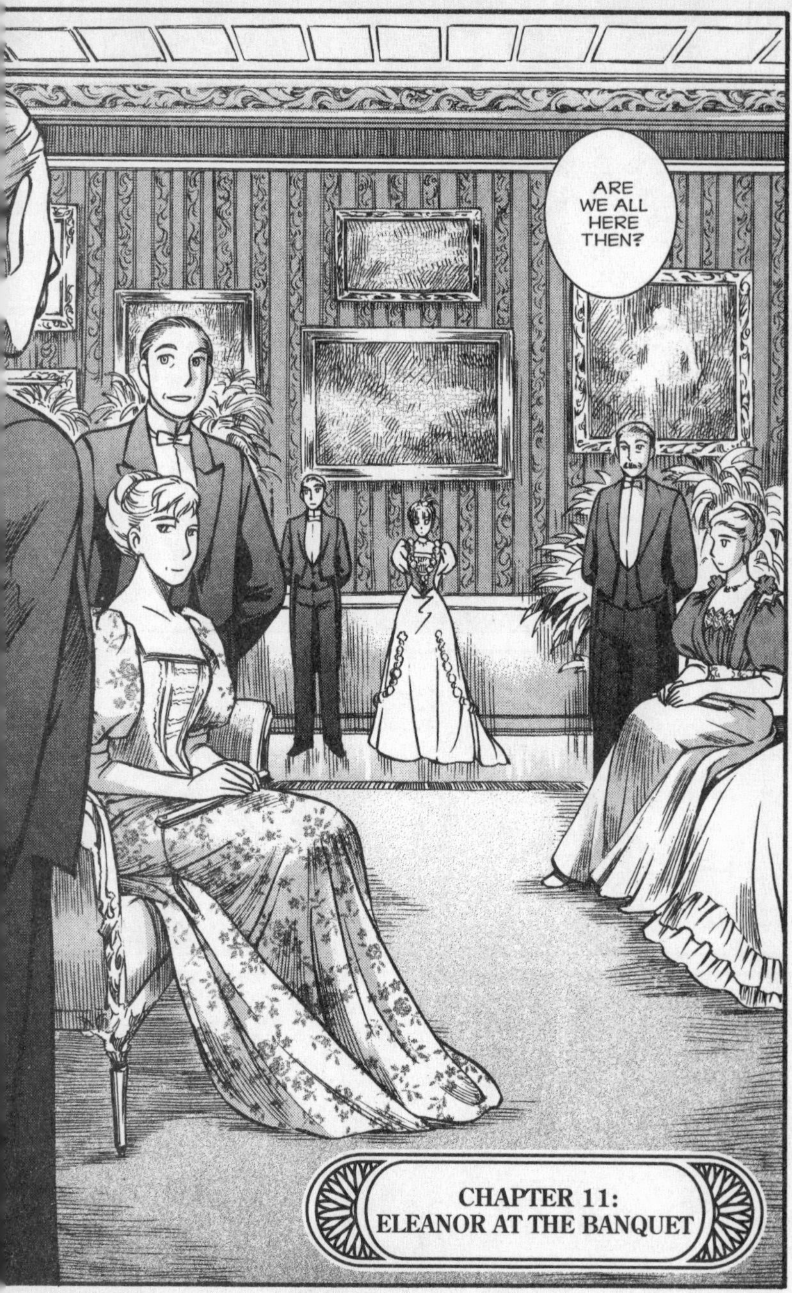
ARE WE ALL HERE THEN?
CHAPTER 11:
ELEANOR AT THE BANQUET

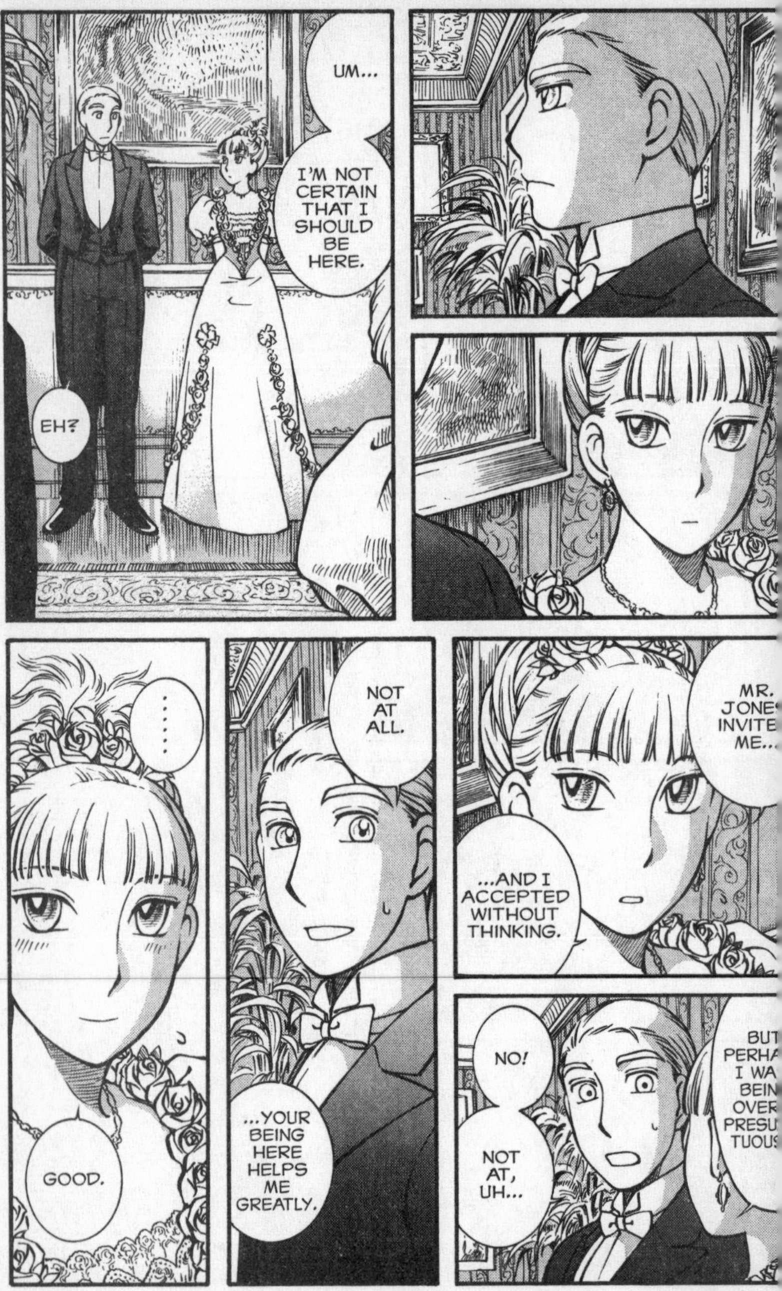

UM...
I'M NOT CERTAIN THAT I SHOULD BE HERE.
EH?
MR. JONES INVITE ME...
...AND I ACCEPTED WITHOUT THINKING.
BUT PERHA I WA BEIN OVER PRESU TUOUS
NO!
NOT AT, UH...
NOT AT ALL.
...YOUR BEING HERE HELPS ME GREATLY.
......
GOOD.

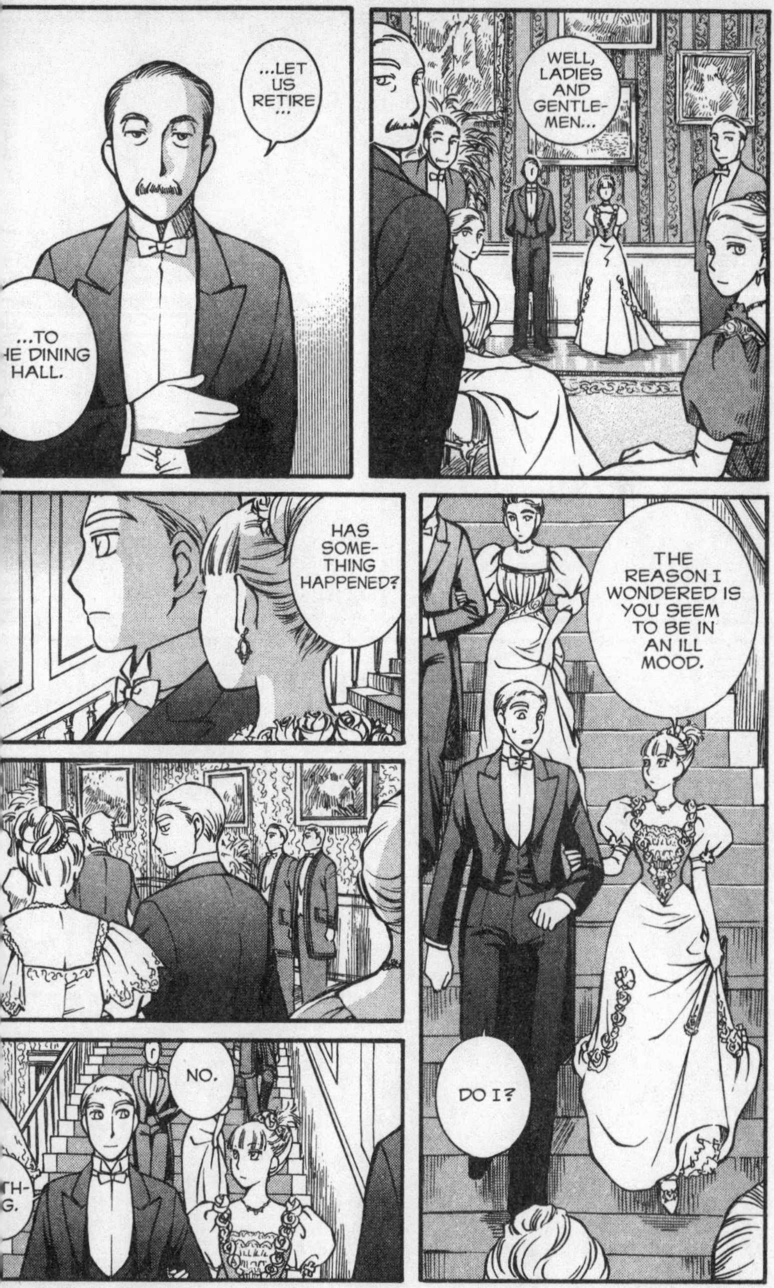
WELL, LADIES AND GENTLE-MEN...
...LET US RETIRE ...
...TO
HE DINING HALL.
THE REASON I WONDERED IS YOU SEEM TO BE IN AN ILL MOOD.
DO I?
HAS SOME-THING HAPPENED?
NO.
TH-
G.

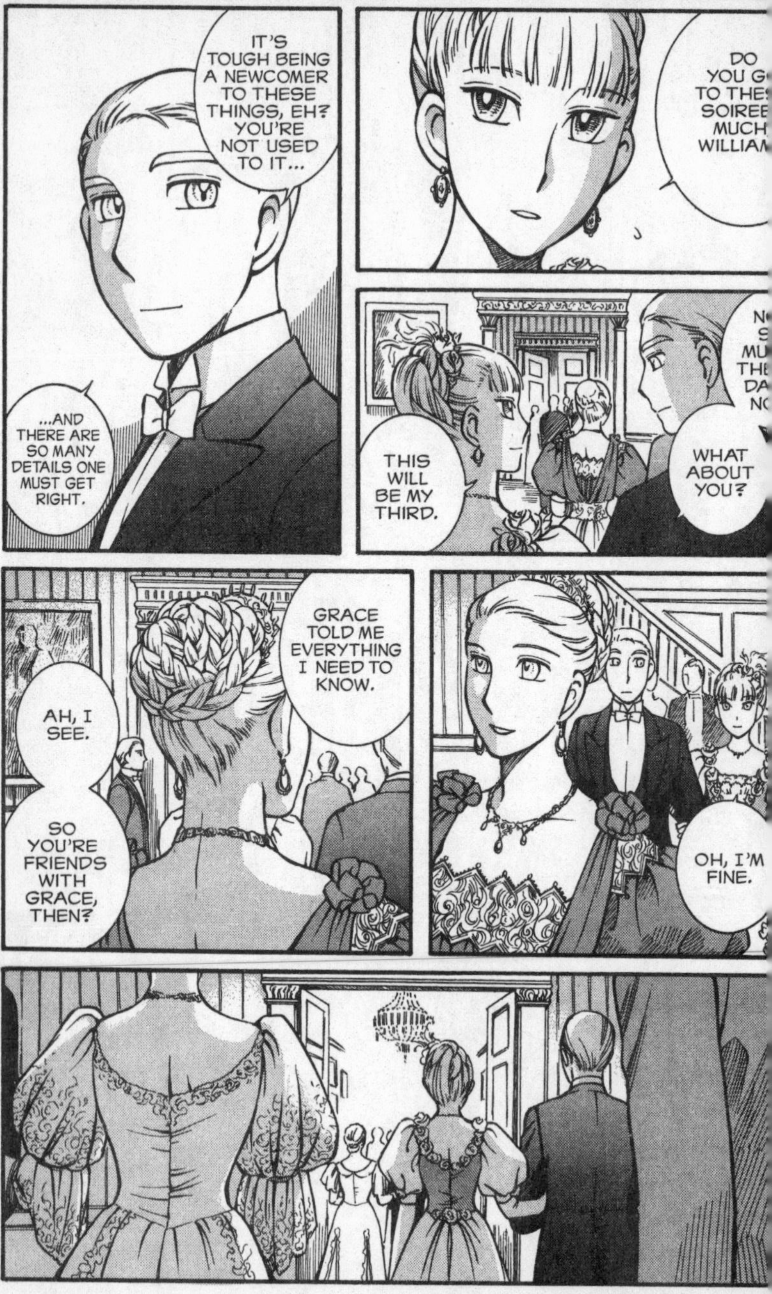
DO YOU G TO THE SOIREE MUCH WILLIAM
WHAT ABOUT YOU?
THIS WILL BE MY THIRD.
IT'S TOUGH BEING A NEWCOMER TO THESE THINGS, EH? YOU'RE NOT USED TO IT...
...AND THERE ARE SO MANY DETAILS ONE MUST GET RIGHT.
OH, I'M FINE.
GRACE TOLD ME EVERYTHING I NEED TO KNOW.
AH, I SEE.
SO YOU'RE FRIENDS WITH GRACE, THEN?

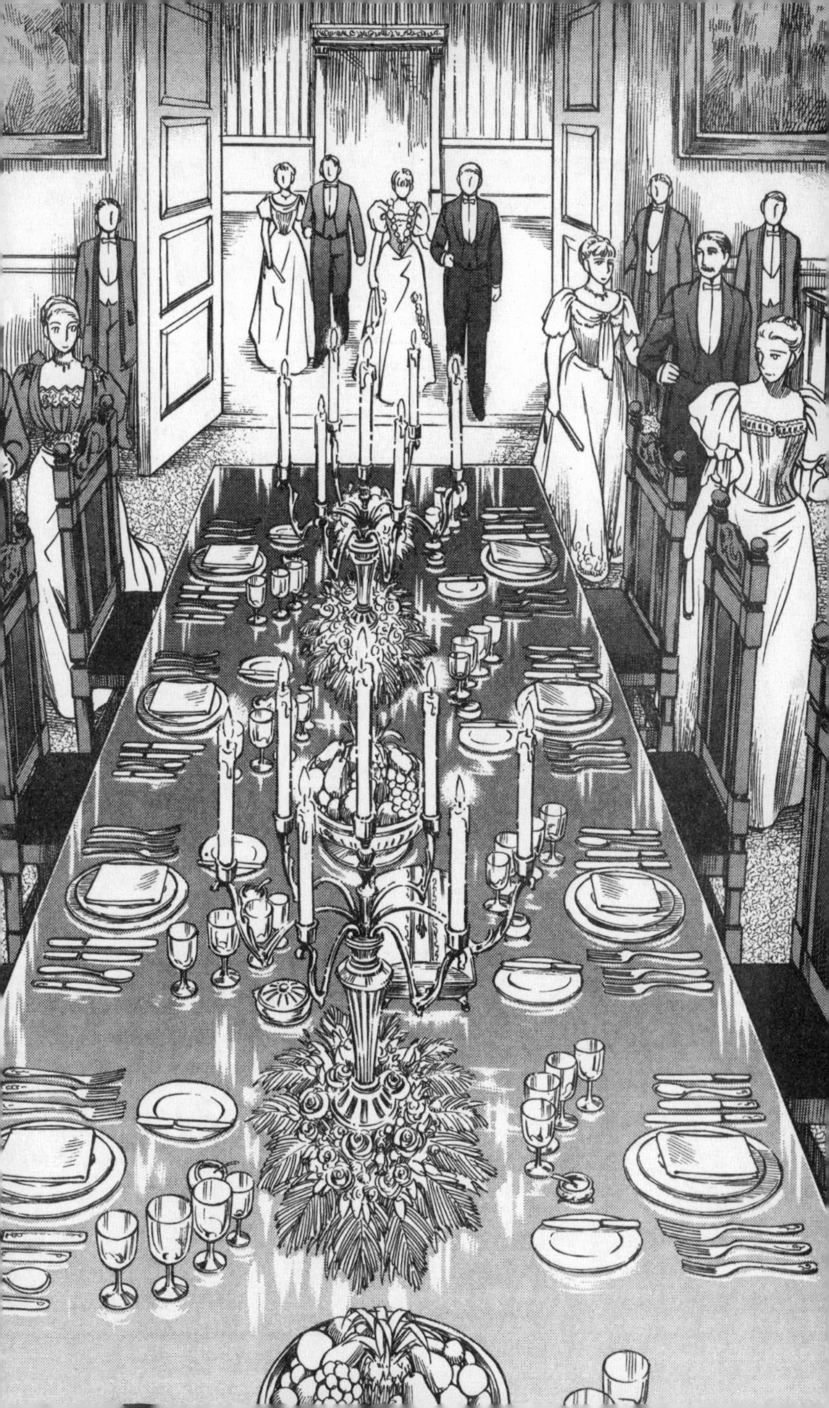

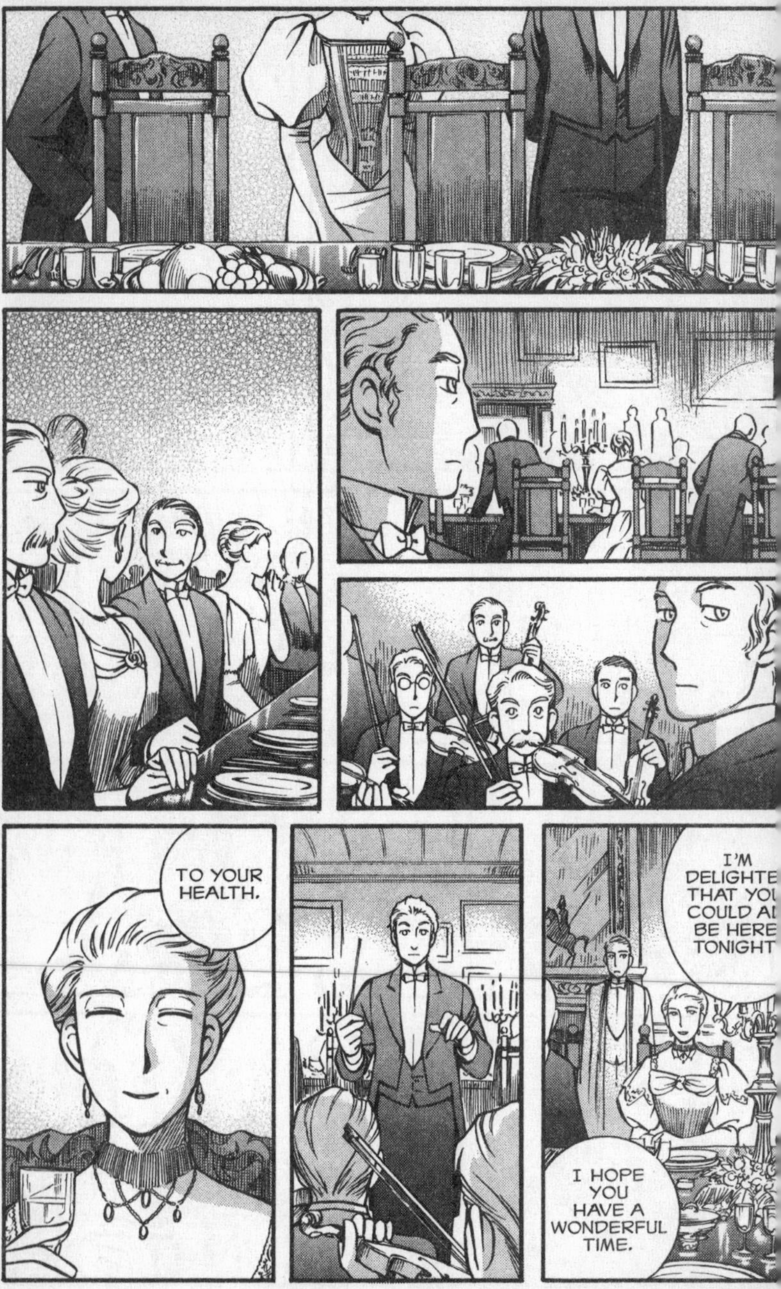
I'M DELIGHTE THAT YOU COULD AL BE HERE TONIGHT
I HOPE YOU HAVE A WONDERFUL TIME.
TO YOUR HEALTH.

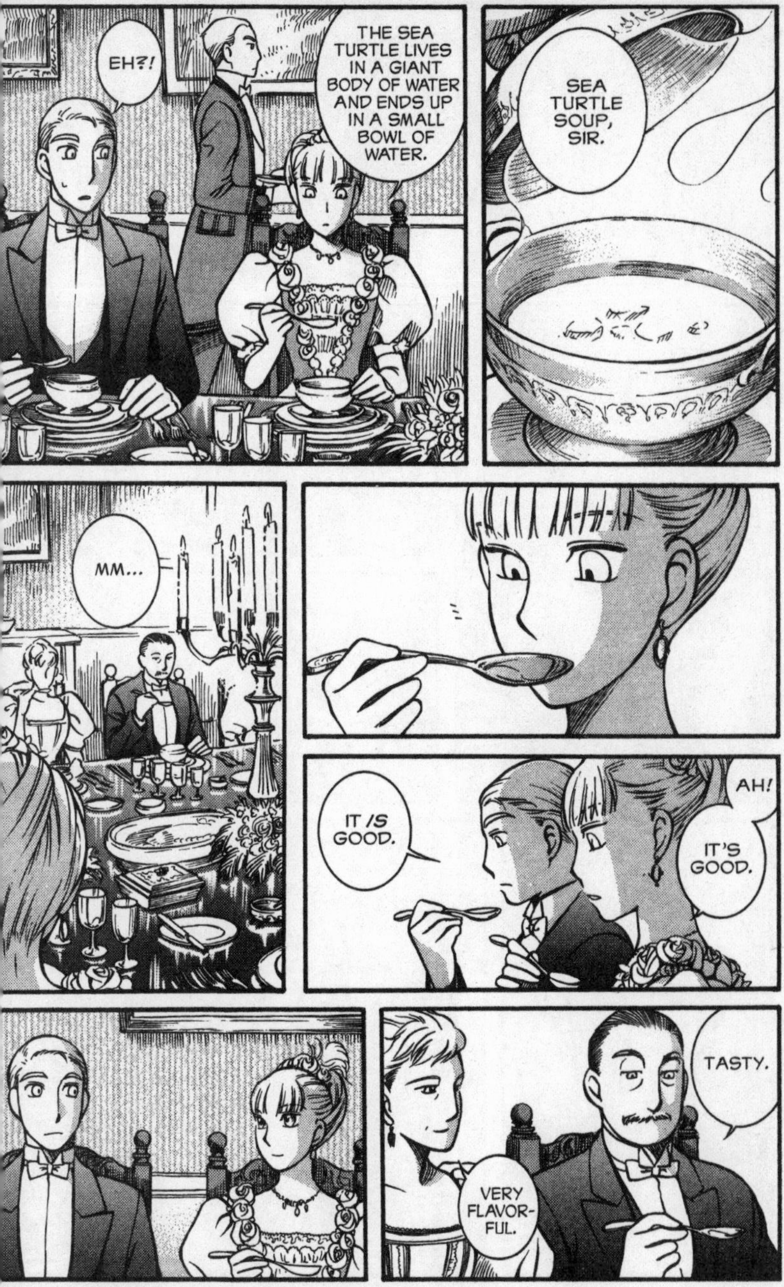
SEA TURTLE SOUP, SIR.
THE SEA TURTLE LIVES IN A GIANT BODY OF WATER AND ENDS UP IN A SMALL BOWL OF WATER.
EH?!
AH!
IT'S GOOD.
IT IS GOOD.
MM...
TASTY.
VERY FLAVOR-FUL.

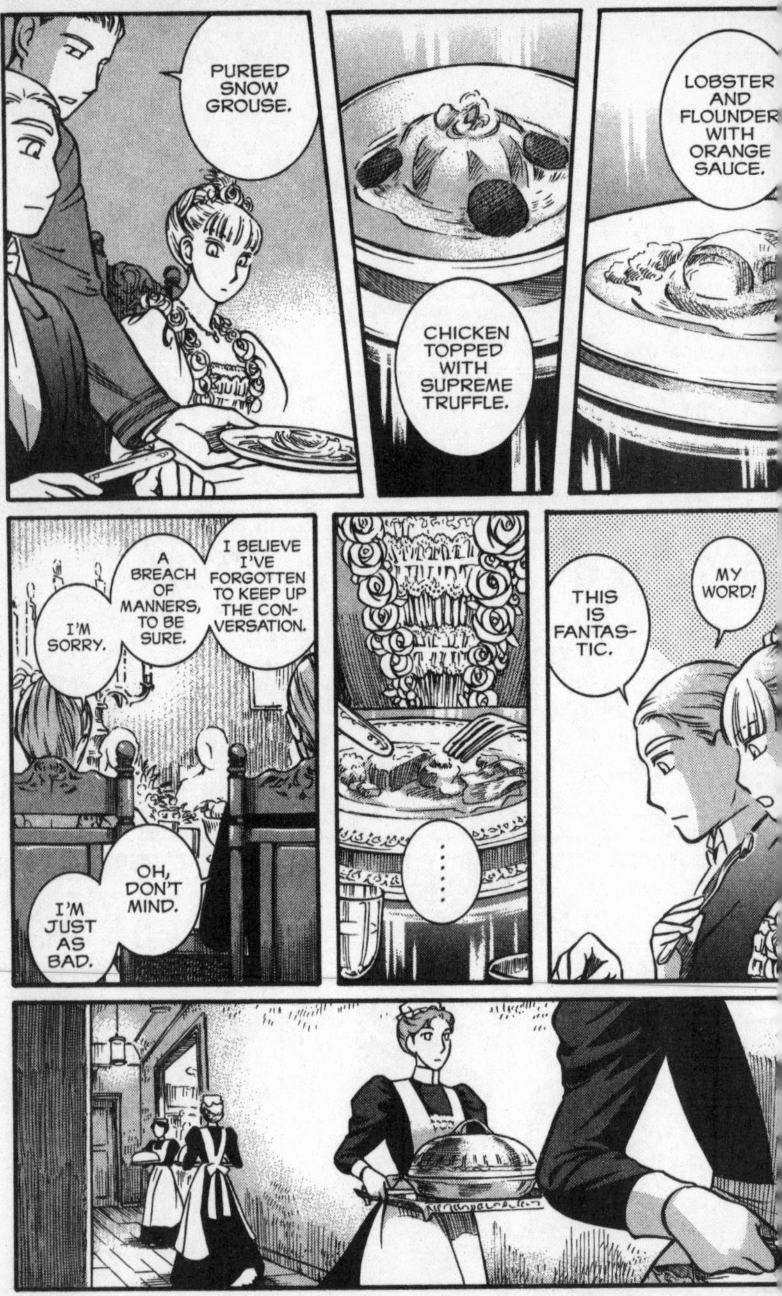
LOBSTER AND FLOUNDER WITH ORANGE SAUCE.
CHICKEN TOPPED WITH SUPREME TRUFFLE.
PUREED SNOW GROUSE.
MY WORD!
THIS IS FANTASTIC.
......
I BELIEVE I'VE FORGOTTEN TO KEEP UP THE CONVERSATION.
A BREACH OF MANNERS, TO BE SURE.
I'M SORRY.
OH, DON'T MIND.
I'M JUST AS BAD.

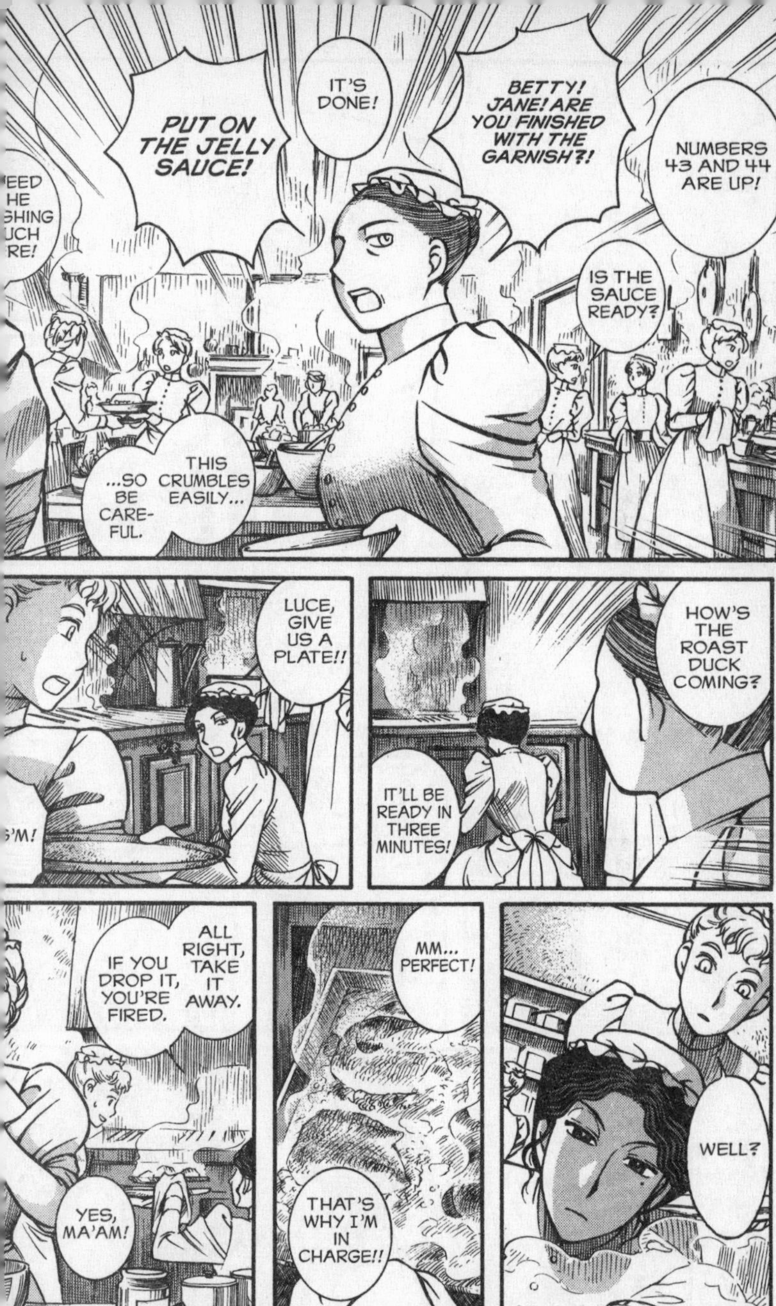
NUMBERS 43 AND 44 ARE UP!
IS THE SAUCE READY?
BETTY! JANE! ARE YOU FINISHED WITH THE GARNISH?!
IT'S DONE!
PUT ON THE JELLY SAUCE!
THIS CRUMBLES EASILY...
...SO BE CAREFUL.
HOW'S THE ROAST DUCK COMING?
IT'LL BE READY IN THREE MINUTES!
LUCE, GIVE US A PLATE!!
WELL?
MM... PERFECT!
THAT'S WHY I'M IN CHARGE!!
ALL RIGHT, TAKE IT AWAY.
IF YOU DROP IT, YOU'RE FIRED.
YES, MA'AM!

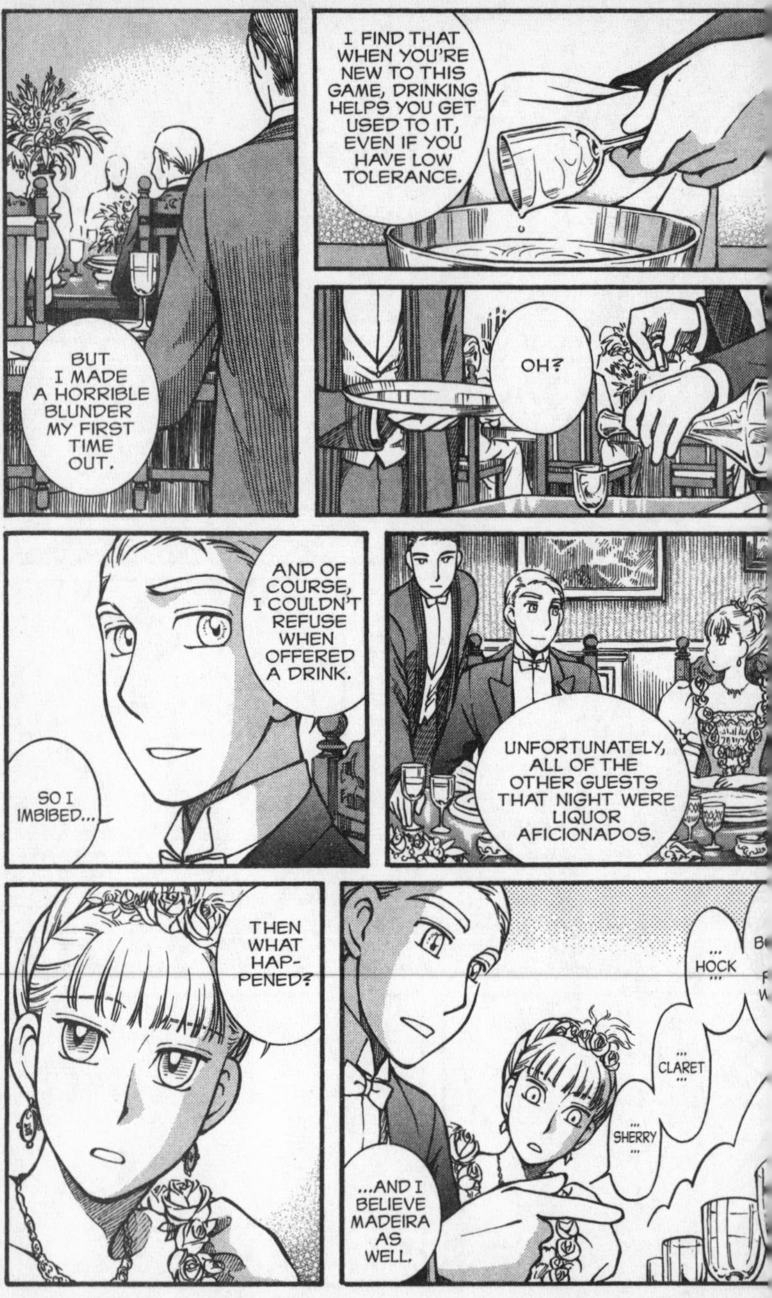
I FIND THAT WHEN YOU'RE NEW TO THIS GAME, DRINKING HELPS YOU GET USED TO IT, EVEN IF YOU HAVE LOW TOLERANCE.
OH?
BUT I MADE A HORRIBLE BLUNDER MY FIRST TIME OUT.
UNFORTUNATELY, ALL OF THE OTHER GUESTS THAT NIGHT WERE LIQUOR AFICIONADOS.
AND OF COURSE, I COULDN'T REFUSE WHEN OFFERED A DRINK.
SO I IMBIBED...
... HOCK ...
... CLARET ...
... SHERRY ...
...AND I BELIEVE MADEIRA AS WELL.
THEN WHAT HAP-PENED?

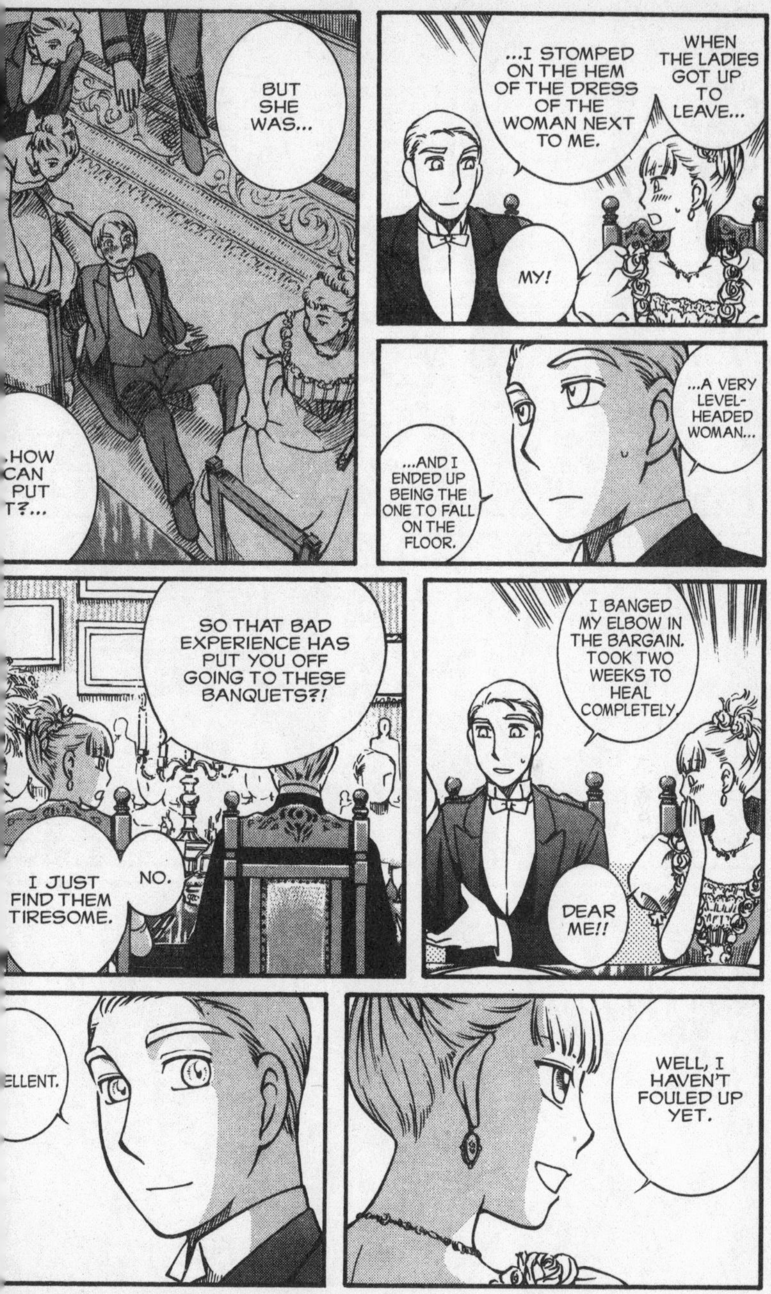
WHEN THE LADIES GOT UP TO LEAVE...
...I STOMPED ON THE HEM OF THE DRESS OF THE WOMAN NEXT TO ME.
MY!
...A VERY LEVEL-HEADED WOMAN...
...AND I ENDED UP BEING THE ONE TO FALL ON THE FLOOR.
BUT SHE WAS...
.HOW CAN PUT T?...
I BANGED MY ELBOW IN THE BARGAIN. TOOK TWO WEEKS TO HEAL COMPLETELY.
DEAR ME!!
SO THAT BAD EXPERIENCE HAS PUT YOU OFF GOING TO THESE BANQUETS?!
NO.
I JUST FIND THEM TIRESOME.
WELL, I HAVEN'T FOULED UP YET.
ELLENT.

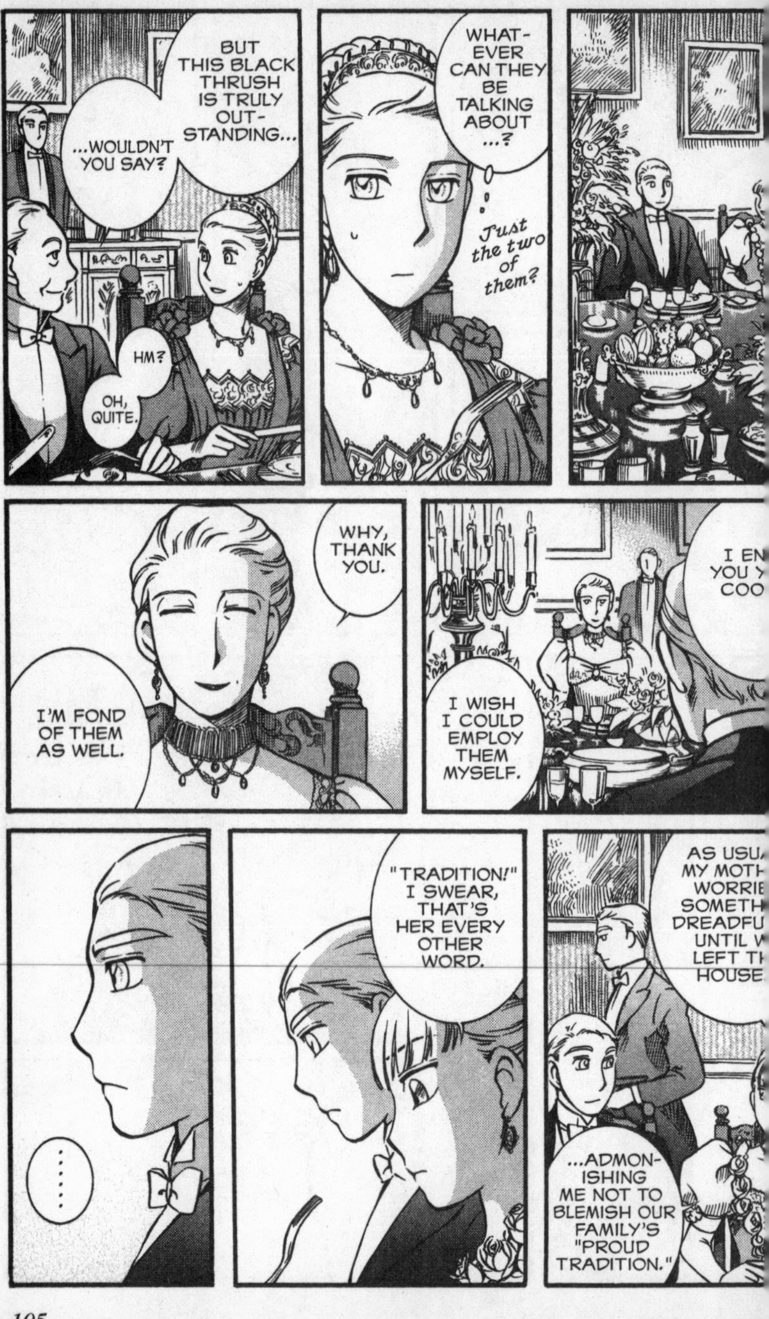
WHATEVER CAN THEY BE TALKING ABOUT...?
Just the two of them?
BUT THIS BLACK THRUSH IS TRULY OUTSTANDING...
...WOULDN'T YOU SAY?
HM?
OH, QUITE.
I EN YOU Y COO
I WISH I COULD EMPLOY THEM MYSELF.
WHY, THANK YOU.
I'M FOND OF THEM AS WELL.
AS USU MY MOTH WORRIE SOMETH DREADFU UNTIL W LEFT TH HOUSE
...ADMONISHING ME NOT TO BLEMISH OUR FAMILY'S "PROUD TRADITION."
"TRADITION!" I SWEAR, THAT'S HER EVERY OTHER WORD.
......

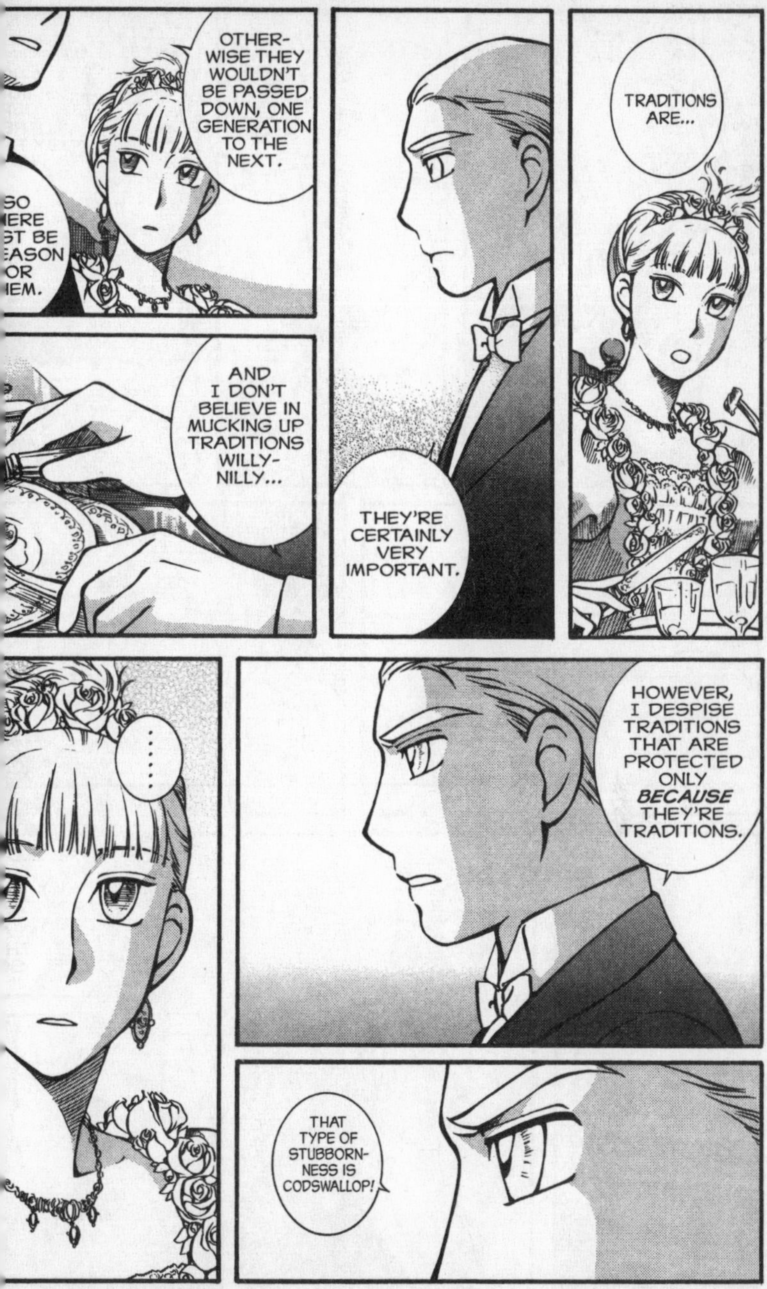
TRADITIONS ARE...
THEY'RE CERTAINLY VERY IMPORTANT.
OTHER-WISE THEY WOULDN'T BE PASSED DOWN, ONE GENERATION TO THE NEXT.
SO HERE ST BE EASON OR HEM.
AND I DON'T BELIEVE IN MUCKING UP TRADITIONS WILLY-NILLY...
HOWEVER, I DESPISE TRADITIONS THAT ARE PROTECTED ONLY *BECAUSE* THEY'RE TRADITIONS.
THAT TYPE OF STUBBORN-NESS IS CODSWALLOP!
......

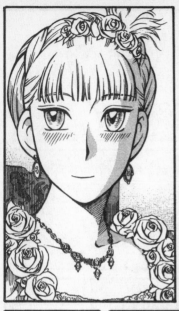

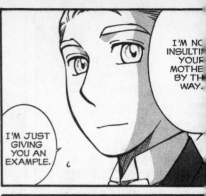

I'M NO[T]
INSULTIN[G]
YOUR
MOTHE[R]
BY TH[E]
WAY.

I'M JUST
GIVING
YOU AN
EXAMPLE.

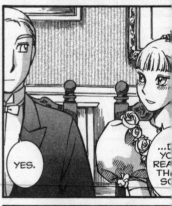

IN [MY]
OPIN[ION]
ANYW[AY]

...YOUR
MOTHER HAS
NOTHING TO
WORRY ABOUT WITH
YOU.

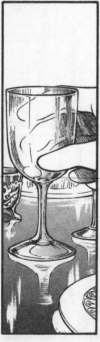

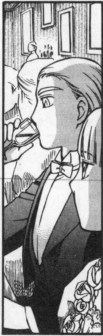

YES.

...D[O]
YO[U]
REA[LLY]
TH[INK]
SO[?]

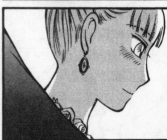

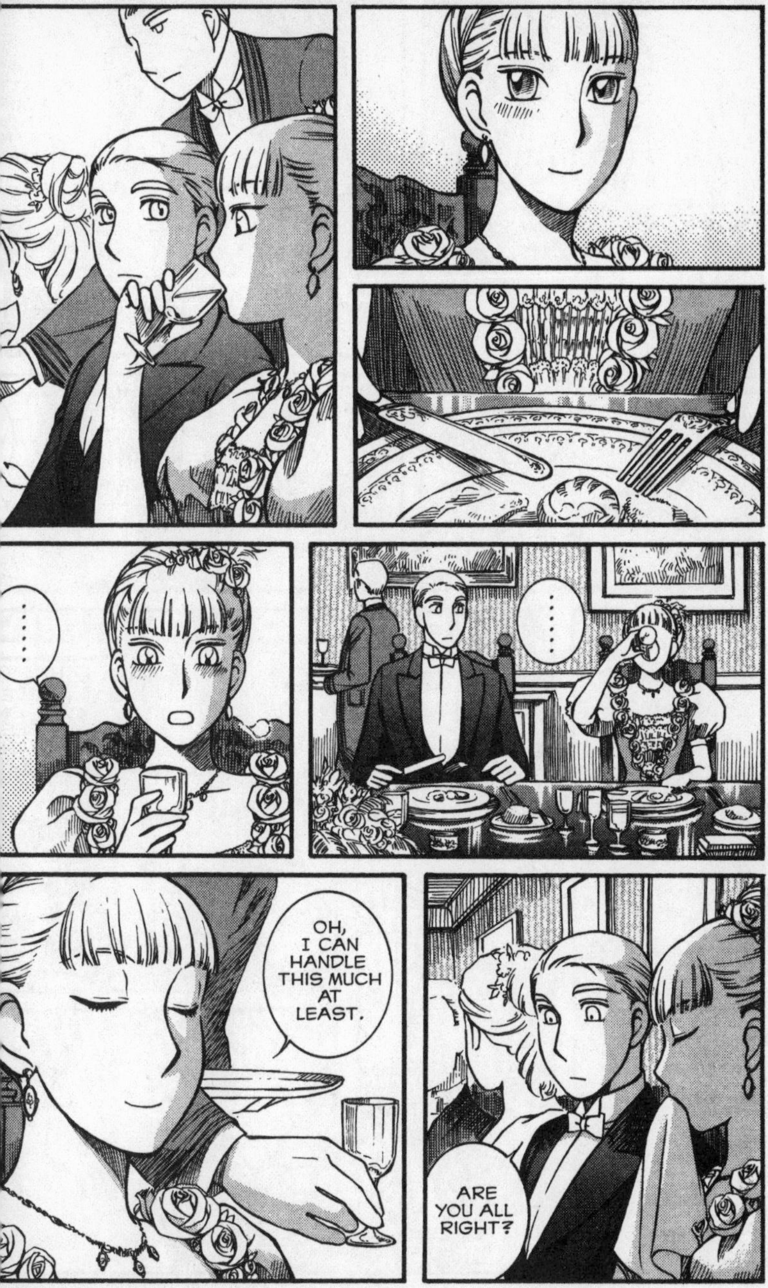
......
......
ARE YOU ALL RIGHT?
OH, I CAN HANDLE THIS MUCH AT LEAST.

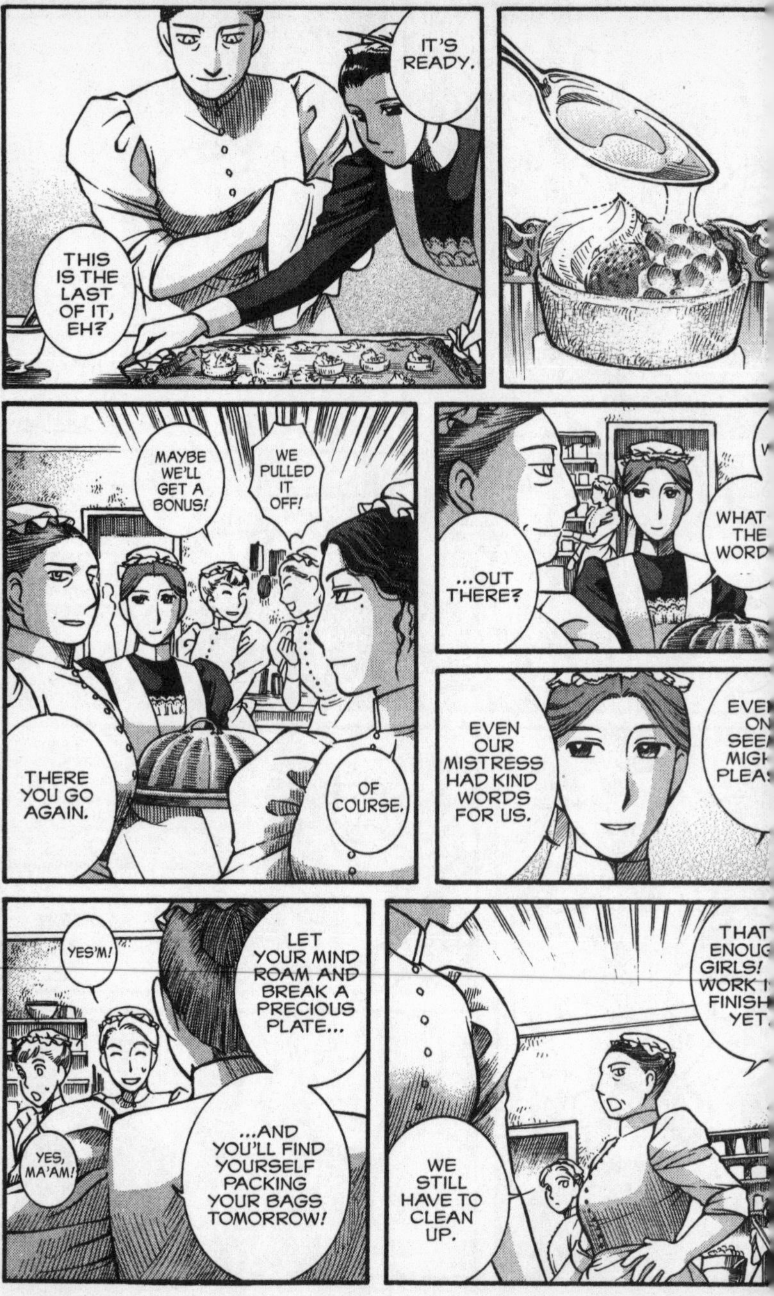
IT'S READY.
THIS IS THE LAST OF IT, EH?
WHAT THE WORD
...OUT THERE?
EVE ON SEE MIGH PLEA
EVEN OUR MISTRESS HAD KIND WORDS FOR US.
WE PULLED IT OFF!
MAYBE WE'LL GET A BONUS!
OF COURSE.
THERE YOU GO AGAIN.
THAT ENOUG GIRLS! WORK I FINISH YET.
WE STILL HAVE TO CLEAN UP.
LET YOUR MIND ROAM AND BREAK A PRECIOUS PLATE...
...AND YOU'LL FIND YOURSELF PACKING YOUR BAGS TOMORROW!
YES'M!
YES, MA'AM!

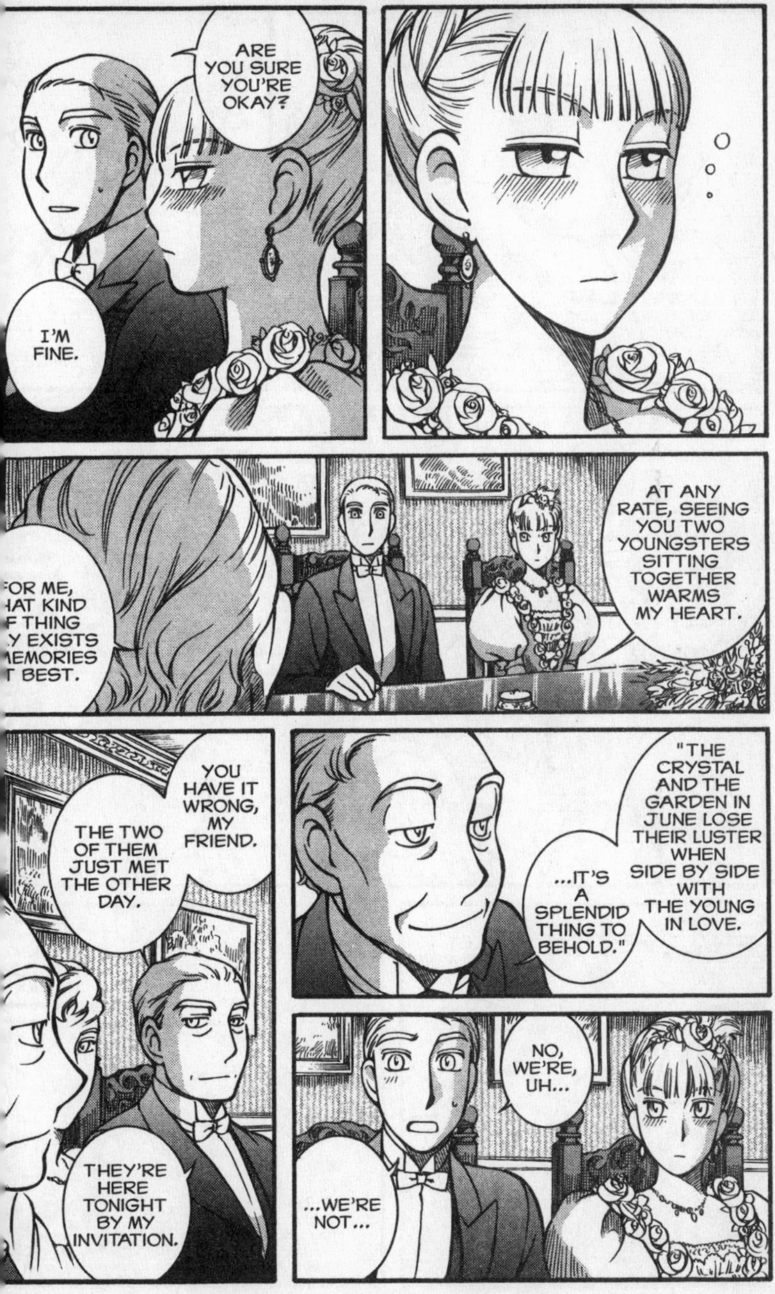
ARE YOU SURE YOU'RE OKAY?
I'M FINE.
AT ANY RATE, SEEING YOU TWO YOUNGSTERS SITTING TOGETHER WARMS MY HEART.
FOR ME, HAT KIND F THING Y EXISTS MEMORIES T BEST.
"THE CRYSTAL AND THE GARDEN IN JUNE LOSE THEIR LUSTER WHEN SIDE BY SIDE WITH THE YOUNG IN LOVE.
...IT'S A SPLENDID THING TO BEHOLD."
NO, WE'RE, UH...
...WE'RE NOT...
YOU HAVE IT WRONG, MY FRIEND.
THE TWO OF THEM JUST MET THE OTHER DAY.
THEY'RE HERE TONIGHT BY MY INVITATION.

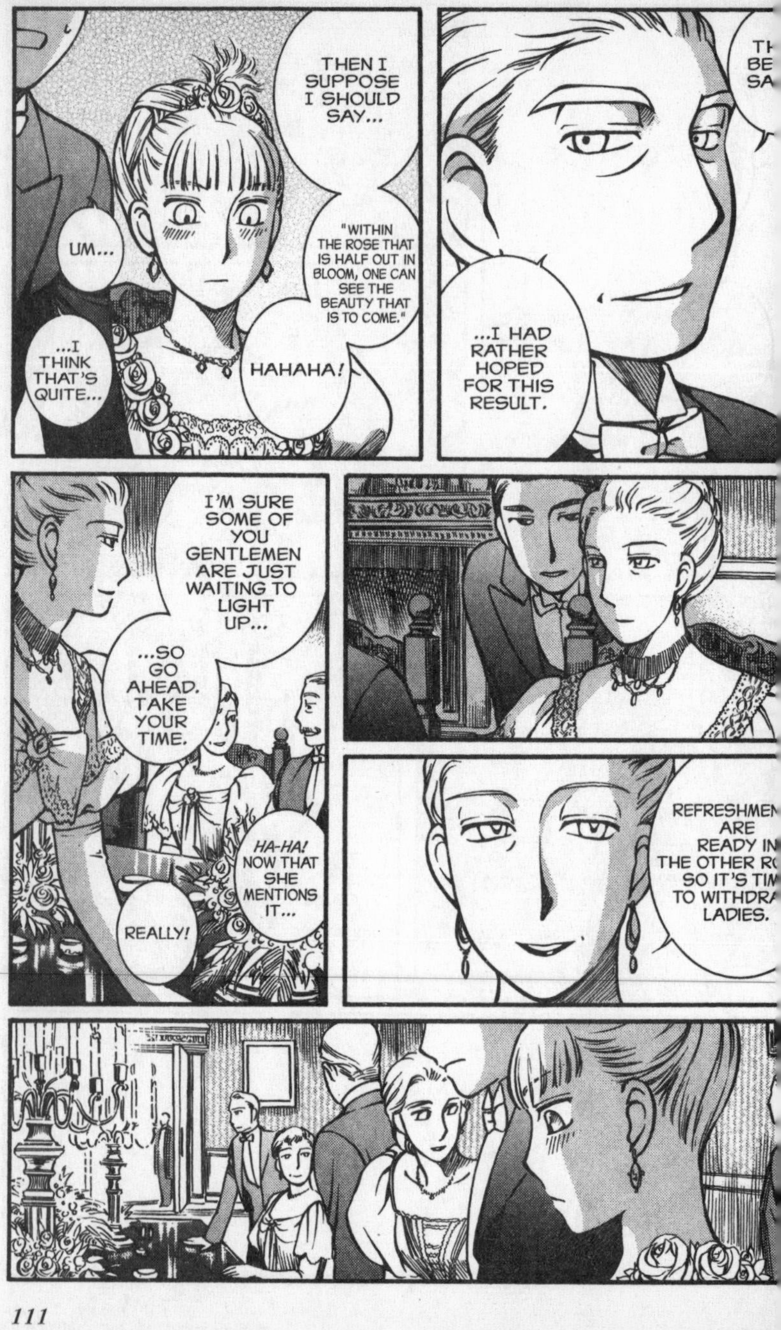
TH BE SA
...I HAD RATHER HOPED FOR THIS RESULT.
THEN I SUPPOSE I SHOULD SAY...
"WITHIN THE ROSE THAT IS HALF OUT IN BLOOM, ONE CAN SEE THE BEAUTY THAT IS TO COME."
HAHAHA!
UM...
...I THINK THAT'S QUITE...
REFRESHMEN ARE READY IN THE OTHER R SO IT'S TIM TO WITHDRA LADIES.
I'M SURE SOME OF YOU GENTLEMEN ARE JUST WAITING TO LIGHT UP...
...SO GO AHEAD. TAKE YOUR TIME.
HA-HA! NOW THAT SHE MENTIONS IT...
REALLY!

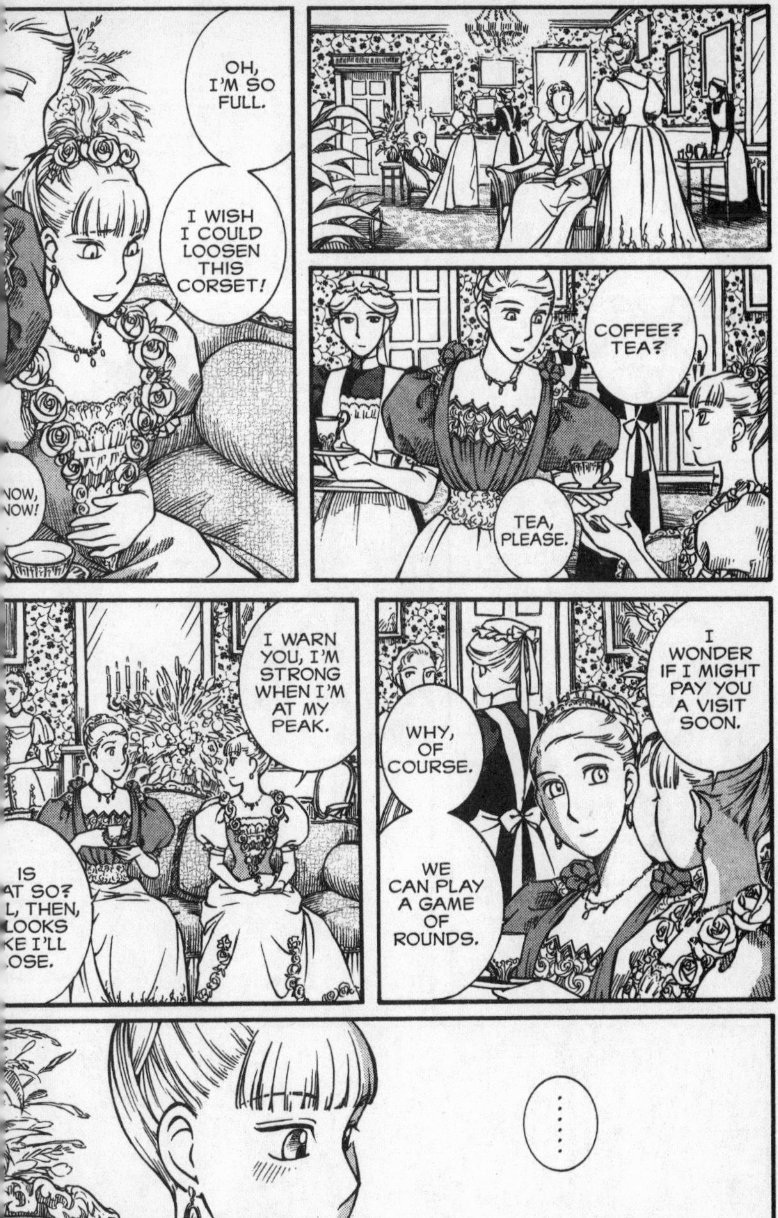
COFFEE? TEA?
TEA, PLEASE.
OH, I'M SO FULL.
I WISH I COULD LOOSEN THIS CORSET!
NOW, NOW!
I WONDER IF I MIGHT PAY YOU A VISIT SOON.
WHY, OF COURSE.
WE CAN PLAY A GAME OF ROUNDS.
I WARN YOU, I'M STRONG WHEN I'M AT MY PEAK.
IS AT SO? L, THEN, LOOKS KE I'LL OSE.
......

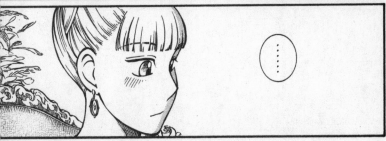

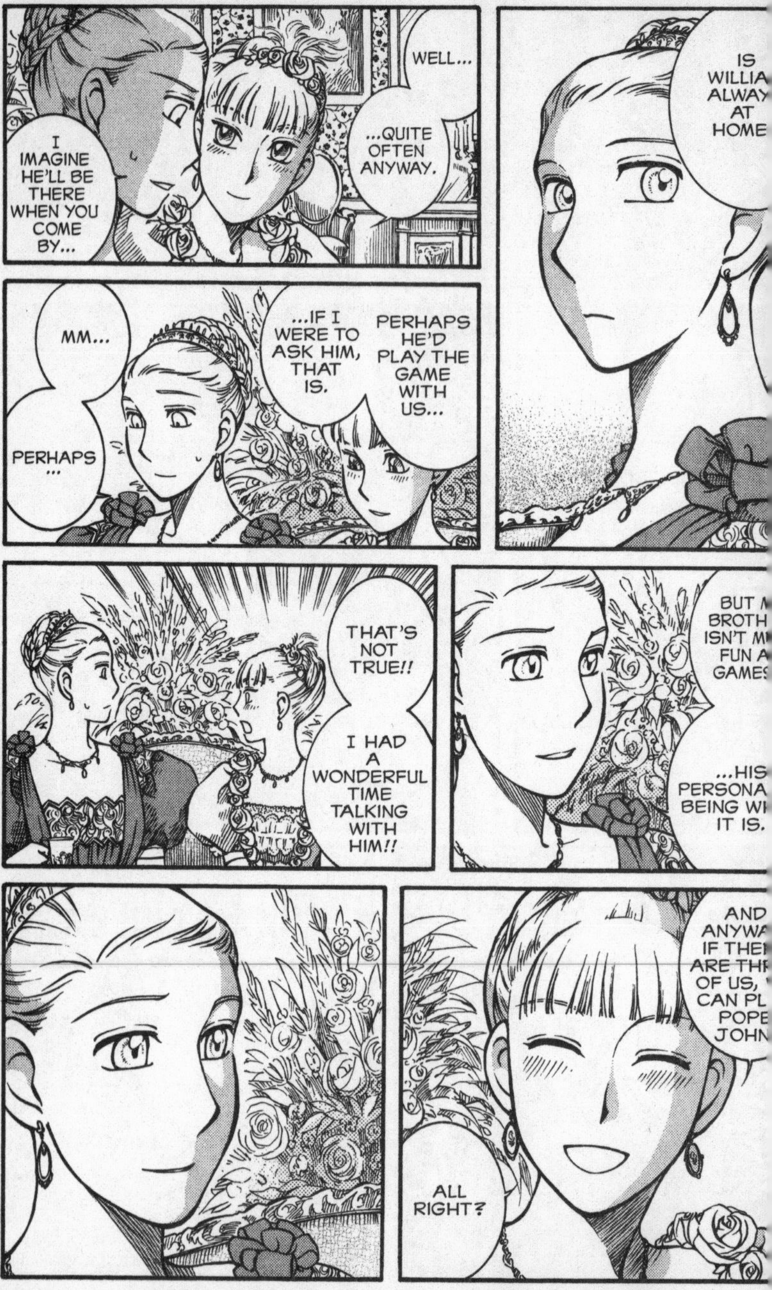

IS WILLIA ALWAY AT HOME
WELL...
...QUITE OFTEN ANYWAY.
I IMAGINE HE'LL BE THERE WHEN YOU COME BY...
PERHAPS HE'D PLAY THE GAME WITH US...
...IF I WERE TO ASK HIM, THAT IS.
MM...
PERHAPS...
BUT M BROTH ISN'T M FUN A GAMES
...HIS PERSONA BEING WI IT IS.
THAT'S NOT TRUE!!
I HAD A WONDERFUL TIME TALKING WITH HIM!!
AND ANYWA IF THE ARE TH OF US, CAN PL POPE JOHN
ALL RIGHT?

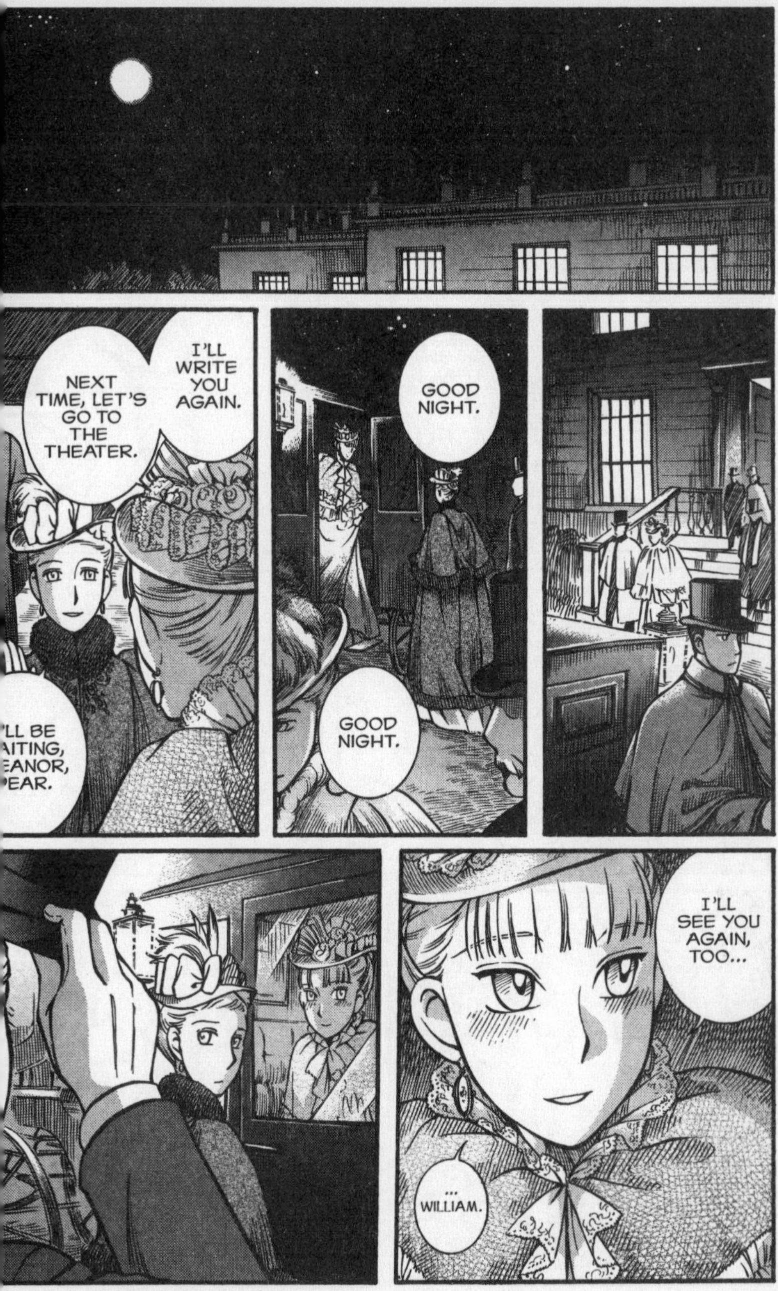
GOOD NIGHT.
GOOD NIGHT.
I'LL WRITE YOU AGAIN.
NEXT TIME, LET'S GO TO THE THEATER.
'LL BE AITING, EANOR, EAR.
I'LL SEE YOU AGAIN, TOO...
... WILLIAM.

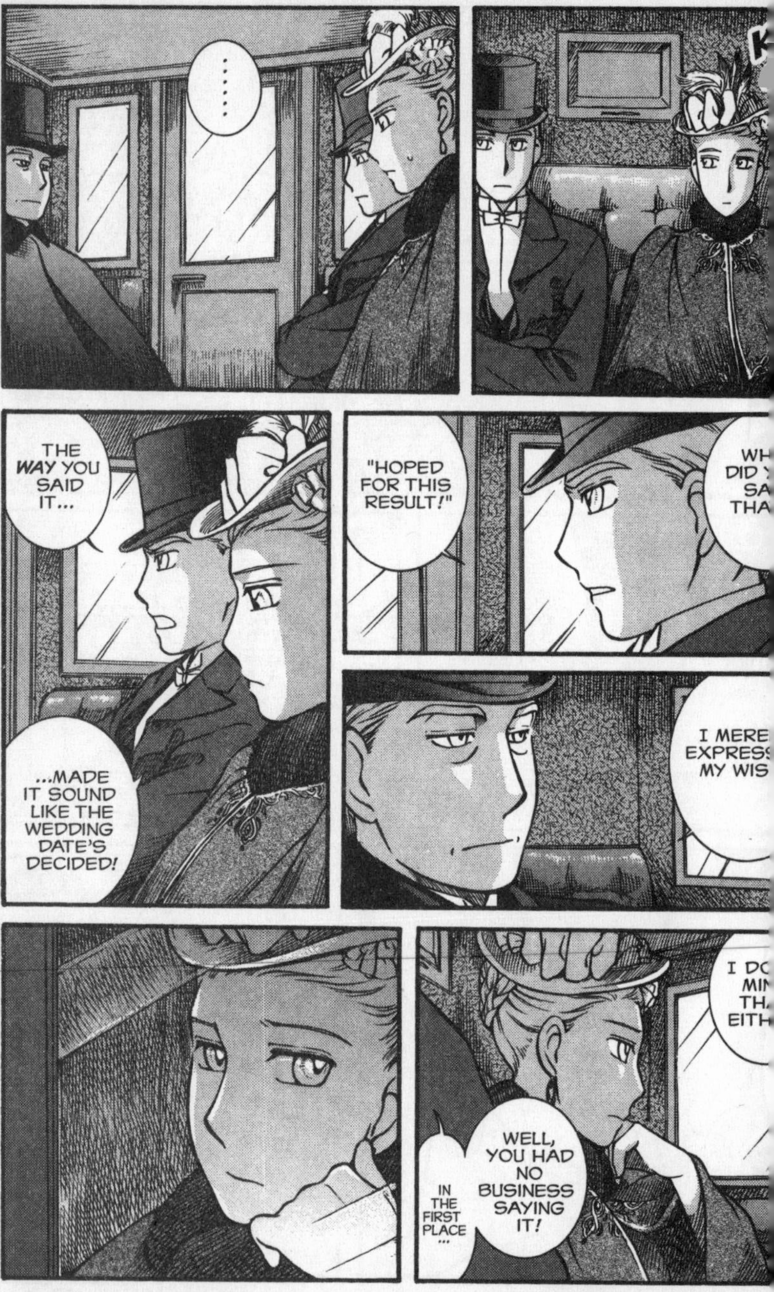
……
"HOPED FOR THIS RESULT!"
THE *WAY* YOU SAID IT...
...MADE IT SOUND LIKE THE WEDDING DATE'S DECIDED!
WELL, YOU HAD NO BUSINESS SAYING IT!
IN THE FIRST PLACE...

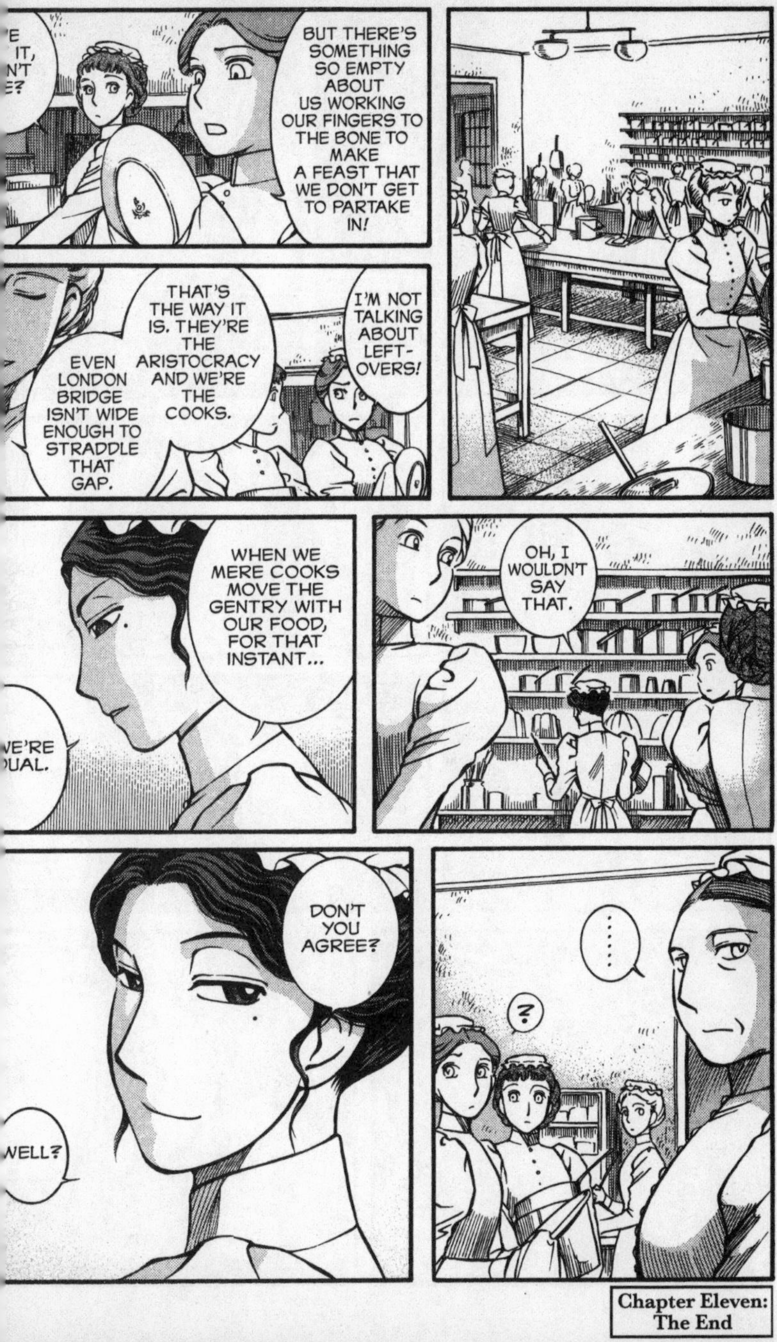
BUT THERE'S SOMETHING SO EMPTY ABOUT US WORKING OUR FINGERS TO THE BONE TO MAKE A FEAST THAT WE DON'T GET TO PARTAKE IN!
I'M NOT TALKING ABOUT LEFT-OVERS!
THAT'S THE WAY IT IS. THEY'RE THE ARISTOCRACY AND WE'RE THE COOKS.
EVEN LONDON BRIDGE ISN'T WIDE ENOUGH TO STRADDLE THAT GAP.
OH, I WOULDN'T SAY THAT.
WHEN WE MERE COOKS MOVE THE GENTRY WITH OUR FOOD, FOR THAT INSTANT...
......
?
DON'T YOU AGREE?
WELL?

Chapter Eleven: The End

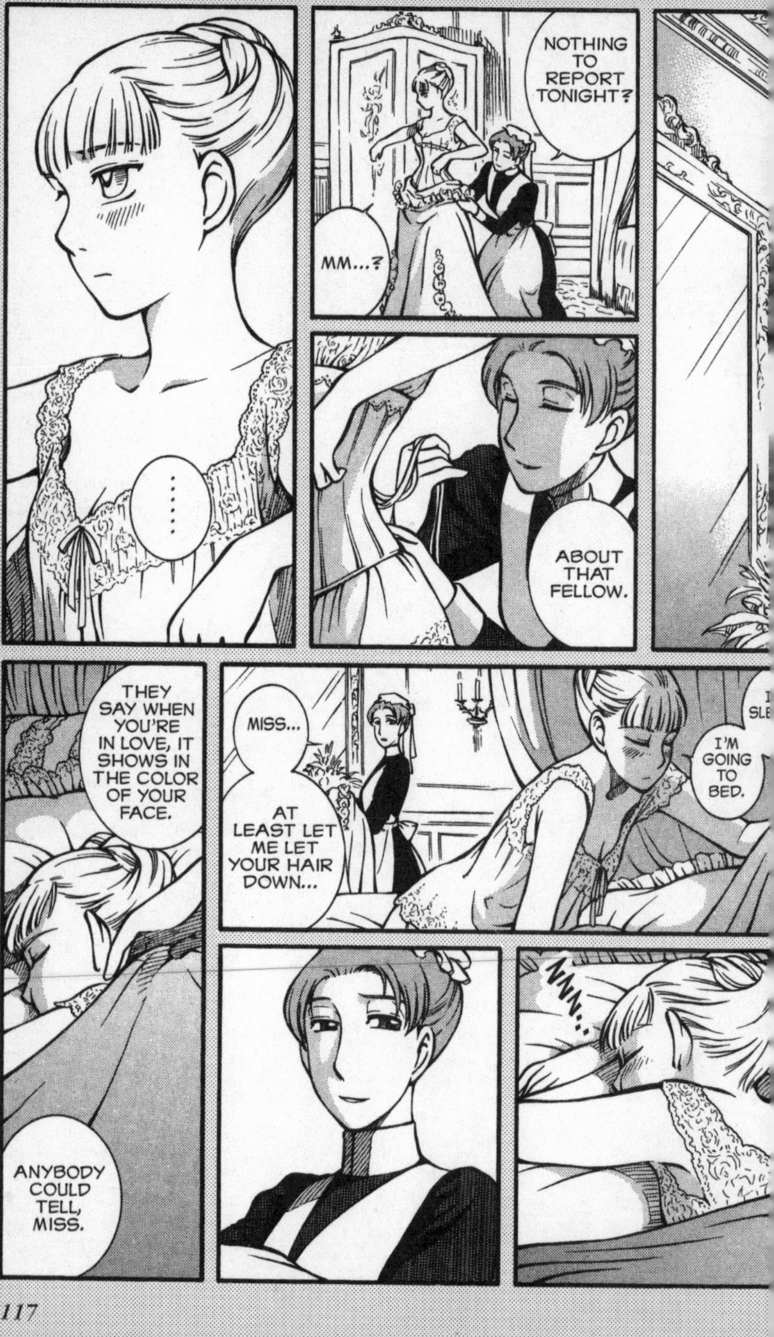
NOTHING TO REPORT TONIGHT?
MM...?
ABOUT THAT FELLOW.
......
I SLE
I'M GOING TO BED.
MISS...
AT LEAST LET ME LET YOUR HAIR DOWN...
NNN...
THEY SAY WHEN YOU'RE IN LOVE, IT SHOWS IN THE COLOR OF YOUR FACE.
ANYBODY COULD TELL, MISS.

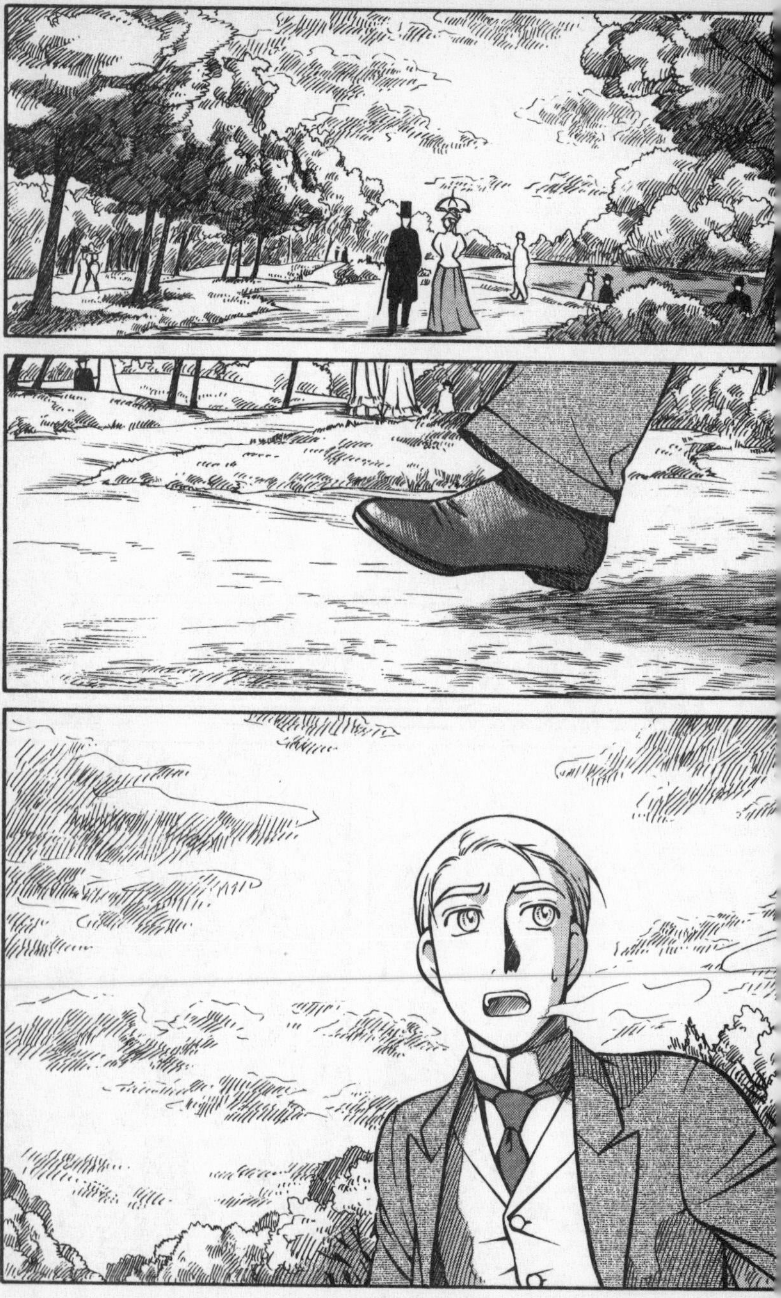

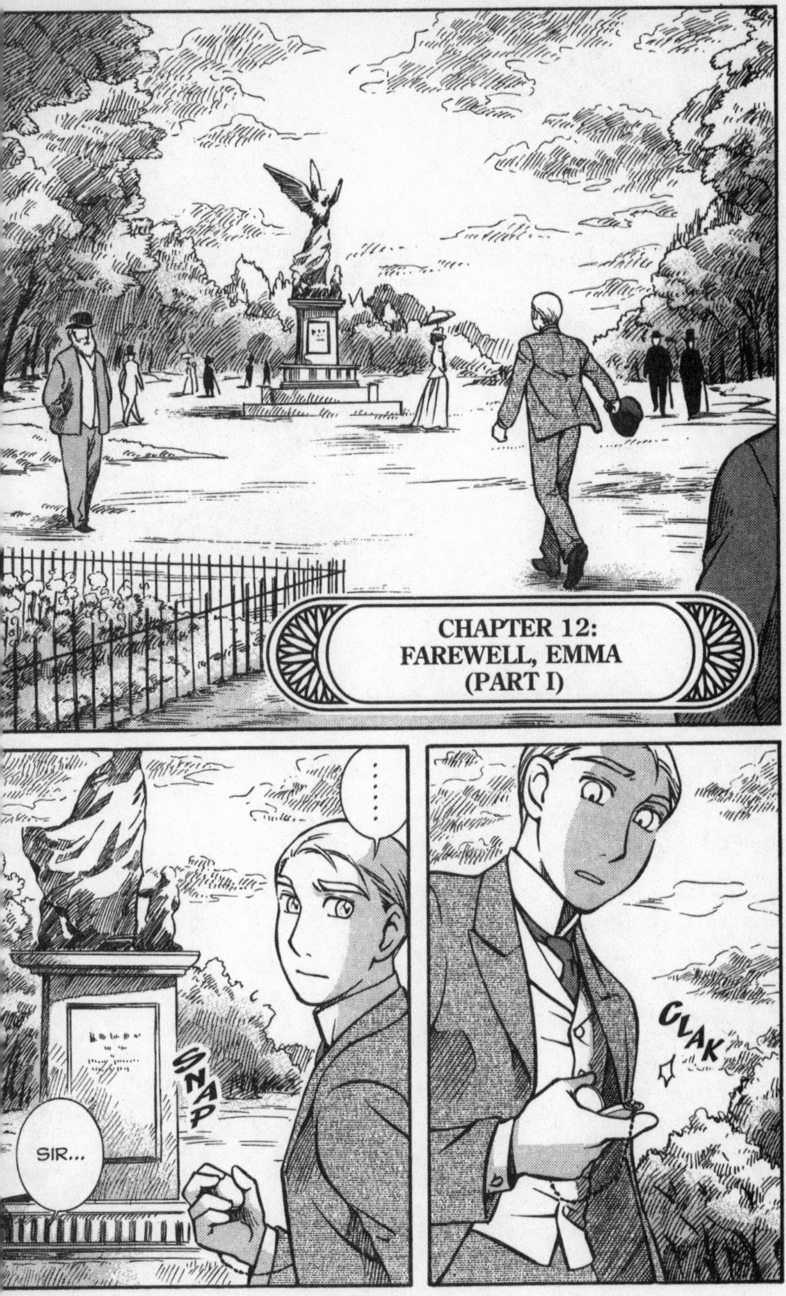
CHAPTER 12:
FAREWELL, EMMA
(PART I)
CLAK
......
SNAP
SIR...

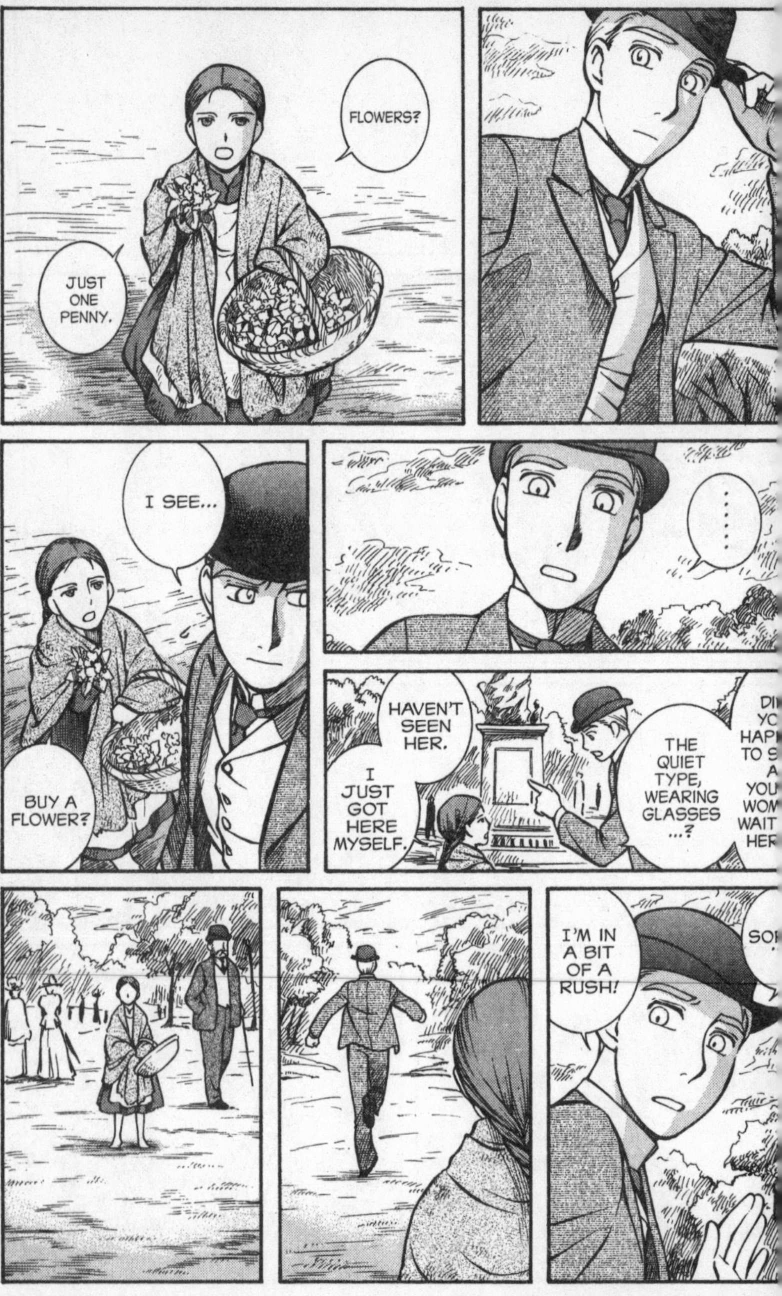
FLOWERS?
JUST ONE PENNY.
......
DI YO HAP TO S A YOU WOM WAIT HER
THE QUIET TYPE, WEARING GLASSES ...?
HAVEN'T SEEN HER.
I JUST GOT HERE MYSELF.
I SEE...
BUY A FLOWER?
SO
I'M IN A BIT OF A RUSH!

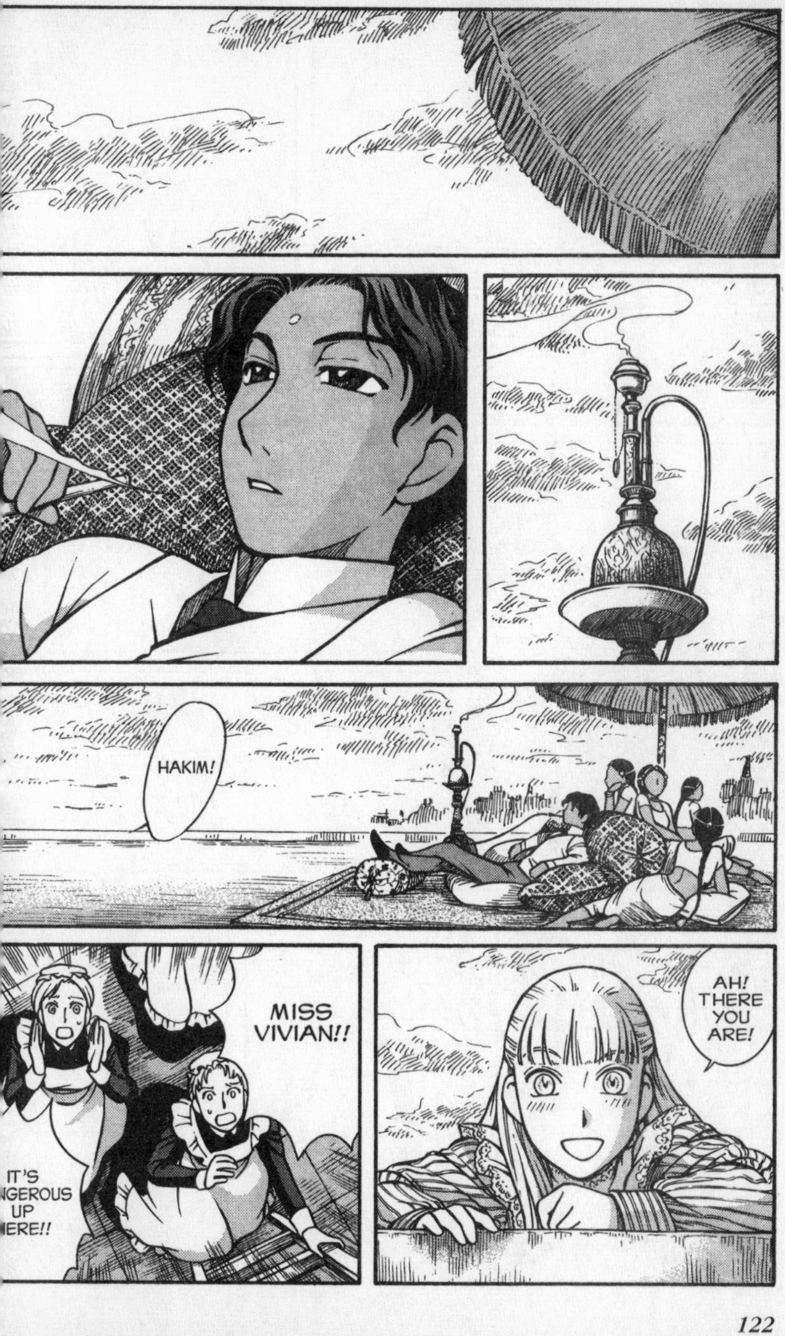
HAKIM!
AH! THERE YOU ARE!
MISS VIVIAN!!
IT'S NGEROUS UP ERE!!

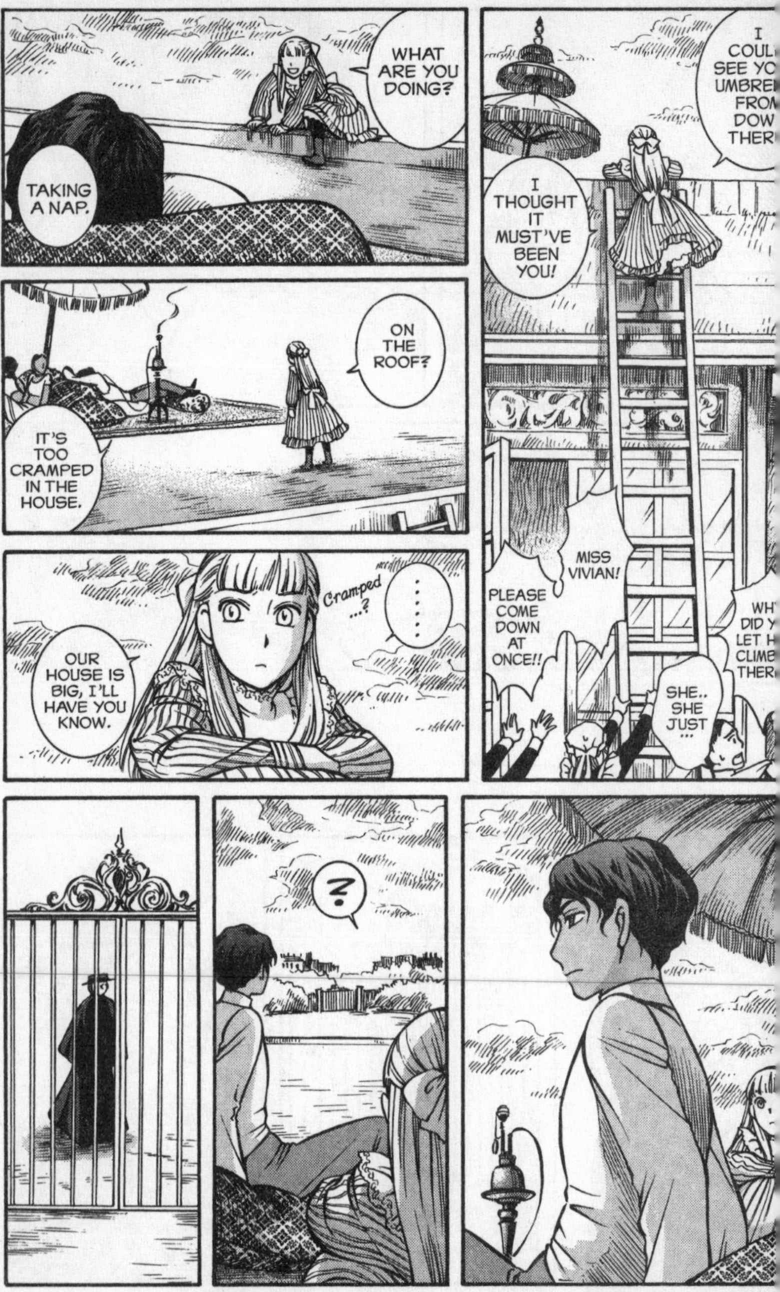
I COUL SEE YO UMBRE FROM DOW THER
I THOUGHT IT MUST'VE BEEN YOU!
MISS VIVIAN!
WH DID Y LET H CLIMB THER
PLEASE COME DOWN AT ONCE!!
SHE.. SHE JUST ...
WHAT ARE YOU DOING?
TAKING A NAP.
ON THE ROOF?
IT'S TOO CRAMPED IN THE HOUSE.
......
Cramped ...?
OUR HOUSE IS BIG, I'LL HAVE YOU KNOW.
?

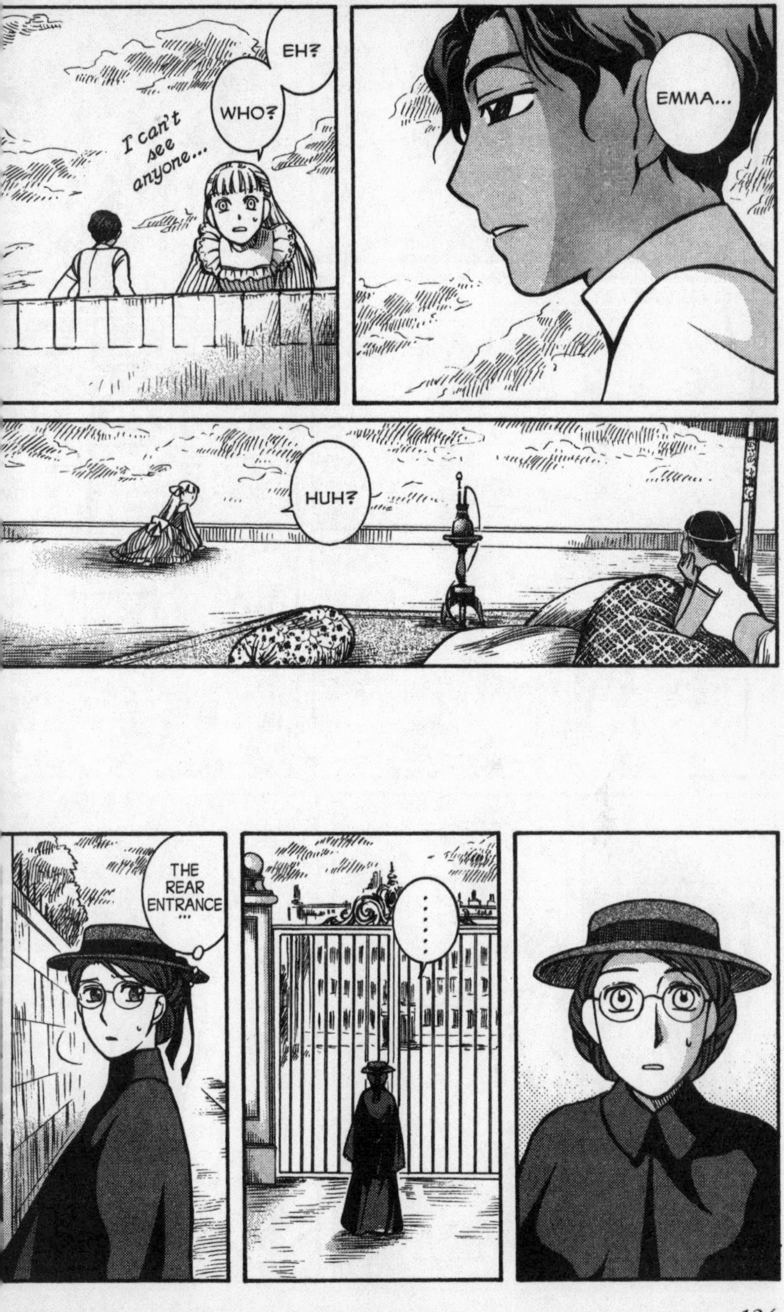
EMMA...
EH?
WHO?
I can't see anyone...
HUH?
......
THE REAR ENTRANCE ...

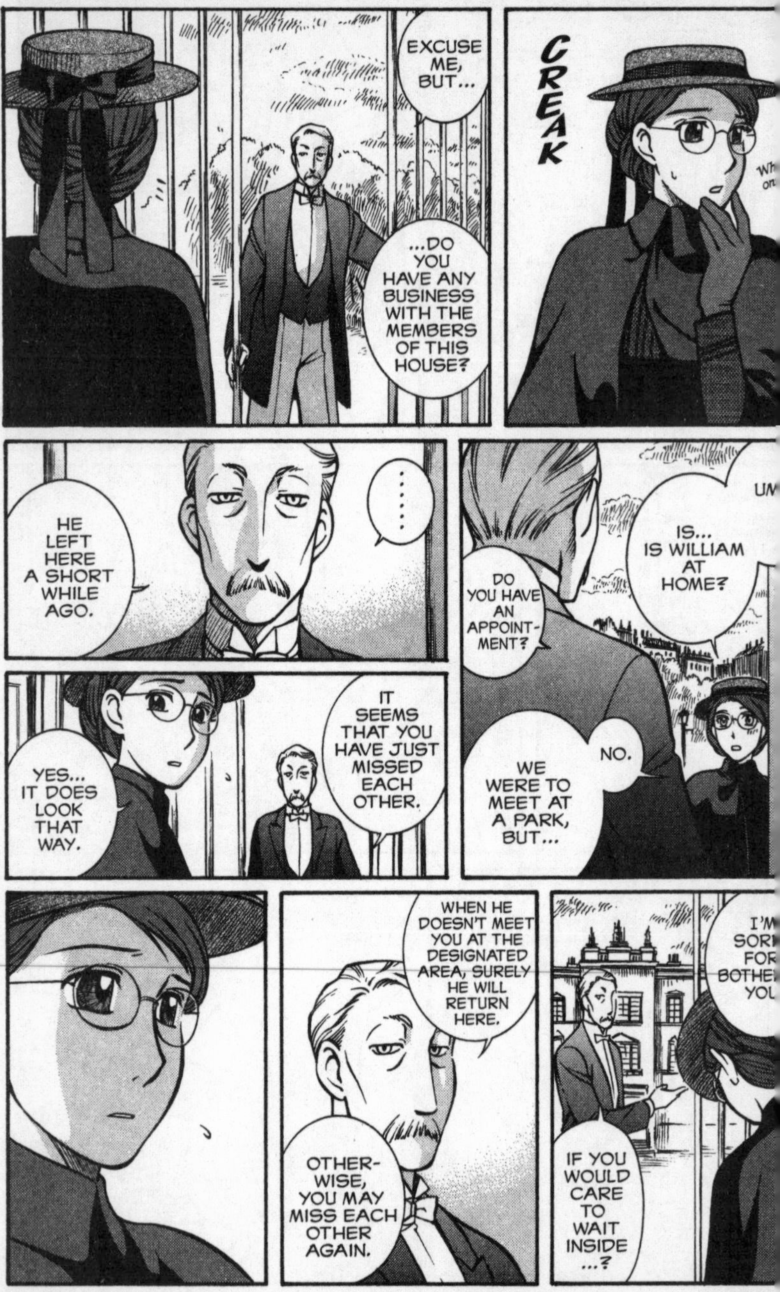
CREAK
EXCUSE ME, BUT...
...DO YOU HAVE ANY BUSINESS WITH THE MEMBERS OF THIS HOUSE?
UM
IS... IS WILLIAM AT HOME?
DO YOU HAVE AN APPOINT-MENT?
NO.
WE WERE TO MEET AT A PARK, BUT...
......
HE LEFT HERE A SHORT WHILE AGO.
IT SEEMS THAT YOU HAVE JUST MISSED EACH OTHER.
YES... IT DOES LOOK THAT WAY.
I'M SOR FOR BOTHE YOU
IF YOU WOULD CARE TO WAIT INSIDE ...?
WHEN HE DOESN'T MEET YOU AT THE DESIGNATED AREA, SURELY HE WILL RETURN HERE.
OTHER-WISE, YOU MAY MISS EACH OTHER AGAIN.

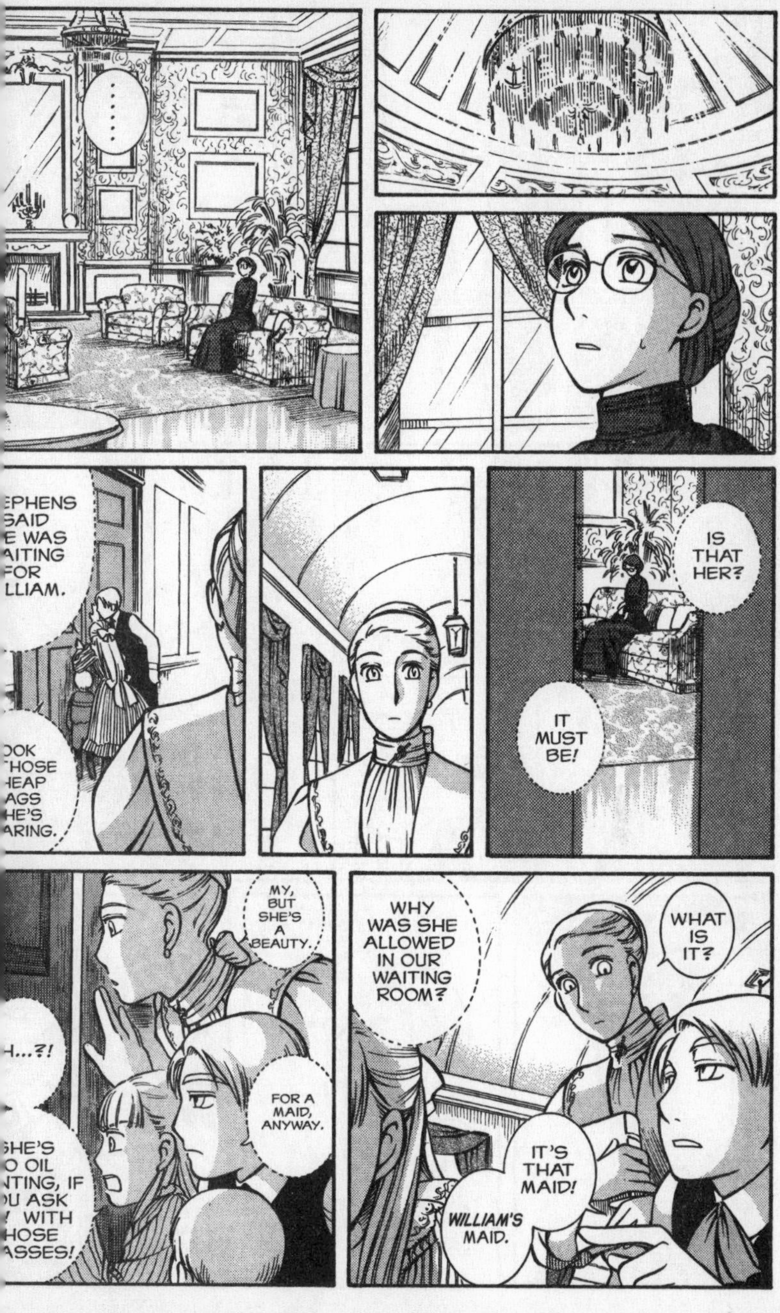
......
IS THAT HER?
IT MUST BE!
EPHENS SAID E WAS AITING FOR LLIAM.
OOK THOSE HEAP AGS HE'S ARING.
WHAT IS IT?
WHY WAS SHE ALLOWED IN OUR WAITING ROOM?
IT'S THAT MAID!
WILLIAM'S MAID.
MY, BUT SHE'S A BEAUTY.
H...?!
FOR A MAID, ANYWAY.
SHE'S O OIL NTING, IF U ASK WITH HOSE ASSES!

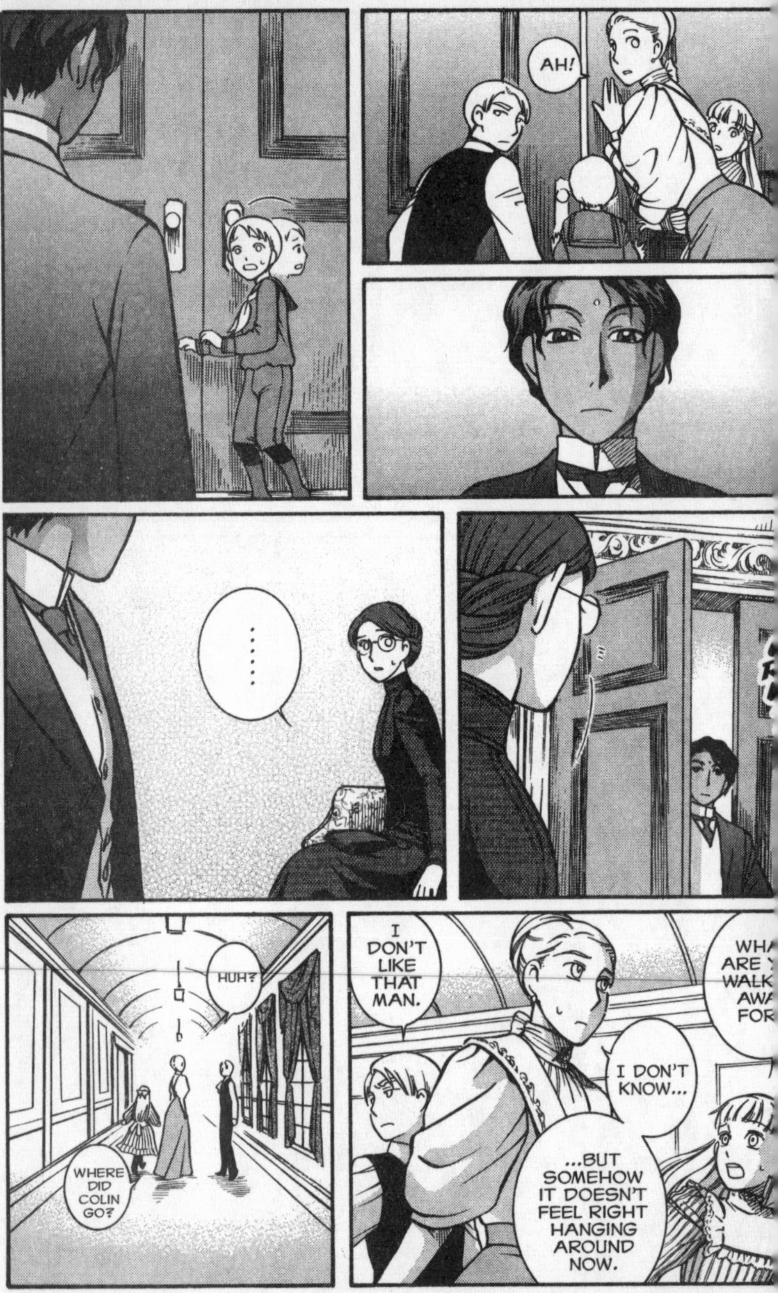
AH!
......
WHA
ARE Y
WALK
AWA
FOR
I DON'T LIKE THAT MAN.
I DON'T KNOW...
...BUT SOMEHOW IT DOESN'T FEEL RIGHT HANGING AROUND NOW.
HUH?
WHERE DID COLIN GO?

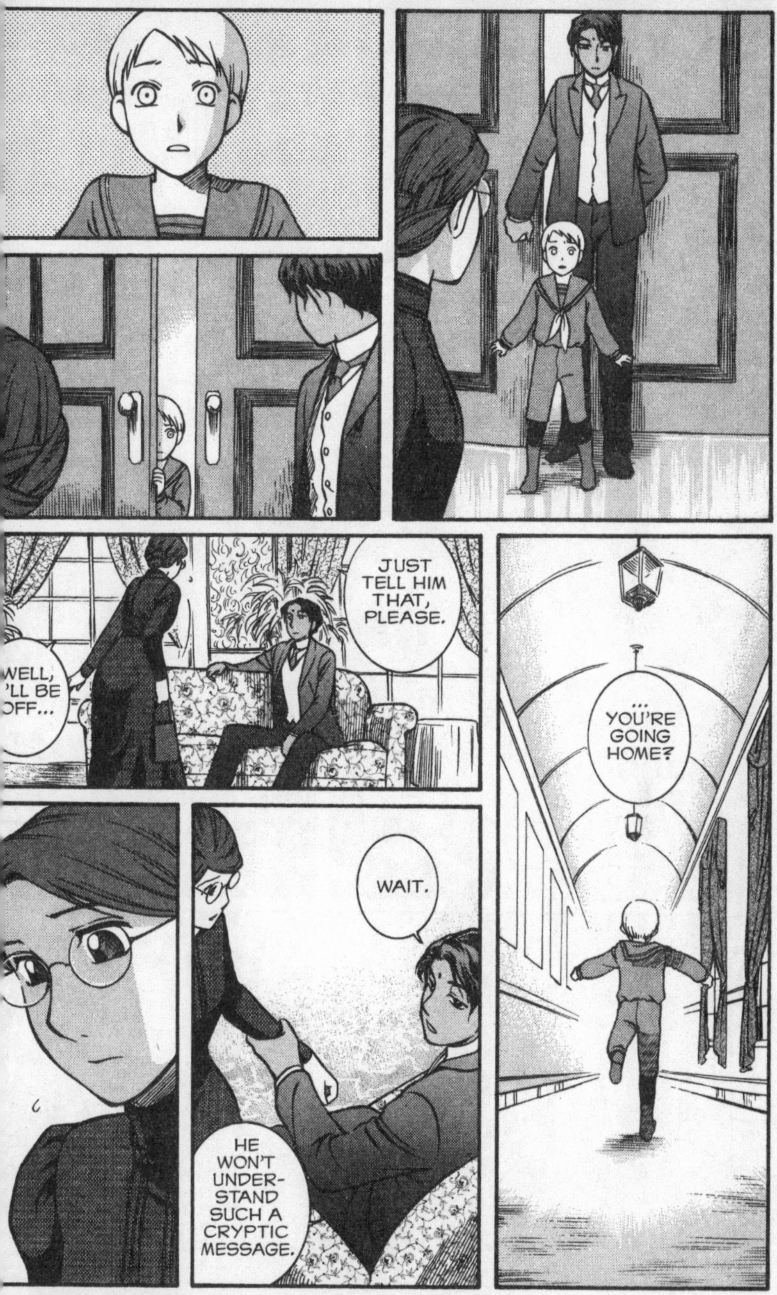
... YOU'RE GOING HOME?
JUST TELL HIM THAT, PLEASE.
WELL, 'LL BE OFF...
WAIT.
HE WON'T UNDER-STAND SUCH A CRYPTIC MESSAGE.

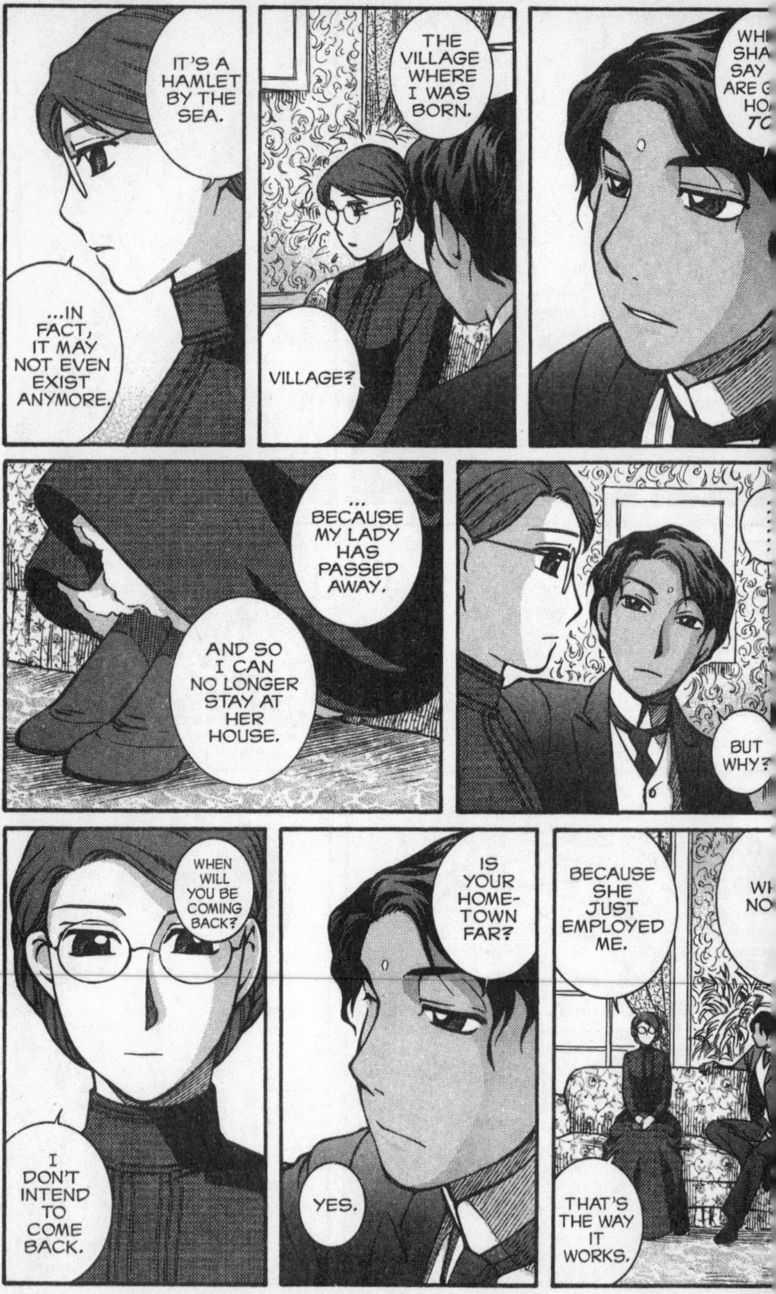
THE VILLAGE WHERE I WAS BORN.
VILLAGE?
IT'S A HAMLET BY THE SEA.
...IN FACT, IT MAY NOT EVEN EXIST ANYMORE.
BUT WHY?
...BECAUSE MY LADY HAS PASSED AWAY.
AND SO I CAN NO LONGER STAY AT HER HOUSE.
BECAUSE SHE JUST EMPLOYED ME.
THAT'S THE WAY IT WORKS.
IS YOUR HOME-TOWN FAR?
YES.
WHEN WILL YOU BE COMING BACK?
I DON'T INTEND TO COME BACK.

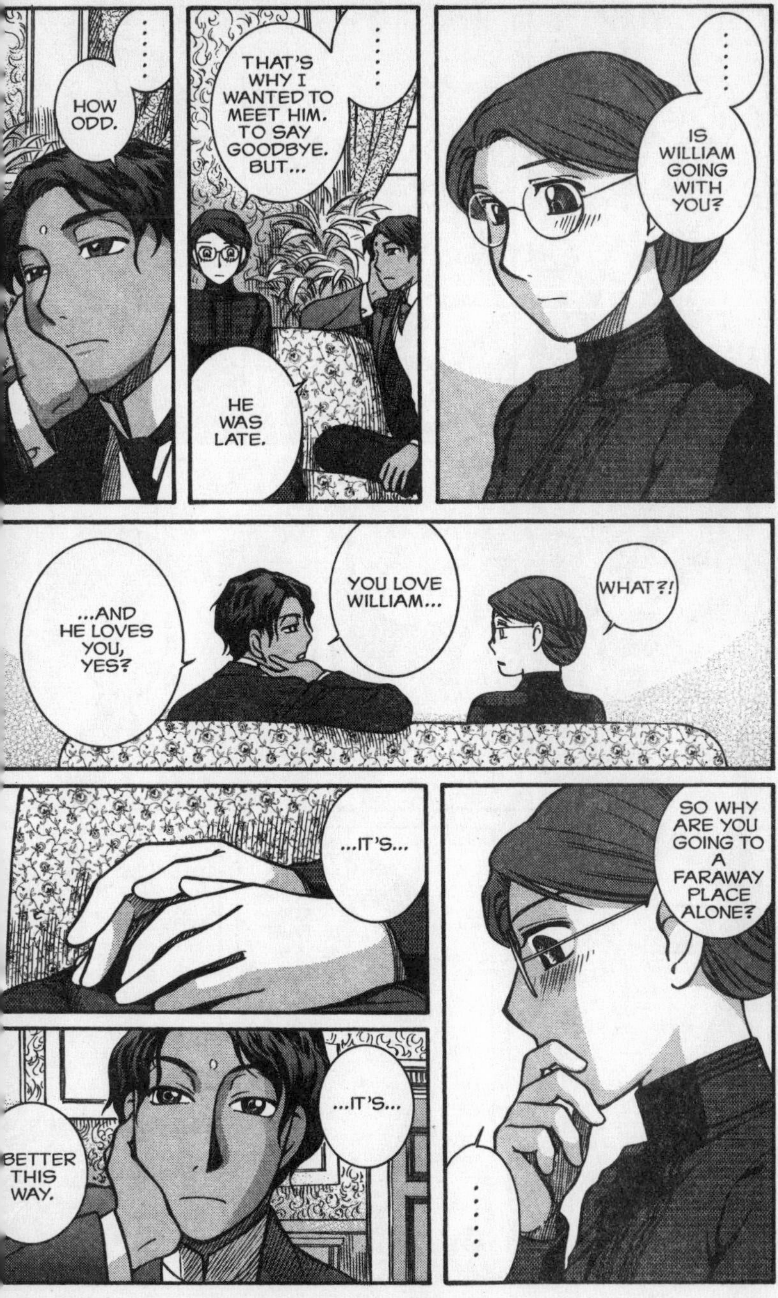
......
IS WILLIAM GOING WITH YOU?
......
THAT'S WHY I WANTED TO MEET HIM. TO SAY GOODBYE. BUT...
HE WAS LATE.
......
HOW ODD.
YOU LOVE WILLIAM...
WHAT?!
...AND HE LOVES YOU, YES?
SO WHY ARE YOU GOING TO A FARAWAY PLACE ALONE?
......
...IT'S...
...IT'S...
BETTER THIS WAY.

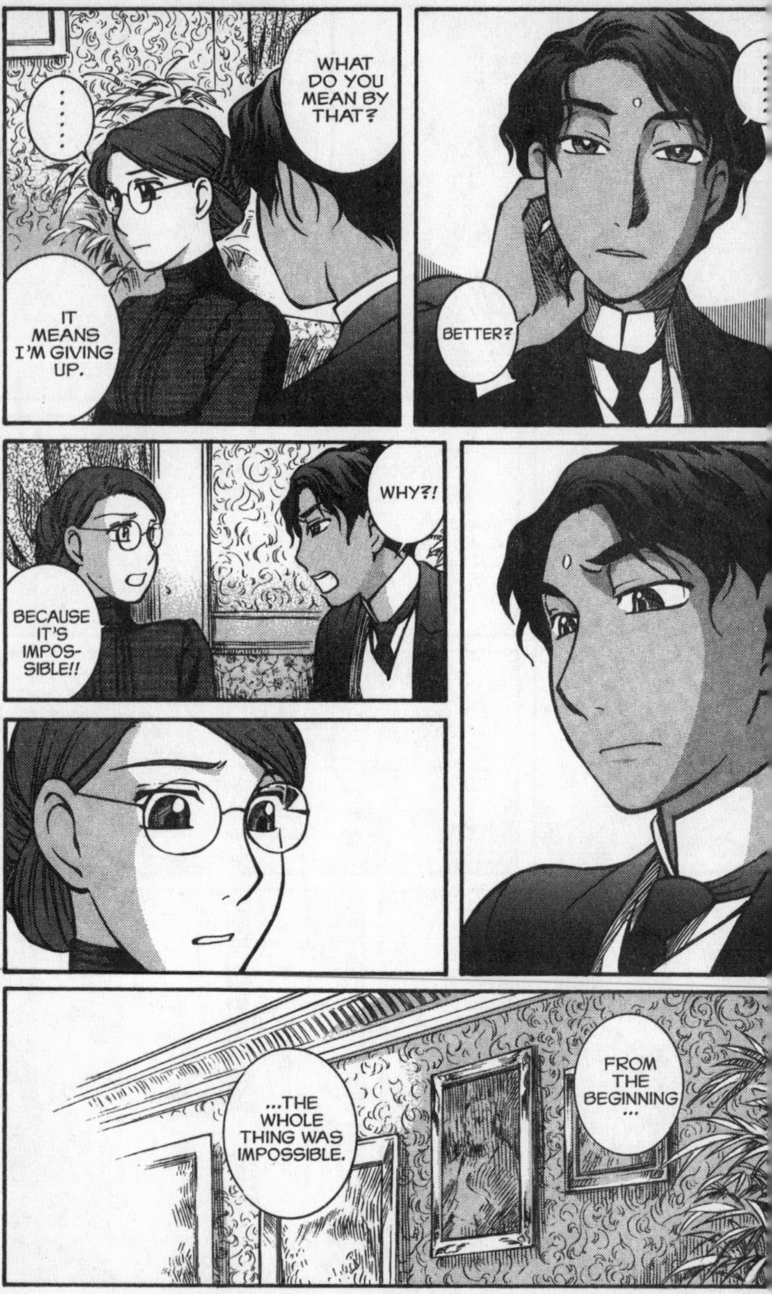
BETTER?
WHAT DO YOU MEAN BY THAT?
......
IT MEANS I'M GIVING UP.
WHY?!
BECAUSE IT'S IMPOS-SIBLE!!
FROM THE BEGINNING...
...THE WHOLE THING WAS IMPOSSIBLE.

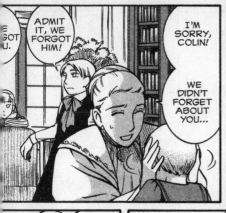

E GOT U.

ADMIT IT, WE FORGOT HIM!

I'M SORRY, COLIN!

WE DIDN'T FORGET ABOUT YOU...

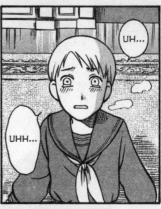

UH...

UHH...

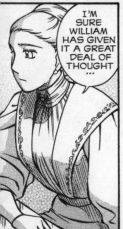

I'M SURE WILLIAM HAS GIVEN IT A GREAT DEAL OF THOUGHT ...

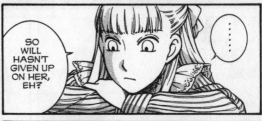

SO WILL HASN'T GIVEN UP ON HER, EH?

. . . .

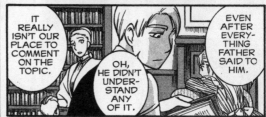

IT REALLY ISN'T OUR PLACE TO COMMENT ON THE TOPIC.

OH, HE DIDN'T UNDERSTAND ANY OF IT.

EVEN AFTER EVERYTHING FATHER SAID TO HIM.

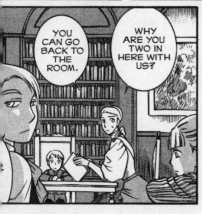

YOU CAN GO BACK TO THE ROOM.

WHY ARE YOU TWO IN HERE WITH US?

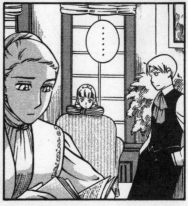

. . . .

132

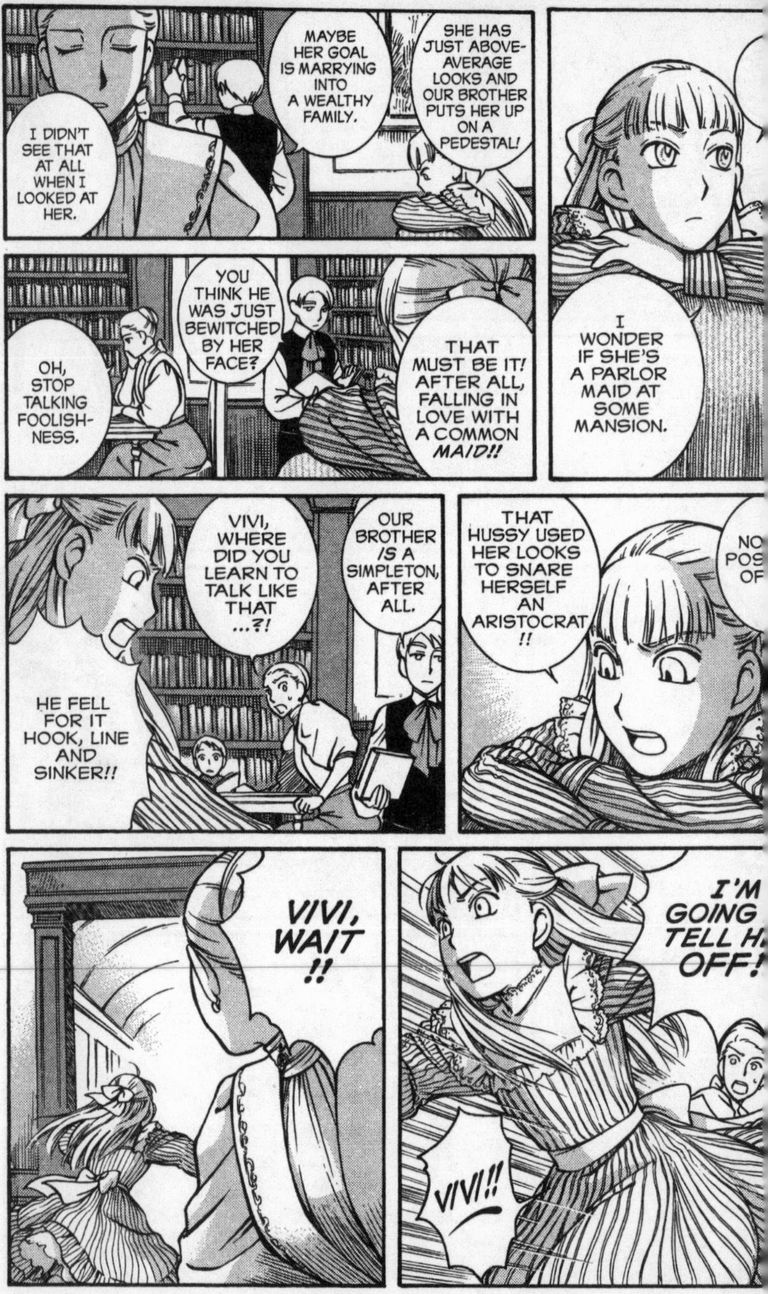
I WONDER IF SHE'S A PARLOR MAID AT SOME MANSION.
SHE HAS JUST ABOVE-AVERAGE LOOKS AND OUR BROTHER PUTS HER UP ON A PEDESTAL!
MAYBE HER GOAL IS MARRYING INTO A WEALTHY FAMILY.
I DIDN'T SEE THAT AT ALL WHEN I LOOKED AT HER.
THAT MUST BE IT! AFTER ALL, FALLING IN LOVE WITH A COMMON *MAID!!*
YOU THINK HE WAS JUST BEWITCHED BY HER FACE?
OH, STOP TALKING FOOLISHNESS.
NO POS OF
THAT HUSSY USED HER LOOKS TO SNARE HERSELF AN ARISTOCRAT!!
OUR BROTHER *IS* A SIMPLETON, AFTER ALL.
VIVI, WHERE DID YOU LEARN TO TALK LIKE THAT ...?!
HE FELL FOR IT HOOK, LINE AND SINKER!!
I'M GOING TELL H OFF!
VIVI!!
VIVI, WAIT!!

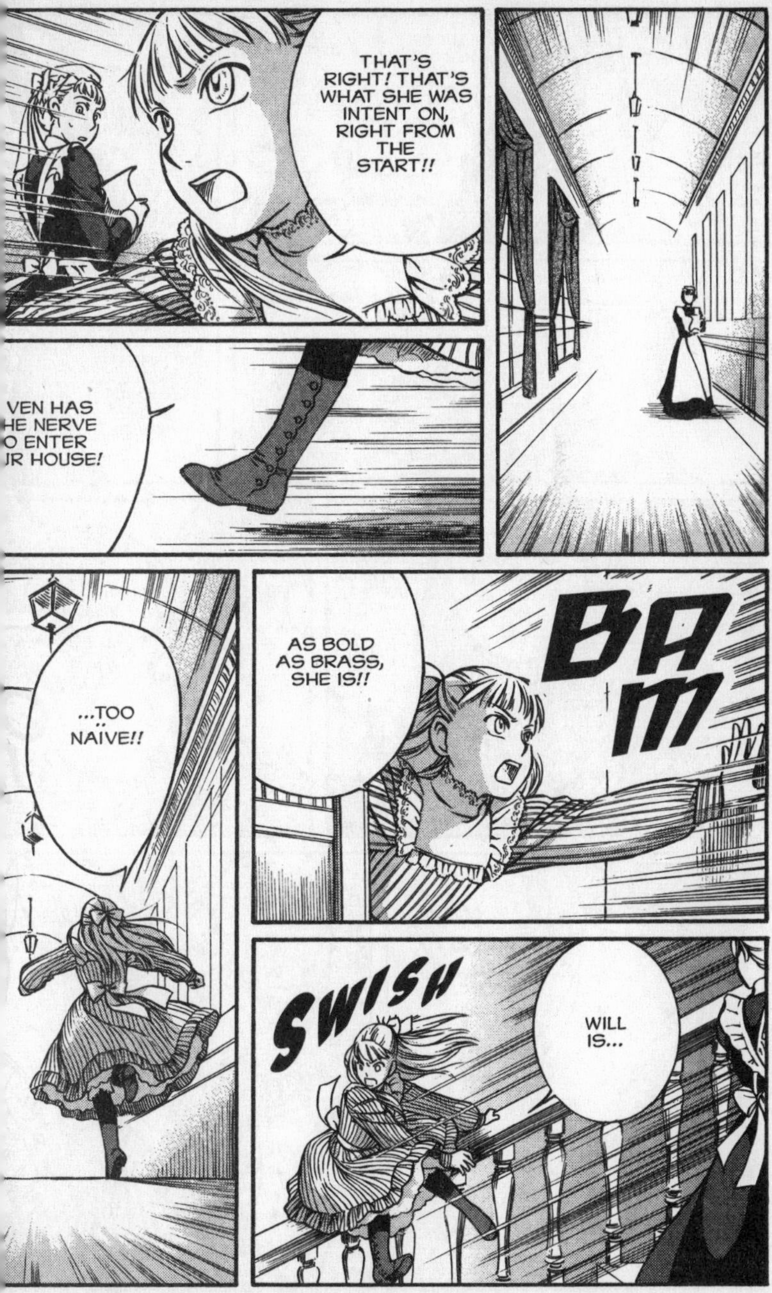
THAT'S RIGHT! THAT'S WHAT SHE WAS INTENT ON, RIGHT FROM THE START!!
VEN HAS HE NERVE O ENTER JR HOUSE!
AS BOLD AS BRASS, SHE IS!!
BAM
SWISH
WILL IS...
...TOO NAIVE!!

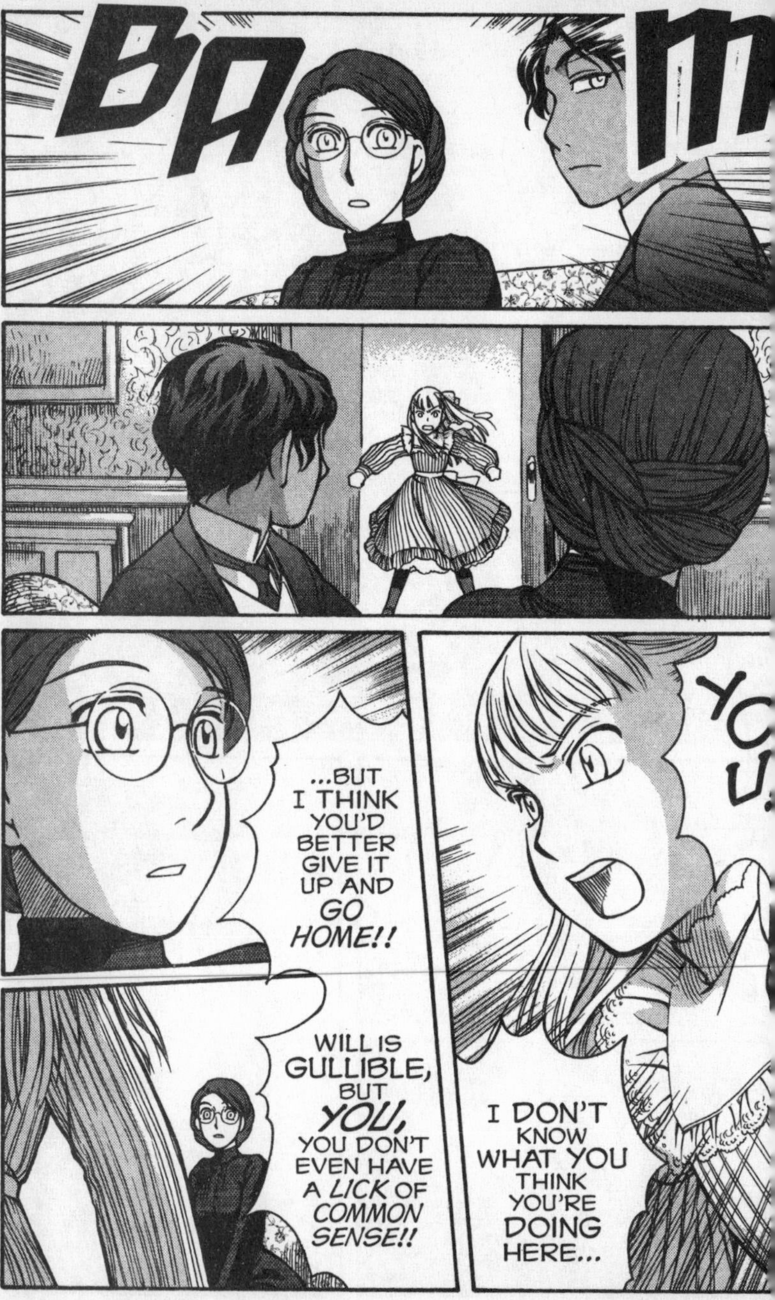
BAM
YOU!
I DON'T KNOW WHAT YOU THINK YOU'RE DOING HERE...
...BUT I THINK YOU'D BETTER GIVE IT UP AND GO HOME!!
WILL IS GULLIBLE, BUT YOU, YOU DON'T EVEN HAVE A LICK OF COMMON SENSE!!

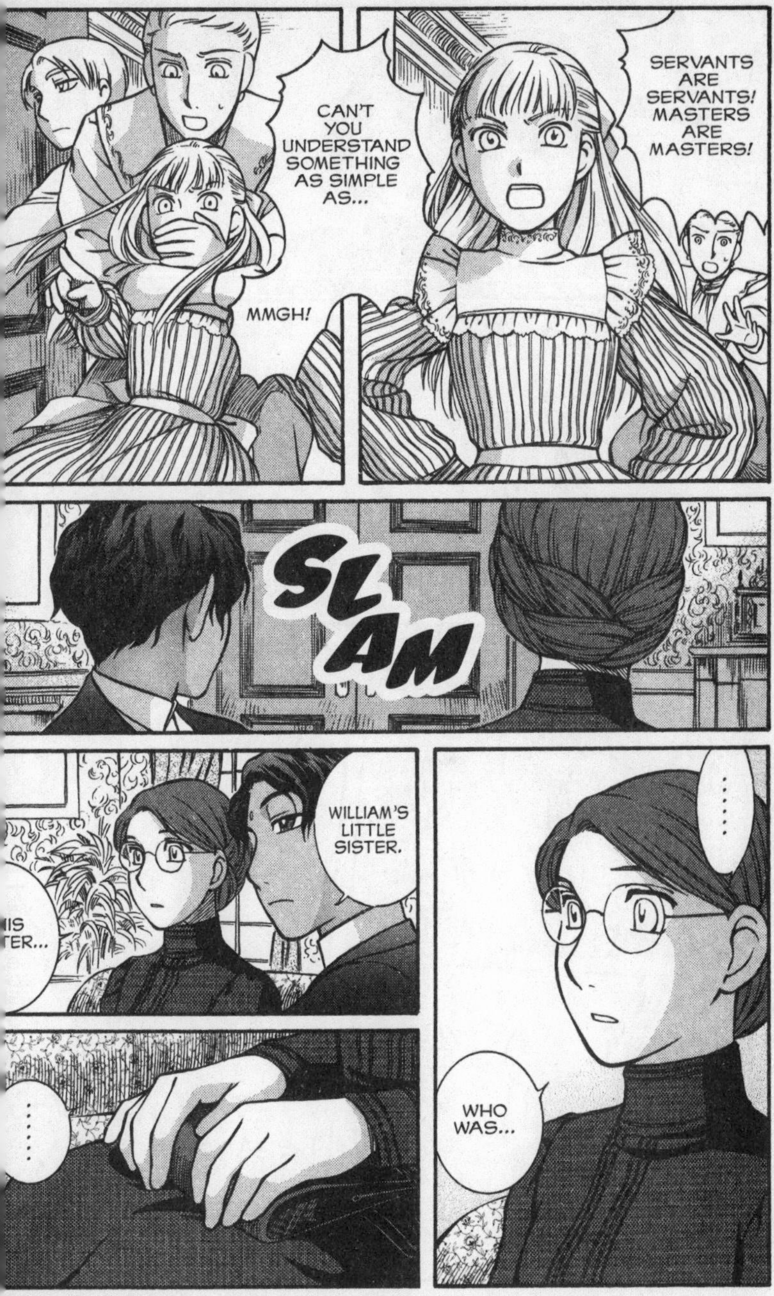
SERVANTS ARE SERVANTS! MASTERS ARE MASTERS!
CAN'T YOU UNDERSTAND SOMETHING AS SIMPLE AS...
MMGH!
SLAM
......
WHO WAS...
WILLIAM'S LITTLE SISTER.
......

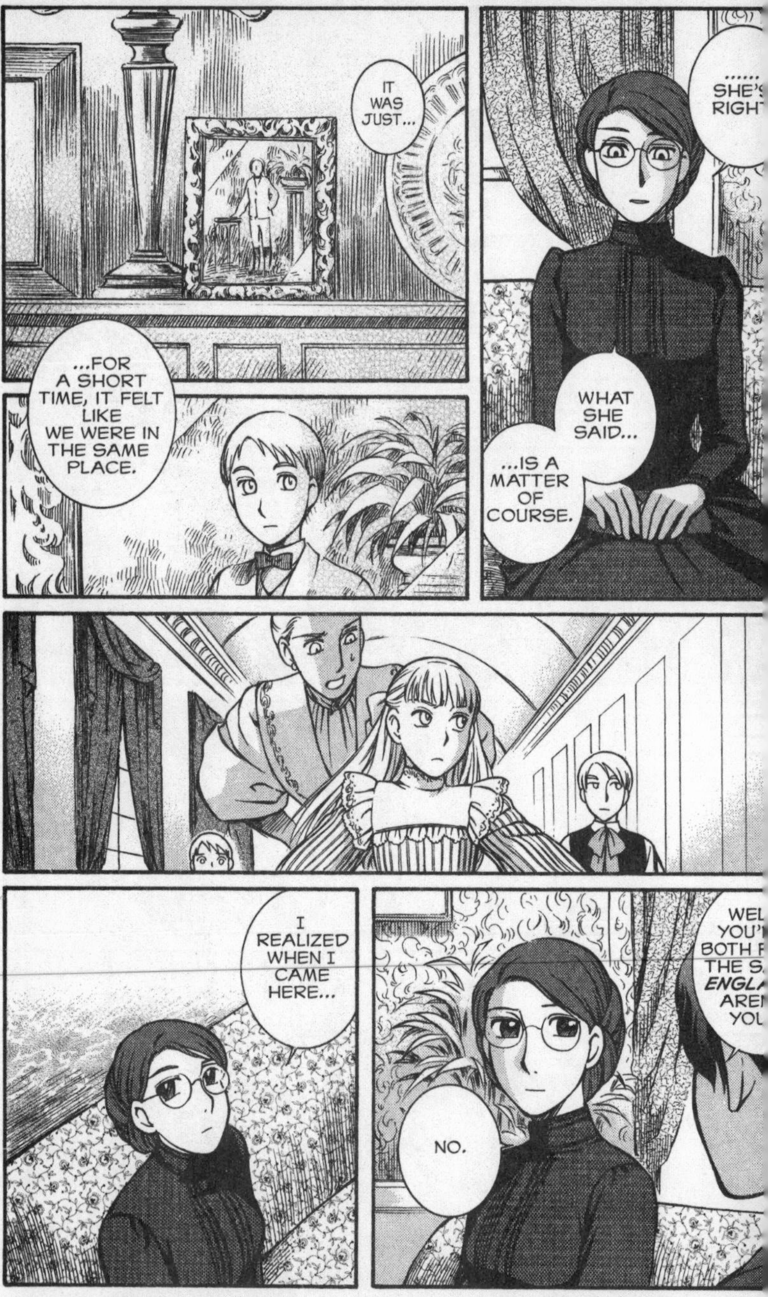
......SHE'S RIGHT
WHAT SHE SAID...
...IS A MATTER OF COURSE.
IT WAS JUST...
...FOR A SHORT TIME, IT FELT LIKE WE WERE IN THE SAME PLACE.
NO.
I REALIZED WHEN I CAME HERE...

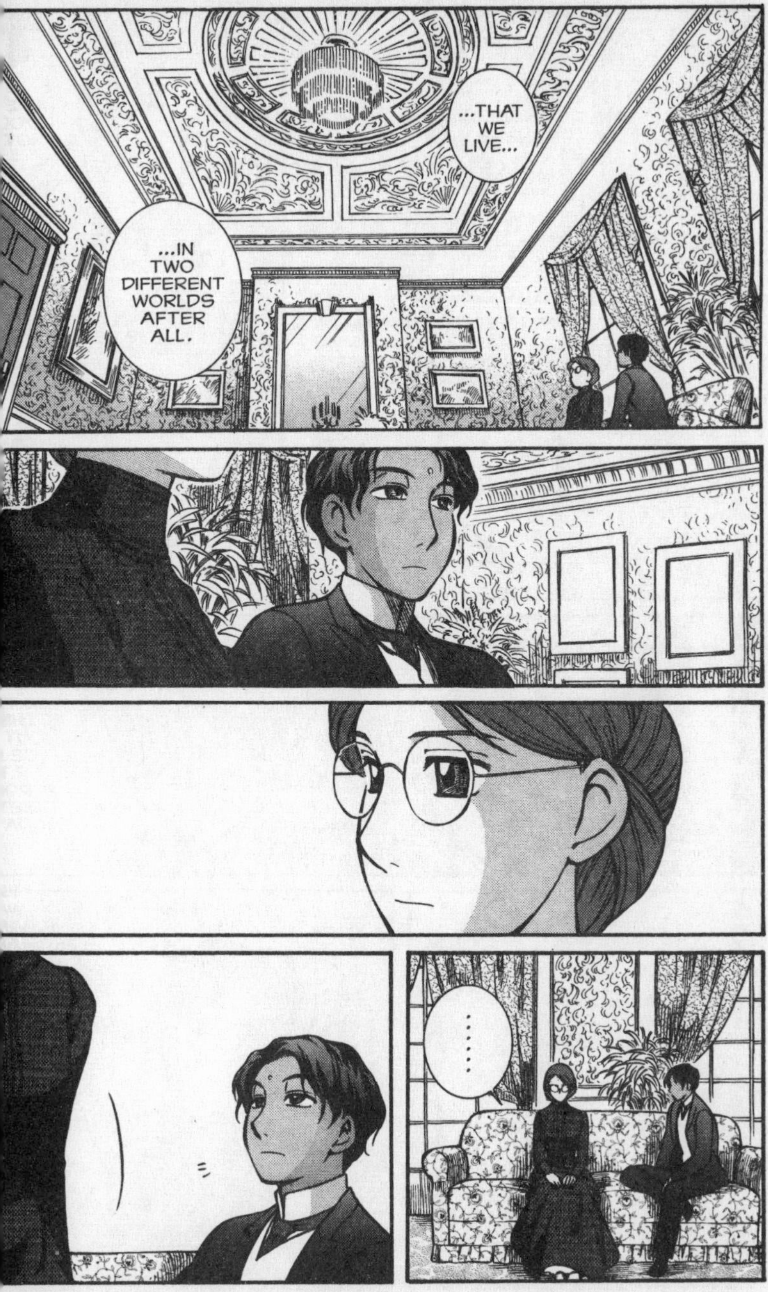
...THAT WE LIVE...
...IN TWO DIFFERENT WORLDS AFTER ALL.
......

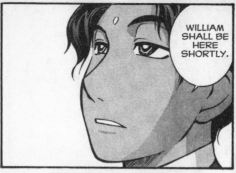

WHERE ARE YOU GOING?
HOME.
WILLIAM SHALL BE HERE SHORTLY.
THAT'S ALL RIGHT.
I'M GOING NOW.
NOW T I THI ABOUT MAYBE BETTER WE DO MEET TODA
THIS ISN'T GOOD.

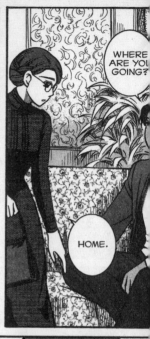

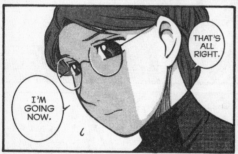

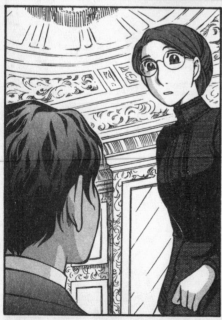

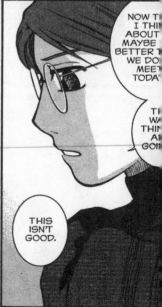

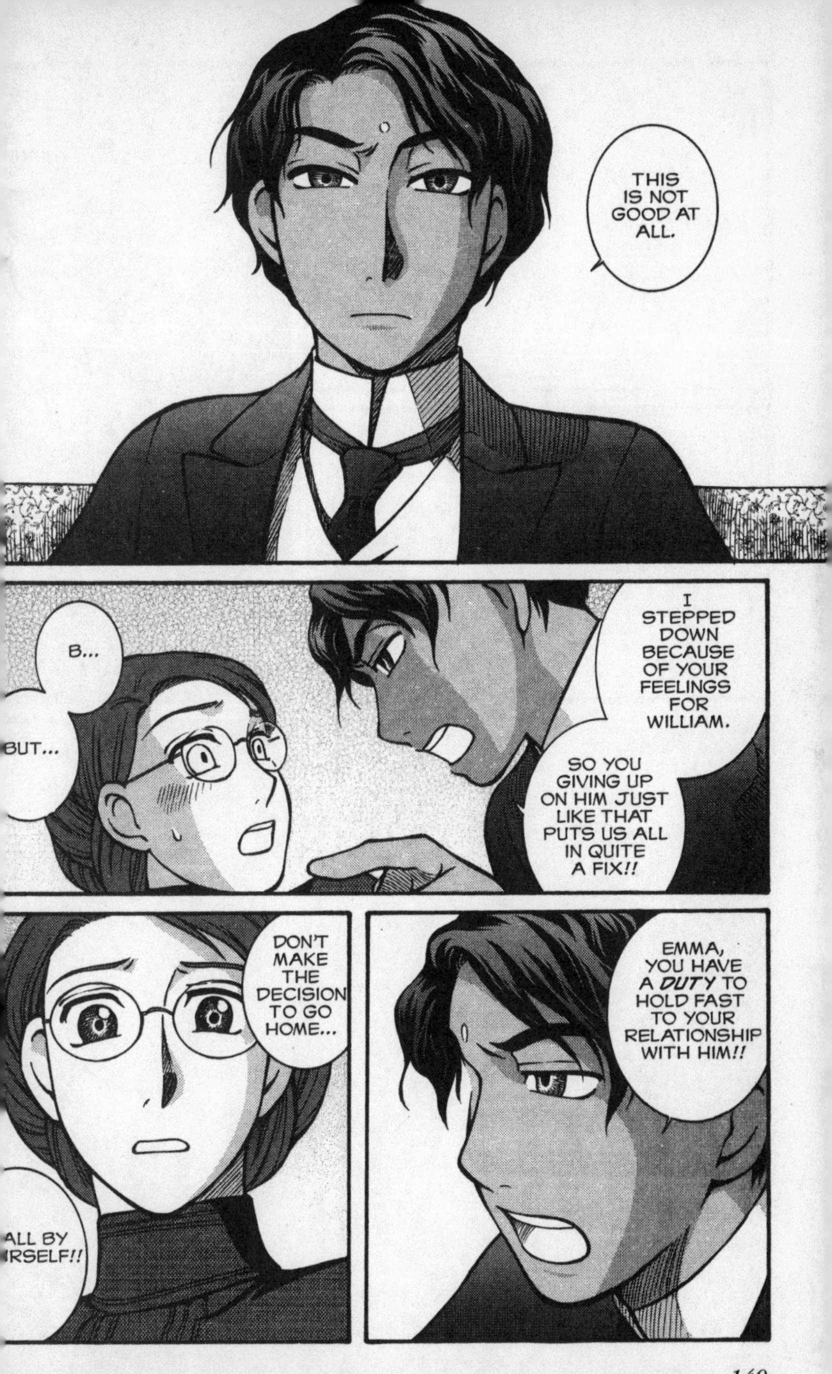
THIS IS NOT GOOD AT ALL.
I STEPPED DOWN BECAUSE OF YOUR FEELINGS FOR WILLIAM.
SO YOU GIVING UP ON HIM JUST LIKE THAT PUTS US ALL IN QUITE A FIX!!
B...
BUT...
EMMA, YOU HAVE A *DUTY* TO HOLD FAST TO YOUR RELATIONSHIP WITH HIM!!
DON'T MAKE THE DECISION TO GO HOME...
ALL BY RSELF!!

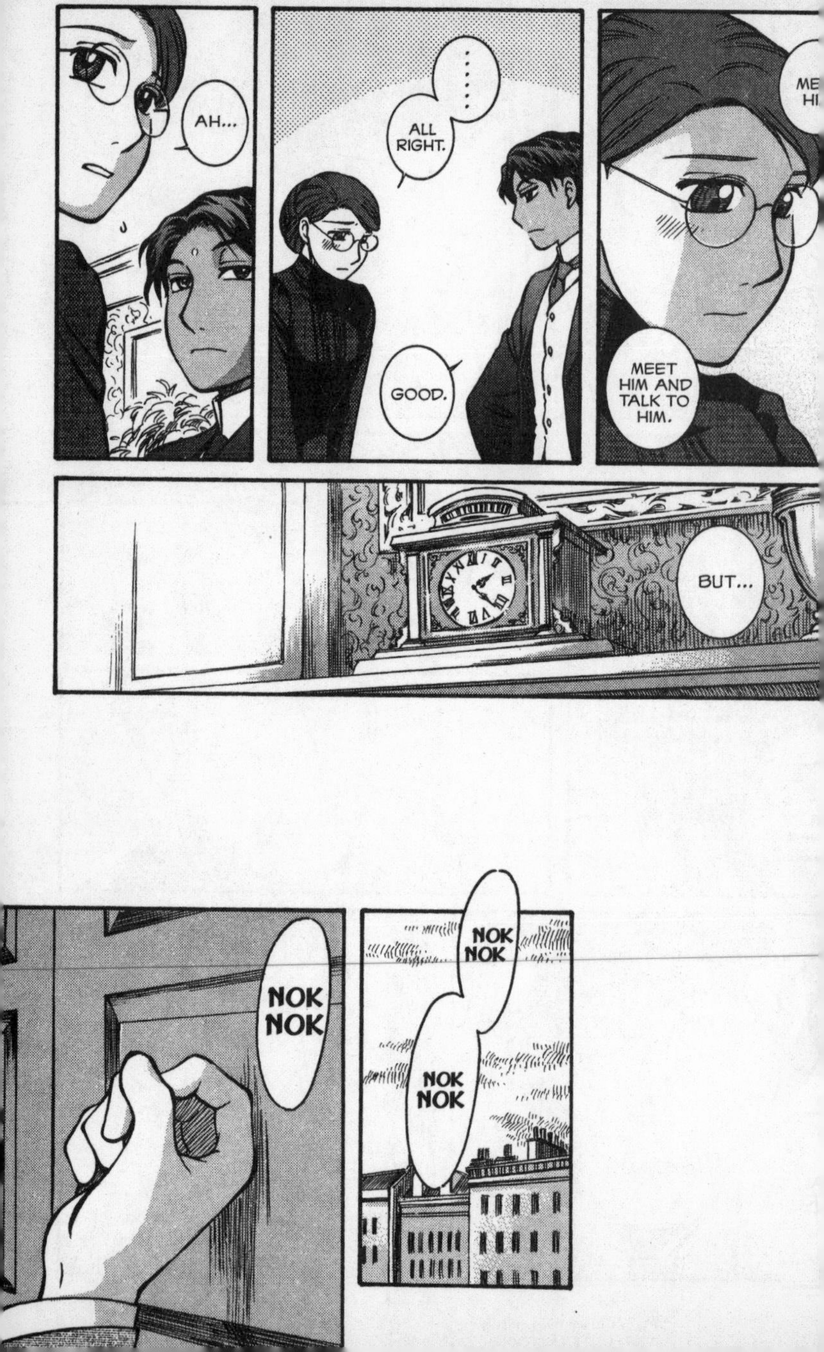
MEET HIM AND TALK TO HIM.
......
ALL RIGHT.
GOOD.
AH...
BUT...
NOK NOK
NOK NOK
NOK NOK

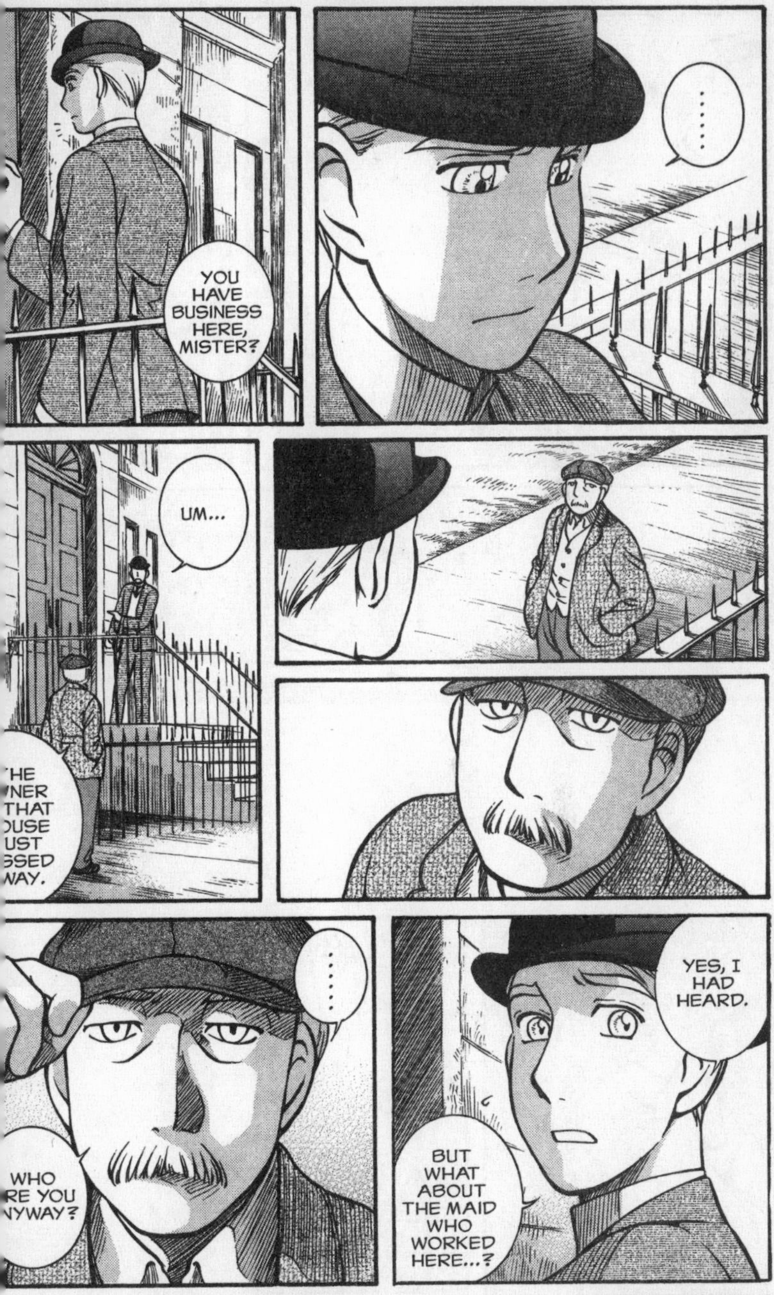
……
YOU HAVE BUSINESS HERE, MISTER?
UM...
HE NER THAT OUSE UST SSED WAY.
YES, I HAD HEARD.
BUT WHAT ABOUT THE MAID WHO WORKED HERE...?
……
WHO RE YOU NYWAY?

Chapter Twelve: The End

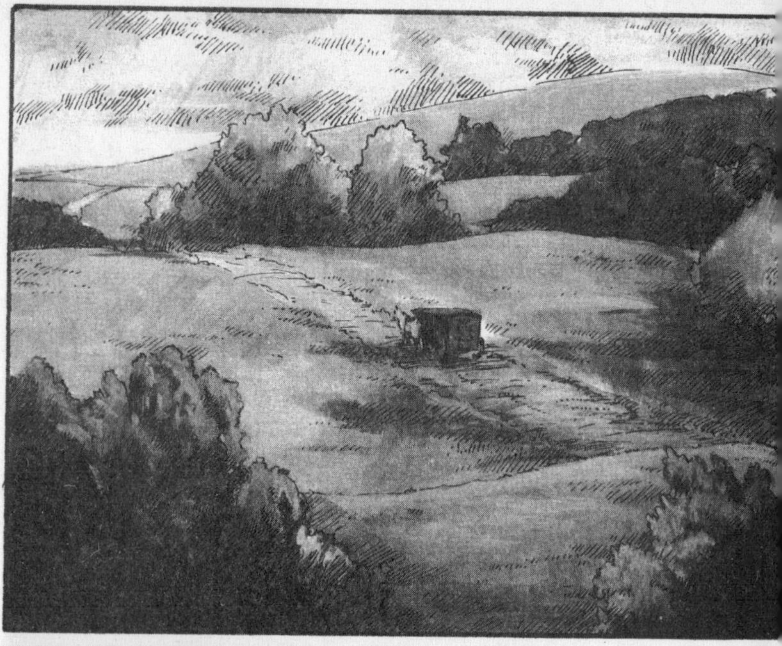

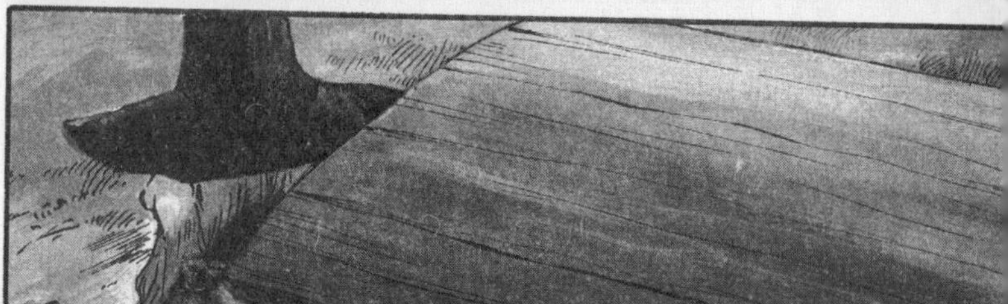

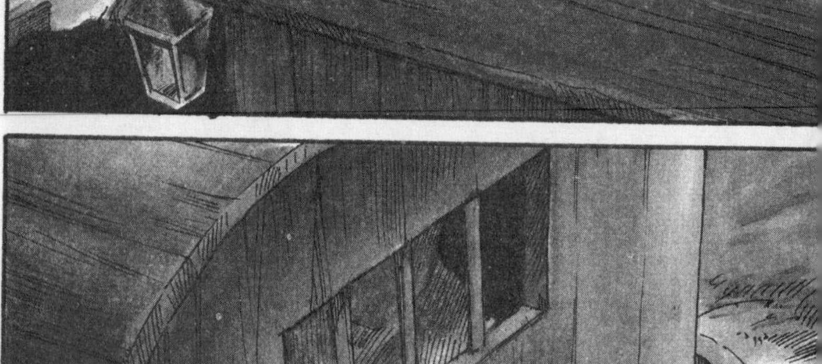

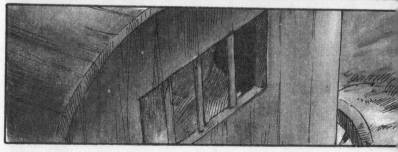

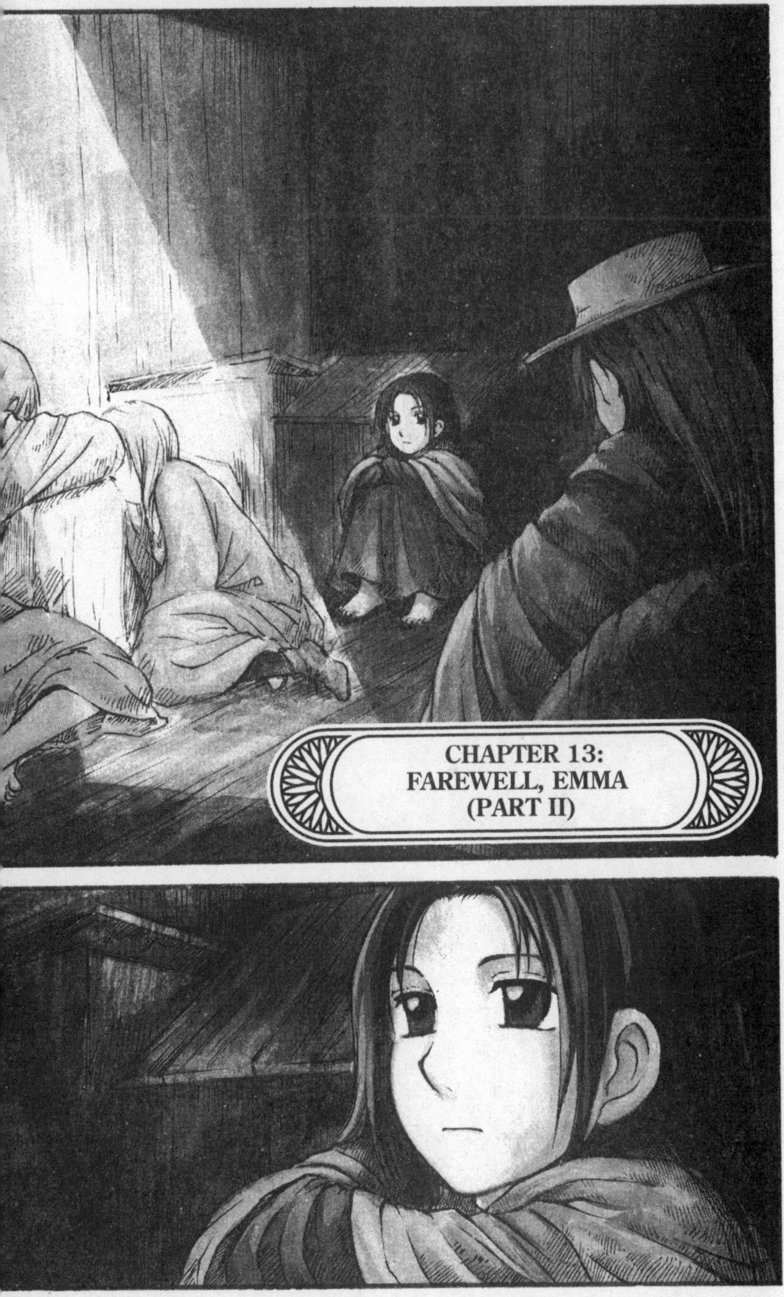
CHAPTER 13:
FAREWELL, EMMA
(PART II)

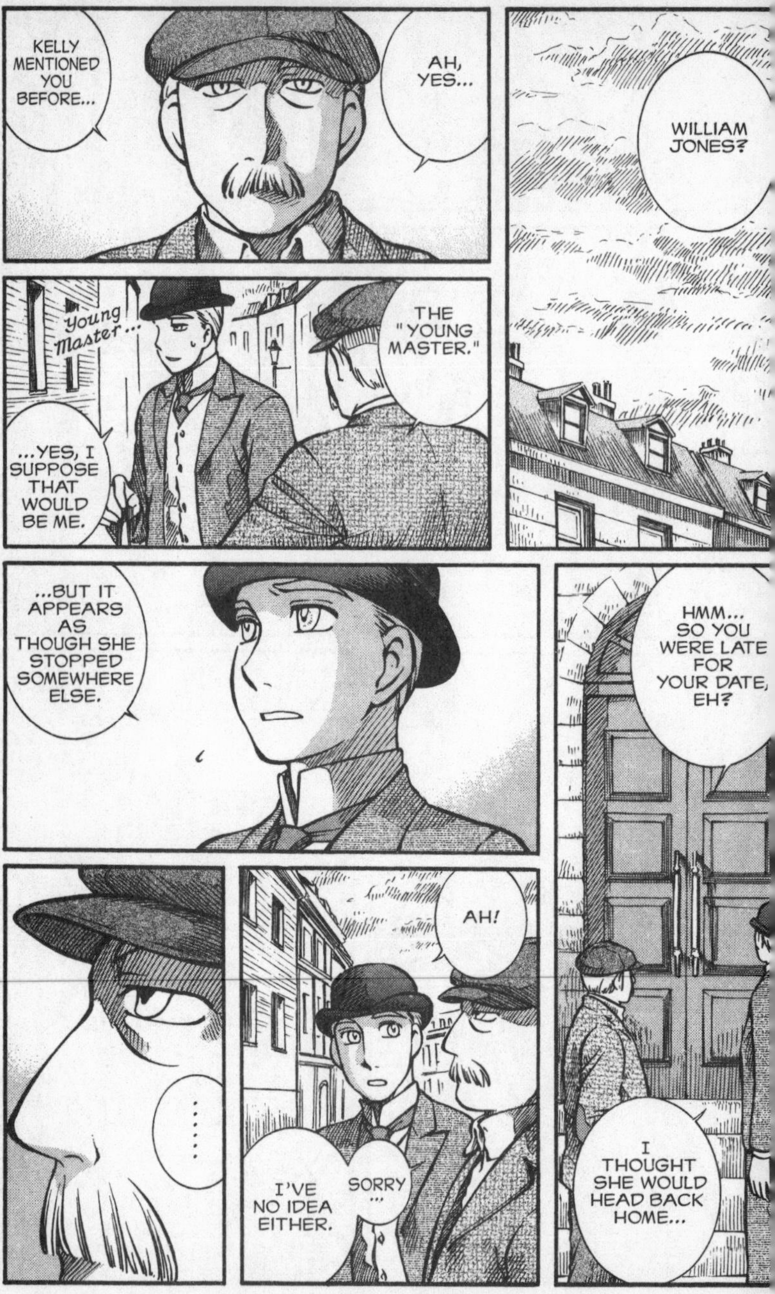
WILLIAM JONES?
AH, YES...
KELLY MENTIONED YOU BEFORE...
THE "YOUNG MASTER."
Young Master...
...YES, I SUPPOSE THAT WOULD BE ME.
HMM... SO YOU WERE LATE FOR YOUR DATE, EH?
I THOUGHT SHE WOULD HEAD BACK HOME...
...BUT IT APPEARS AS THOUGH SHE STOPPED SOMEWHERE ELSE.
AH!
SORRY...
I'VE NO IDEA EITHER.
......

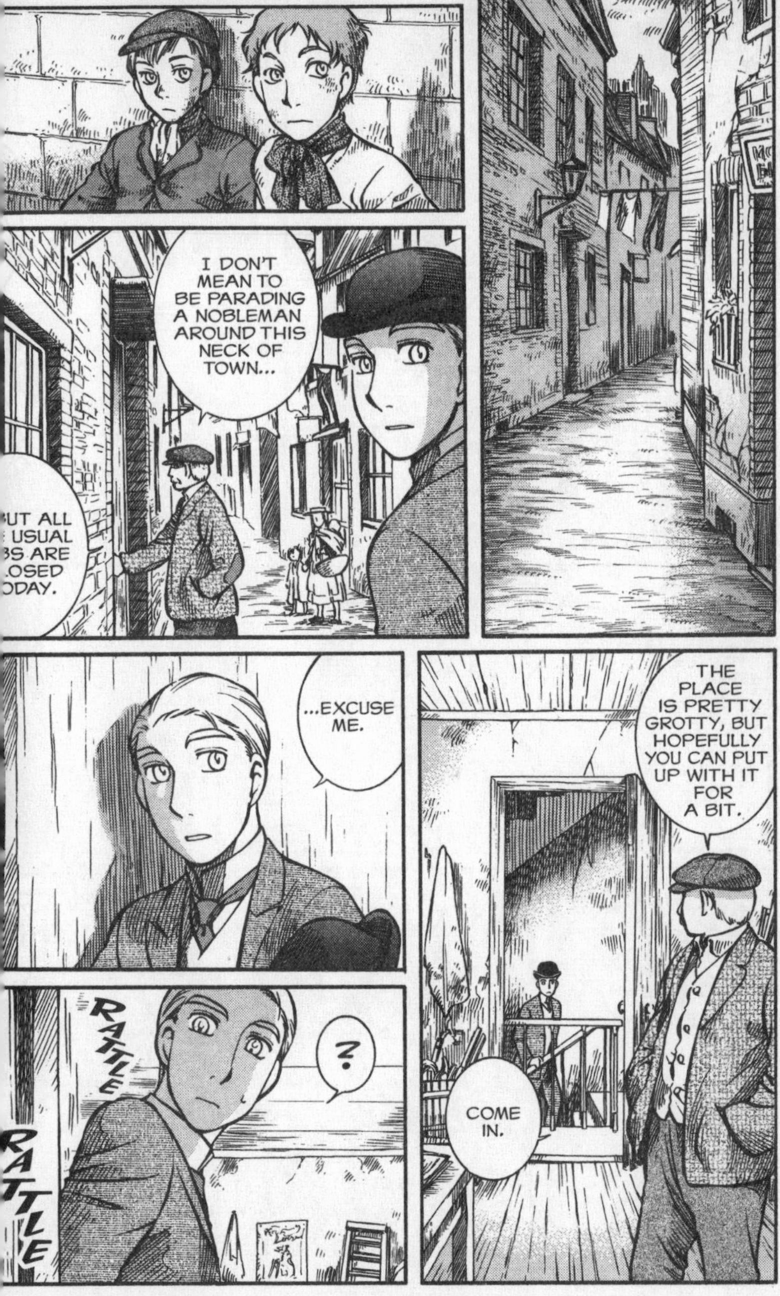
I DON'T MEAN TO BE PARADING A NOBLEMAN AROUND THIS NECK OF TOWN...
UT ALL E USUAL BS ARE OSED ODAY.
THE PLACE IS PRETTY GROTTY, BUT HOPEFULLY YOU CAN PUT UP WITH IT FOR A BIT.
COME IN.
...EXCUSE ME.
RATTLE
RATTLE
?

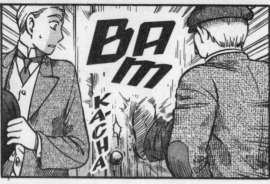

BAM
KACHA

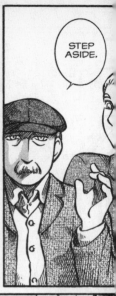

STEP ASIDE.

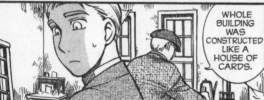

WHOLE BUILDING WAS CONSTRUCTED LIKE A HOUSE OF CARDS.

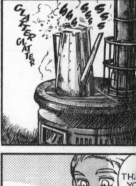

CLATTER CLATTER
sss sss

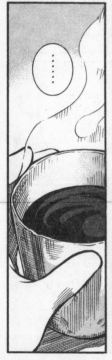

. . . . .

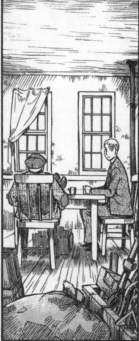

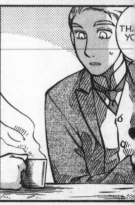

TH..
YO..

147

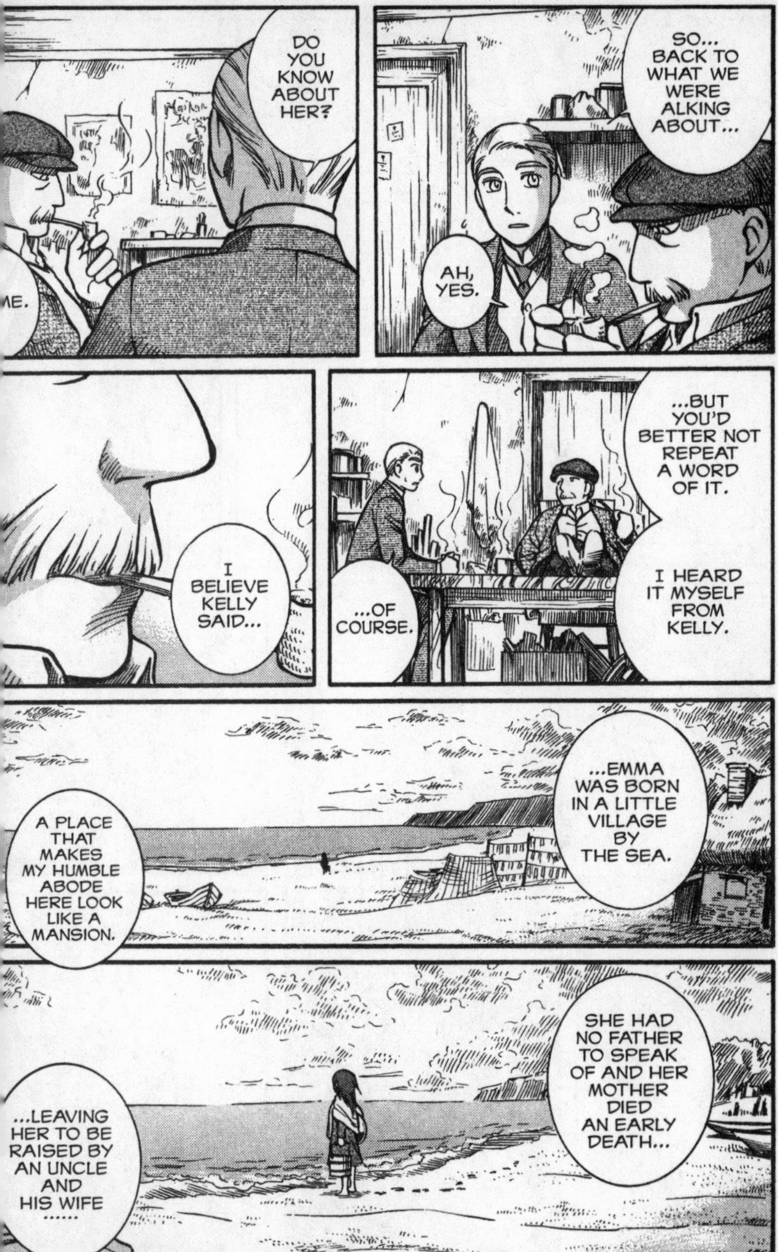

SO... BACK TO WHAT WE WERE ALKING ABOUT...
AH, YES.
DO YOU KNOW ABOUT HER?
ME.
...BUT YOU'D BETTER NOT REPEAT A WORD OF IT.
I HEARD IT MYSELF FROM KELLY.
...OF COURSE.
I BELIEVE KELLY SAID...
...EMMA WAS BORN IN A LITTLE VILLAGE BY THE SEA.
A PLACE THAT MAKES MY HUMBLE ABODE HERE LOOK LIKE A MANSION.
SHE HAD NO FATHER TO SPEAK OF AND HER MOTHER DIED AN EARLY DEATH...
...LEAVING HER TO BE RAISED BY AN UNCLE AND HIS WIFE ......

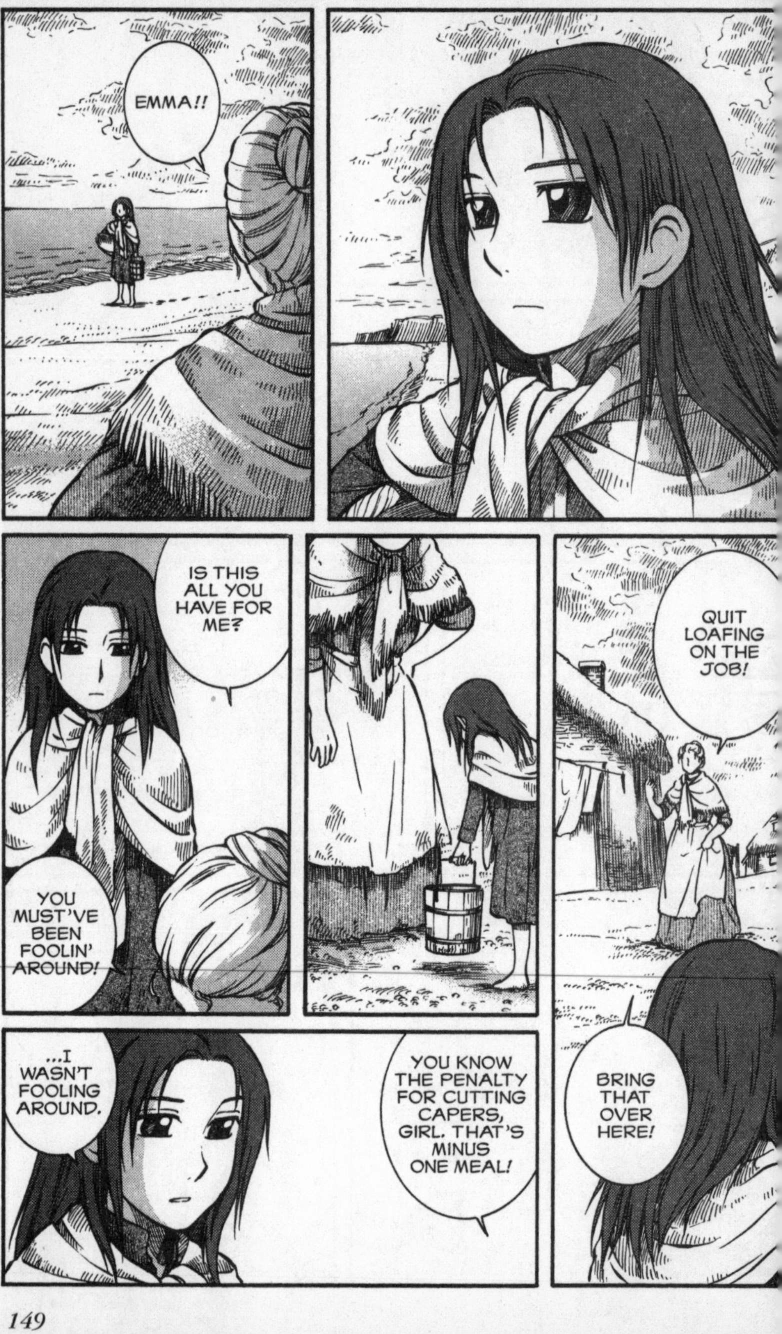
EMMA!!
QUIT LOAFING ON THE JOB!
IS THIS ALL YOU HAVE FOR ME?
YOU MUST'VE BEEN FOOLIN' AROUND!
BRING THAT OVER HERE!
YOU KNOW THE PENALTY FOR CUTTING CAPERS, GIRL. THAT'S MINUS ONE MEAL!
...I WASN'T FOOLING AROUND.

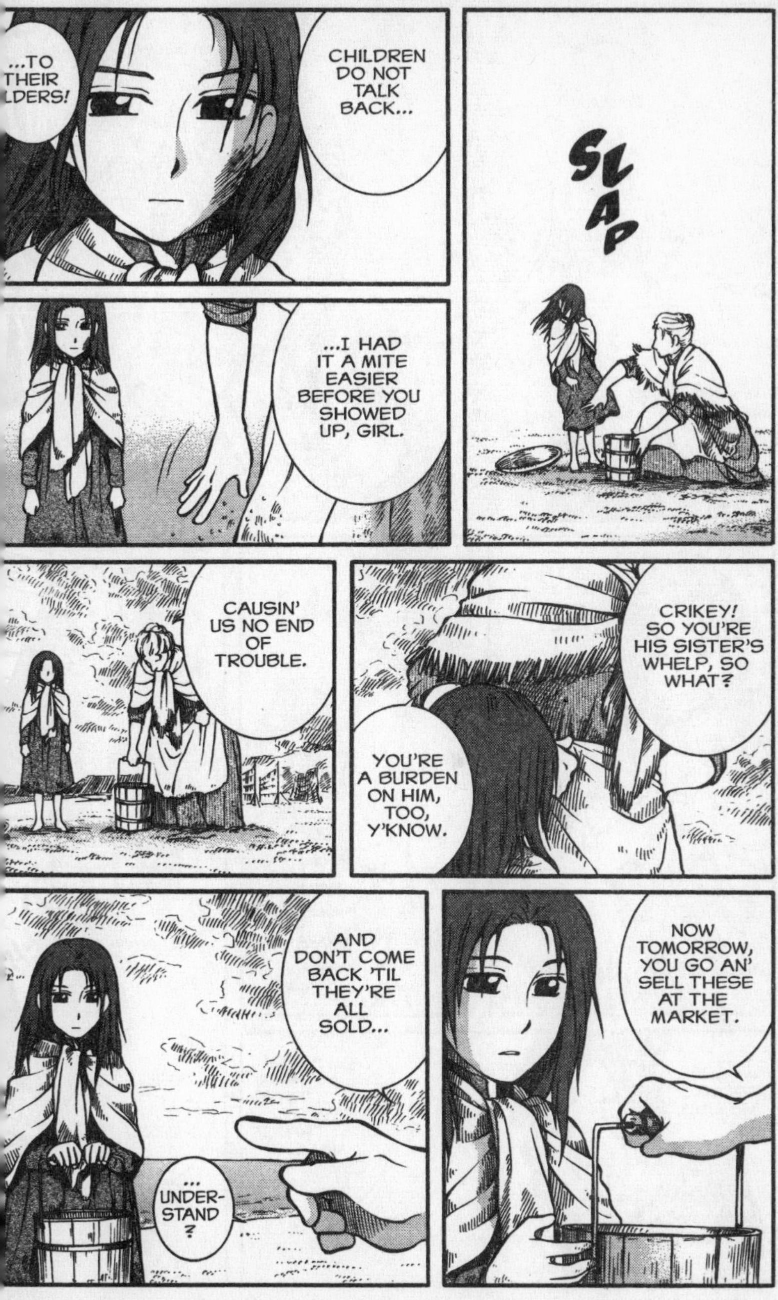
SLAP
CHILDREN DO NOT TALK BACK...
...TO THEIR LDERS!
...I HAD IT A MITE EASIER BEFORE YOU SHOWED UP, GIRL.
CRIKEY! SO YOU'RE HIS SISTER'S WHELP, SO WHAT?
YOU'RE A BURDEN ON HIM, TOO, Y'KNOW.
CAUSIN' US NO END OF TROUBLE.
NOW TOMORROW, YOU GO AN' SELL THESE AT THE MARKET.
AND DON'T COME BACK 'TIL THEY'RE ALL SOLD...
...UNDERSTAND?

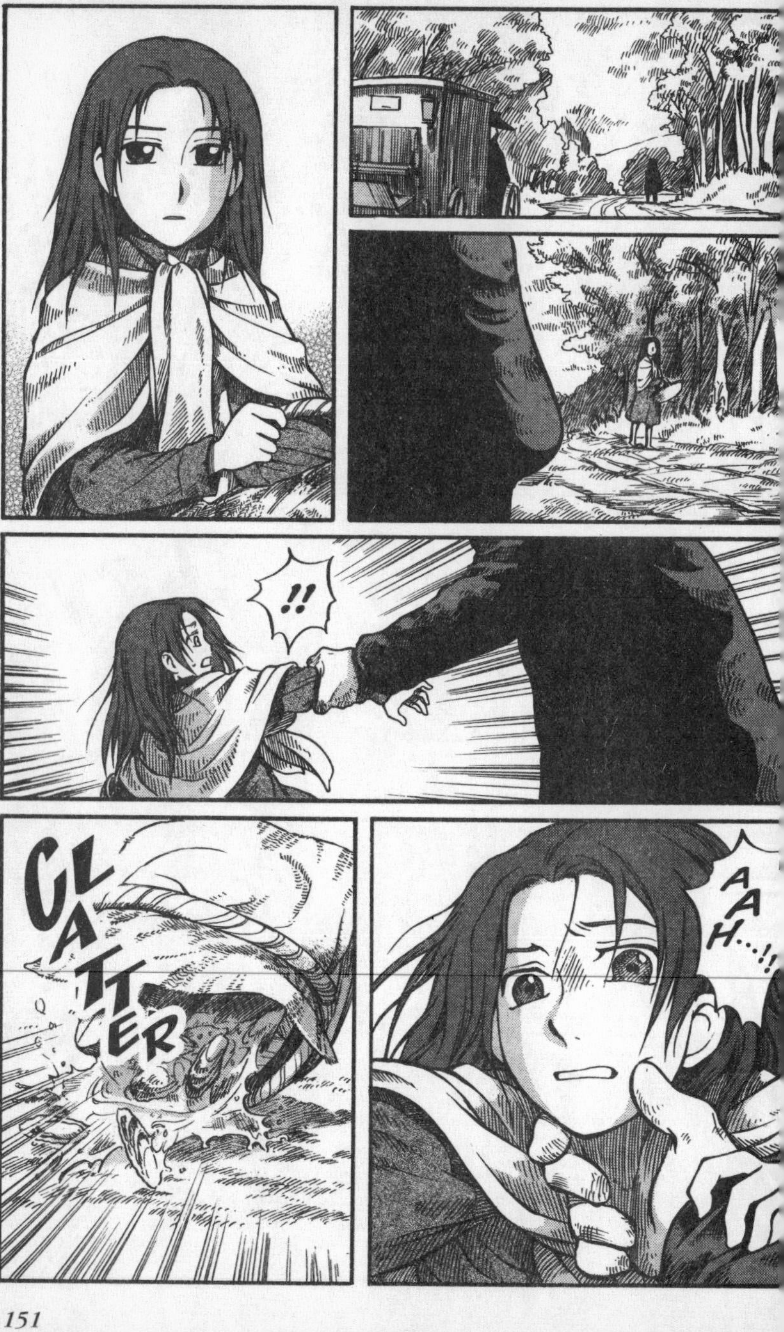
!!
AAH...!!
CLATTER

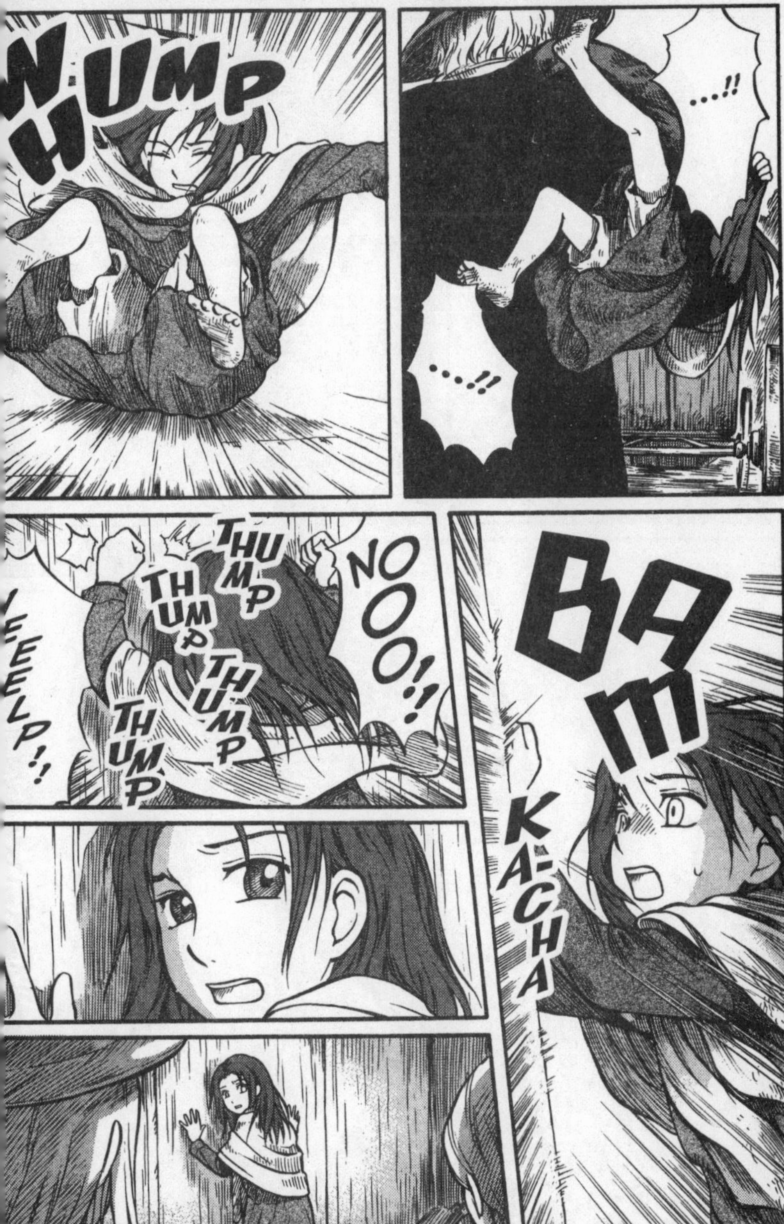
...!!
...!!
HUMP
BAM
KA-CHA
NOOO!!
THUMP
THUMP
THUMP
THUMP
EEEELP!!

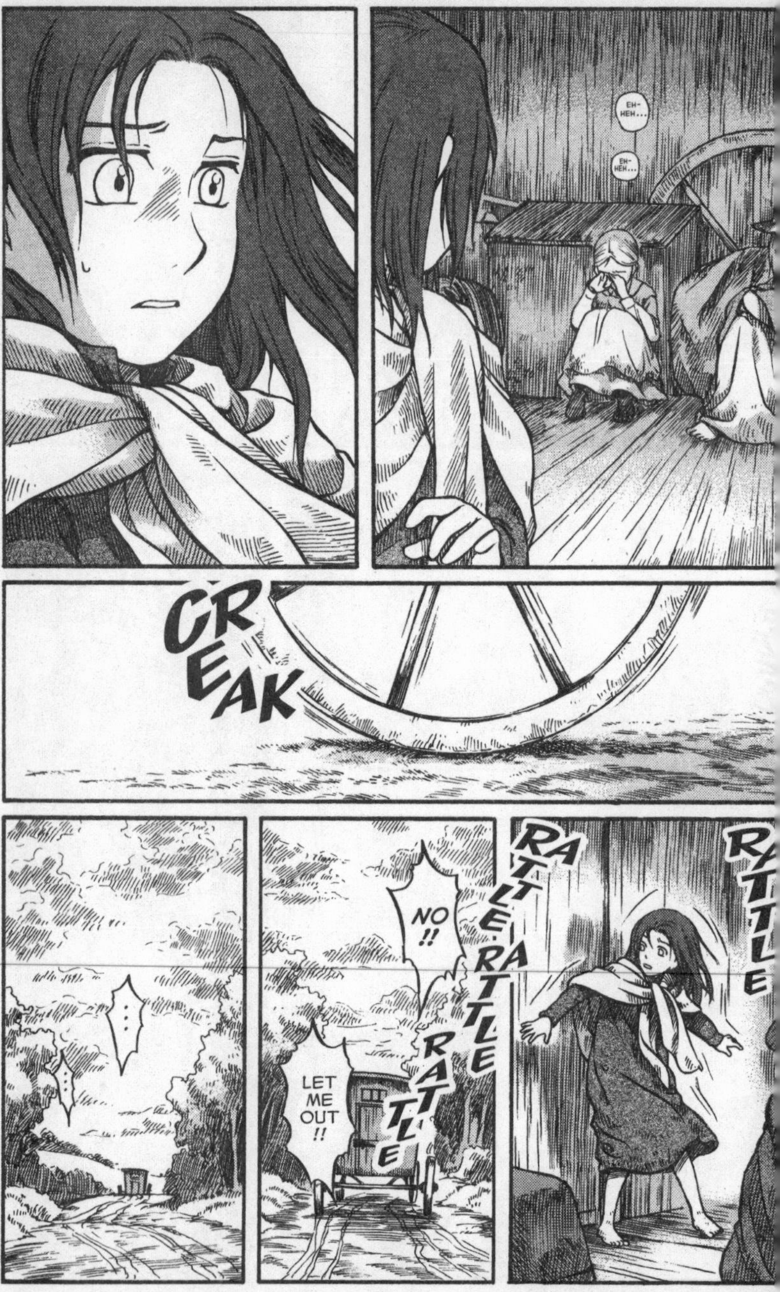
EH-HEH...
EH-HEH...
CREAK
RATTLE
RATTLE·RATTLE
RATTLE
NO!!
LET ME OUT!!
...
...

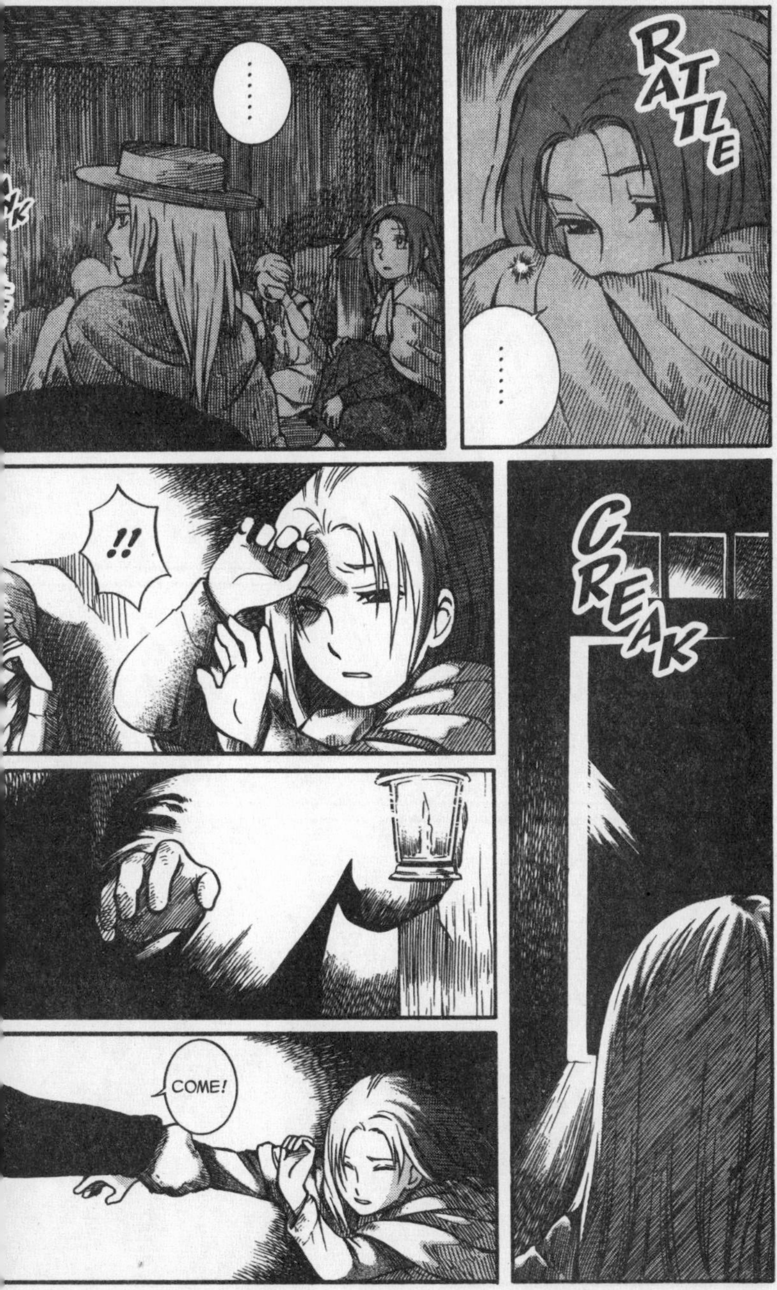
RATTLE
......
......
CREAK
!!
COME!

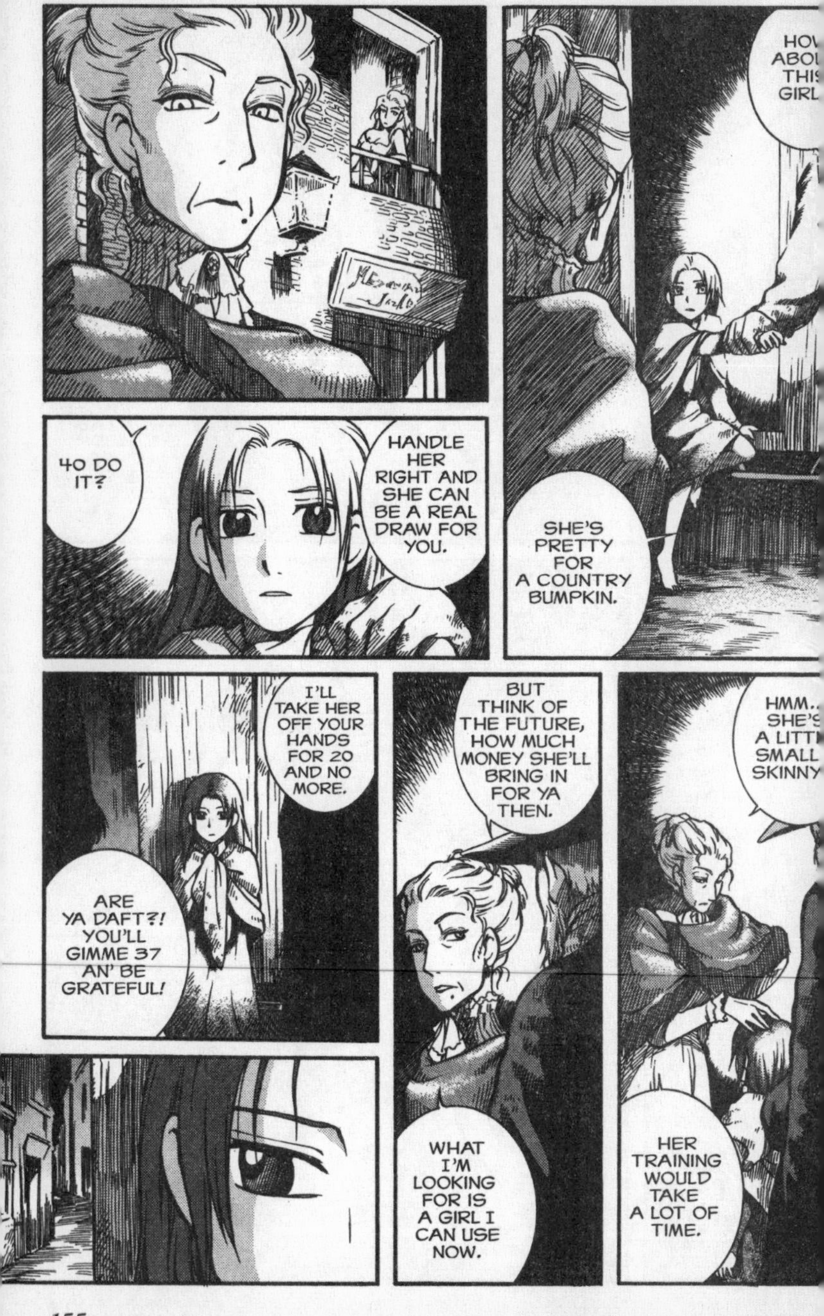
HOW ABOU THIS GIRL
SHE'S PRETTY FOR A COUNTRY BUMPKIN.
HANDLE HER RIGHT AND SHE CAN BE A REAL DRAW FOR YOU.
40 DO IT?
HMM.. SHE'S A LITT SMALL SKINNY
HER TRAINING WOULD TAKE A LOT OF TIME.
BUT THINK OF THE FUTURE, HOW MUCH MONEY SHE'LL BRING IN FOR YA THEN.
WHAT I'M LOOKING FOR IS A GIRL I CAN USE NOW.
I'LL TAKE HER OFF YOUR HANDS FOR 20 AND NO MORE.
ARE YA DAFT?! YOU'LL GIMME 37 AN' BE GRATEFUL!

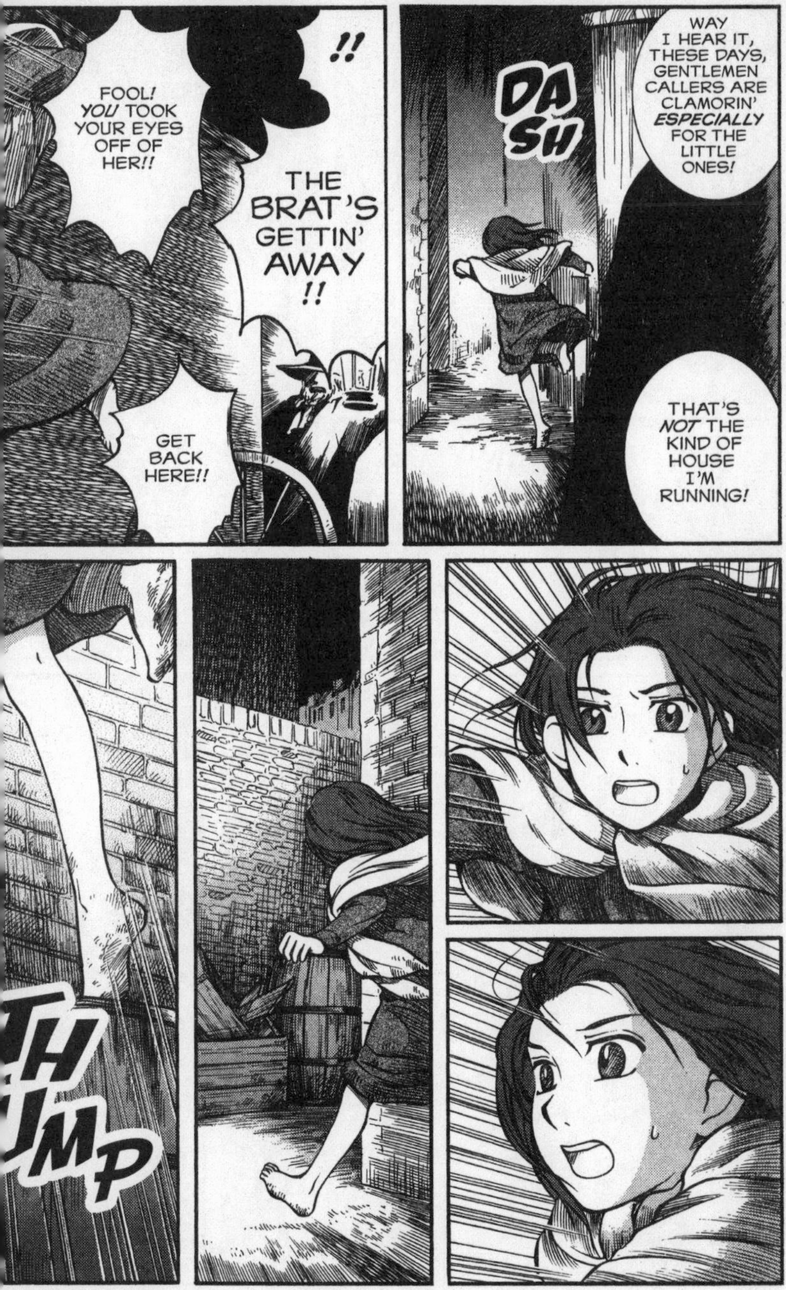

WAY I HEAR IT, THESE DAYS, GENTLEMEN CALLERS ARE CLAMORIN' *ESPECIALLY* FOR THE LITTLE ONES!
DASH
THAT'S *NOT* THE KIND OF HOUSE I'M RUNNING!
!!
FOOL! *YOU* TOOK YOUR EYES OFF OF HER!!
THE BRAT'S GETTIN' AWAY!!
GET BACK HERE!!
THMP

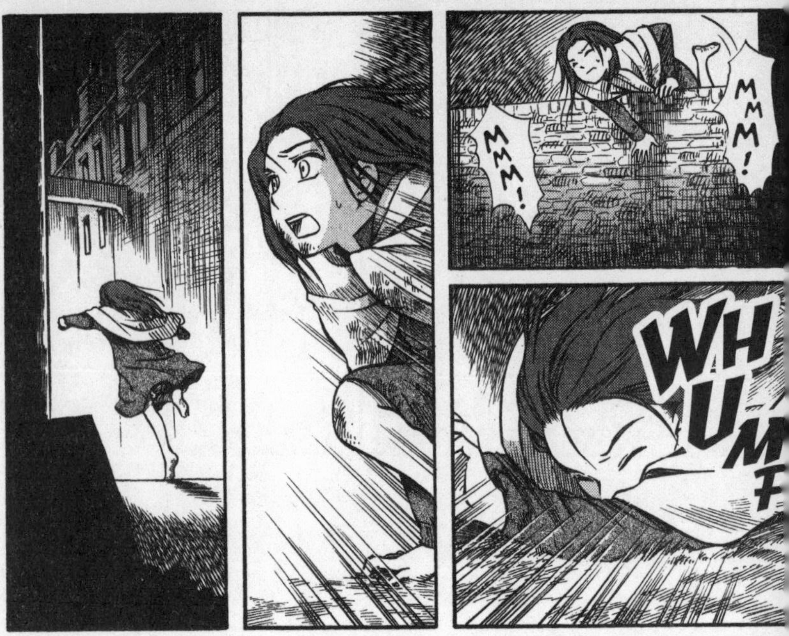
MMM!
MMM!
WHUMF

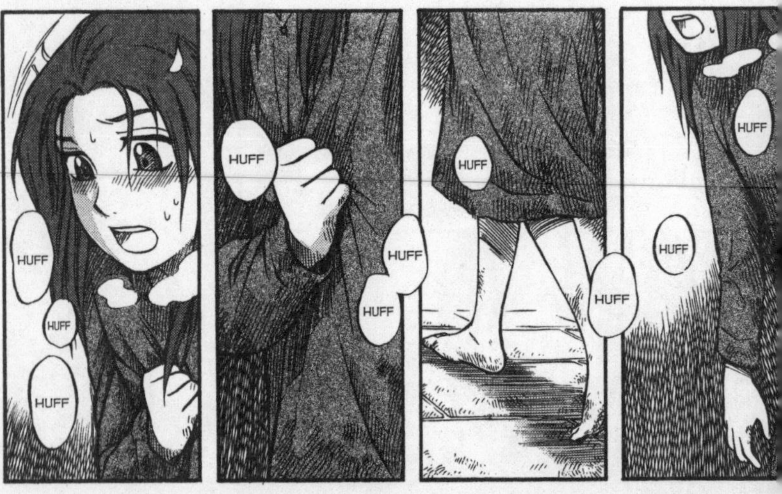
HUFF
HUFF
HUFF
HUFF
HUFF
HUFF
HUFF
HUFF
HUFF
HUFF

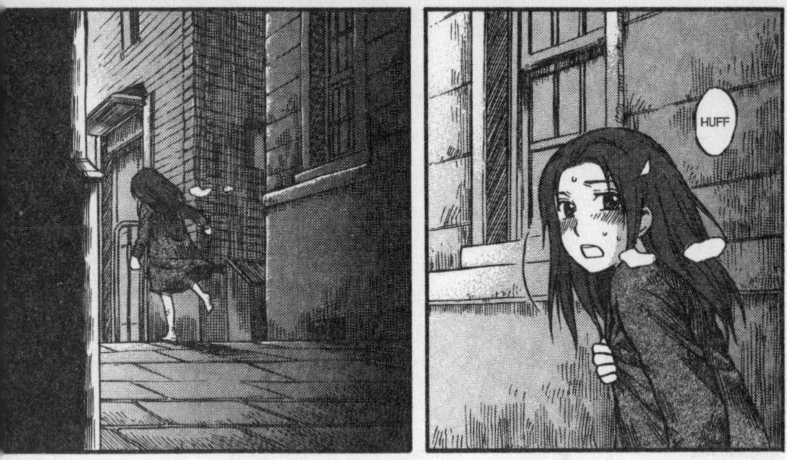
HUFF

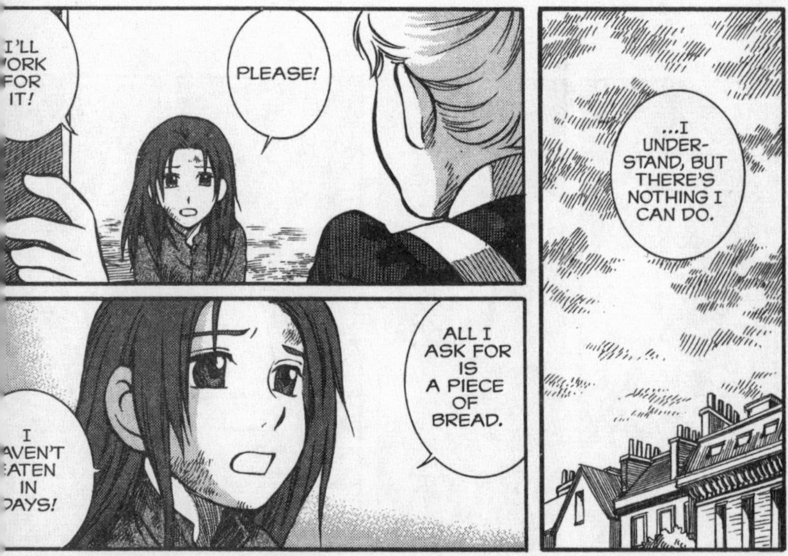
...I UNDERSTAND, BUT THERE'S NOTHING I CAN DO.
PLEASE!
I'LL ORK FOR IT!
ALL I ASK FOR IS A PIECE OF BREAD.
I AVEN'T ATEN IN AYS!

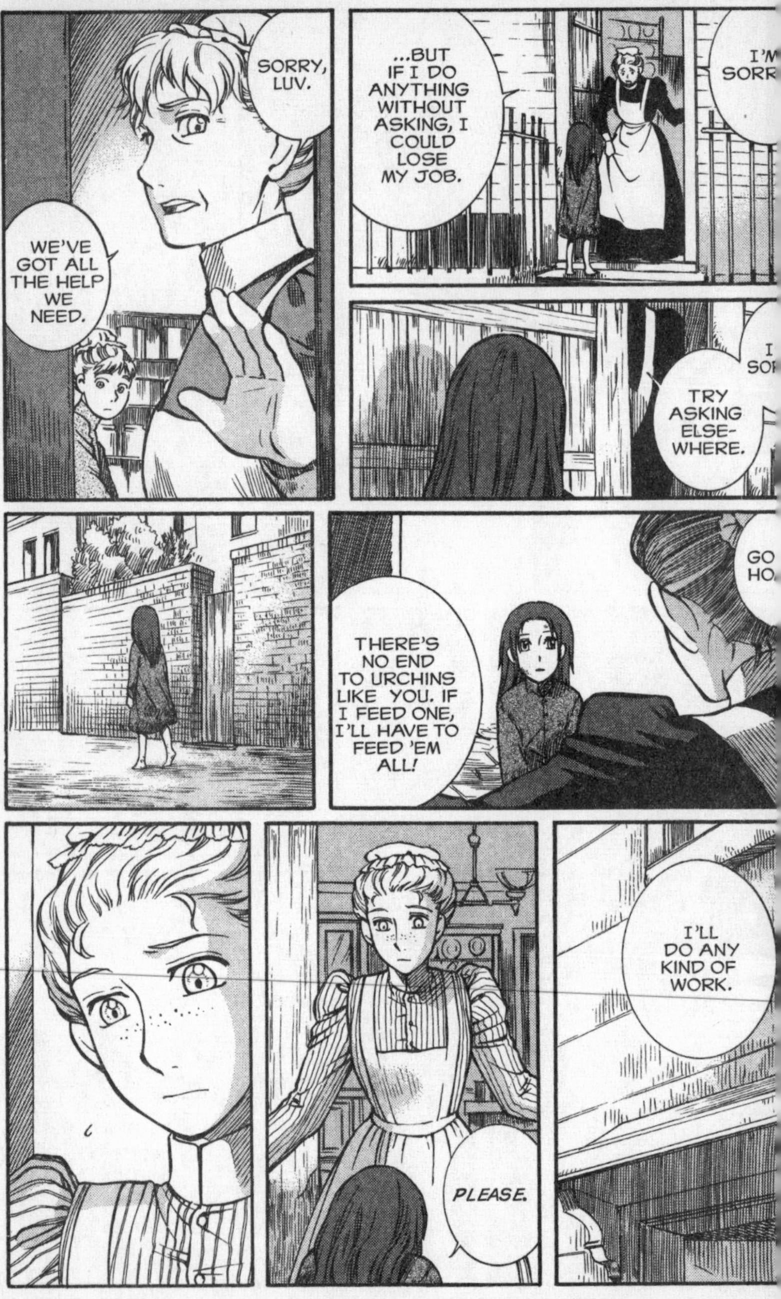
I'M SORR
...BUT IF I DO ANYTHING WITHOUT ASKING, I COULD LOSE MY JOB.
I SOR
TRY ASKING ELSE-WHERE.
SORRY, LUV.
WE'VE GOT ALL THE HELP WE NEED.
GO HO
THERE'S NO END TO URCHINS LIKE YOU. IF I FEED ONE, I'LL HAVE TO FEED 'EM ALL!
I'LL DO ANY KIND OF WORK.
PLEASE.

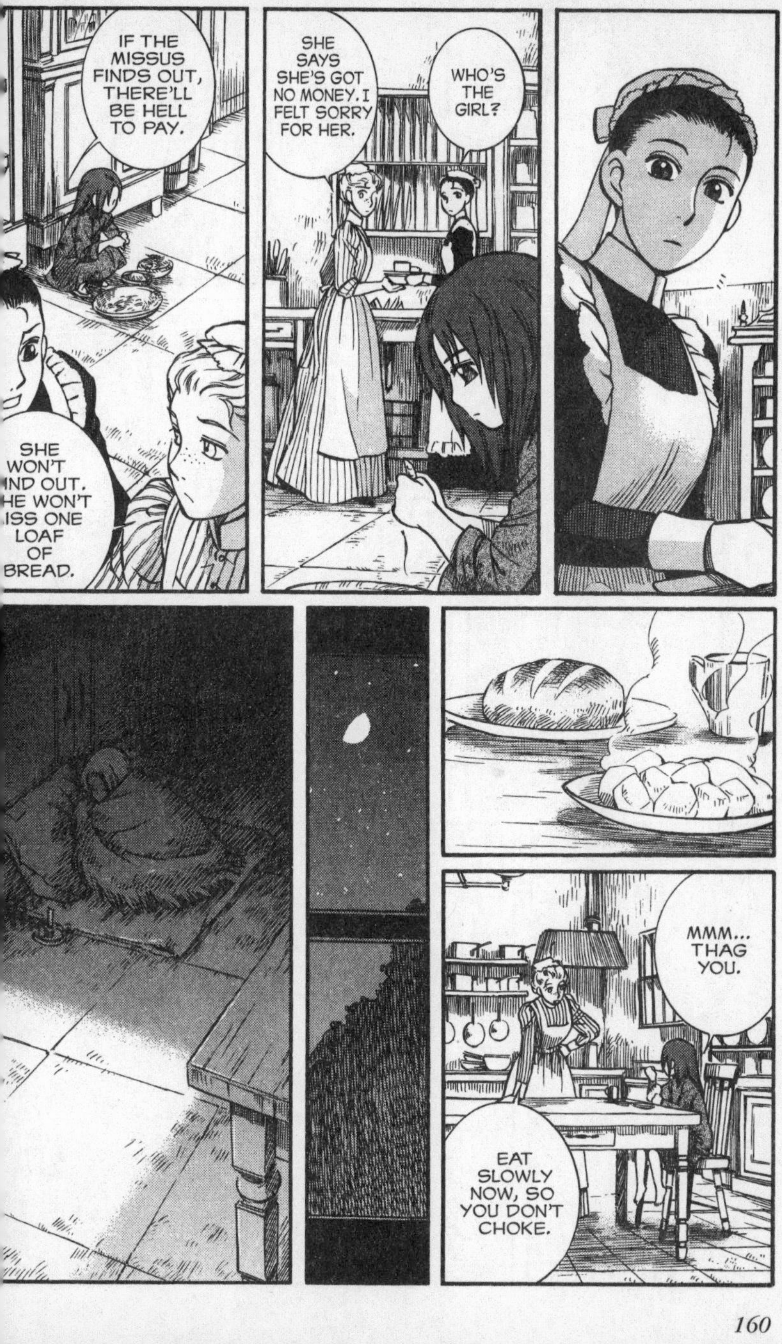
WHO'S THE GIRL?
SHE SAYS SHE'S GOT NO MONEY. I FELT SORRY FOR HER.
IF THE MISSUS FINDS OUT, THERE'LL BE HELL TO PAY.
SHE WON'T IND OUT. HE WON'T ISS ONE LOAF OF BREAD.
MMM... THAG YOU.
EAT SLOWLY NOW, SO YOU DON'T CHOKE.

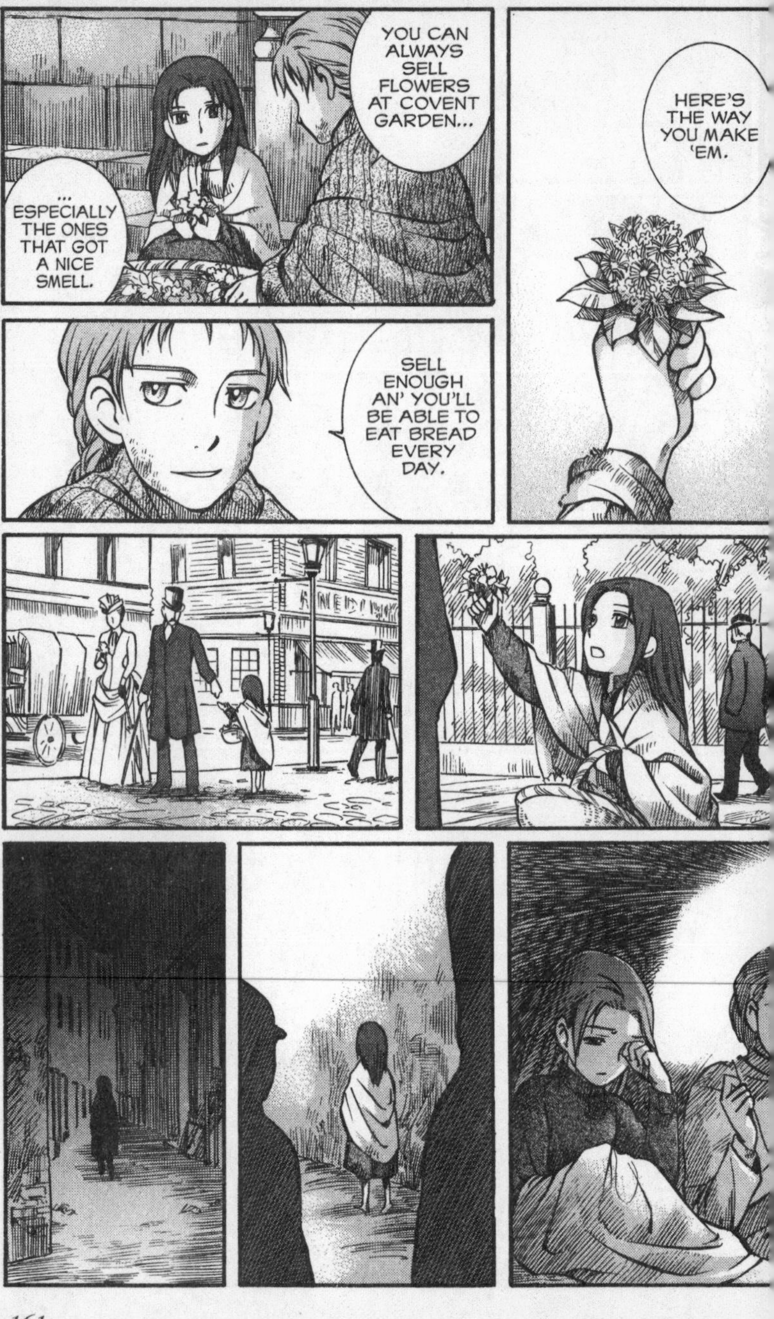
HERE'S THE WAY YOU MAKE 'EM.
YOU CAN ALWAYS SELL FLOWERS AT COVENT GARDEN...
... ESPECIALLY THE ONES THAT GOT A NICE SMELL.
SELL ENOUGH AN' YOU'LL BE ABLE TO EAT BREAD EVERY DAY.

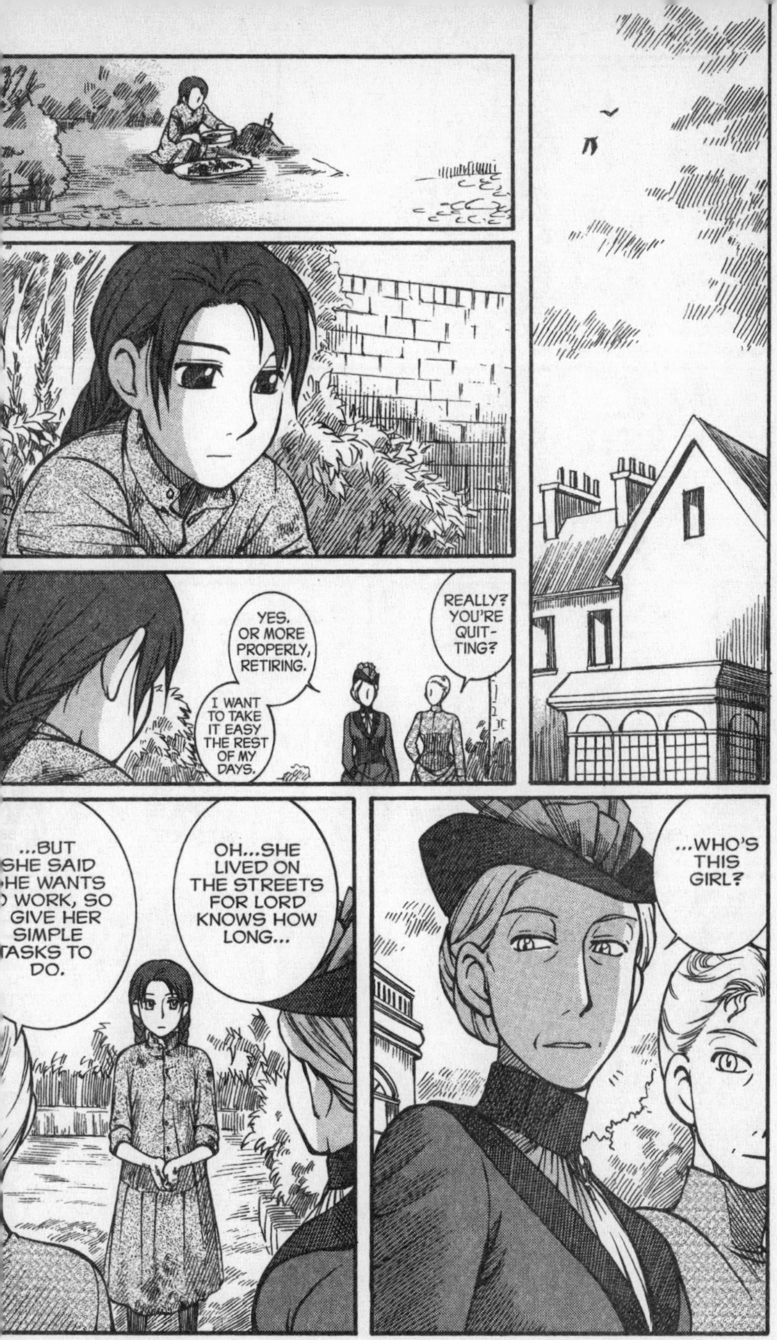
REALLY? YOU'RE QUIT-TING?
YES. OR MORE PROPERLY, RETIRING.
I WANT TO TAKE IT EASY THE REST OF MY DAYS.
...WHO'S THIS GIRL?
OH...SHE LIVED ON THE STREETS FOR LORD KNOWS HOW LONG...
...BUT SHE SAID HE WANTS O WORK, SO GIVE HER SIMPLE TASKS TO DO.

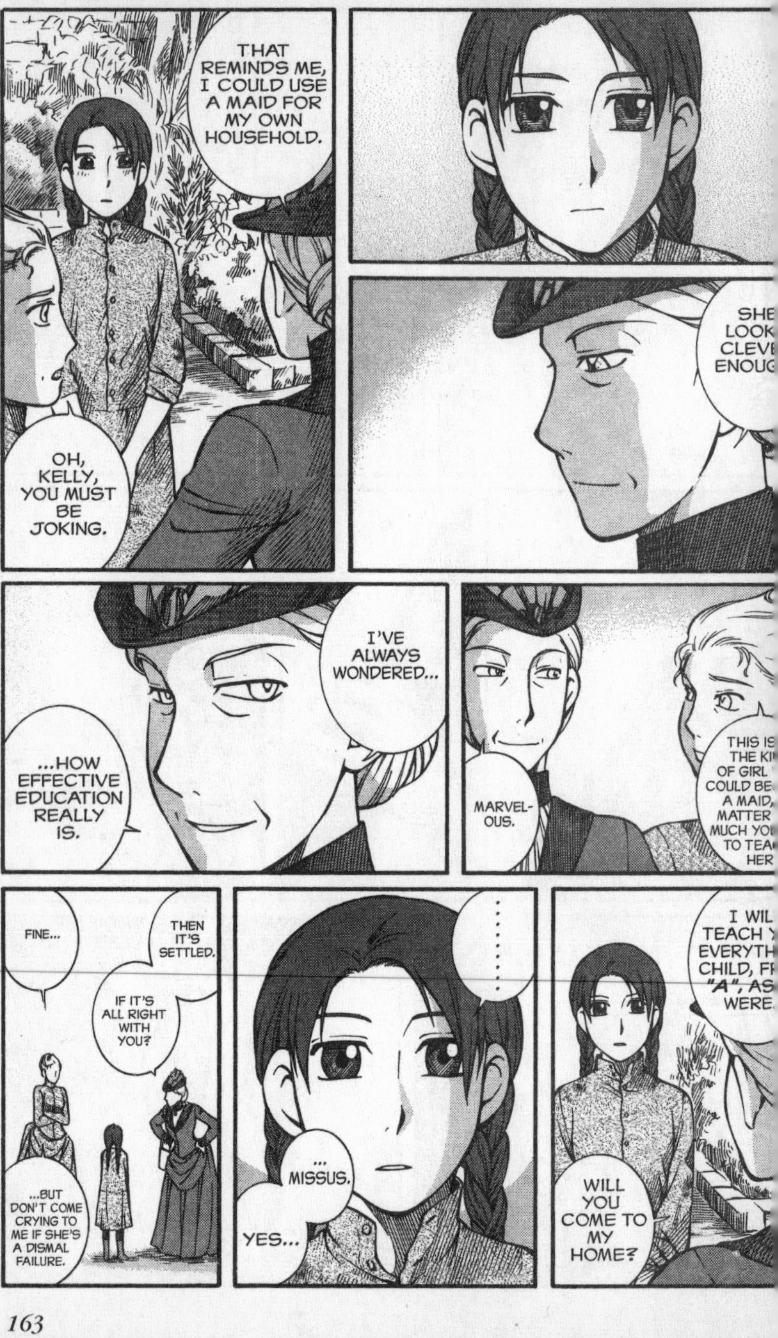
SHE LOOK CLEVE ENOUG
THAT REMINDS ME, I COULD USE A MAID FOR MY OWN HOUSEHOLD.
OH, KELLY, YOU MUST BE JOKING.
THIS IS THE KI OF GIRL COULD BE A MAID, MATTER MUCH YO TO TEA HER
MARVEL-OUS.
I'VE ALWAYS WONDERED...
...HOW EFFECTIVE EDUCATION REALLY IS.
I WIL TEACH Y EVERYTH CHILD, FR "A", AS WERE.
WILL YOU COME TO MY HOME?
......
... MISSUS.
YES...
THEN IT'S SETTLED.
FINE...
IF IT'S ALL RIGHT WITH YOU?
...BUT DON'T COME CRYING TO ME IF SHE'S A DISMAL FAILURE.

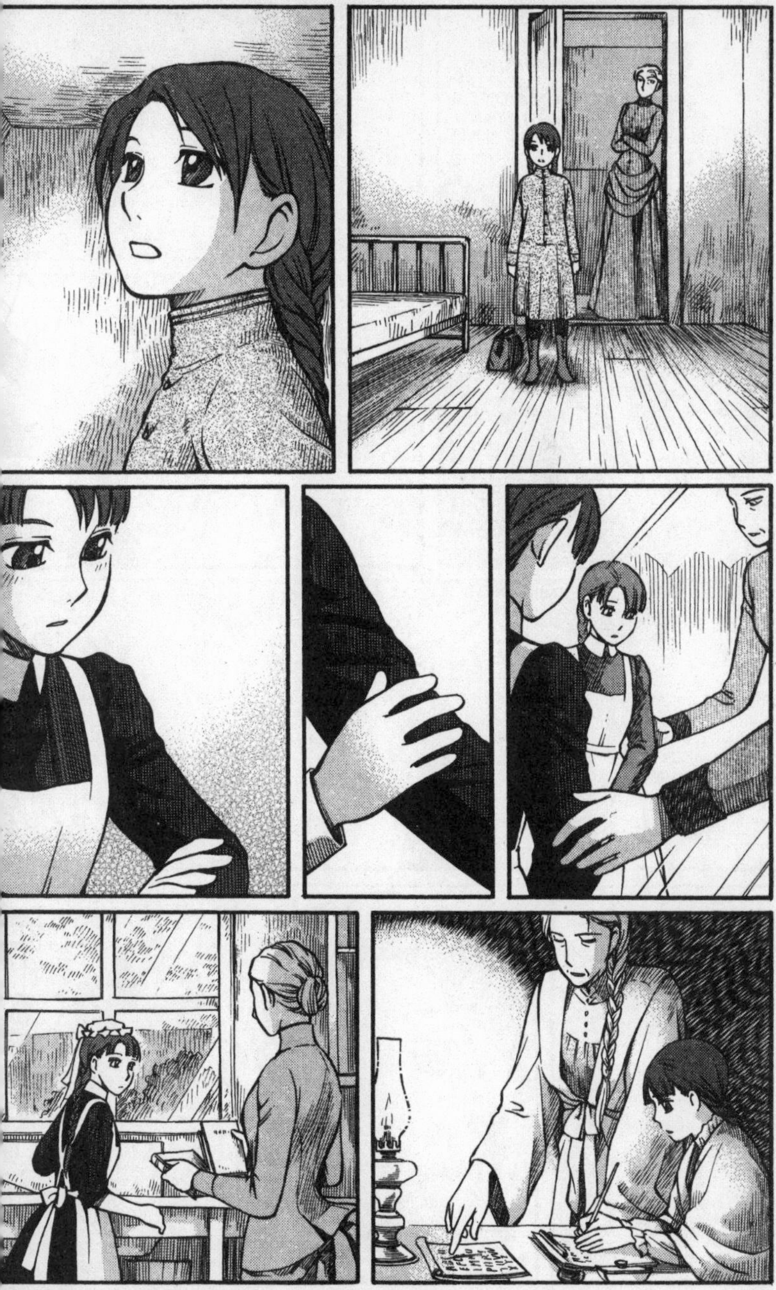

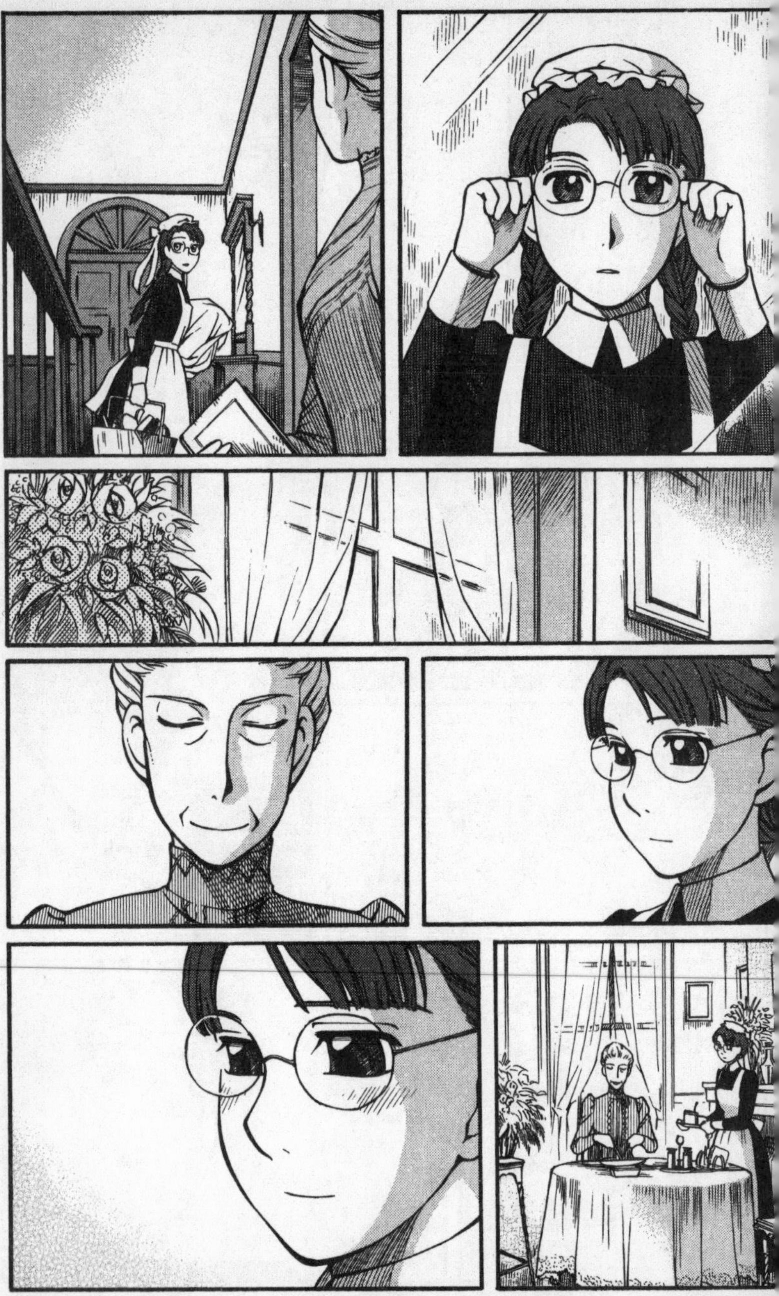

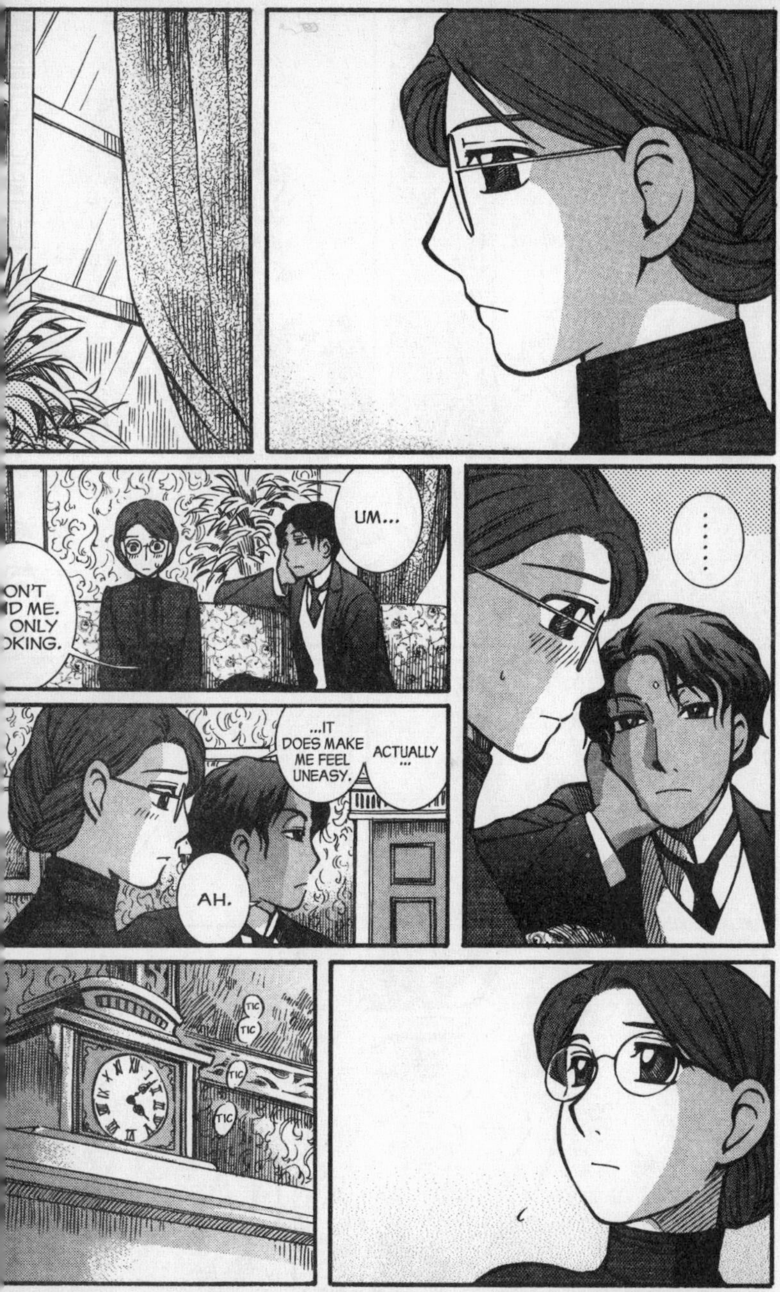
......
UM...
ON'T D ME. ONLY OKING.
ACTUALLY ...
...IT DOES MAKE ME FEEL UNEASY.
AH.
TIC
TIC
TIC
TIC

Chapter Thirteen: The End

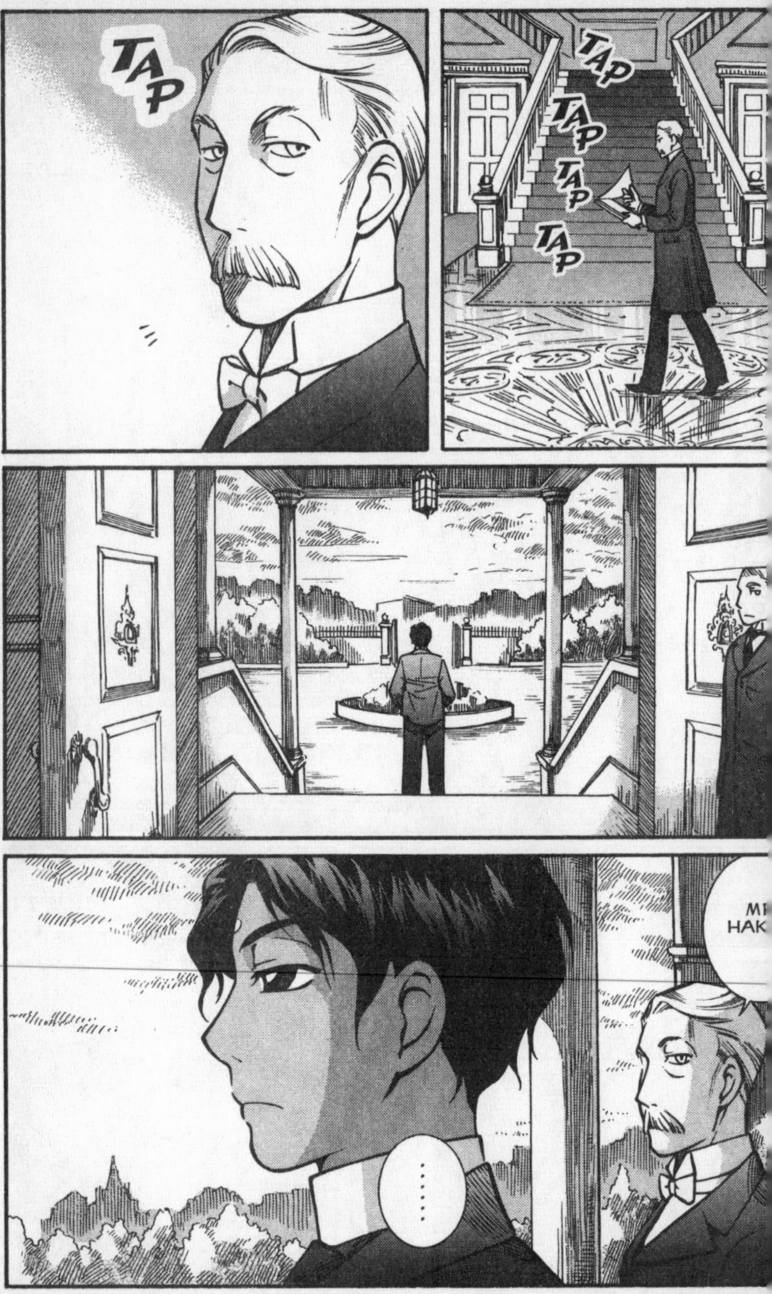
TAP
TAP
TAP
TAP
TAP
MR
HAK
......

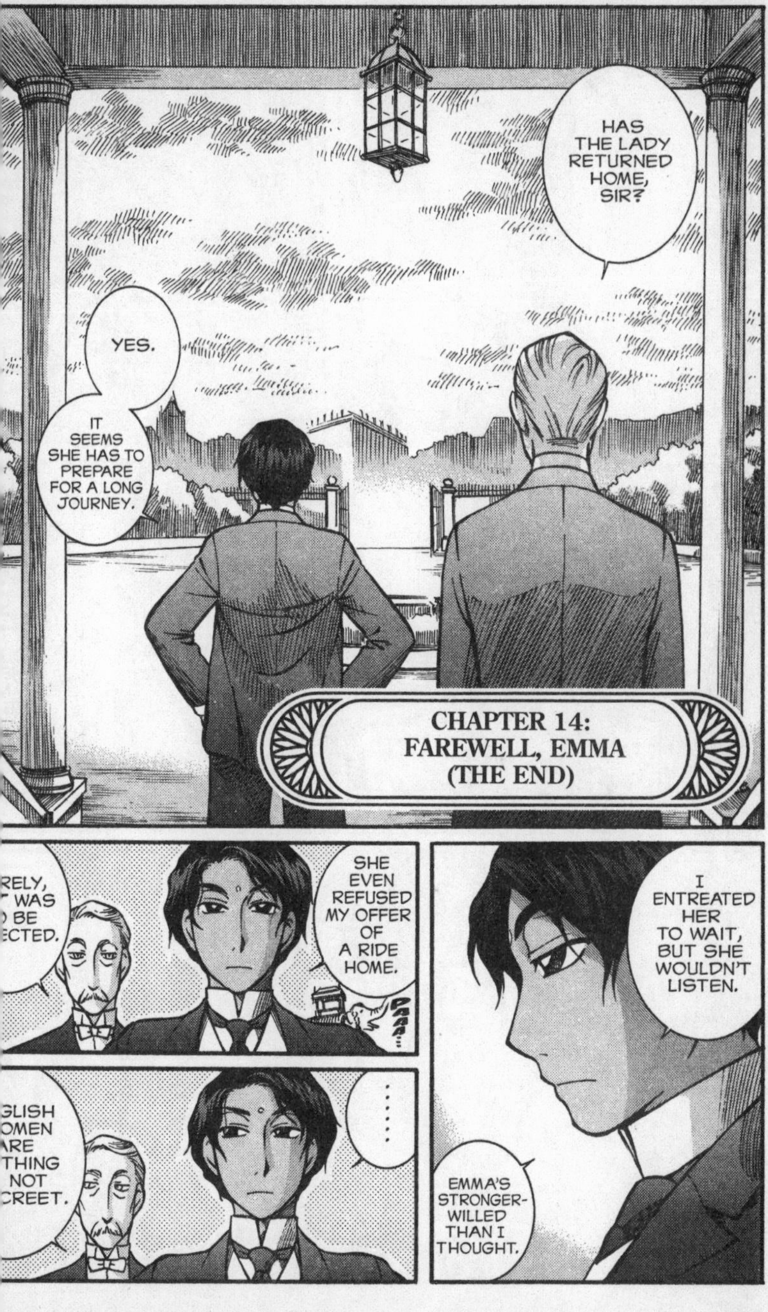
HAS THE LADY RETURNED HOME, SIR?
YES.
IT SEEMS SHE HAS TO PREPARE FOR A LONG JOURNEY.
CHAPTER 14: FAREWELL, EMMA (THE END)
I ENTREATED HER TO WAIT, BUT SHE WOULDN'T LISTEN.
EMMA'S STRONGER-WILLED THAN I THOUGHT.
SHE EVEN REFUSED MY OFFER OF A RIDE HOME.
RELY, T WAS D BE ECTED.
......
GLISH OMEN ARE THING NOT CREET.

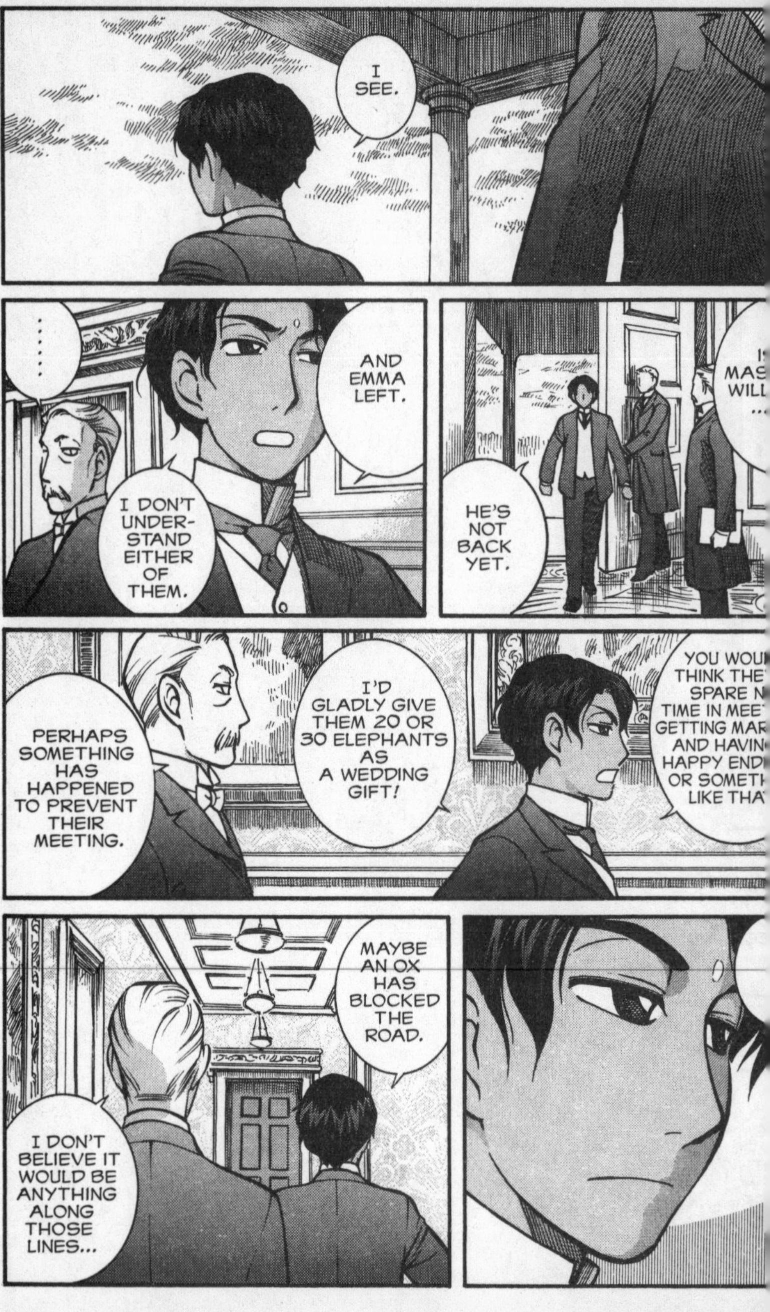
I SEE.
HE'S NOT BACK YET.
AND EMMA LEFT.
......
I DON'T UNDER-STAND EITHER OF THEM.
I'D GLADLY GIVE THEM 20 OR 30 ELEPHANTS AS A WEDDING GIFT!
PERHAPS SOMETHING HAS HAPPENED TO PREVENT THEIR MEETING.
MAYBE AN OX HAS BLOCKED THE ROAD.
I DON'T BELIEVE IT WOULD BE ANYTHING ALONG THOSE LINES...

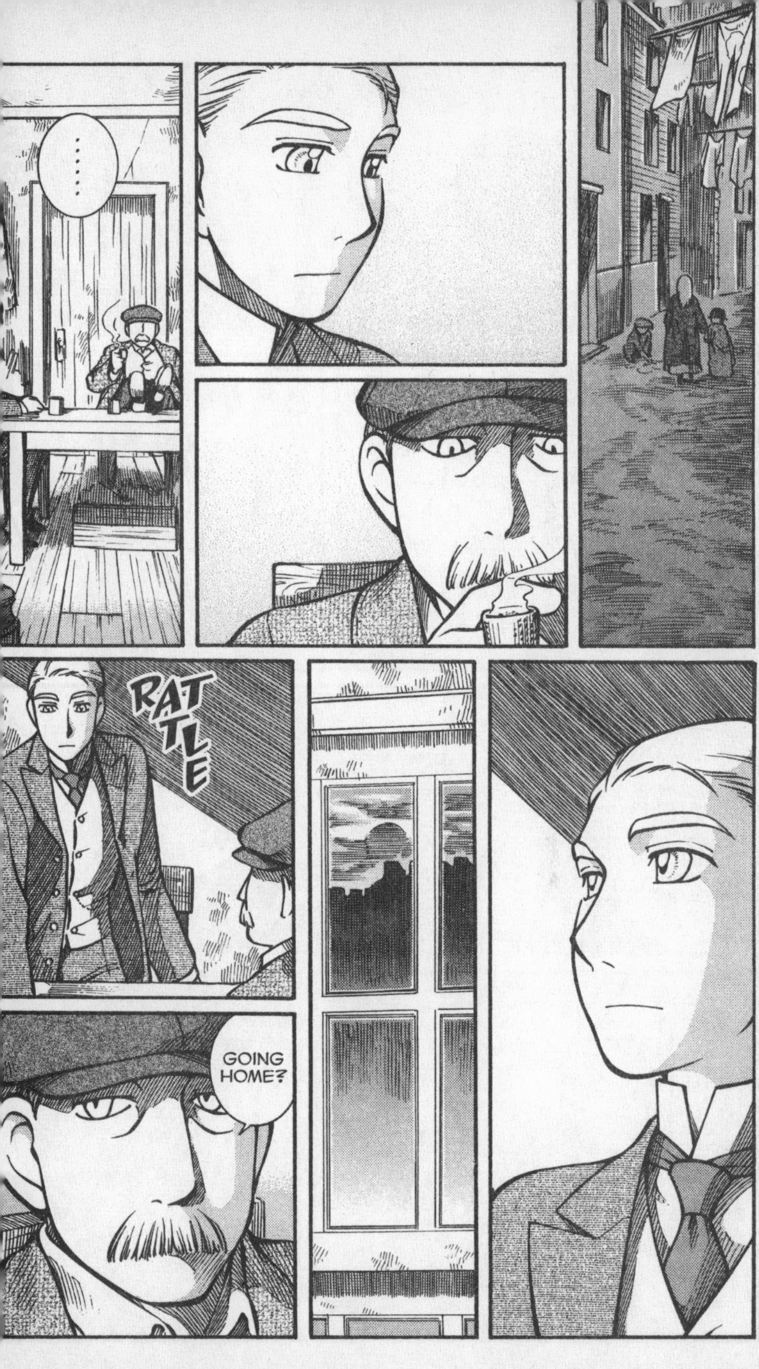
......
RATTLE
GOING HOME?

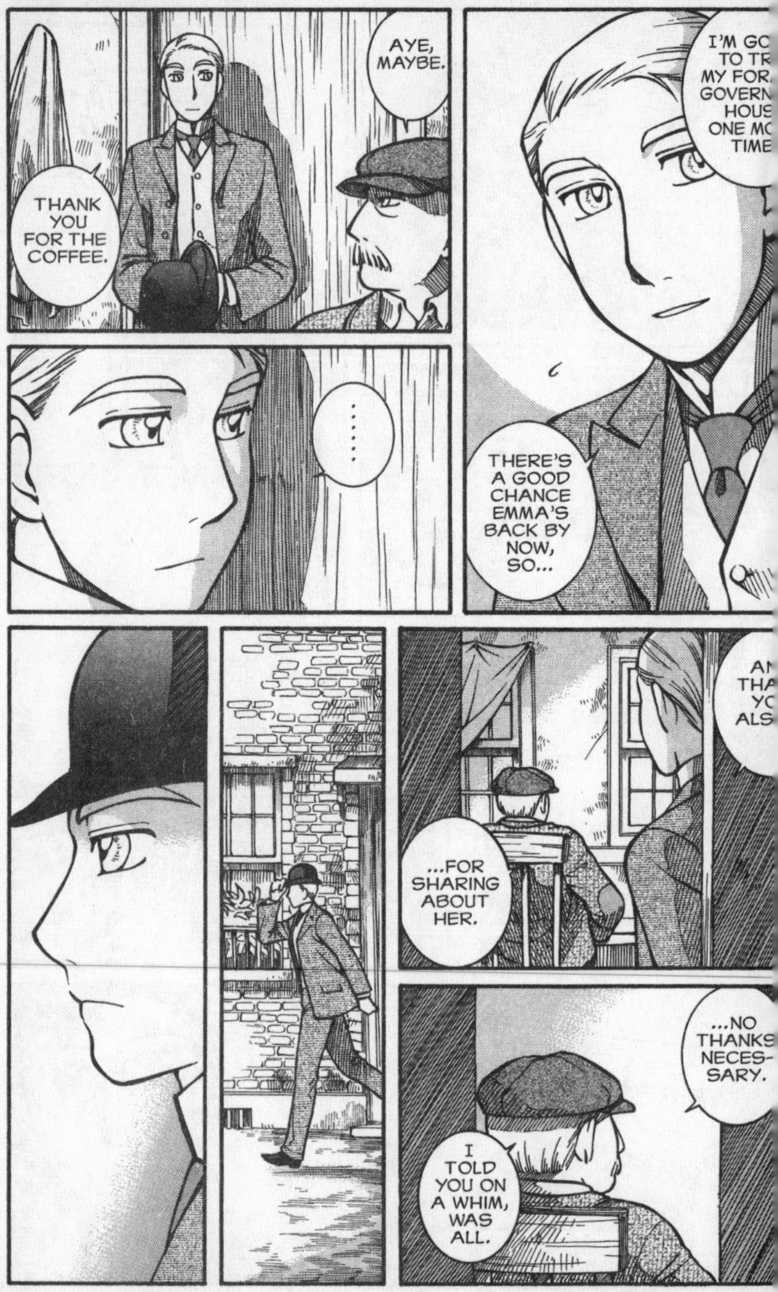
I'M GO TO TR MY FOR GOVERN HOUS ONE MO TIME
THERE'S A GOOD CHANCE EMMA'S BACK BY NOW, SO...
AYE, MAYBE.
THANK YOU FOR THE COFFEE.
......
AN THA YO ALS
...FOR SHARING ABOUT HER.
...NO THANKS NECES-SARY.
I TOLD YOU ON A WHIM, WAS ALL.

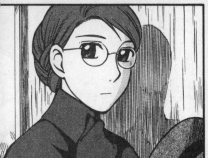

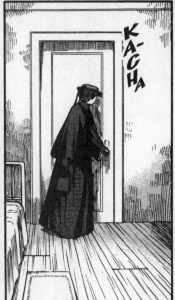

KA-
CHA

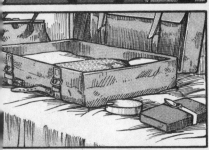

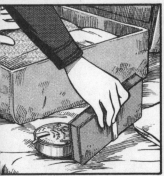

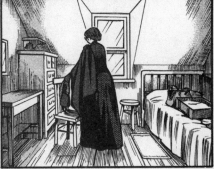

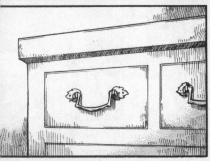

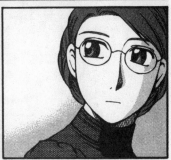

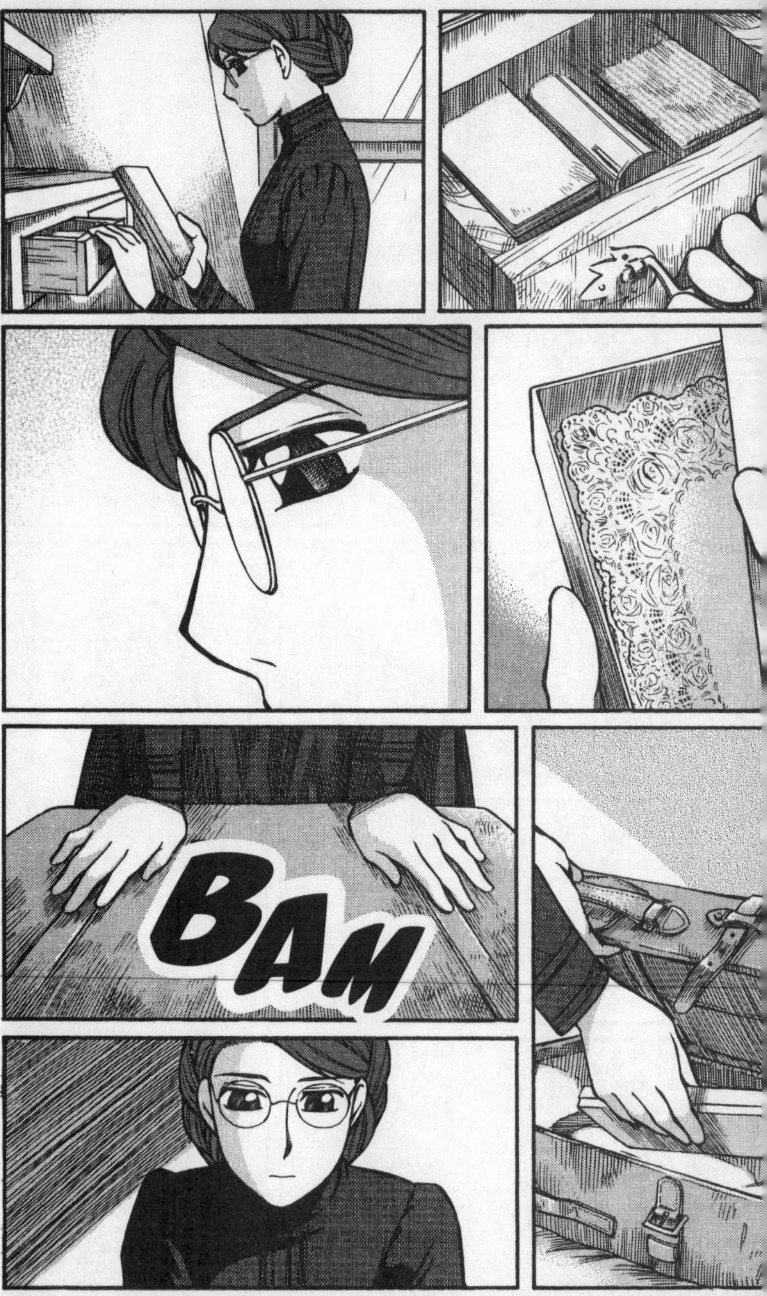
BAM

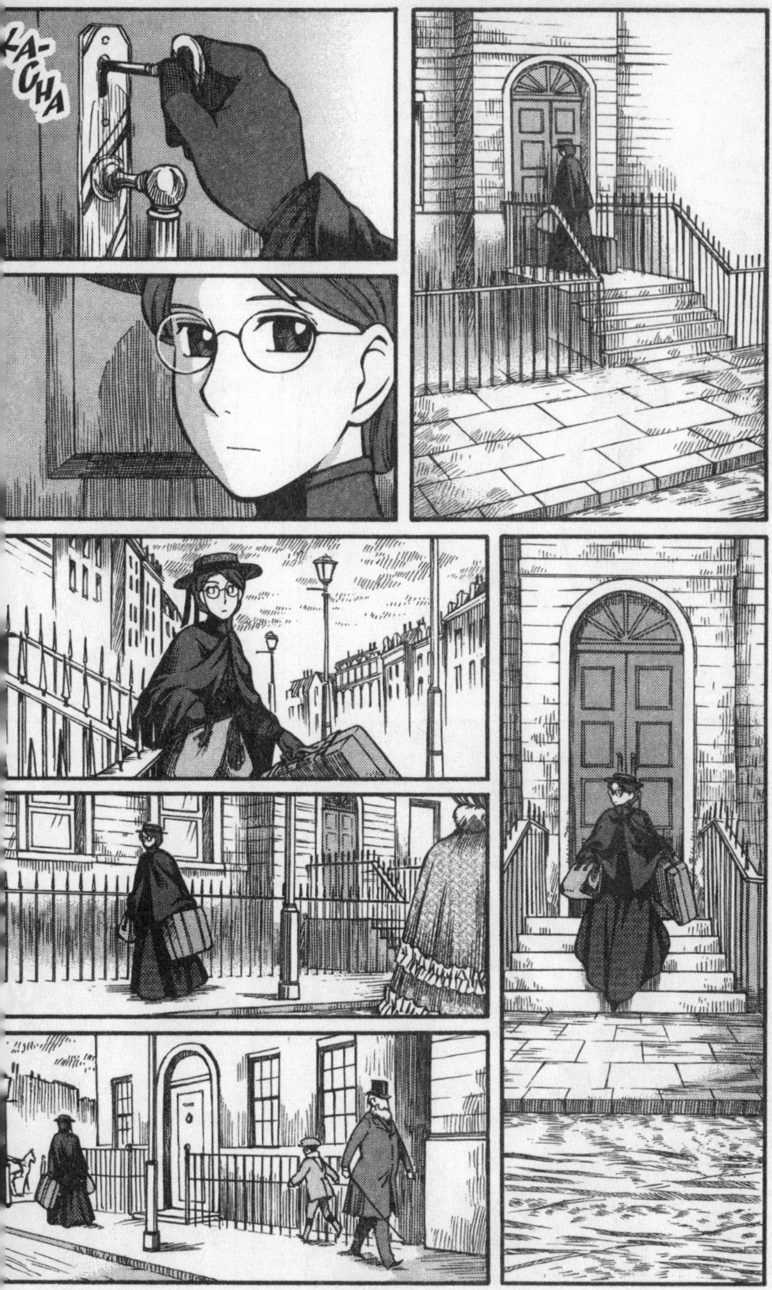
KA-
CHA

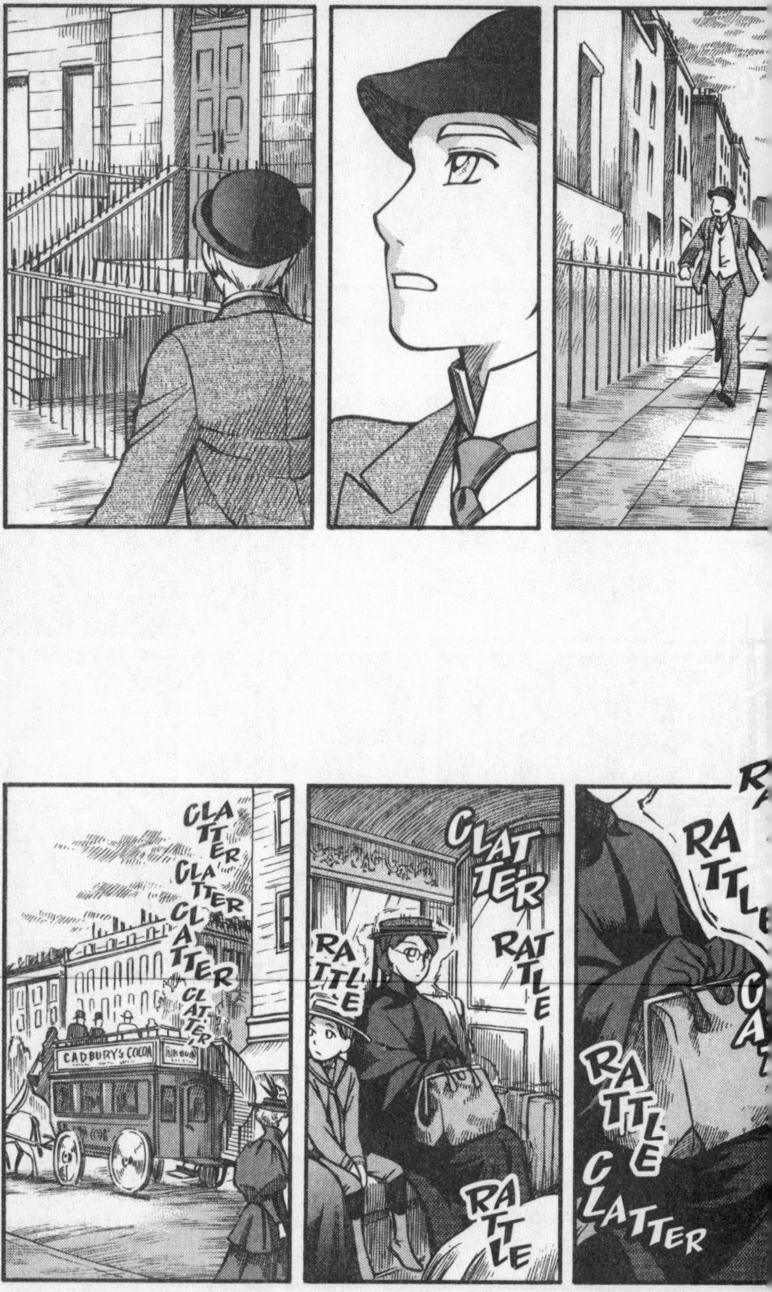
RATTLE
RATTLE
CLATTER
CLATTER
RATTLE
RATTLE
RATTLE
CLATTER
CLATTER
CLATTER
CLATTER
CADBURY'S COCOA

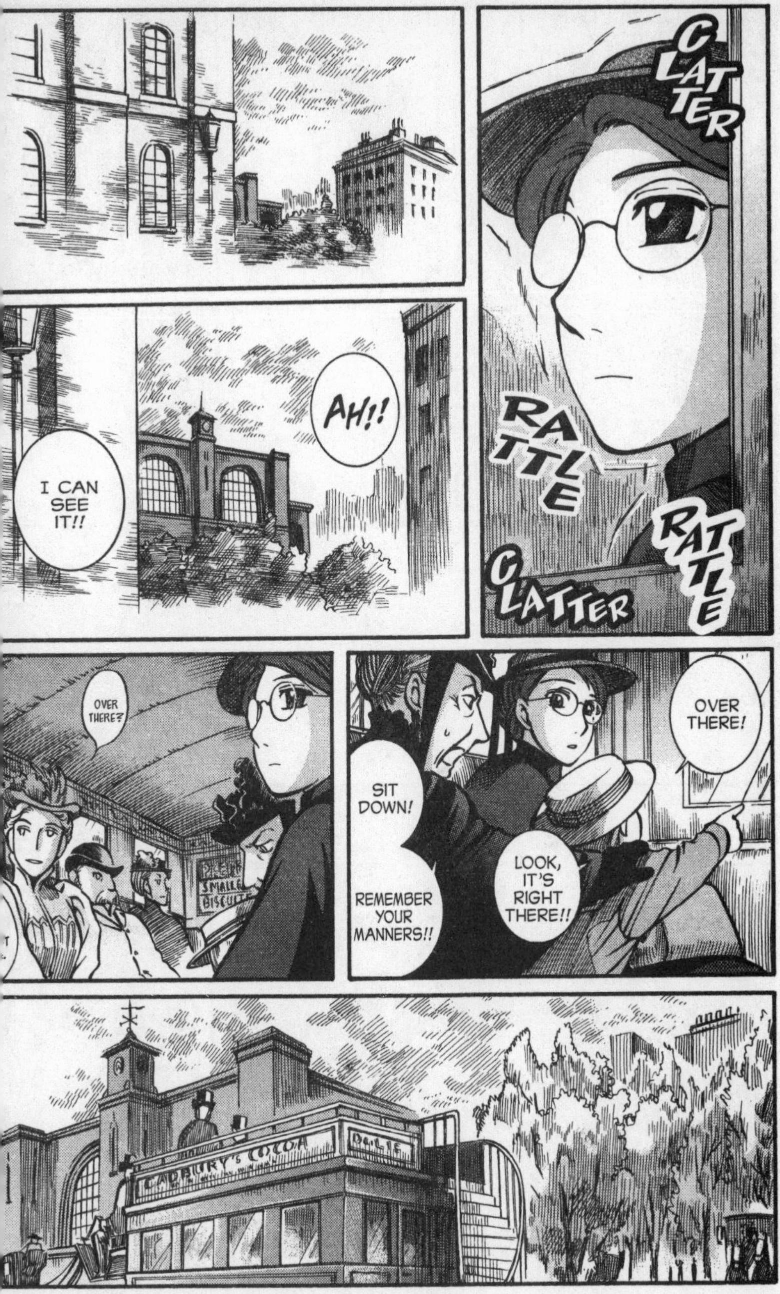
CLATTER
RATTLE
RATTLE
CLATTER
AH!!
I CAN SEE IT!!
OVER THERE!
LOOK, IT'S RIGHT THERE!!
SIT DOWN!
REMEMBER YOUR MANNERS!!
OVER THERE?
CADBURY'S COCOA

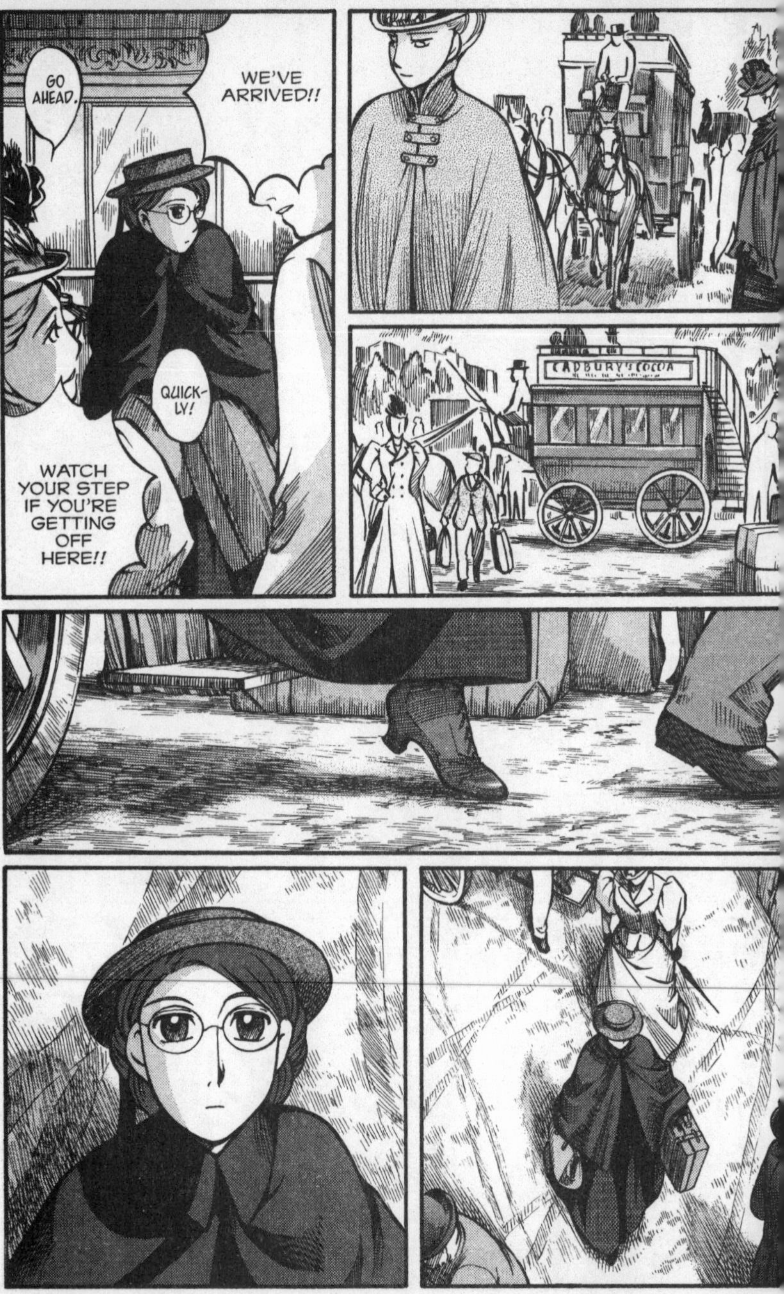
CADBURY'S COCOA
WE'VE ARRIVED!!
GO AHEAD.
QUICKLY!
WATCH YOUR STEP IF YOU'RE GETTING OFF HERE!!

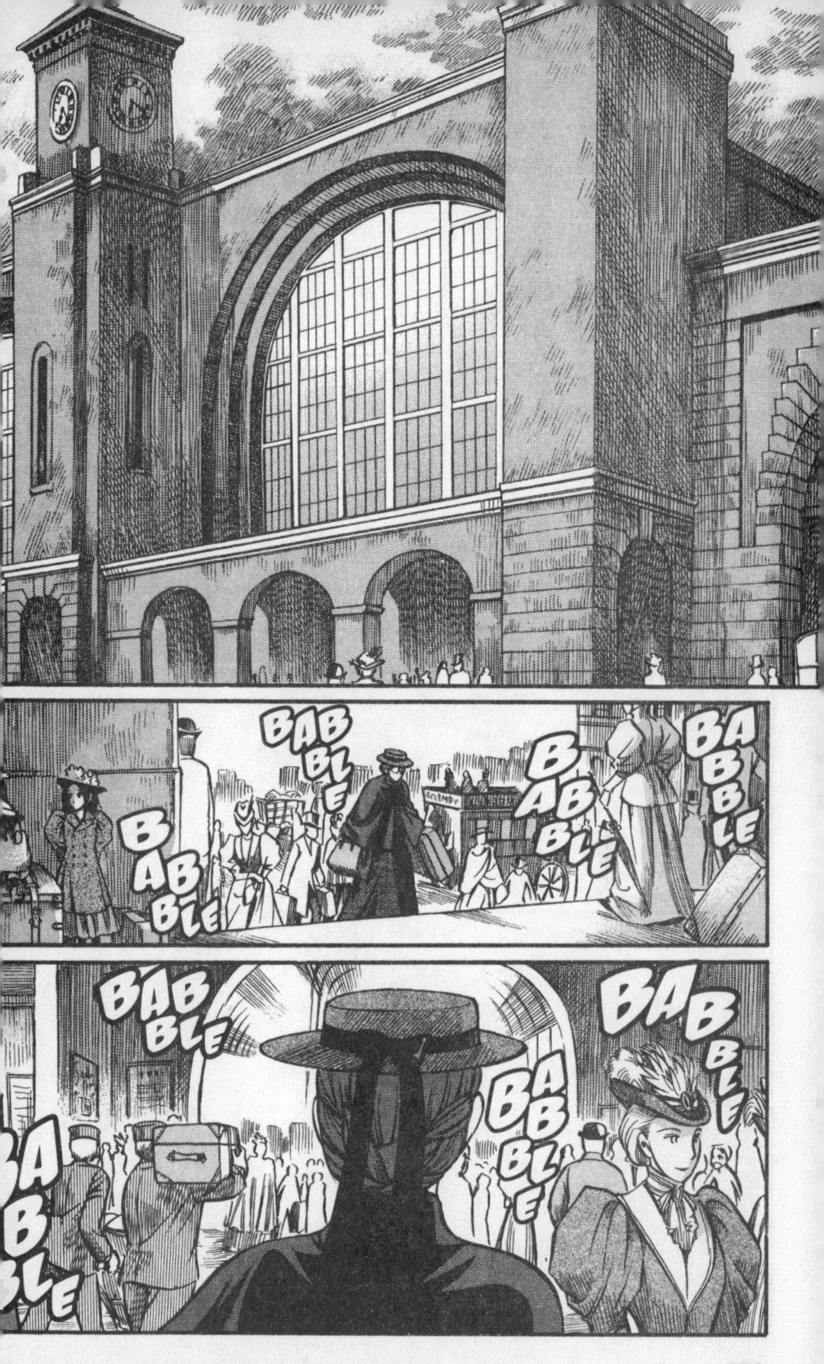
BABBLE
BABBLE
BABBLE
BABBLE
BABBLE
BABBLE
BABBLE
BABBLE

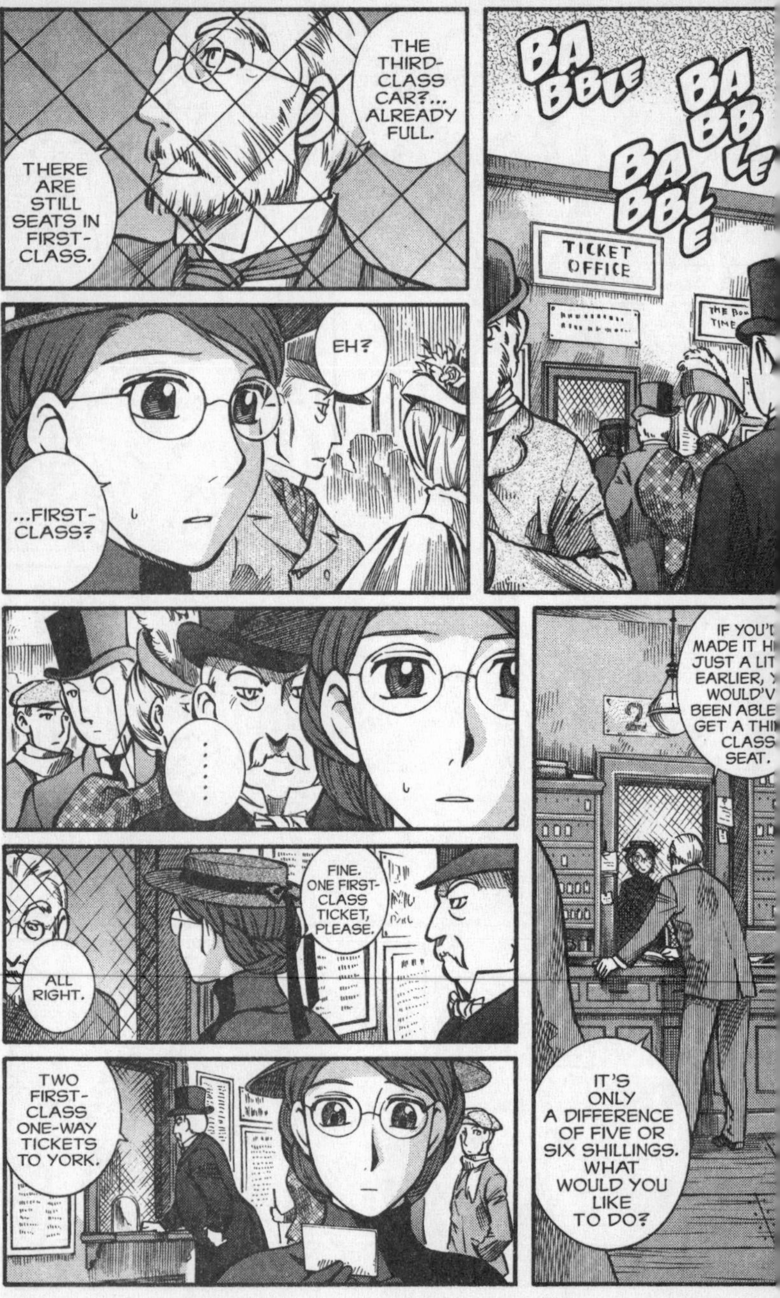
BABBLE BABBLE BABBLE
TICKET OFFICE
THE THIRD-CLASS CAR?... ALREADY FULL.
THERE ARE STILL SEATS IN FIRST-CLASS.
EH?
...FIRST-CLASS?
IF YOU'D MADE IT H JUST A LIT EARLIER, Y WOULD'V BEEN ABLE GET A THI CLASS SEAT.
IT'S ONLY A DIFFERENCE OF FIVE OR SIX SHILLINGS. WHAT WOULD YOU LIKE TO DO?
......
FINE. ONE FIRST-CLASS TICKET, PLEASE.
ALL RIGHT.
TWO FIRST-CLASS ONE-WAY TICKETS TO YORK.

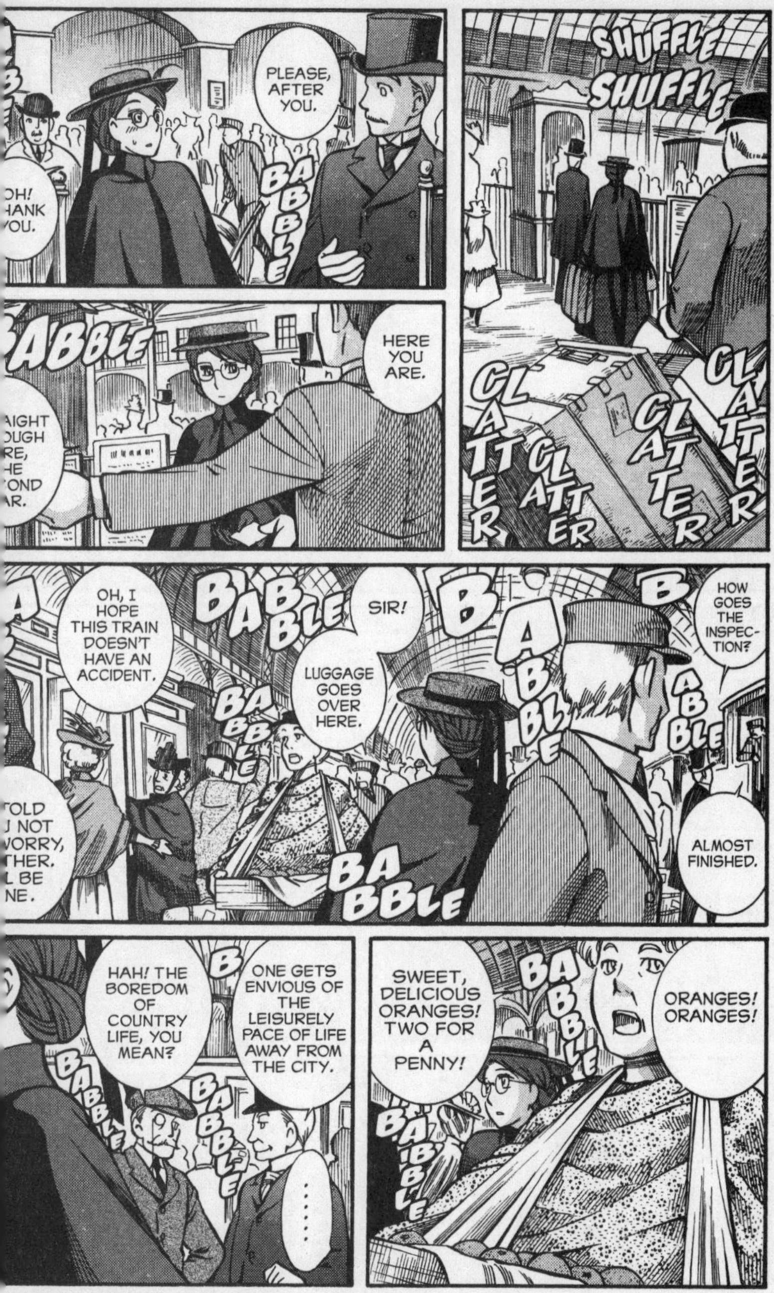
SHUFFLE
SHUFFLE
PLEASE, AFTER YOU.
BABBLE
OH! HANK YOU.
CLATTER
CLATTER
CLATTER
CLATTER
HERE YOU ARE.
BABBLE
AIGHT OUGH RE, HE COND AR.
HOW GOES THE INSPECTION?
BABBLE
ALMOST FINISHED.
BABBLE
SIR!
LUGGAGE GOES OVER HERE.
BABBLE
BABBLE
OH, I HOPE THIS TRAIN DOESN'T HAVE AN ACCIDENT.
BABBLE
TOLD U NOT WORRY, THER. L BE NE.
ORANGES! ORANGES!
BABBLE
SWEET, DELICIOUS ORANGES! TWO FOR A PENNY!
BABBLE
ONE GETS ENVIOUS OF THE LEISURELY PACE OF LIFE AWAY FROM THE CITY.
BABBLE
HAH! THE BOREDOM OF COUNTRY LIFE, YOU MEAN?
......
BABBLE

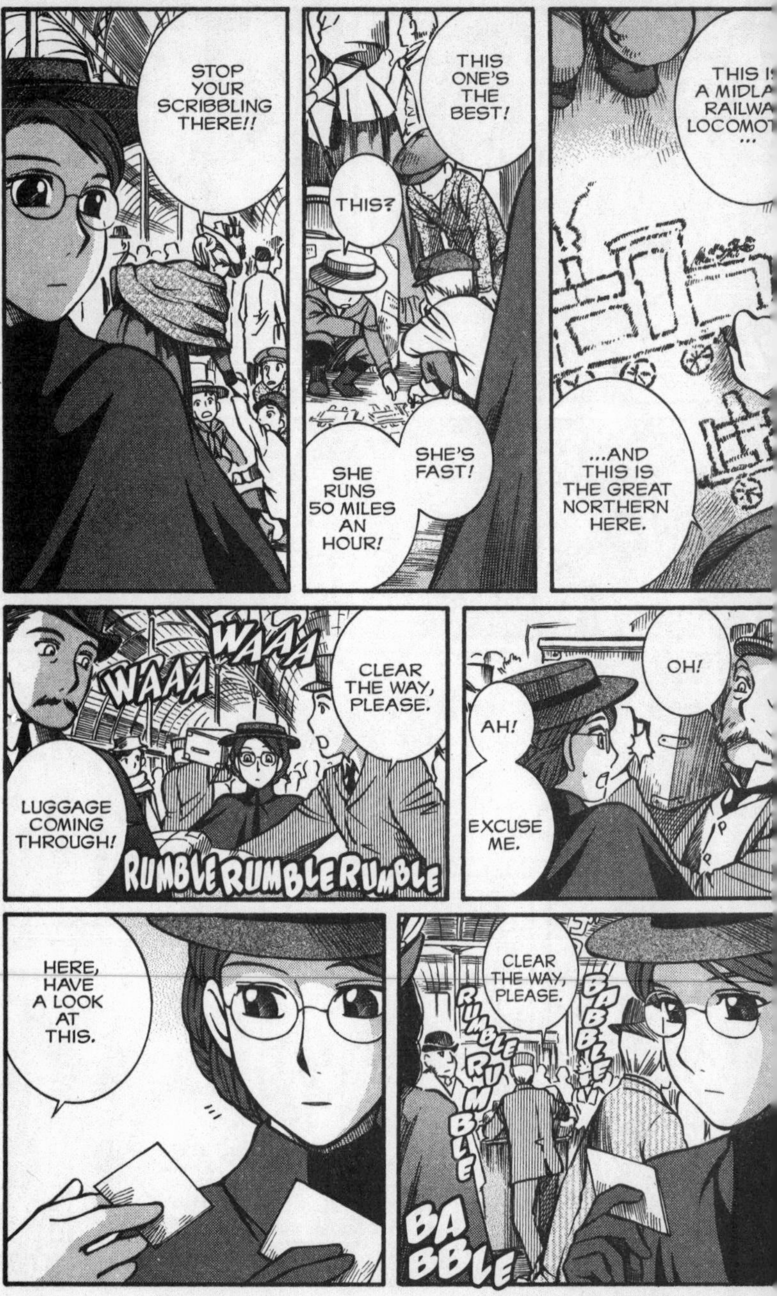
THIS IS A MIDLA RAILWA LOCOMOT ...
...AND THIS IS THE GREAT NORTHERN HERE.
THIS ONE'S THE BEST!
THIS?
SHE'S FAST!
SHE RUNS 50 MILES AN HOUR!
STOP YOUR SCRIBBLING THERE!!
OH!
AH!
EXCUSE ME.
CLEAR THE WAY, PLEASE.
WAAA
WAAA
LUGGAGE COMING THROUGH!
RUMBLE RUMBLE RUMBLE
CLEAR THE WAY, PLEASE.
BABBLE
RUMBLE RUMBLE
BABBLE
HERE, HAVE A LOOK AT THIS.

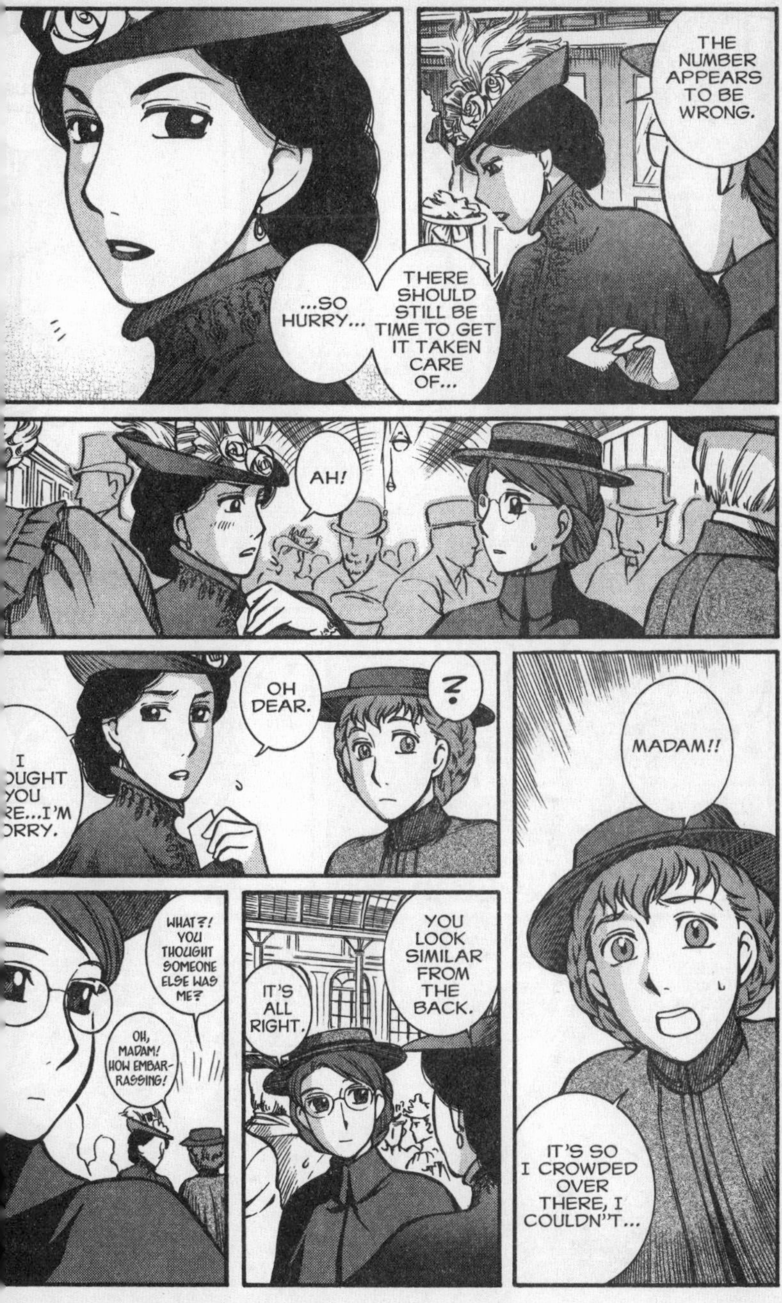
THE NUMBER APPEARS TO BE WRONG.
THERE SHOULD STILL BE TIME TO GET IT TAKEN CARE OF...
...SO HURRY...
AH!
MADAM!!
IT'S SO I CROWDED OVER THERE, I COULDN'T...
?
OH DEAR.
I OUGHT YOU RE...I'M ORRY.
YOU LOOK SIMILAR FROM THE BACK.
IT'S ALL RIGHT.
WHAT?! YOU THOUGHT SOMEONE ELSE WAS ME?
OH, MADAM! HOW EMBARRASSING!

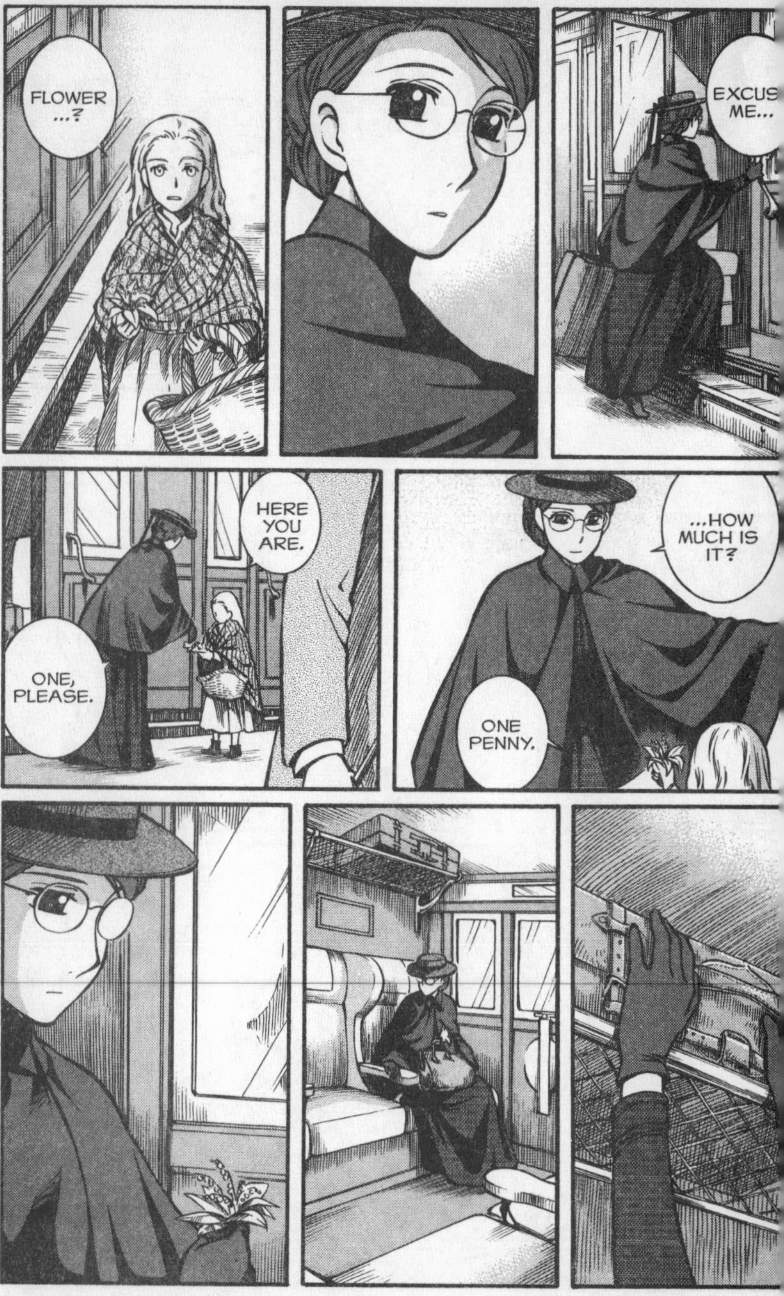
EXCUS ME...
FLOWER ...?
...HOW MUCH IS IT?
ONE PENNY.
HERE YOU ARE.
ONE, PLEASE.

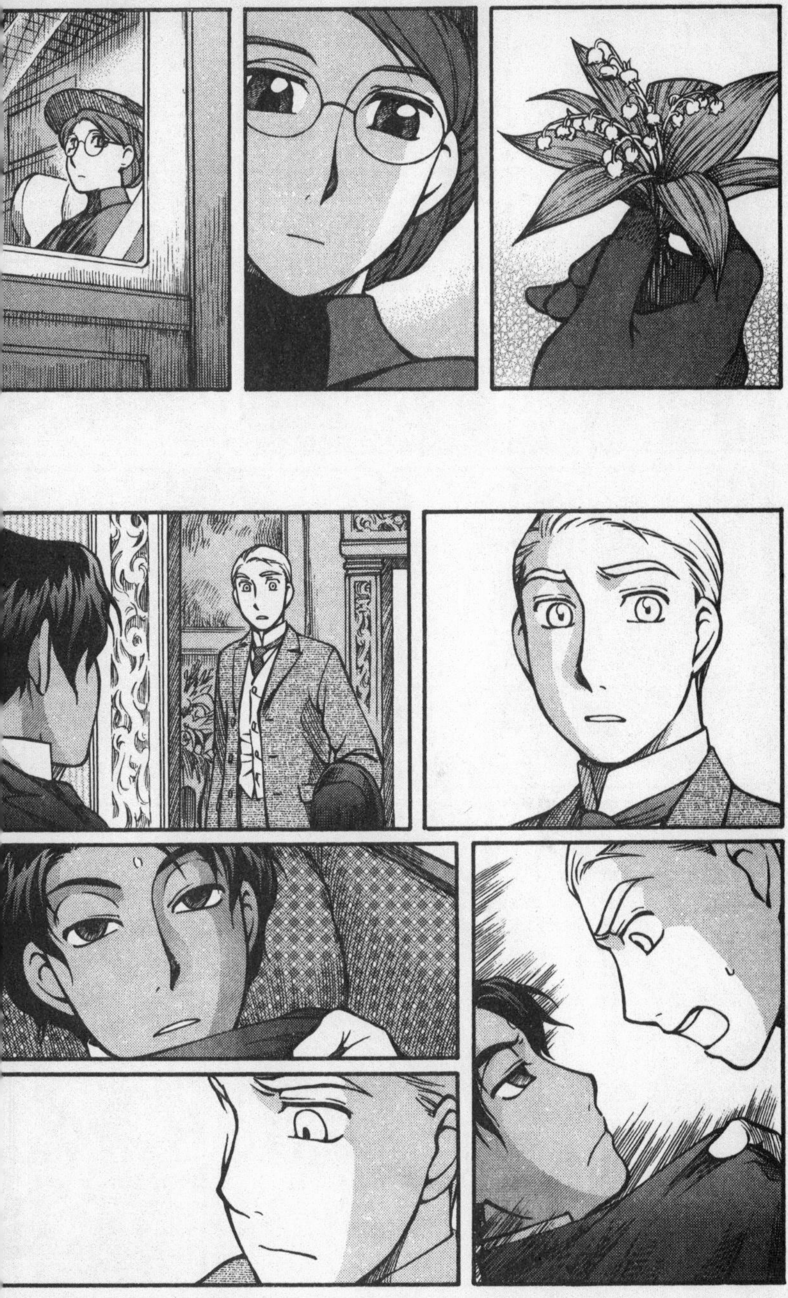

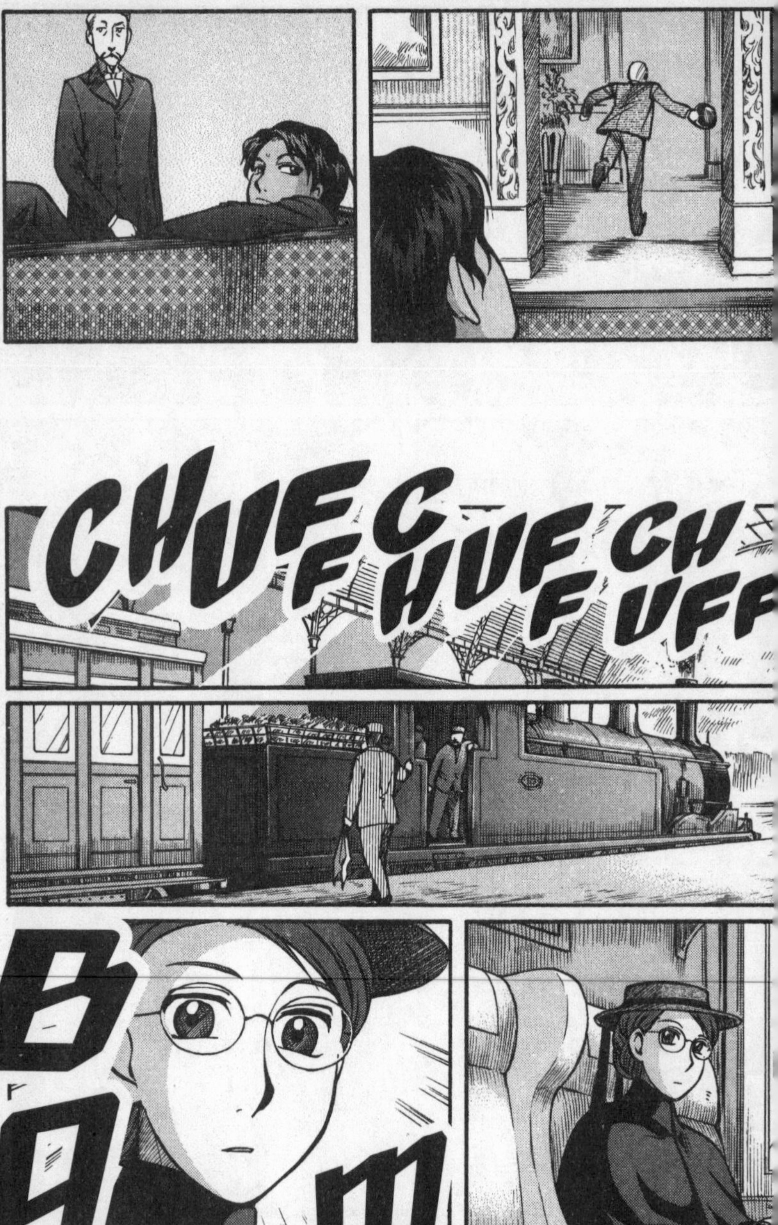
CHUFF
CHUFF
CHUFF
BAM

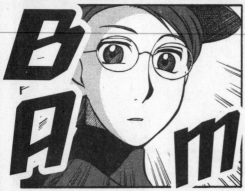

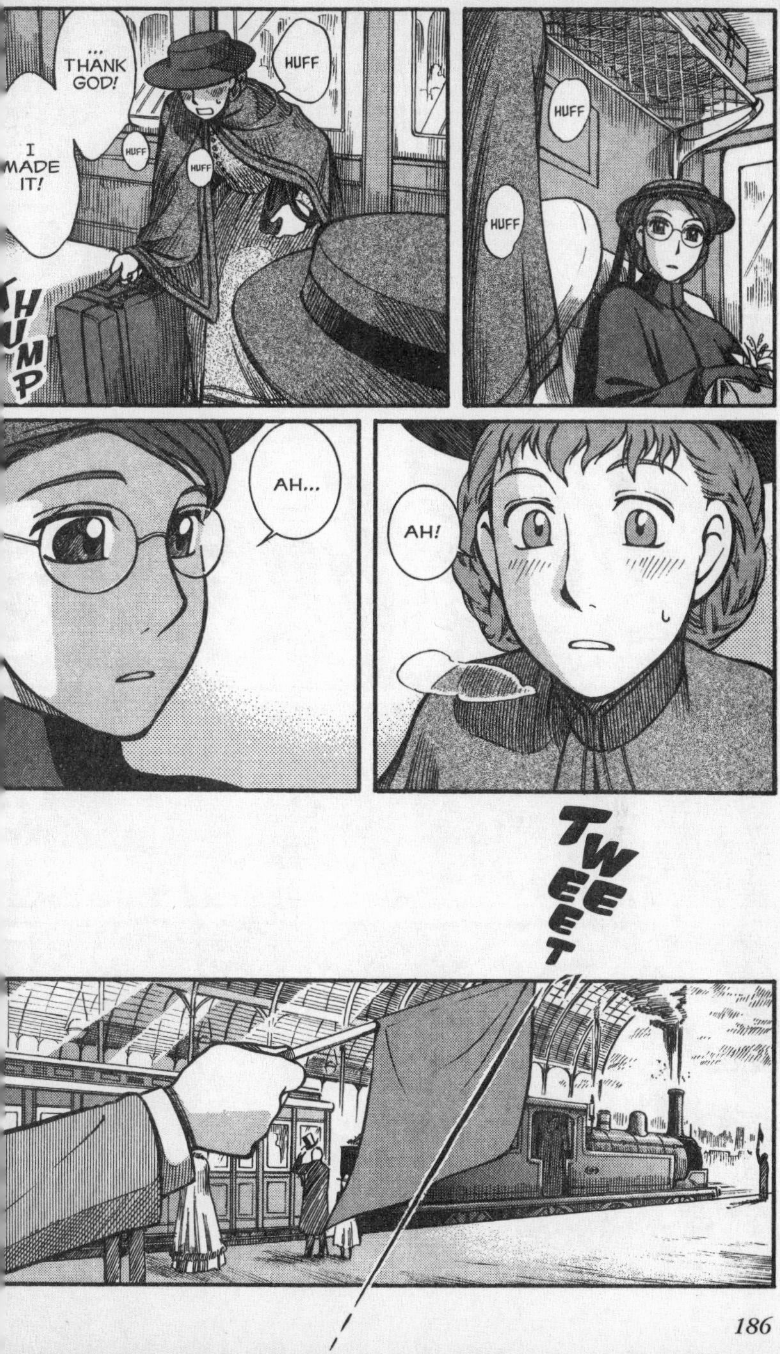
HUFF
HUFF
HUFF
... THANK GOD!
I MADE IT!
HUFF
HUFF
THUMP
AH!
AH...
TWEET

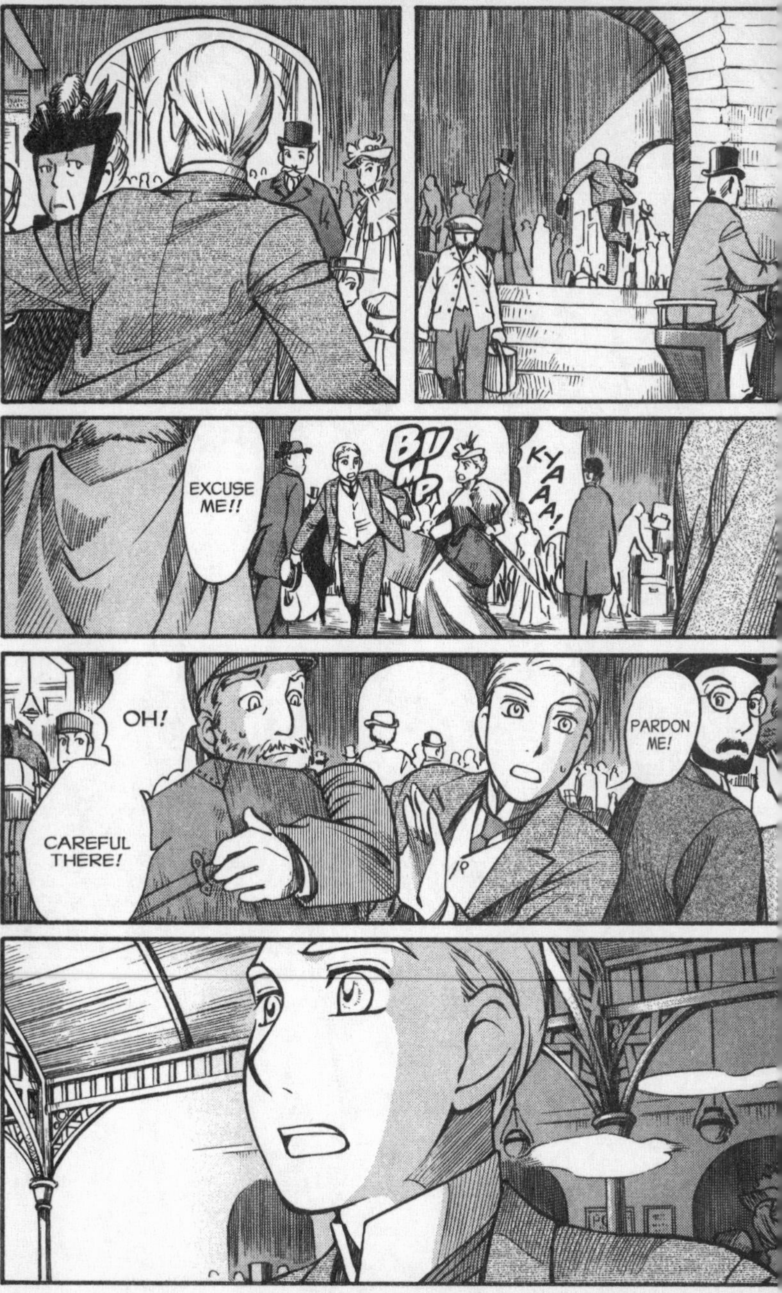
KYAAA!
BUMP
EXCUSE ME!!
PARDON ME!
OH!
CAREFUL THERE!

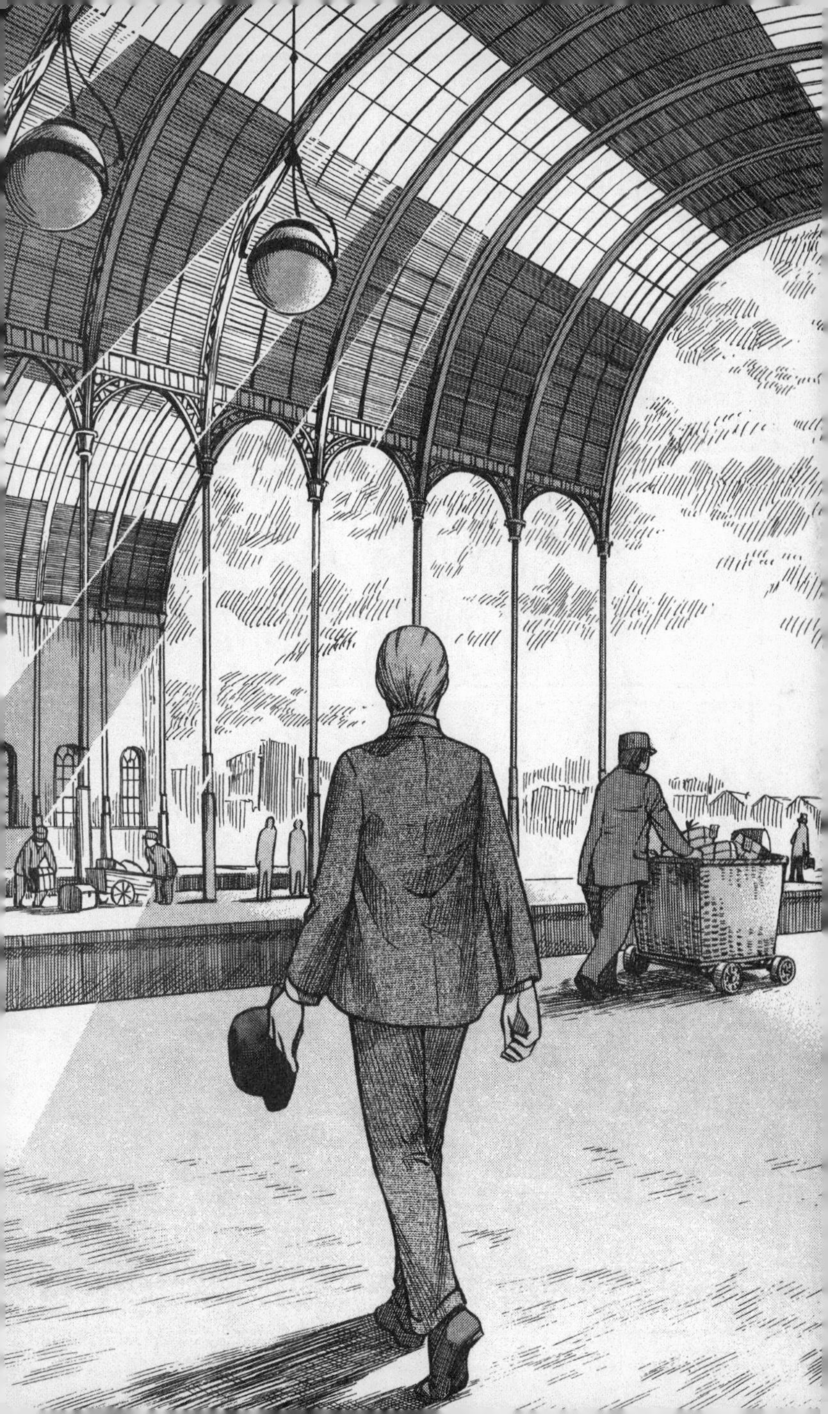

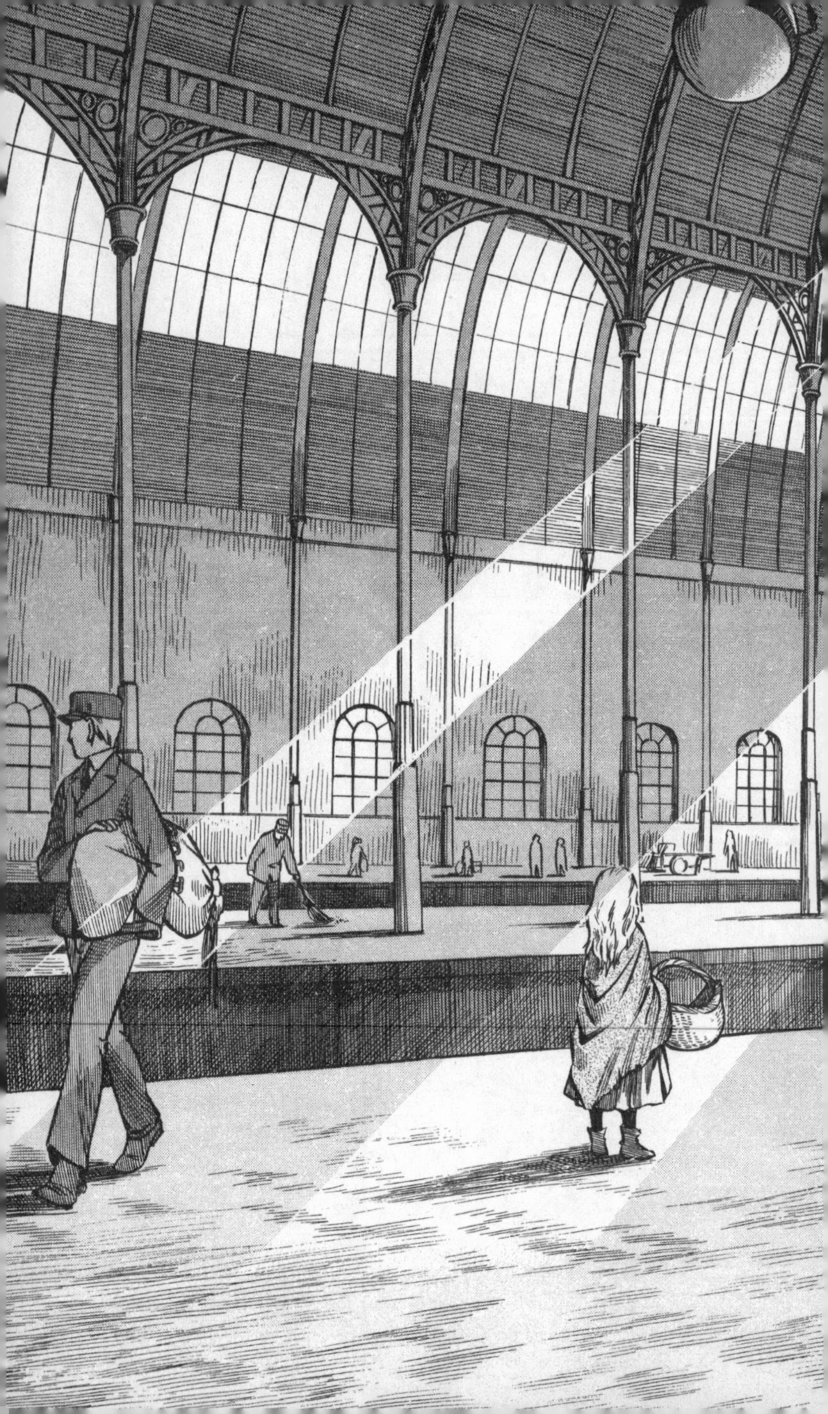

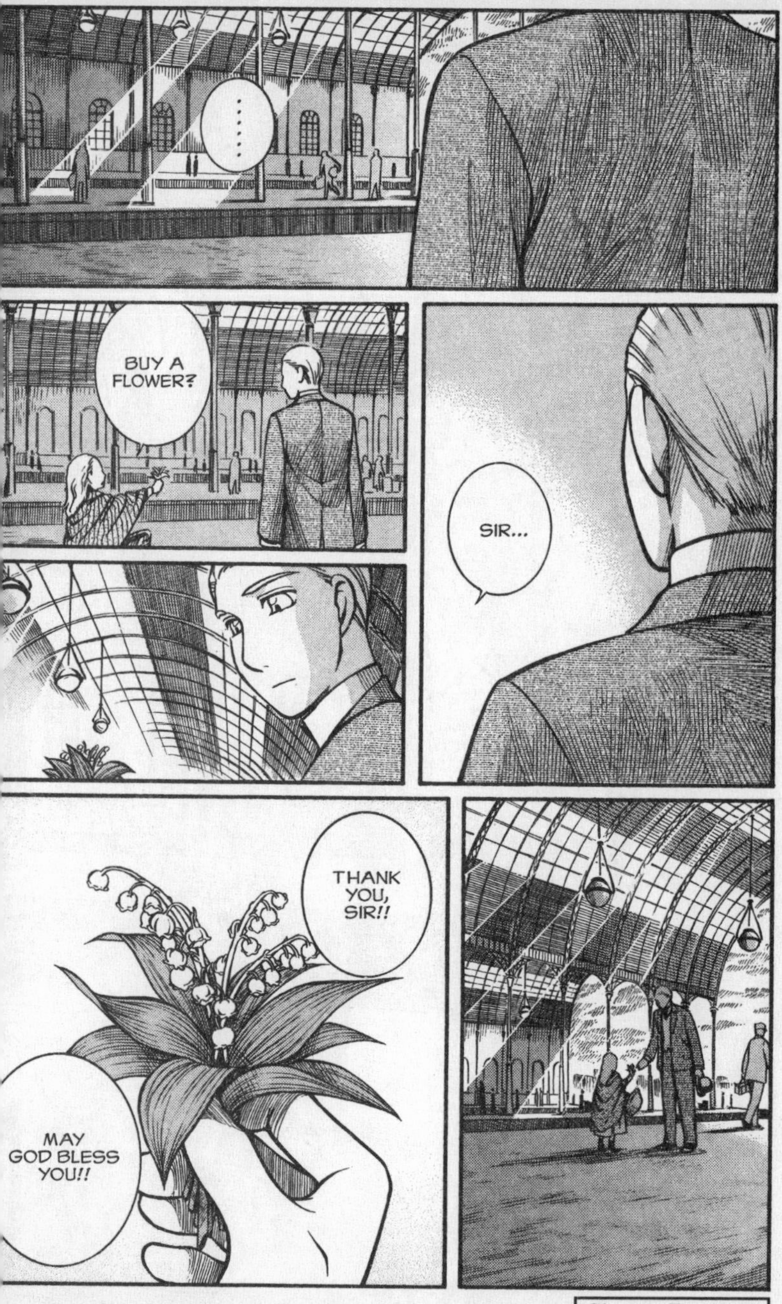
......
SIR...
BUY A FLOWER?
THANK YOU, SIR!!
MAY GOD BLESS YOU!!

Chapter Fourteen:
The End

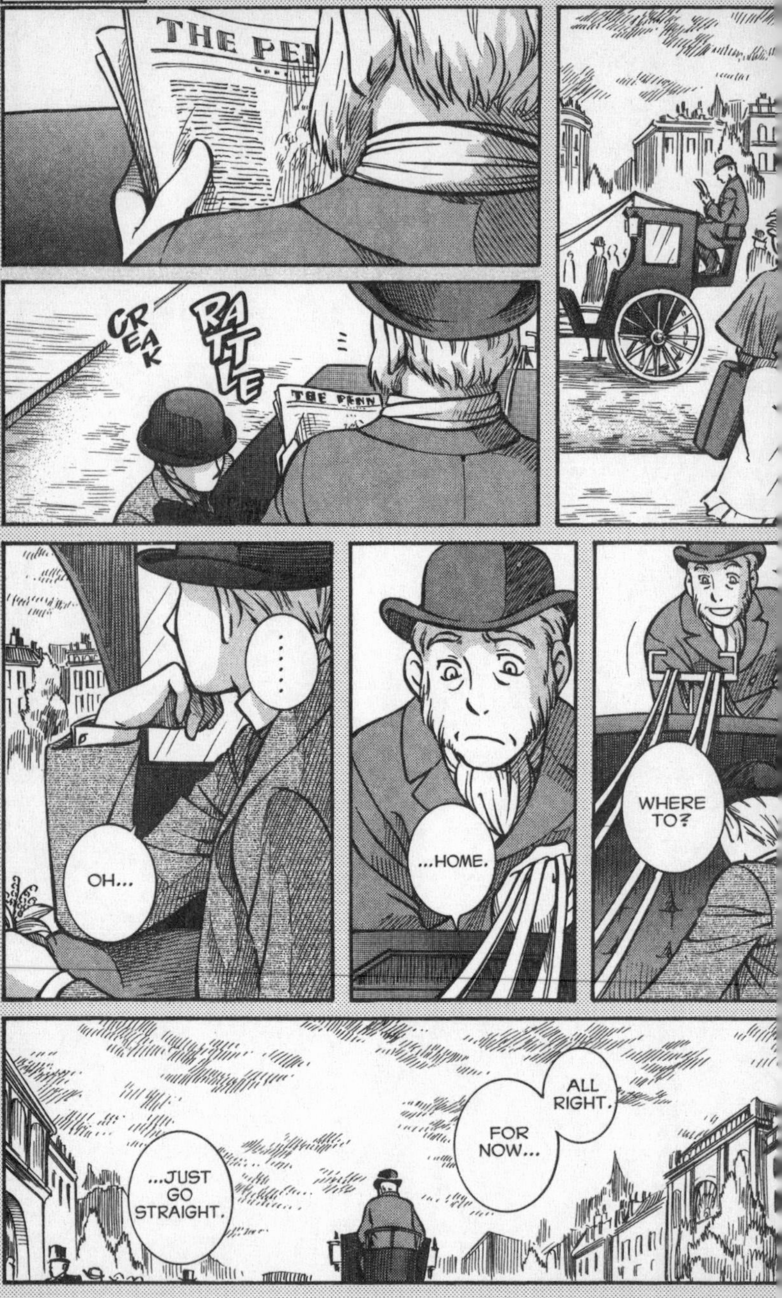
THE PE
CREAK
RATTLE
THE PENN
WHERE TO?
...HOME.
......
OH...
ALL RIGHT.
FOR NOW...
...JUST GO STRAIGHT.

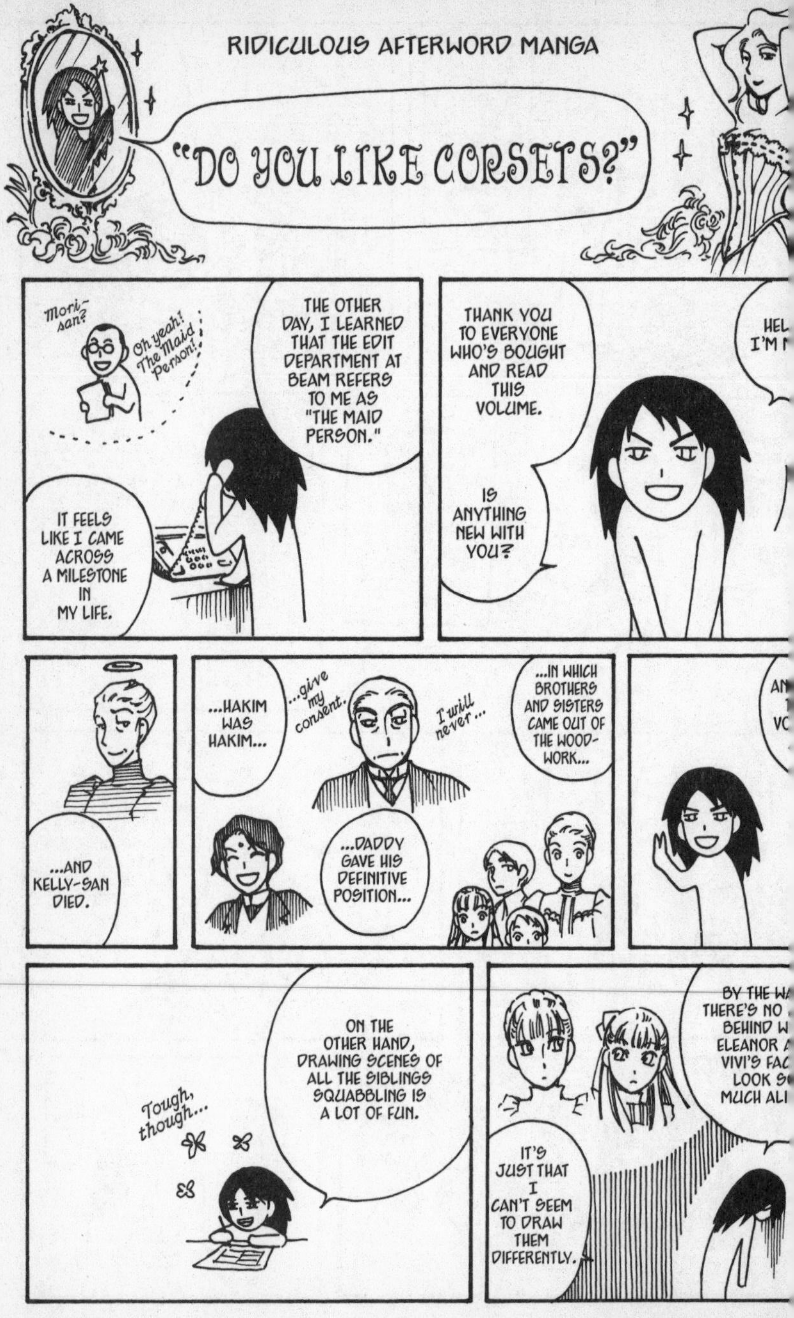
RIDICULOUS AFTERWORD MANGA
"DO YOU LIKE CORSETS?"
HEL I'M N
THANK YOU TO EVERYONE WHO'S BOUGHT AND READ THIS VOLUME.
IS ANYTHING NEW WITH YOU?
THE OTHER DAY, I LEARNED THAT THE EDIT DEPARTMENT AT BEAM REFERS TO ME AS "THE MAID PERSON."
Mori-san?
Oh yeah! The Maid Person!
IT FEELS LIKE I CAME ACROSS A MILESTONE IN MY LIFE.
AN T VC
...IN WHICH BROTHERS AND SISTERS CAME OUT OF THE WOODWORK...
I will never...
...give my consent.
...HAKIM WAS HAKIM...
...DADDY GAVE HIS DEFINITIVE POSITION...
...AND KELLY-SAN DIED.
BY THE WA THERE'S NO BEHIND W ELEANOR A VIVI'S FAC LOOK S MUCH ALI
IT'S JUST THAT I CAN'T SEEM TO DRAW THEM DIFFERENTLY.
ON THE OTHER HAND, DRAWING SCENES OF ALL THE SIBLINGS SQUABBLING IS A LOT OF FUN.
Tough, though...

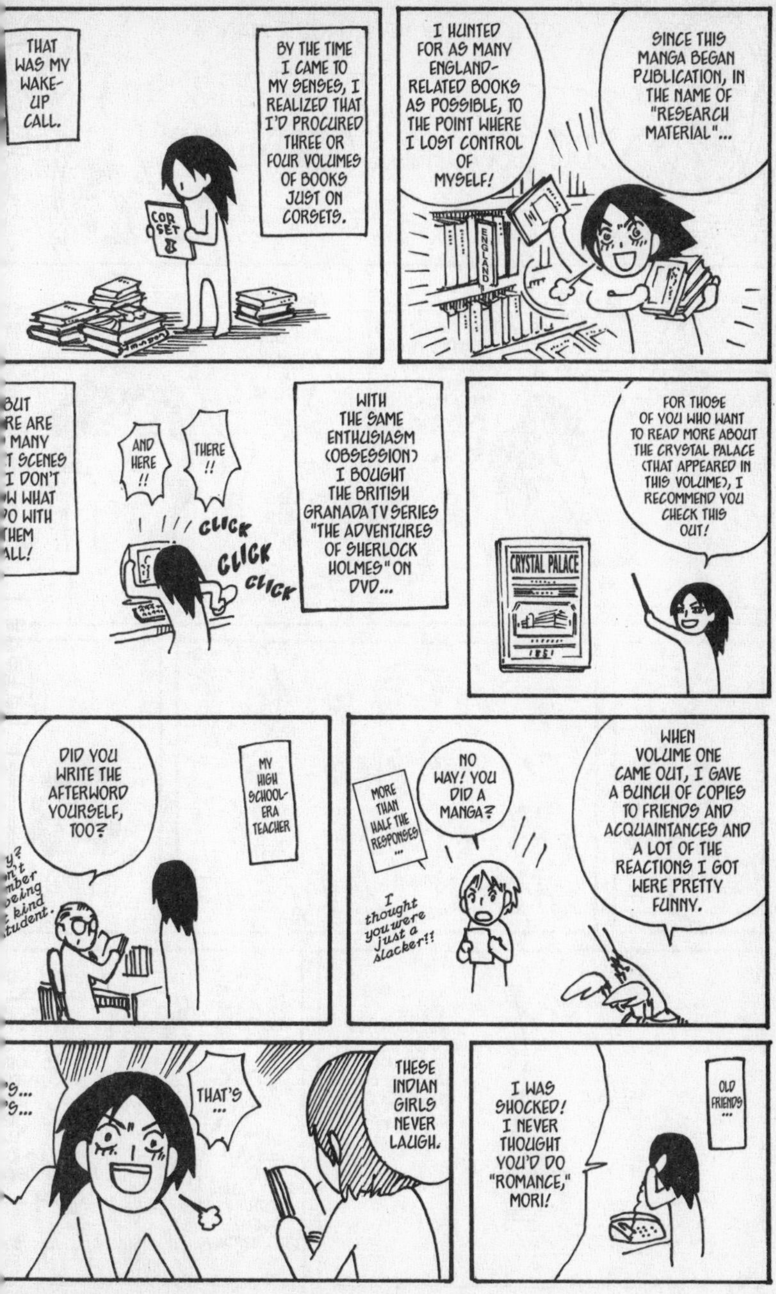
SINCE THIS MANGA BEGAN PUBLICATION, IN THE NAME OF "RESEARCH MATERIAL"...
I HUNTED FOR AS MANY ENGLAND-RELATED BOOKS AS POSSIBLE, TO THE POINT WHERE I LOST CONTROL OF MYSELF!
ENGLAND
BY THE TIME I CAME TO MY SENSES, I REALIZED THAT I'D PROCURED THREE OR FOUR VOLUMES OF BOOKS JUST ON CORSETS.
CORSET
THAT WAS MY WAKE-UP CALL.
FOR THOSE OF YOU WHO WANT TO READ MORE ABOUT THE CRYSTAL PALACE (THAT APPEARED IN THIS VOLUME), I RECOMMEND YOU CHECK THIS OUT!
CRYSTAL PALACE
1851
WITH THE SAME ENTHUSIASM (OBSESSION) I BOUGHT THE BRITISH GRANADA TV SERIES "THE ADVENTURES OF SHERLOCK HOLMES" ON DVD...
THERE!!
AND HERE!!
CLICK CLICK CLICK
BUT RE ARE MANY T SCENES I DON'T W WHAT DO WITH THEM ALL!
WHEN VOLUME ONE CAME OUT, I GAVE A BUNCH OF COPIES TO FRIENDS AND ACQUAINTANCES AND A LOT OF THE REACTIONS I GOT WERE PRETTY FUNNY.
NO WAY! YOU DID A MANGA?
MORE THAN HALF THE RESPONSES...
I thought you were just a slacker!!
MY HIGH SCHOOL-ERA TEACHER
DID YOU WRITE THE AFTERWORD YOURSELF, TOO?
OLD FRIENDS...
I WAS SHOCKED! I NEVER THOUGHT YOU'D DO "ROMANCE," MORI!
THESE INDIAN GIRLS NEVER LAUGH.
THAT'S...

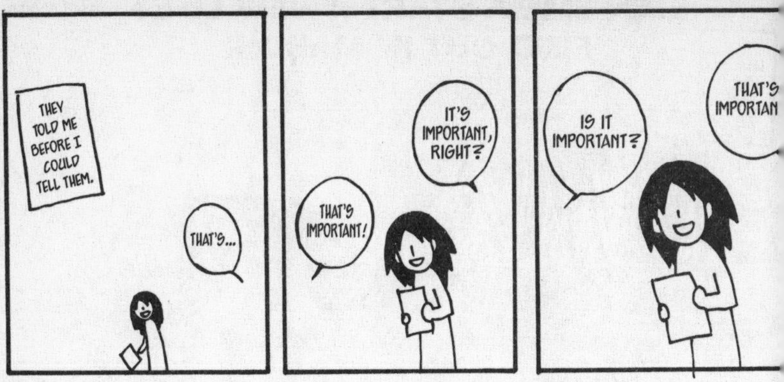
THAT'S IMPORTAN
IS IT IMPORTANT?
IT'S IMPORTANT, RIGHT?
THAT'S IMPORTANT!
THEY TOLD ME BEFORE I COULD TELL THEM.
THAT'S...

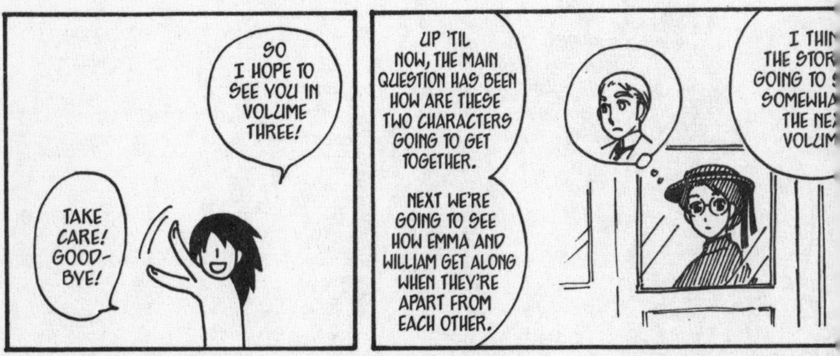
I THI THE STOR GOING TO SOMEWHA THE NE VOLUM
UP 'TIL NOW, THE MAIN QUESTION HAS BEEN HOW ARE THESE TWO CHARACTERS GOING TO GET TOGETHER.
NEXT WE'RE GOING TO SEE HOW EMMA AND WILLIAM GET ALONG WHEN THEY'RE APART FROM EACH OTHER.
SO I HOPE TO SEE YOU IN VOLUME THREE!
TAKE CARE! GOOD-BYE!

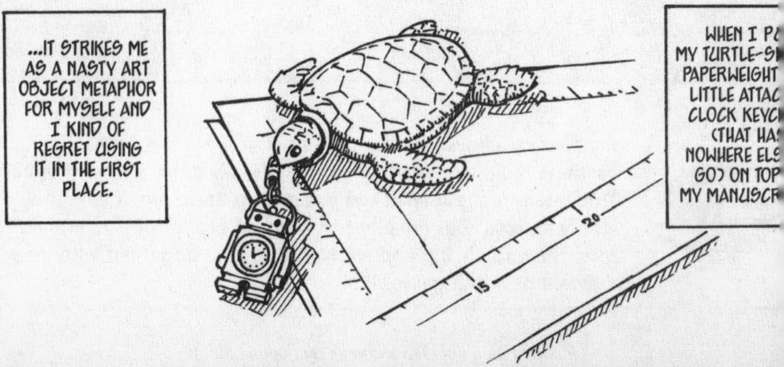
WHEN I P MY TURTLE-S PAPERWEIGHT LITTLE ATTAC CLOCK KEYC (THAT HA NOWHERE ELS GO) ON TOP MY MANUSCR
20
15
...IT STRIKES ME AS A NASTY ART OBJECT METAPHOR FOR MYSELF AND I KIND OF REGRET USING IT IN THE FIRST PLACE.

CAN EMMA START A NEW LIFE? FIND OUT IN MARCH!

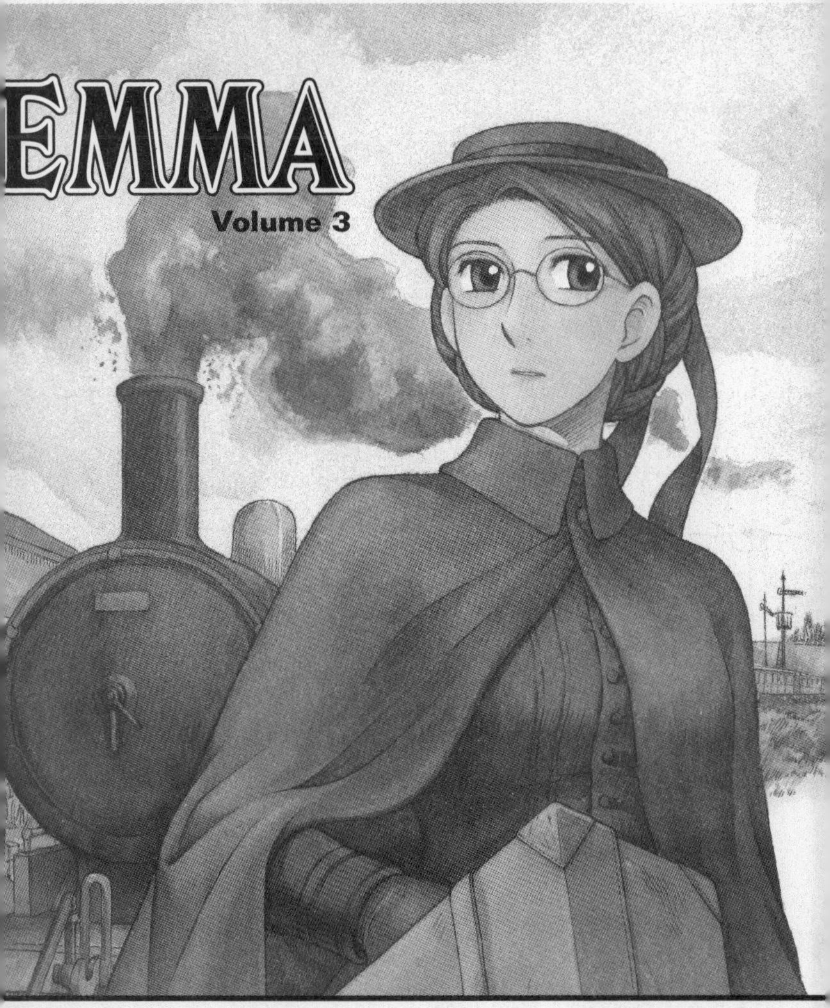
EMMA
Volume 3

By Kaoru Mori. On the train back to her hometown, Emma meets Tasha, a maid working at a wealthy family's mansion in the country. This fateful encounter leads to Emma getting employment with the family as well. But despite her years of experience as a maid for Mrs. Stownar, living and working at a mansion filled with servants is a whole new ball game.

MORE VISIONS REVEALED
AND AVAILABLE NOW!

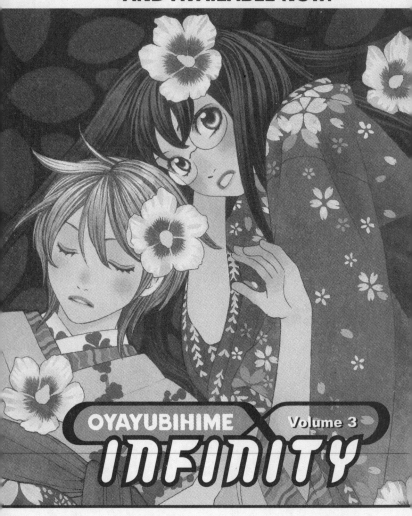

OYAYUBIHIME Volume 3

INFINITY

By Toru Fujieda. Kanoko and Mike try to piece together the my
surrounding the tragic life of Agemaki. Can Kanoko really be Age
reincarnated? And does that make her destined to be with Tsuchiy
who thinks he's destined to be with Kanoko's sister Mayu? And w
is Mike's motivation for wanting to hide the truth from Tsubame?
always, confusion reigns when the butterfly birthmarks touch and
visions of the past are ignited.

OYAYUBIHIME INFINITY (OYAYUBIHIME ∞) Vol. 3 © 2005 Toru Fujieda/Akitashoten.

THE FATE OF EARTH HANGS IN THE BALANCE! AVAILABLE NOW!

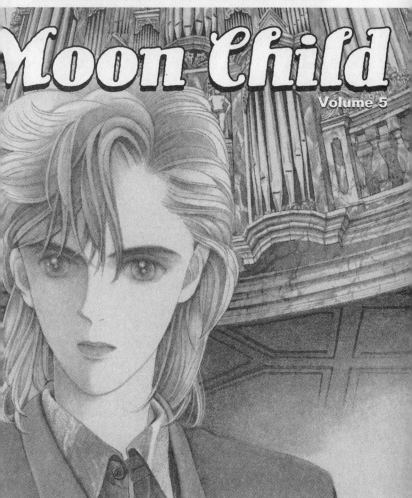

Moon Child
Volume 5

By Reiko Shimizu. Teruto has possessed the rich and powerful Gil Owen and is using him to wreak havoc in New York. Will Teruto hasten the destruction foretold in the mer-people's prophecies? Only Jimmy has the power to stop him by maturing into the beautiful female form he's destined to take and falling in love with a mer-man in order to save Earth. And no one dares predict who he'll choose.

MOON CHILD © 1988 Reiko Shimizu/HAKUSENSHA, INC.

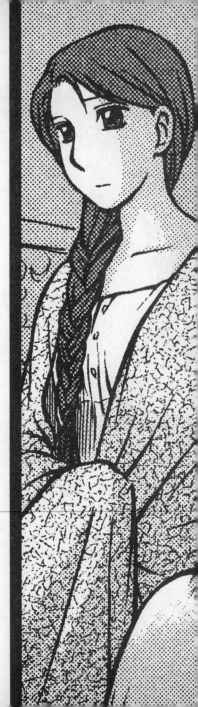

Jim Lee
    Editorial Director
John Nee
    VP—Business Development
Hank Kanalz
    VP—General Manager, WildStorm
Paul Levitz
    President & Publisher
Georg Brewer
    VP—Design & DC Direct Creative
Richard Bruning
    Senior VP—Creative Director
Patrick Caldon
    Executive VP—Finance & Operations
Chris Caramalis
    VP—Finance
John Cunningham
    VP—Marketing
Terri Cunningham
    VP—Managing Editor
Stephanie Fierman
    Senior VP—Sales & Marketing
Alison Gill
    VP—Manufacturing
Lillian Laserson
    Senior VP & General Counsel
Paula Lowitt
    Senior VP—Business & Legal Affairs
David McKillips
    VP—Advertising & Custom Publishing
Gregory Noveck
    Senior VP—Creative Affairs
Cheryl Rubin
    Senior VP—Brand Management
Jeff Trojan
    VP—Business Development, DC Direct
Bob Wayne
    VP—Sales

EMMA Vol. 2 © 2003 KAORU MORI. All Rights Reserved.
First published in Japan in 2003 by ENTERBRAIN, INC.

EMMA Volume 2, published by WildStorm Productions, an
imprint of DC Comics, 888 Prospect St. #240, La Jolla, CA
92037. English Translation © 2007. All Rights Reserved.
English translation rights in U.S.A. and Canada arranged by
ENTERBRAIN, INC. through Tuttle-Mori Agency, Inc., Tokyo.
The stories, characters, and incidents mentioned in this
magazine are entirely fictional. Printed on recyclable paper.
WildStorm does not read or accept unsolicited submissions
of ideas, stories or artwork. Printed in Canada.

DC Comics, a Warner Bros. Entertainment Company.

Sheldon Drzka – Translation and Adaptation
Janice Chiang – Lettering
Larry Berry – Design
Jim Chadwick – Editor

ISBN:1-4012-1133-X
ISBN-13: 978-1-4012-1133-2

the pages in this book were created—and are printed here—in Japanese RIGHT-to-LEFT format. No artwork has been reversed or altered, so you can read the stories the way the creators meant for them to be read.

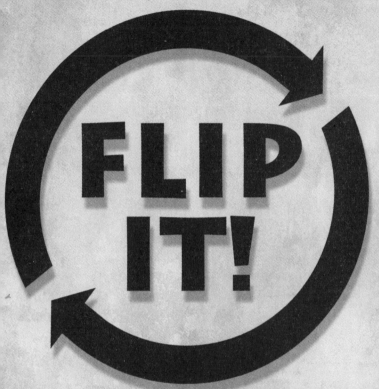

RIGHT TO LEFT?!

Traditional Japanese manga starts at the upper right-hand corner, and moves right-to-left as it goes down the page. Follow this guide for an easy understanding.

For more information and sneak previews, visit cmxmanga.com. Call 1-800-COMIC BOOK for the nearest comics shop or head to your local book store.

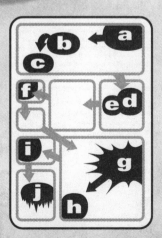

MARGARET E.

W9-CCE-943

741
.5
MOR
V2

Mori, Kaoru.
Emma, v. 2 /
36110002308596 $9.99